The Many Paths of Change in International Law

The Many Paths of Change in International Law

Edited by

NICO KRISCH AND EZGI YILDIZ

OXFORD
UNIVERSITY PRESS

OXFORD
UNIVERSITY PRESS

Great Clarendon Street, Oxford, OX2 6DP,
United Kingdom

Oxford University Press is a department of the University of Oxford.
It furthers the University's objective of excellence in research, scholarship,
and education by publishing worldwide. Oxford is a registered trade mark of
Oxford University Press in the UK and in certain other countries

First Edition published in 2023

Published in the United States of America by Oxford University Press
198 Madison Avenue, New York, NY 10016, United States of America

British Library Cataloguing in Publication Data
Data available

Library of Congress Control Number: 2023944953

ISBN 978–0–19–887784–4

DOI: 10.1093/oso/9780198877844.001.0001

Printed and bound by
CPI Group (UK) Ltd, Croydon, CR0 4YY

Preface

Dynamism is perhaps *the* defining characteristic of the modern world. The speed at which the world changes seems to be ever increasing, so much so that it often appears out of control. As Anthony Giddens wrote thirty years ago, 'living in the modern world is … like being aboard a careering juggernaut', and his diagnosis has only become more obvious today. Entire sociological theories are now built around the notion of social acceleration, and we live, in Hartmut Rosa's words, on 'slipping slopes'.

This dynamism poses serious problems for any form of governance, and in particular for law. Law in modernity is ensnared in a perennial tension—meant to guarantee stability and predictability, it also needs to change and adapt at an ever-faster pace in order to make good on the promise of ordering society. Between stability and change, between the past and the future, law is caught in an uneasy oscillation, never able to cater fully to either. Legal institutions in the modern state have found ways of coping with this oscillation, by establishing legal fixed points in the continuing process of social, political, and economic change, and by revising these rapidly in a continuous exercise of reflexivity through legislation and administrative regulation.

On the international plane, however, we find few comparable tools—treaties, seemingly closest to domestic statutes, are too difficult and slow to negotiate and amend to be able to strike a similar balance. Secondary rulemaking by international organizations is largely limited to non-binding forms. Change is then a core challenge for international law, but we do not understand it all too well. We do not know how, realistically, more dynamic adaptation could be achieved in an international legal order built around diverse, sovereign states. But we also do not even know very well how international law actually changes—how dynamic it really is, and the factors that facilitate or hinder this dynamism.

This volume is an attempt to fill this gap. It comes out of a project we have been heading for a few years, on 'The Paths of International Law'. With our team (which included Dorothea Endres, Nina Kiderlin, and Pedro Martínez Esponda, all of whom also have chapters in this book) we have sought to get a better understanding of the ways in which international law actually changes—the actors, institutions, and conditions that matter in change processes. For this, we took a deliberate distance from the doctrinal categories in which international lawyers typically study change—these exclude by definition many instances in which new rights, obligations, and understandings of international legal norms have come about outside traditional, state-centred processes.

The present volume is the fruit of a collaboration that began with a workshop we hosted in Geneva in the summer of 2019. The energy in the room was extraordinary, and not just because of the beautiful views of Lake Geneva outside our workshop venue. It was especially the conversations across disciplinary boundaries—between lawyers, sociologists, and international relations scholars in particular—that worked exceptionally well, and we decided to continue these in a smaller group with a view to producing a joint volume. An authors' workshop and various conference panels later, we are happy that the conversation has continued and that contributions have all come together to make for a stimulating whole which, we hope, will find many readers.

The beauty of a volume of this kind is that it is held together by a common theme—the paths of change in international law—but explores this theme in a great many directions, driven by the backgrounds and curiosities of the different contributors, to whom we owe many thanks. We learn about Raphael Lemkin and Donald Trump, about subsidies as well as search and rescue at sea, and about rights activists and authoritarian antipreneurs. Only Godot, impressively present in his absence at the 2019 workshop, remains outside this time. International law's social life, the actors behind it, come to life here in a way which, for international lawyers at least, is rare. And international law emerges from this volume as more dynamic than usually catches the eye—but still within limits, and often caught between rival visions of whether it should change or in what direction.

Apart from our team and the contributors, we would also like to thank Matthew Daminato for his help with editing; Clarissa Brack Burdeu, Camila Morais Silva, and Sylvia Nissim at the Graduate Institute's Global Governance Centre for their administrative and logistical support; and Robert Cavooris and Lane Berger at Oxford University Press for steering the process of publication. Last but not least, we are grateful to the European Research Council whose funding has made our research, the workshops, as well as the open access publication possible. We hope you, the readers, will enjoy the fruits.

Nico Krisch and Ezgi Yildiz

Acknowledgements

This book is part of 'The Paths of International Law: Stability and Change in the International Legal Order', a project that has received funding from the European Union's Horizon 2020 research and innovation programme under grant agreement No 740634. Funded by the European Union. Views and opinions expressed are however those of the author(s) only and do not necessarily reflect those of the European Union or the European Research Council Executive Agency. Neither the European Union nor the granting authority can be held responsible for them.

erc

European Research Council

Established by the European Commission

Summary Contents

V. SITUATING CHANGE

VI. EPILOGUE

Detailed Contents

List of Contributors

BS Chimni: Professor of International Law, Jindal Global Law School, Sonipat, India

Jaye Ellis: Associate Professor, McGill University, Montreal, Canada

Dorothea Endres: PhD Researcher in International Law, Graduate Institute of International and Development Studies, Geneva, Switzerland; Research Assistant, Faculty of Law, University of Geneva

Nina Teresa Kiderlin: PhD Researcher in Anthropology and Sociology, Graduate Institute of International and Development Studies, Geneva, Switzerland

Nico Krisch: Professor of International Law, Graduate Institute of International and Development Studies, Geneva, Switzerland

Jeff Kucik: Associate Professor of Political Science and Law (by courtesy) at the University of Arizona

Pedro Martínez Esponda: Professor of International Law at Universidad Iberoamericana in Mexico City, Mexico

Mark A Pollack: Professor of Political Science and Law, Temple University, Philadelphia, PA, USA

Sergio Puig: Evo DeConcini Professor of Law and Director, International Trade and Business Law Program at the University of Arizona

Tonya Putnam: Research Scholar, Columbia University, New York, NY, USA

Nina Reiners: Associate Professor for Human Rights and Social Sciences at the Centre for Human Rights, University of Oslo, Norway; Associated Researcher, Graduate Institute of International and Development Studies, Geneva, Switzerland

Wayne Sandholtz: Professor and John A McCone Chair in International Relations, Department of Political Science and International Relations and Gould School of Law, University of Southern California, USA

Seline Trevisanut: Professor of International Law and Sustainability, Utrecht University, Utrecht, The Netherlands

Ingo Venzke: Professor of International Law and Social Justice, University of Amsterdam, Amsterdam, The Netherlands

Wouter Werner: Professor in International Law, Vrije Universiteit Amsterdam, Amsterdam, The Netherlands

Ezgi Yildiz: Assistant Professor of International Relations, California State University, Long Beach, CA, USA

Fuad Zarbiyev: Associate Professor of International Law, Graduate Institute of International and Development Studies, Geneva, Switzerland

List of Abbreviations

AALCO	Asian-African Legal Consultative Organization
AB	Appellate Body
ACtHPR	African Court on Human and Peoples' Rights
AP I	First Additional Protocol to the Geneva Conventions
API	American Petroleum Institute
BARCO OFOG	Barcelona Convention Offshore Oil and Gas Group
CBD	1992 Convention on Biological Diversity
CCPR	UN Human Rights Committee
CEDAW	UN Convention on the Elimination of all forms of Discrimination Against Women
CEITs	countries with economies in transition
CELAC	Community of Latin American and Caribbean States
CERD	Committee on the Elimination of All Forms of Racial Discrimination
CESCR	UN Committee for Economic, Social and Cultural Rights
CoP	Community of Practice
COP	Conference of the Parties
COR	corporate ocean responsibility
CPA	Comprehensive Plan of Action
CPTPP	Comprehensive and Progressive Agreement for Trans-Pacific Partnership
CSO	civil society organizations
CSR	corporate social responsibility
CVDs	countervailing duties
DISERO	Disembarkation Resettlement Offers
DPH	direct participation in hostilities
DRC	Democratic Republic of the Congo
DSB	Dispute Settlement Body
DSM	Dispute Settlement Mechanism
EAC	East African Community
EB	enforcement branch
ECOSOC	Economic and Social Council
ECOWAS	Economic Community of West African States
ECHR	European Convention of Human Rights
ECtHR	European Court of Human Rights
EEZ	exclusive economic zone
EIA	environmental impact assessment
ERTs	expert review teams
ExCom	Executive Committee

FAL	IMO Facilitation Committee
FB	facilitative branch
FtAIL	Feminist Approaches to International Law
GAIR	Guardian Angels International Rescue
GATT	General Agreement on Tariffs and Trade
GHG	greenhouse gas
HELCOM	Helsinki Commission
HI	historical institutionalism
IACtHR	Inter-American Court of Human Rights
ICC	International Chamber of Commerce
ICC	International Criminal Court
ICESCR	International Covenant on Economic, Social and Cultural Rights
ICISS	International Commission on Intervention and State Sovereignty
ICJ	International Commission of Jurists
ICJ	International Court of Justice
ICRC	International Committee of the Red Cross
ICS	International Chamber of Shipping
ICSID	International Centre for Settlement of Investment Disputes
IEC	International Electrotechnical Commission
IEL	international environmental law
IFC	International Finance Corporation
IGO	intergovernmental organization
IHL	international humanitarian law
IHRL	international human rights law
ILC	International Law Commission
ILO	International Labour Organization
IMO	International Maritime Organization
INF Treaty	Intermediate-Range Nuclear Forces Treaty
IO	international organization
IOGP	International Association of Oil and Gas Producers
IOM	International Organization for Migration
IPCC	Intergovernmental Panel on Climate Change
IR	international relations
IRENA	International Renewable Energy Agency
IRF	International Regulators' Forum
ITO	International Trade Organization
IUU	illegal, unreported, and unregulated
JCPOA	Joint Comprehensive Plan of Action
KORUS	Korea Free Trade Agreement
LoAC	Laws of Armed Conflict
LOSC	Law of the Sea Convention
LRA	Lord Resistance Army
MEAs	within multilateral environmental agreements
MNCs	multinational corporations
MOP	Meeting of the Parties

MPIA	Multiparty Interim Appeal-Arbitration Arrangement
MSC	Maritime Safety Committee
NAFTA	North American Free Trade Agreement
NAM	Non-Aligned Movement
NATO	North Atlantic Treaty Organization
NDCs	Nationally Determined Contributions
NGO	non-governmental organization
NHRI	National Human Rights Institutions
NMEs	non-market economies
NPM	New Public Management
OECD	Organisation for Economic Co-operation and Development
OHCHR	Office of the High Commissioner for Human Rights
ONUCA	UN Observadores de las Naciones Unidas en Centro America (UN Peacekeeping Mission in Central America)
OPOL	Offshore Pollution Liability Association
OSPAR Convention	Convention for the Protection of the Marine Environment of the North-East Atlantic
PATHS	paths of International Law
PLO	Palestine Liberation Organization
R2P	responsibility to protect
RASRO	Rescue at Sea Resettlement Offers
RCEP	Regional Comprehensive Economic Partnership
ROPME	Regional Organization for the Protection of the Marine Environment
SAR	search and rescue
SAR Convention	Search and Rescue Convention 1979
SCM Agreement	Agreement on Subsidies and Countervailing Measures
SCO	Shanghai Cooperation Organization
SD	standard deviation
SDGs	Sustainable Development Goals
SD-NSA	self-defence against non-state actors
SEA	Strategic Environmental Assessment
SG	Secretary General
SOE	state-owned enterprises
SOLAS Convention	Convention on the Safety of Life at Sea 1974
SPA	Specially Protected Areas
START Treaty	Strategic Arms Reduction Treaty
TLC	transnational lawmaking coalition
TLO	transnational legal order
TPP	Trans Pacific Partnership
TRIMS	Trade Related Investment Measures
TWAIL	Third World Approaches to International Law
UDHR	Universal Declaration of Human Rights
UNGA	UN General Assembly
UN	United Nations

UNAMIR	UN Assistance Mission for Rwanda
UNAVEM I	UN Angola Verification Mission I
UNFCCC	UN Framework Convention on Climate Change
UNGOMAP	UN Good Offices Mission in Afghanistan and Pakistan
UNHCR	UN High Commissioner for Refugees
UNHRC	UN Human Rights Council
UNIIMOG	UN Iran-Iraq Military Observer Group
UNODC	UN Office on Drugs and Crime
UNSC	UN Security Council
UNTAG	UN Transition Assistance Group
UPR	Universal Periodic Review
USMCA	US Mexico Canada Agreement
USSR	Union of Soviet Socialist Republics
USTR	US Trade Representative
VCLT	Vienna Convention on the Law of Treaties
V-Dem	Varieties of Democracy
WHO	World Health Organization
WTO	World Trade Organization

PART I
INTRODUCTION

1

The Many Paths of Change in International Law

A Frame

*Nico Krisch** *and Ezgi Yildiz***

1. Introduction

International politics is in constant flux. States' interests, status, and power are shifting; norms governing appropriate behaviour are getting stronger or weaker, emerging or decaying, or changing complexion and content. It is stability, rather than mutability, that requires an explanation in politics. International law, on the other hand, appears much less fluid. While it will often reflect the shifting political constellations of its time to some extent, it is not merely the mirror image of politics, nor does it track political change immediately or in its entirety. Some changes in politics will make a quick impact, some a much slower one, and yet some will fail to leave a mark on the law.

How and when political change translates into new (interpretations of) international legal rules is not well understood so far. Existing approaches portray legal change as a result of power constellations, of the properties of the norms at issue, or as a phenomenon that depends on a new confluence of state interests. But they can hardly account for the dynamic, and varied, picture that emerges when we look at change processes in different areas of international law. Moreover, most approaches focus on treaties, but treaty-making faces a high threshold, and major new agreements are few and far between. Instead, the more frequent forms of change through reinterpretation or shifts in customary rules tend to remain out of view, but it is through these that many broader transformations find reflection in the international legal order.

This volume seeks to take us closer to an understanding of how change happens in international law, and consequently of the factors that facilitate or hinder the reception of political transformations in the international legal order. In this,

* Professor of International Law, Graduate Institute of International and Development Studies, Geneva, Switzerland.

** Assistant Professor of International Relations, California State University, Long Beach, CA, USA.

Nico Krisch and Ezgi Yildiz, *The Many Paths of Change in International Law: A Frame* In: *The Many Paths of Change in International Law*. Edited by: Nico Krisch and Ezgi Yildiz, Oxford University Press. © Nico Krisch and Ezgi Yildiz 2023.
DOI: 10.1093/oso/9780198877844.003.0001

it places particular emphasis on the different pathways through which change occurs and the authorities that play a central role situated on each of these pathways. These vary across issue-areas and institutional contexts, and they are subject to change and transformation themselves. Without properly accounting for these pathways—and the social and political dynamics associated with them—we cannot begin to build a broader, more systematic account of the ways in which change processes unfold.

In this introduction, we seek to set the scene for this inquiry by clarifying core concepts and developing an instrumentarium that helps us structure the analysis of change processes in international law. We begin by taking stock of some of the key attempts at understanding international legal change in the past, focusing on recent scholarship at the intersection between international law and international relations (section 2). Addressing the shortcomings of these attempts, we build an ideal-typical model of the stages and pathways of change processes in the international legal order (section 3). Starting from a micro-level, focusing on the actors initiating, processing, and receiving attempts at changing international legal rules, we then zoom out again to develop conjectures about the factors that condition the speed, ease, and success of change processes (section 4). Understanding these conditions can help us to account for the significant variation across the different fields of international law. We then use this framework to introduce and situate the contributions to this volume and their findings with a view to developing the contours of a bigger picture of international legal change (section 5).

The picture that emerges from this endeavour is one of change processes in multiple sites, at different speeds, and involving diverse actors—and with a significant variation across the different areas of international law. It is a picture not of revolution but of polycentric reform efforts, but nevertheless, one that, we hope, will give us a clearer understanding of the dynamics of, and forces behind, much consequential change—and that will help us to better appreciate the complex politics of international law.

2. Change and Stasis in International Law

The question of change is central to international law—even more so than in other legal orders because of a lack of legislative mechanisms that would allow adapting legal rules to changing circumstances—and it has accordingly been of concern to international lawyers for centuries. The issue became particularly salient in the early twentieth century when calls for the 'peaceful change' of treaties (often concluded in highly unequal relations) gained political strength, and the absence of an international legislature was widely lamented.[1] Hersch Lauterpacht devoted a large

[1] Sir John Fischer Williams, *International Change and International Peace* (OUP, H Milford 1932).

part of his seminal work on 'The Function of Law in the International Community' to the issue, yet just as many lawyers before and after, his treatment of the question focused particularly on the doctrinal categories through which change could be rationalized, such as the '*clausula rebus sic stantibus*' or the notion of '*abus de droit*'.[2] Tellingly, though, he pointed to the relatively limited extent of the problem in international, as opposed to domestic, law. In his assessment, international law at the time was 'more static than any other law not only because of the absence of an international legislature, but principally because it regulate[d] relations which are not in themselves liable to be affected in a decisive manner by economic and other changes'. He concluded that '[o]nly when the political organization of the international community has undergone a fundamental change, so as to regulate in detail the life of its individual members in its internal aspects—only then will it be possible to speak of a constant flux of changes necessitating legislative remedies'.[3]

The question continued to be discussed during the Cold War,[4] but it has been the turn to an international law of 'governance', with a significant impact on domestic politics in many areas,[5] that has—as foreseen by Lauterpacht—brought the problem to the fore with yet greater urgency. Many have pointed to the structural difficulties of bringing about effective regulation on issues of global concern, such as climate change,[6] and to the limits on adapting existing international law to changing political views, as in the case of world trade law for environmental and development concerns, or in investment law for concerns about domestic regulation in the public interest.[7] Many of these limits derive from the high hurdles for change through the traditional categories of international law. Treaties require the consent of the parties to begin with, and usually the agreement of all parties is seen as necessary for their adaptation through 'subsequent practice'. And customary international law requires, according to standard doctrine, a widespread and uniform practice of nearly all states.

While these difficulties may have led actors to seek solutions outside the formal international legal order,[8] there are also indications that they have led to adaptations of the traditionally rigid ways of making formal law. This is especially the

[2] Hersch Lauterpacht, *The Function of Law in the International Community* (2nd edn, OUP 2011).
[3] ibid 257–58.
[4] Antonio Cassese and Joseph HH Weiler (eds), *Change and Stability in International Law-Making* (Walter de Gruyter 1988).
[5] Joseph HH Weiler, 'The Geology of International Law—Governance, Democracy and Legitimacy' (2004) 64 Zeitschrift für ausländisches öffentliches Recht und Völkerrecht 547.
[6] David G Victor, *Global Warming Gridlock: Creating More Effective Strategies for Protecting the Planet* (CUP 2011); Thomas Hale, David Held, and Kevin Young, *Gridlock: Why Global Cooperation Is Failing When We Need It Most* (Polity 2013).
[7] Andrew Lang, *World Trade Law after Neoliberalism: Reimagining the Global Economic Order* (OUP 2011); Muthucumaraswamy Sornarajah, *Resistance and Change in the International Law on Foreign Investment* (CUP 2015).
[8] Nico Krisch, 'The Decay of Consent: International Law in an Age of Global Public Goods' (2014) 108 American Journal of International Law 1.

case in a number of specialized issue-areas, such as (international) environmental law, human rights law, humanitarian law, criminal law, or the law of international organizations.[9] Tendencies towards a more dynamic approach to legal change have also been observed in core areas of general international law, such as state responsibility,[10] the law on the use of force,[11] or customary law,[12] typically with particular attention to the influence of international institutions on the development of international law.[13] Most existing accounts remain, however, limited to particular contexts and issues,[14] and many are driven by normative precommitments in favour of particular mechanisms for (or limitations to) change.[15] Moreover, observed differences in perceptions about the applicable secondary rules among actors have not been taken up systematically.[16] The greater dynamism visible in some areas is then often treated as exceptional, also because it tends to be contested on normative grounds.[17] Broader attempts at restating the norms of international legal change—especially in the United Nations (UN) International Law Commission (ILC)—tend to return to traditional conceptualizations of subsequent practice or customary law.[18]

[9] Monica Hakimi, 'Secondary Human Rights Law' (2009) 34 Yale Journal of International Law 596; Julian Arato, 'Treaty Interpretation and Constitutional Transformation: Informal Change in International Organizations' (2013) 38 Yale Journal of International Law 289; Alexander Grabert, *Dynamic Interpretation in International Criminal Law: Striking a Balance between Stability and Change* (Herbert Utz Verlag 2015); Yuval Shany, 'Sources and the Enforcement of International Law: What Norms Do International Law-Enforcement Bodies Actually Invoke?' in Samantha Besson and Jean d'Aspremont (eds), *The Oxford Handbook of the Sources of International Law* (OUP 2017); Jutta Brunnée, 'Sources of International Environmental Law: Interactional Law' in Besson and d'Aspremont (eds), The Oxford Handbook of the Sources of International Law; Sandesh Sivakumaran, 'Making and Shaping the Law of Armed Conflict' (2018) 71 Current Legal Problems 119.

[10] James Crawford, 'The International Court of Justice and the Law of State Responsibility' in CJ Tams and J Sloan (eds), *The Development of International Law by the International Court of Justice* (OUP 2013).

[11] Monica Hakimi and Jacob Katz Cogan, 'The Two Codes on the Use of Force' (2016) 27 European Journal of International Law 257.

[12] Anthea Roberts, 'Traditional and Modern Approaches to Customary International Law: A Reconciliation' [2001] American Journal of International Law 757; Niels Petersen, 'Der Wandel des Ungeschriebenen Völkerrechts im Zuge der Konstitutionalisierung' (2008) 46 Archiv des Völkerrechts 502; Curtis A Bradley, 'Customary International Law Adjudication as Common Law Adjudication' in Bradley (ed), *Custom's Future: International Law in a Changing World* (CUP 2016).

[13] Ingo Venzke, *How Interpretation Makes International Law: On Semantic Change and Normative Twists* (OUP 2012).

[14] For exceptions, see Michael P Scharf, *Customary International Law in Times of Fundamental Change: Recognizing Grotian Moments* (CUP 2013); Georg Nolte (ed), *Treaties and Subsequent Practice* (OUP 2013).

[15] See eg Rebecca Crootof, 'Change Without Consent: How Customary International Law Modifies Treaties' (2016) 41 Yale Journal of International Law.

[16] Hakimi and Cogan (n 11); Lauri Mälksoo, *Russian Approaches to International Law* (OUP 2015).

[17] Marcelo G Kohen, 'Keeping Subsequent Agreements and Practice in Their Right Limits' in Georg Nolte (ed), *Treaties and Subsequent Practice* (OUP 2013).

[18] International Law Commission, 'Subsequent Agreements and Subsequent Practice in Relation to the Interpretation of Treaties: Text of the Draft Conclusions Provisionally Adopted by the Drafting Committee on First Reading' (2016); International Law Commission, 'Identification of Customary International Law: Text of the Draft Conclusions Provisionally Adopted by the Drafting Committee' (2016).

In the growing interdisciplinary literature at the boundary between international law and international relations, the question of change has surprisingly attracted only limited attention.[19] Much of this literature—especially that operating in a rational-choice framework—seeks to explain or understand the creation of, or compliance with, particular norms at a given point, without paying much attention to the dynamics of changing legal norms over time. Andrew Guzman's influential account is a good example here: concerned primarily with the relevance of international legal rules for state behaviour, he starts from a fixed content of these rules and focuses on the factors that may drive states to comply with them. In terms of law-creation and change, only treaty-making comes into clearer view.[20] The latter point is also remarkable for many prominent engagements with international law by international relations scholars. The path-breaking 'legalization' project,[21] or Barbara Koremenos' recent work focus almost exclusively on treaties and treaty design.[22] The dynamic construction of international law over time remains largely outside the picture.

This is somewhat different for constructivist approaches that pay particular attention to the processes through which norms are socially constructed. However, the constructivist literature on norm development, for the most part, does not address international law specifically.[23] When it does, it often sees legal norms merely as reflections of social norms as they have evolved, without theorizing the more complicated ways in which the two are related.[24] Such a close linkage is, for example, characteristic of the prominent work of Jutta Brunnée and Stephen Toope, for whom international legal norms—understood as social norms—rest on shared understandings within a community of practice. Their particularly legal character stems from a grounding in an inclusive 'practice of legality', a requirement derived primarily from normative considerations, but one that leaves the possible (and actual) distance between social and legal norms out of sight.[25]

Broader accounts of change in international law as such have thus remained relatively isolated. One of these, by Wayne Sandholtz and Kendall Stiles, adopts a constructivist frame and views legal change as driven primarily by norm

[19] See eg Jeffrey L Dunoff and Mark A Pollack (eds), *Interdisciplinary Perspectives on International Law and International Relations: The State of the Art* (CUP 2012).

[20] Andrew T Guzman, *How International Law Works: A Rational Choice Theory* (OUP 2008).

[21] Judith L Goldstein and others (eds), *Legalization and World Politics* (MIT Press 2001).

[22] Barbara Koremenos, *The Continent of International Law: Explaining Agreement Design* (CUP 2016).

[23] Martha Finnemore and Kathryn Sikkink, 'International Norm Dynamics and Political Change' (1998) 52 International Organization 887. But see also Martha Finnemore and Stephen J Toope, 'Alternatives to "Legalization": Richer Views of Law and Politics' (2001) 55 International Organization 743.

[24] Christian Reus-Smit, 'The Politics of International Law' in C Reus-Smit (ed), *The Politics of International Law* (CUP 2004).

[25] Jutta Brunnée and Stephen J Toope, *Legitimacy and Legality in International Law. An Interactional Account* (CUP 2010).

tensions: cycles of action produce arguments over existing norms and shift the normative space step by step. The focus here is primarily on discursive change rather than transformation through treaties or political action, and they emphasize the internal dynamics of international law.[26] Another broad account has been advanced by Paul Diehl and Charlotte Ku, who combine a focus on internal tensions in the law (mainly between what they call the 'operating' and the 'normative' systems in international law) with an appreciation of external factors that help to move international law from one punctuated equilibrium to another.[27] They emphasize sudden rather than gradual forms of change, and much of their argument centres on 'legislative' interventions, especially the adoption of new treaties, rather than processes of change internal to the legal system. Moreover, they mostly propose a theoretical framework with possible pathways and relevant factors, and they use empirical cases as illustration rather than for systematic analysis.

Their focus on sudden change is shared by a recent attempt at theorizing change in customary international law by Pierre-Hugues Verdier and Erik Voeten.[28] Verdier and Voeten start from a precedent-based explanation of why countries comply with customary norms and link it to a tipping-point model of change, with long periods of stability punctuated by periods of rapid change. This account offers valuable starting points and provides a well-grounded critique of prominent approaches that dismiss customary law's relevance outright, but it has difficulties explaining the relative stickiness of customary rules even as state interests change, or the ways in which the influence of power relations is qualified in the modification of customary law.[29]

Some of these problems are addressed by the recent practice-based constructivist literature that focuses on incremental change, in particular, through subsequent state practice. For example, Mark Raymond's analysis on social practices of rulemaking, interpretation, and application comes from this tradition. It highlights the role of secondary rules for the success or failure of states' change attempts.[30] Zoltán Búzás and Erin Graham have helpfully employed the notion of 'emergent flexibility' to explain how creative rule users successfully change rules that lack design flexibility.[31] Yet, these approaches remain underspecified when it comes to

[26] Wayne Sandholtz, 'Dynamics of International Norm Change: Rules against Wartime Plunder' (2008) 14 European Journal of International Relations 101; Wayne Sandholtz and Kendall W Stiles, *International Norms and Cycles of Change* (OUP 2009).

[27] Paul F Diehl and Charlotte Ku, *The Dynamics of International Law* (CUP 2010).

[28] Pierre-Hugues Verdier and Erik Voeten, 'Precedent, Compliance, and Change in Customary International Law: An Explanatory Theory' (2014) 108 American Journal of International Law 389.

[29] See eg Michael Byers, *Custom, Power and the Power of Rules: International Relations and Customary International Law* (CUP 1999); Stephen Toope, 'Powerful but Unpersuasive? The Role of the United States in the Evolution of Customary International Law' in M Byers and G Nolte (eds), *United States Hegemony and the Foundations of International Law* (CUP 2003).

[30] Mark Raymond, *Social Practices of Rule-Making in World Politics* (OUP 2019)3.

[31] Zoltán I Búzás and Erin R Graham, 'Emergent Flexibility in Institutional Development: How International Rules Really Change' (2020) 64 International Studies Quarterly 821.

understanding variations in the success of efforts at reshaping law through subsequent practice.

The picture that emerges from existing engagements with change in international law is one that raises more questions than it provides answers. There is a gulf between different accounts as to the degree of stability or flexibility of international law—while some, especially from the legal side, emphasize high hurdles for change, others, especially from the more interdisciplinary realm, highlight greater flexibility. There is also a contrast between those who identify gradual change as the main pathway for flexibility and those who focus on sudden instances of change. Power- or interest-based accounts are challenged by alternatives that emphasize the dynamics internal to normative processes. State-centric accounts compete with those which focus on the role of international institutions or, as is often the case in the general literature on norm change, civil society organizations. Many of these contrasts relate to broader disagreements about the nature of international politics, and the empirical evidence on international law as such remains scattered. And most of them—those of lawyers as well as political scientists—provide accounts that work across the different fields of international law, and across different historical periods, thus downplaying the enormous variation in the ways of international legal change that can be gleaned from anecdotal evidence.

3. The Process of Change

In this volume, we seek to reconstruct the many paths of change in the different fields of international law, especially in change processes that cannot be reduced to treaty-making. Treaties are the most prominent path for modifying the law, and they have been widely studied, but treaties are relatively rare occurrences given how difficult they are to conclude. Observers have also found treaty-making to have stagnated over the past two decades.[32] On the other hand, much change in international law runs on different tracks—involving state action, courts, expert bodies, etc. We know much less about the shape or operation of these latter ways of change and understanding them better is at the centre of our interest. In this section, we introduce core concepts and categories that help to provide building blocks for an account of such informal change in international law.

By change, we understand any modification of the burden of argument for a particular position on the content of the law.[33] This conception goes well beyond

[32] Robert A Denemark and Matthew J Hoffmann, 'Just Scraps of Paper? The Dynamics of Multilateral Treaty-Making' (2008) 43 Cooperation and Conflict 185; Joost Pauwelyn, Ramses A Wessel, and Jan Wouters, 'When Structures Become Shackles: Stagnation and Dynamics in International Lawmaking' (2014) 25 European Journal of International Law 733.

[33] This account of legal change goes back to a suggestion in Ingo Venzke, 'What Makes for a Valid Legal Argument?' (2014) 27 Leiden Journal of International Law 811.

the idea that change requires the replacement of one norm with another, typically underlying doctrinal approaches. It instead acknowledges that there are different degrees of change, some more limited, others more radical, and that no clear line can be drawn between a mere change in interpretation and the appearance of a new rule. At any given point in time, we will be confronted with various interpretations of a given norm, with some positions being more widely accepted than others. Change occurs when, at a second point in time, the scope of possible interpretations or the weight of particular positions in legal discourse has shifted. This may or may not correspond with doctrinal reconstructions of what the law is—at times, the law practised by actors in a given field will differ from what, say, an application of the doctrinal requirements for new customary law would result in. Here we are primarily interested in the 'law in action' or 'in discourse', in order to allow us to detect the distance that may exist with the 'law in the books' and to understand the dynamics behind actual change processes in international law.

3.1 Practices and Authorities

International law's operation is typically portrayed as centred on states, with other actors making an appearance largely in supporting roles. Doctrinal lawyers understand international law as interstate law, created by and generating obligations for states. Rational-choice scholars focus on state interests to explain treaty-making and compliance. And even constructivists, more open to other norm entrepreneurs at the initial stages of change processes, often focus exclusively on states when they seek to assess whether norms have actually changed.

This focus stands in some contrast with real-world examples of international legal change in which states play only a supporting role.[34] Especially in areas where courts have become central actors, it is often these courts—rather than the views or practices of states—that become a reference point for understanding whether a norm has changed and what it entails at a given point. The European Court of Human Rights shifted understandings of European human rights law, for example in the area of LGBT rights, even though a sizeable number of member states had not embraced such a shift.[35] The World Trade Organization (WTO) Appellate Body (AB) was, for more than two decades, the focal point of action in world trade law, redefining the law even in the face of opposition by important states.[36] But

[34] Nico Krisch and Ezgi Yildiz, 'From Drivers to Bystanders: The Varying Roles of States in International Legal Change' (May 23, 2023). <https://ssrn.com/abstract=4456773> <http://dx.doi.org/10.2139/ssrn.4456773>.

[35] See Laurence R Helfer and Erik Voeten, 'International Courts as Agents of Legal Change: Evidence from LGBT Rights in Europe' (2014) 68 International Organization 77.

[36] Gregory Shaffer, Manfred Elsig. and Sergio Puig, 'The Extensive (But Fragile) Authority of the WTO Appellate Body' (2016) 79 Law and Contemporary Problems 237.

also beyond the realm of courts we find examples of authorities central to change processes—the UN High Commissioner for Refugees when it comes to the interpretation of the 1951 Geneva Convention,[37] the International Committee of the Red Cross for the development of international humanitarian law,[38] or the ILC, an expert body, for the codification of the law of state responsibility[39] or clarifying the rules of treaty interpretation, as Fuad Zarbiyev explains in his contribution to this volume.[40]

These examples point not only to a limited role of states, but also to a variation in the role of other institutions that is not easily reduced to formal mandates. Some courts have developed far-reaching authority in their issue-areas, while others have not.[41] Some international organizations are key legal players in their domain, while others play a secondary part, and variation is yet more pronounced in the role of expert bodies and private institutions. We can only account for this variation if we take into consideration the social processes through which the authority of different actors is generated. These processes are not necessarily the same across international law, but often vary across its different fields. International law today can be understood as comprising multiple social fields with their own structures of actors, authorities, boundaries, and fundamental norms. These fields are differentiated along issue-areas and regions, national boundaries as well as practical and academic contexts.[42] The differences are visible according to the experts recognized in each field, and in the institutions whose views and pronouncements are seen to matter.[43] As emphasized by Giovanni Mantilla, the International Committee of the Red Cross (ICRC) is widely accepted as an authority when it comes to the interpretation of international humanitarian law.[44] In human rights, different institutions and actors struggle for influence; Nina Reiners' contribution to this volume highlights the ways in which bodies such as the UN Committee on Economic, Social and Cultural Rights cultivate authority by forming network-based informal coalitions.[45] Other fields, such as international environmental law, have not produced a similar institutional authority, and different constellations of actors and texts matter there. At the same time, as Dorothea Endres shows in her

[37] Ingo Venzke, 'Semantic Authority' in Jean d'Aspremont and Sahib Singh (eds), *Concepts for International Law* (Edward Elgar 2019).

[38] Giovanni Mantilla, *Lawmaking under Pressure: International Humanitarian Law and Internal Armed Conflict* (Cornell University Press 2020).

[39] James Crawford, *The International Law Commission's Articles on State Responsibility: Introduction, Text and Commentaries* (CUP 2002).

[40] Zarbiyev, this volume.

[41] Karen Alter, Laurence Helfer. and Mikael Madsen, 'How Context Shapes the Authority of International Courts' (2016) 79 Law and Contemporary Problems 1.

[42] Nico Krisch, 'The Many Fields of (German) International Law' in A Roberts and others (eds), *Comparative International Law* (OUP 2018).

[43] See also Venzke, *How Interpretation Makes International Law* (n 13); Anthea Roberts, *Is International Law International?* (OUP 2017).

[44] Mantilla (n 38).

[45] Reiners, this volume.

chapter, we can often observe divergences within a given field regarding who and what counts as authority, leaving authority contested.[46]

The different fields of international law are linked with one another, but they do not form a common whole. What kinds of arguments are acceptable in legal discourse is endogenously defined through the practices of law within each social field—practices that typically connect with, but also generate variations on, rules about sources and interpretations in other areas and 'general' international law. Approaching these as 'practices' in a narrower sense appears fruitful also because they are not simply external to actors and thus at their disposal to accept, reject, or modify.[47] They instead provide the structure in which actors operate. These practices are not just discourses in an ideational realm but are embodied by actors: proper participants in legal interactions are only those who understand 'how to' make legal arguments, how to work within the field. Being an international lawyer (or an international human rights lawyer, international criminal lawyer, etc) is largely defined by the practical mastery of key techniques.[48]

An interest in practices, and communities of practice, has recently gained more traction in the international legal realm, especially in the work of Jutta Brunnée and Stephen Toope, and Tanja Aalberts and Ingo Venzke.[49] Such a focus can save us from falling into the trap of reproducing the entrenched dichotomies between 'agency and structure', 'material and discursive' factors, and 'continuity and change'.[50] The particular role of practices in linking agency and structure also helps make sense of the stickiness of law.[51] Practices, as structures in which actors operate, appear as stable in the first place. However, they are not immutable but instead subject to reflection, contestation, and reinterpretation as long as they continue to be recognized as the frame for the identity of actors within the field.[52] Change in the 'ground rules' of practice within the fields of international law is thus likely to be gradual and slow. At the same time, those ground rules establish under what conditions ordinary legal change is recognized—what acts or statements suffice to bring about a modification of existing norms. These conditions may be strict or permissive; they may erect high hurdles or allow for rapid change.

46 Endres, this volume.

47 Christian Bueger and Frank Gadinger, *International Practice Theory* (2nd edn, Springer 2018).

48 See Nikolas M Rajkovic, Tanja Aalberts, and Thomas Gammeltoft-Hansen (eds), *The Power of Legality: Practices of International Law and Their Politics* (CUP 2016).

49 eg Jutta Brunnée and Stephen J Toope, *Legitimacy and Legality in International Law: An Interactional Account* (CUP 2010); Tanja Aalberts and Ingo Venzke, 'Moving Beyond Interdisciplinary Turf Wars: Towards an Understanding of International Law as Practice' in André Nollkaemper and others (eds), *International Law as a Profession* (CUP 2017).

50 Emanuel Adler and Vincent Pouliot, 'International Practices' (2011) 3 International Theory 1.

51 Ezgi Yildiz, 'Enduring Practices in Changing Circumstances: A Comparison of the European Court of Human Rights and the Inter-American Court of Human Rights' (2020) 34 Temple International & Comparative Law Journal 309.

52 Ted Hopf, 'Change in International Practices' (2018) 24 European Journal of International Relations 687.

As an example: the ground rules of international law may themselves be resistant to change but they allow for (relatively quick) legal change through the adoption of treaties. In some fields, they may recognize particular authorities, such as the courts mentioned before, as central to processes of norm change. In others, they may assign a greater role to domestic courts, or pronouncements of diplomatic gatherings.

3.2 Pathways

The practices in each field produce different pathways along which change can travel. International lawyers traditionally focus on state-centric forms in keeping with their established doctrine of sources, and they have been hesitant to broaden this focus, in part for normative reasons.[53] But as already highlighted, we can actually observe a much greater variety of forms and processes leading to change in legal practice, and the mix of available pathways varies significantly from issue-area to issue-area.

In order to structure our inquiry, we here identify five main, ideal-typical pathways present in different contexts. Each path has its own operating logic and relies on a certain vested authority. Propositions for a change in meaning are bound to be more successful if they stem from, or are ratified by, an actor, or set of actors, recognized as authority.[54] Each path also comes with its own mechanisms through which change occurs or upon which actors rely to propose change attempts.

1. *The state action path.* On this path, change is identified when states modify their behaviour and make corresponding statements, as in the traditional image of change in customary international law and subsequent practice to treaties. This path derives its legitimacy from the authority of states. Although change attempts may be initiated by a few states, their success depends on building a broader consensus around the suggested change. The mechanism of change typically consists of two steps: proposing a new norm or establishing a new practice (which destabilizes existing understandings, pushes existing boundaries, or goes beyond set standards), and then building consensus around these new understandings. Traditionally, such consensus was thought to require virtually universal acceptance or acquiescence, but the actual threshold may be lower in practice.

[53] eg Michael Wood, 'International Organizations and Customary International Law' (2015) 48 Vanderbilt Journal of Transnational Law 609.

[54] Venzke, *How Interpretation Makes International Law* (n 13); for a relevant overview of different sources of authority, see Deborah D Avant, Martha Finnemore, and Susan K Sell, 'Who Governs the Globe?' in Deborah Avant, Martha Finnemore, and Susan K Sell (eds), *Who Governs the Globe?* (CUP 2010).

2. *The multilateral path.* Here change is generated as a result of statements issued by many states within the framework of an international organization. It relies on the collective authority of states, but also the institutional authority of the organization that serves as a forum. A resolution adopted by the UN Human Rights Council, for example, will often appear more authoritative than a collective statement by the same states outside the organizational framework. Change attempts on this path are typically realized by means of the introduction of new ideas via declarations and soft law documents as well as the adoption of formal treaties, which might shift opinion on customary rules or the interpretation of existing agreements even if they are not universally ratified.
3. *The bureaucratic path.* Change on this path is identified as the result of decisions or statements produced by international organizations in contexts that do not involve the direct participation of states in the decision-making processes. It relies on delegated authority or bureaucratic authority deriving from expertise, capacity, and procedures, though it might also reflect principled (moral) authority. Sources of authority will often be mixed and depend on the particular organ in question. The UN's ILC, for example, derives its weight from both its mandate and the recognized expertise of its members. This path typically operates through the production of texts for purposes of clarification and interpretation and thus in a more technical vein. Although such attempts may sometimes involve new norms and organizational mission creep, they usually avoid open pretensions to legal change.
4. *The judicial path.* Change in this form is recognized as the result of decisions and findings of courts and quasi-judicial bodies. It relies on judicial expert authority and often also on the delegation from states. Change typically comes about through mechanisms of (broader or narrower) interpretation or channelling of views expressed in other legal instruments (both soft and hard)—without open claims to effecting change. International courts are the typical anchor of this path, but institutions such as the UN human rights treaty bodies or the OECD National Contact Points feature here as well just as much as national courts when they interpret international (rather than national) law.
5. *The private authority path.* Change in this modality follows statements or reports by recognized authorities in a private capacity without a clear affiliation to or mandate from states or international organizations. This path's claim to legitimacy is built upon authority from expertise, capacity, or principle, potentially also on inclusive procedures. Its mechanisms for change are often solution-oriented interventions in specific issue-areas, and they are realized through the production of technical manuals, standards, and regulations—responding to new demands not (yet) addressed through other pathways.

But, in more exceptional cases such as the ICRC, private authority can also weigh heavily in facilitating a lasting change of established rules.

These paths are ideal-typical, and they are not mutually exclusive—often enough they will run in parallel or crisscross, bolstering or undercutting each other. The interactions between pathways produce a range of effects from solidifying legal change by creating focal points, to giving grounds for (further) legal contestation by providing alternative interpretations. They will also often appear in a sequential way, with some pathways building on others, for example, the judicial on the private authority one.

Change in international law is then rarely the result of the activation of a single pathway. Only where an authority is consolidated and sufficiently focal in a particular context will it alone shift an accepted understanding of legal rules. The European Court of Human Rights might be such an example, at least within certain bounds. Otherwise, change will typically be the result of an accumulation of statements produced in the same or different pathways, sometimes in quick succession, at other times over a significant period of time. These statements will typically serve initially to irritate and destabilize prior understandings and then (potentially) reconsolidate in the direction of a new, settled rule or interpretation. Yet such consolidation will often be a matter of degree, with a certain amount of contestation frequently persisting for a long time.

3.3 Stages

Change does not travel along these pathways by itself but is pursued in and through them by political and societal actors. In order to better understand the actors and dynamics relevant to change processes, we can usefully conceptualize pathways as consisting of three stages, each of which is crucial for the process to be successfully completed.

The first is the *selection stage*, where change agents choose and activate a pathway to realize their vision of change. They may sometimes activate more than one pathway contemporaneously to increase their legitimacy claims or to undercut the legitimacy of rival interpretations. Potential change agents include governments, but also individuals, companies, scholars, experts, or other interested parties. Different actors will have different pathways available to them. Private actors will typically have access to a much more limited range than governments (and sometimes depend on the latter to take up their cause). Actors' choices in this respect are likely to be only boundedly rational as they usually are not able to fully assess the benefits and drawbacks of each pathway, and they will often follow established authorities in a field unless they have significant reasons to choose others.[55] Yet,

[55] See Joseph Jupille, Walter Mattli, and Duncan Snidal, *Institutional Choice and Global Commerce* (CUP 2013).

in some cases, actors might even attempt to create new pathways—for example, new bodies within international organizations, or independent groups of experts such as that assembled to produce the Maastricht Principles on Extraterritorial Obligations of States.[56]

The second, central stage is that of *construction*. Here the actors and authorities associated with the particular pathway process the change attempts and generate statements about the status of the norm in question—confirming or refuting the change attempt, finding some middle ground, etc—or avoid expressing their positions. This processing and position-taking may help create a new norm or clarify an existing one and, in some instances, this results in rejecting proposed new definitions and revoking the change attempt altogether. These statements are then used by change agents (as well as their opponents, as the case may be) to build legitimacy and bolster support for their cause. If the selection stage is often dominated by activist modes of engagement with a choice between different fora, the construction stage tends to follow a different logic. On many pathways, actors engage in interpretation rather than law-creation and are thus constrained by expectations of legal continuity rather than change. This is especially true for judicial and quasi-judicial actors, but also for expert bodies within and outside international organizations. In more political contexts, where change agents may be able to pursue change openly, such constraints are lessened. However, in all forms, we often observe attempts at consensus-building—or other forms of legitimacy-enhancing strategies—that are more pronounced than those at the selection stage.

The third is the *reception stage*, where the outcome of the construction stage is appraised by a broader range of actors; it is here that change attempts are accepted, partially accepted, or rejected—or held in suspense when change is recognized as potential yet not complete. The relevant actors typically include especially state representatives—executive, legislative, as well as judicial ones—but also international courts, scholars, and other experts. Who counts as a relevant participant depends on the structure of the field—in some fields, for example human rights law, civil society organizations will play some role, in others less so, and recognition as a relevant actor is bound to be the subject of struggles itself. Actors in the reception stage will assess a proposed change on substance but also on pedigree. If the actors and institutions at the construction stage are recognized as authorities, many actors in the field will defer to them even if they disagree with the result.

These three stages will often be consecutive, but this does not necessarily mean that they are always neatly separated and that every change process follows through them linearly. Feedback from the reception stage may come in while the construction phase is still underway; selection and construction stages may overlap; and

[56] Olivier De Schutter and others, 'Commentary to the Maastricht Principles on Extraterritorial Obligations of States in the Area of Economic, Social and Cultural Rights' (2012) 34 Human Rights Quarterly 1084.

change agents may also pursue new paths to build on ongoing construction processes in other fora. The chapter by Jeff Kucik and Sergio Puig provides a good example of feedback effects as they show how the WTO AB adapts its jurisprudence in response to states' non-compliance with earlier decisions.[57] Moreover, the different stages may be repeated multiple times in different pathways in the overall change process. The notion of stages, therefore, should not be understood strictly in the sense of temporal phases but instead as a useful heuristic that helps us capture the different dynamics and actor constellations that are present at different points in the change process.

Which path actors choose or activate will depend on their awareness of existing options, and on the availability of these options. It is also likely to depend on the change agents' assessment of the degree to which the institutions and actors associated with a given path are receptive to their cause, and on the likely impact that a certain path might have on a successful outcome.[58] For a non-governmental organization (NGO) keen on developing the interpretation of women's rights, an expert body in the field of human rights, and especially one associated with the UN Convention on the Elimination of all forms of Discrimination Against Women (CEDAW), will appear as more receptive than, say, the ILC or an intergovernmental body such as the UN General Assembly. Yet in order to consolidate a given interpretation, a stronger authority might be needed. If initially, a change agent might choose the path of least resistance, it may at a later stage seek to activate a path that promises a greater impact, also beyond the narrow field of human rights practitioners. The result will often be a staged approach in which each step builds on the outcome of a previous one, expanding influence and scope with each iteration if the institutional structure of the respective field so allows, and thus accumulating authority over time.

As they go through their different stages, change processes also vary significantly as to their pace or modes, and one of the objectives of our project is to understand the conditions determining such variation. As mentioned above, many existing accounts focus on punctuated equilibria, with long periods of stability interrupted by sudden and short periods of movement.[59] This picture may be accurate for treaty-making episodes, but it may not be as fitting to describe other modes of change, captured in more gradualist accounts. Gradual change has recently found greater theoretical attention,[60] and we expect it to be the dominant form when change processes centrally involve actors—especially judges or experts—who, as a result of their particular role, cannot openly claim to be engaged in change as such and thus

[57] Kucik and Puig, this volume.

[58] See also Jupille, Mattli, and Snidal (n 55).

[59] Paul F Diehl and Charlotte Ku, *The Dynamics of International Law* (CUP 2010).

[60] James Mahoney and Kathleen Thelen, 'A Theory of Gradual Institutional Change' in James Mahoney and Kathleen Thelen (eds), *Explaining Institutional Change: Ambiguity, Agency, and Power* (CUP 2010).

have to avoid the appearance of taking big steps.[61] Wouter Werner demonstrates how this plays out for expert authorities engaged in change through restatements.[62]

4. Conditions of Change

When is an attempt at changing international law successful? Traditional legal doctrine focuses almost exclusively on state positions and demands near-unanimity of support or acquiescence among states (or treaty parties). In reality, the threshold appears lower—change seems to be accepted in many instances with less support by, or even in the face of objections from, states. Yet which factors condition the success of change processes is not clear. The existing literature focuses especially on two groups of factors—pertaining to state positions and norm properties, much along the lines of rationalist and constructivist approaches. Yet we argue that in addition to these, two further groups of factors, both related to the pathways sketched above, are likely to be important: one related to the institutional structure of the respective context and one concerning discursive openings facilitating legal shifts. The importance of these latter factors is suggested by approaches drawing on historical and discursive institutionalism, both less prominent in international relations but potentially powerful in the context of a field as discursively oriented as international law.

The factors laid out here certainly cannot explain all variation and should, in any event, not be understood in a deterministic fashion. As Ingo Venzke reminds us in his chapter, change processes always contain an element of contingency, of paths not taken even if they could have been, of individual actors shaping developments even if structural constraints make their success unlikely.[63] In this sense, the factors presented here only increase the likelihood of success without in any way determining it. Still, we believe that they go a long way towards explaining the outcomes of informal change processes.

4.1 State Positions

Most observers agree that the success of change in international legal norms depends in large part on how strongly it is supported and opposed by states. Where there is unanimity, or near-unanimity, among states, change is likely to

[61] See eg Ezgi Yildiz, 'A Court with Many Faces: Judicial Characters and Modes of Norm Development in the European Court of Human Rights' (2020) 31 European Journal of International Law 73; Ezgi Yildiz, *Between Forbearance and Audacity: The European Court of Human Rights and the Norm Against Torture* (CUP 2023).

[62] Werner, this volume.

[63] Venkze, this volume.

occur smoothly and quickly. In the realm of customary law, notions such as 'instant custom' or different forms of 'modern custom' give expression to this fact, downplaying the need for consistency of practice or statements over time.[64]

Yet below this threshold, conditions are less well-defined. More state support certainly means a higher probability of success, but what thresholds must be met remains disputed. The literature on norm change in international politics often focuses on a need for support from a critical mass—sometimes thought to be around one-third—of states to reach a 'tipping point' and declench a norm cascade that brings the rest of states to the table.[65] Others focus on 'broad support', but without a clear specification of what this implies—potentially a majority of states, but in certain circumstances also a smaller number.[66] Yet other thresholds are likely to apply when it comes to legal change, as opposed to norm change in general.

Not all states are equal in these processes, and most accounts emphasize the need for powerful states to support change efforts, or the need for critical states—those particularly active in a domain—to be on board.[67] International law mitigates power differentials to some extent because of its expectations of sovereign equality, and great powers do not always seem to be indispensable for norm change to occur. Examples show successful change processes without great powers—and sometimes against the objections of some of them.[68] Nina Kiderlin's chapter on changes in world trade law despite fervent objections from the US provides an interesting example of such processes while also showing the increasing clout of China at the WTO.[69] Recent literature also shows that great powers do not always effect change through rapidly enforced substantial change proposals. They may effectuate fundamental and yet informal changes through seemingly apolitical moves—by incrementally altering the assumptions around the appropriateness of certain standards or behaviour patterns.[70] They might also intentionally keep norms unstable in order to leave more room for manoeuvre, as Pedro Martínez Esponda finds in his contribution.[71]

Some of the variation in terms of necessary state support might be related to the salience of the norm in question—to the degree to which an attempt at norm

[64] Anthea Elizabeth Roberts, 'Traditional and Modern Approaches to Customary International Law: A Reconciliation' (2001) 95 The American Journal of International Law 757.

[65] Finnemore and Sikkink (n 23).

[66] Wayne Sandholtz, 'International Norm Change' [2017] Oxford Research Encyclopedia of Politics <www.oxfordre.com/abstract/10.1093/acrefore/9780190228637.001.0001/acrefore-9780190228637-e-588> accessed 10 December 2022.

[67] ibid; Finnemore and Sikkink (n 23) 901.

[68] Toope (n 29); see also Adam Bower, *Norms Without the Great Powers: International Law and Changing Social Standards in World Politics* (OUP 2017).

[69] Kiderlin, this volume.

[70] Alexander E Kentikelenis and Sarah Babb, 'The Making of Neoliberal Globalization: Norm Substitution and the Politics of Clandestine Institutional Change' (2019) 124 American Journal of Sociology 1720, 1722.

[71] Martínez Esponda, this volume.

change attracts attention by high-level policymakers or public opinion. On an issue with relatively limited salience, change may happen more smoothly, and objections by some states may not appear as too consequential (and may not be pursued through an investment of significant diplomatic capital). When it comes to issues with high salience, in contrast, states' engagement is likely to be stronger and they are less likely to stand on the sidelines if change processes concern them. For example, as Mark Pollack skilfully shows, the Trump administration spent a considerable amount of energy in derailing the established rules and institutions of international trade law—an issue-area that was (and is) highly salient.[72] At the same time, such increased salience might also lead to deadlock as compromise is more difficult to achieve, potentially driving change onto other than state-driven paths.

4.2 Norm Properties

A second set of factors often thought to influence the likelihood of change attempts' success are the properties of the norm(s) in question.[73] These concern in the first place the stability of prior understandings: the more settled and uncontested an existing (interpretation of a) norm is, the higher the threshold for change. If, on the other hand, competing interpretations are already in circulation, even if they are not (yet) dominant, change efforts can create linkages with these to further destabilize the existing norm and its interpretation. The proximity of a proposed new norm or interpretation to existing ones is then likely to be a significant factor. This is sometimes captured as 'norm adjacency'[74]—when a new claim can present itself as the development of an existing norm rather than a radically new proposition, it faces a lower hurdle in legal discourses.

This is equally relevant when change efforts draw on competing legal norms. If the change of one norm can be argued for by reference to another existing and widely accepted norm, destabilization as a matter of law can be achieved more easily.[75] For example, the availability of international human rights law helped to undermine state official immunities which were otherwise widely recognized.[76] And the rise of international environmental law gave campaigners a potent tool to challenge and redirect free trade rules that stood in tension with environmental

72 Pollack, this volume.

73 eg Miriam Bradley, 'Unintended Consequences of Adjacency Claims: The Function and Dysfunction of Analogies between Refugee Protection and IDP Protection in the Work of UNHCR' (2019) 25 Global Governance: A Review of Multilateralism and International Organizations 620.

74 Finnemore and Sikkink (n 23).

75 See Nico Krisch, Francesco Corradini, and Lucy Lu Reimers, 'Order at the Margins: The Legal Construction of Interface Conflicts over Time' (2020) 9 Global Constitutionalism 343.

76 Pedro José Martínez Esponda, 'Change in International Law Through Informal Means: The Rise of Exceptions to State Official Immunity for International Crimes' (2019) 9 Revista Latinoamericana de Derecho Internacional (LADI) 175, 190.

protection.[77] In the same vein, Seline Trevisanut's chapter demonstrates how human rights law and environmental law helped actors impart new understandings and practices to shape the future of the oceans.[78] We can expect a similar effect, though to a lesser extent, if competing norms are less widely shared (eg if they are part of a treaty ratified by a sub-group of states) or are of a lesser legal pedigree, as in the case of informal norms or soft law.[79]

The stability and rigidity of an existing norm then determine how high the justificatory burden for a change attempt will be. When the burden is low, small shifts in circumstances can trigger norm change. When the burden is higher, change agents need a stronger justification and will often have to take a slower road by first destabilizing existing understandings and then reconsolidating new ones.

Another important dimension that has not received much attention from the literature concerns the purpose and direction of a new norm or understanding as *more permissive or more constraining* than an existing one. For change proposals that seek to open a broader scope for action—such as widening self-defence against non-state actors or expanding port state jurisdiction over vessels engaged in illegal, unreported, and unregulated (IUU) fishing[80]—relatively limited support and positive appraisal may often be sufficient for actors. Destabilizing current understandings, especially in areas of international law that are relatively under- (or un-) institutionalized, might be enough to create the possibility for action. Pursuing change by means of destabilization can be attractive, as Pedro Martínez Esponda shows in his contribution. Yet it also appears to be an option primarily for powerful actors who can bear the costs of (international or domestic) contestation which will often be significant as long as a new meaning has not been re-stabilized. BS Chimni draws our attention to this very fact and emphasizes how power asymmetries can explain the variations in the way change attempts are pursued.[81]

On the other hand, introducing new constraints on or requirements for state action—such as those that limit trade in endangered species or those that require states to prevent domestic violence[82]—often seems to call for a higher threshold, with more buy-in from a critical number of actors and a higher degree of consensus necessary to shift accepted understandings. Change agents then often need to re-stabilize the new norm, often by securing supportive statements from focal institutions or from the accumulation of more dispersed authorities, making this process longer and more burdensome than the one described for permissive norms.

[77] Lucy Lu Reimers, 'International Trade Law: Legal Entanglement on the WTO's Own Terms' in Nico Krisch (ed), *Entangled Legalities Beyond the State* (CUP 2021).

[78] Trevisanut, this volume.

[79] Gregory Shaffer and Mark A Pollack, 'Hard vs. Soft Law: Alternatives, Complements and Antagonists in International Governance' (2010) 94 Minnesota Law Review 706.

[80] Pedro Martínez Esponda, Dorothea Endres, and Ezgi Yildiz (eds), *Paths of Change in International Law: Case Studies* (2023).

[81] Chimni, this volume.

[82] Martínez Esponda, Endres, and Yildiz (n 80).

4.3 Institutional Support

A third set of factors has found less attention in the literature on international norm change, but is, we conjecture, at least equally important: the existence, shape, and accessibility of institutions and authorities. This might seem obvious for those who study change through the lens of historical sociology or historical institutionalism. For them, existing processes and institutions are central to understanding how new change processes unfold and what shape they take.[83] Elements of path dependence and institutional constraints are less prominent in other theoretical approaches, but constructivists, too, have long been attentive to the power of institutions in making and implementing norms,[84] and the positive influence of institutional statements' on norms' strength.[85] Likewise, rational-choice-oriented scholars have come to emphasize the ways in which existing institutional arrangements shape the choices of actors, especially under circumstances of bounded rationality.[86]

In our context, institutional factors are likely to have significant consequences for a number of elements in the change processes. They will, first, condition whether a change attempt evolves into a change process at all. For non-state norm entrepreneurs, in particular, access to certain pathways of change is crucial. Where they can directly engage an international court or expert body, they can more easily generate visibility and potentially gain authority for their cause. Where this is not the case—for example, because an existing court is only accessible for states, or because the only available pathways in a certain area are intergovernmental in character—they face a much higher threshold for getting a change attempt off the ground. However, they can creatively overcome this hurdle by forming coalitions with alternative authorities, as Nina Reiners explains in her chapter in this volume. Likewise, even for states, institutions in some areas are more receptive than in others—compare only the UN Security Council with the more inclusive institutions in international environmental governance. And there are areas with no, or weak, dedicated institutions; this may apply to many questions of general international law, especially where the jurisdiction of the International Court of Justice depends on (scattered) individual acceptance by states. In such areas, states may seek to bring their change proposals to receptive fields or institutions.

[83] See Wolfgang Streeck and Kathleen Thelen (eds), *Beyond Continuity: Institutional Change in Advanced Political Economies* (OUP 2005); Orfeo Fioretos, 'Historical Institutionalism in International Relations' (2011) 65 International Organization 367.

[84] Michael N Barnett and Martha Finnemore, 'The Politics, Power, and Pathologies of International Organizations' (1999) 53 International Organization 699.

[85] Beth A Simmons and Hyeran Jo, 'Measuring Norms and Normative Contestation: The Case of International Criminal Law' (2019) 4 Journal of Global Security Studies 18; Michal Ben-Josef Hirsch and Jennifer M Dixon, 'Conceptualizing and Assessing Norm Strength in International Relations' [2020] European Journal of International Relations 18.

[86] Jupille, Mattli, and Snidal (n 55).

Institutional factors can be expected to condition all three stages of a change process. They define the selection stage in that the existence of available institutions will channel most of the action by change agents, especially so if there is one widely accepted focal institution through which change usually occurs.[87] In the construction stage, the orientation and composition of an institution very much determine whether a certain cause will be taken up or not. And in the reception stage, much depends on the social position of the authority involved in the construction—whether it is regarded as a central authority or merely a marginal voice. In this sense, it usually matters decisively whether support for a change attempt comes from a broad majority in the UN General Assembly or from a privately assembled group of experts on a given issue. Without clear institutional authority in favour of a change proposal, we surmise that it is unlikely that a new understanding becomes consolidated.

The relevance of institutional factors becomes particularly visible when we consider their effects in calibrating the other factors mentioned above. Both as regards state positions and norm properties we have observed significant variation, and this variation may, to an extent, be driven by the institutional context in which a given change process takes place. In an area with a strong focal institution—for example, a court—the required support from states is likely to be lower than in a context in which—as in traditional customary law development—change occurs through the unstructured interaction of states. Likewise, we can expect certain norm properties to matter more in some institutional contexts. The norm adjacency mentioned above is important for gathering political support for a new norm or a new understanding of it. But it will be of particular importance in contexts defined by a preponderance of legal skills—especially courts or expert bodies, and generally all those in which actors draw their authority from legal expertise rather than other sources. Such actors need to stay within the bounds of legal interpretation, and the plausibility of their positions will depend on their adjacency claims to existing norms, judicial findings, and the legal discourse more generally.

In all these respects, the institutional landscape in a given context is likely to influence how smoothly and quickly a change process unfolds and whether it is successful. It will also influence to what extent actors will choose or create other avenues than formally *legal* ones to pursue their agendas. Where existing pathways of change in international law prove too rigid, actors may shift to other fora. This is very visible in the business and human rights context—after attempts at establishing human rights obligations for transnational corporations were frustrated in the UN in the early 2000s, activists continued to pursue their agenda primarily through non-binding norms as well as in domestic fora. As in other

[87] Whether such focalization occurs depends on certain circumstance. See Ezgi Yildiz and Umut Yüksel, 'The Defocalizing Effect of International Courts: Evidence from Maritime Delimitation Practices' (2022) 23 German Law Journal 413

contexts, traditional international law here was displaced by other normativities, or at least pushed to the side through a process of layering, in the language of historical institutionalists.[88] In a similar vein, Jaye Ellis's chapter shows how actors in international environmental governance turned from norms and rules to performance-oriented metrics as the main driver of change, and how these metrics began to operate alongside (and in interaction with) legal norms.[89]

4.4 Discursive Openings

A fourth set of potential factors pertains to the relation of legal norms with their ideational environment. When this gap grows, and especially when it grows suddenly or over a short time span, pressure towards an adaptation of the law rises. In such circumstances, we would expect international legal change to occur more easily than otherwise.

This expectation aligns with the role critical junctures play in historical institutionalism. A distinct feature of such junctures is thought to be 'the loosening of the constraints of structure to allow for agency or contingency to shape divergence from the past, or divergence across cases'.[90] In our context, this should affect the more structural constraints on change deriving from institutional rules and norm stability, and consequently the scope of necessary state support. During a critical juncture—for example, the end of World War II, the outrage over the Bosnian genocide, or the attacks of 9/11—international legal change is likely to occur even if previous norms are stable and state support is relatively weak. This might also imply that change can occur through other paths than those typically considered central in a field, or that a new path can be created more easily. The sudden establishment of individual criminal responsibility in internal armed conflicts by the newly created International Criminal Tribunal for the former Yugoslavia after the Bosnian war might be an example of such a facilitated shift.[91] More generally, scholars have observed the particular movement of international law in times of crisis, and they have even portrayed international law as a 'discipline of crisis'.[92]

[88] Streeck and Thelen (n 83) 18–30.

[89] Ellis, this volume.

[90] Hillel David Soifer, 'The Causal Logic of Critical Junctures' (2012) 45 Comparative Political Studies 1572, 1573; Paul Pierson, *Politics in Time: History, Institutions, and Social Analysis* (Princeton University Press 2004); Giovanni Capoccia and R Daniel Kelemen, 'The Study of Critical Junctures: Theory, Narrative, and Counterfactuals in Historical Institutionalism' (2007) 59 World Politics 341.

[91] Martínez Esponda, Endres, and Yildiz (n 80).

[92] Hilary Charlesworth, 'International Law: A Discipline of Crisis' (2002) 65 The Modern Law Review 377; see also W Michael Reisman, 'International Incidents: Introduction to a New Genre in the Study of International Law' in W Michael Reisman and Andrew R Willard (eds), *International Incidents: The Law That Counts in World Politics* (Princeton University Press 2014); Fleur Johns, Richard Joyce, and Sundhya Pahuja (eds), *Events: The Force of International Law* (Routledge 2010).

True critical junctures are few and far between, but the effects of discursive openings should be observable also in less extreme cases. Shifts in discourses have been found to foster institutional change in general, and they can also reshape international law—which is, after all, a particularly discursive institution itself and one that requires constant justification through broader normative argument.[93] As Tonya Putnam explains, the reformulation of atrocity prevention under the Genocide Convention without any amendment to the treaty text benefited from such discursive shifts.[94] Whenever new ideas—cognitive or moral—are widely held and contrast with existing legal norms or understandings, they create an opportunity space for actors to pursue legal change.[95] This facilitates such change—even though the likelihood will be significantly higher if the new ideas can be linked to some pre-existing norms and if they meet receptive institutions, as discussed in the previous subsections. The newly arisen sense that the moral implications of automated weapons systems require an adaptation of the laws of war creates urgency for such a change, but the change process still needs to find institutional support and will benefit from a linkage with existing rules.[96] Likewise, the increasing salience of the climate change discourse has created pressure for change in other areas of the law, for example, refugee protection. Yet, the full realization of this change needed receptive institutions—such as the UN Human Rights Committee and the UN General Assembly—to lend claims to the reinterpretation by an authority with significant weight.[97]

4.5 Combined Effects

These four groups of potential factors behind successful change are not independent from one another. There might be minimum thresholds—for state support especially, and perhaps also for institutional availability without which it might be difficult to consolidate a new norm in some contexts. But beyond that, what is required in one group appears to depend on the presence or absence of factors from another group. Norm adjacency is likely to be more important in certain

[93] Vivien A Schmidt, 'The State and Political Economic Change: Beyond Rational Choice and Historical Institutionalism to Discursive Institutionalism' in Mario Telò (ed), *State, Globalization and Multilateralism: The Challenges of Institutionalizing Regionalism* (Springer Netherlands 2012).

[94] Putnam, this volume.

[95] See also Antje Wiener, *Contestation and Constitution of Norms in Global International Relations* (CUP 2018).

[96] eg R Charli Carpenter, 'Vetting the Advocacy Agenda: Network Centrality and the Paradox of Weapons Norms' (2011) 65 International Organization 69; Ingvild Bode and Hendrik Huelss, 'Autonomous Weapons Systems and Changing Norms in International Relations' (2018) 44 Review of International Studies 393.

[97] See eg UN Human Rights Committee, Views of 24 October 2019, No 2728/2016, *Teitiota v New Zealand*; UNGA, 'The Human Right to a Clean, Healthy and Sustainable Environment' (26 July 2022) 76th session (A/76/L.75).

institutional contexts (eg in courts) but less so in the presence of significant discursive opening and probably also when there is widespread state support for change. On the other hand, widespread state support might be less important if a strong focal institution exists, when permissive norm change is sought, or when there is a critical juncture facilitating change. In this vein, the inability of states to collectively agree on norm adaptation in the political bodies of the WTO may not have frustrated change attempts but reoriented them towards the organization's dispute settlement system which had already gained significant authority.[98] The different factors are thus interdependent—mutually reinforcing, but in certain circumstances also potential substitutes for one another.

5. The Structure of the Volume

Change processes are manifold, and the way they transpire will depend on the specific set of circumstances, some of which we discuss in the previous section. These include but are not limited to the configuration of actor and interest constellations, the socio-political context, the characteristics of the sites of change, as well as the timing and the ambition of change proposals—ie their form, scope, reach, and potential impact. The present volume is organized around four themes, each exploring different dynamics present in many paths of change in international law. In particular, we take a closer look at *strategies*, *forms*, and *forces* of change, and we then reflect on how to *situate* these change processes and their varied implications in international law and politics.

5.1 Strategies of Change

Strategy is an essential part of the toolkit for change processes, and it is often tailored to the means and ends of change attempts, argues Mark Pollack in his analysis of the Trump administration and its lasting legacy in Chapter 2. Pollack distinguishes between traditional and hostile change agents—while the former seeks to influence the content of the law by resorting to means such as negotiation, interpretation, and adjudication, the latter employs more aggressive means with the ultimate purpose of circumventing and undermining international rules. On the basis of this distinction, Pollack examines the practices of the Trump administration in relation to four international trade-related episodes. He finds that while the evidence is mixed, overall, the Trump administration appears to be a 'genuinely disruptive or hostile change agent' whose objective is to weaken the international

[98] See Nicolas Lamp, 'Discord, Deference, Opportunism, and Pragmatism: How WTO Members Became Bystanders in the Development of WTO Law', manuscript on file with the authors.

rule of law rather than simply to reshape the content of specific norms. Moreover, the destructive legacies left by the Trump administration are, in Pollack's assessment, long-lasting and often difficult to reverse.

Strategies also come in different shades, and actors might resort to tactics other than advocating for or against a given change attempt, as we see in Chapter 3 by Pedro Martínez Esponda on the right to self-defence against non-state actors—a norm left in the twilight zone. The norm's unstable status is actively cultivated by actors that favour wide room for manoeuvre instead of clearly constraining rules. The norm-instability, in this case, has been intentional and sustained by at least four different strategies of destabilization: multilateral ambiguity, selective protest, compromised support, and cryptic precedent. Martínez Esponda argues that while the law on the use of force is particularly prone to such destabilization, norm instability is a widely present phenomenon across different fields of international law.

In Chapter 4, Nina Reiners highlights the role of expert bodies, working in close collaboration with civil society actors, in shaping international law through interpretation. Calling this symbiotic relationship 'transnational lawmaking coalitions' (TLC), Reiners explains how TLCs come together and what strategies they employ to generate change. She relies on interviews and primary and secondary sources to trace the involvement of TLCs in the interpretation of the right to decent working conditions by the Committee on Economic, Social and Cultural Rights, and the creation of a right to abortion, on the basis of the right to life, by the UN Human Rights Committee. Reiners argues that when formed around personal relationships that spread across different epistemic communities or professional or advocacy networks, TLCs can generate and propel change attempts without the involvement of state actors. Reiners' study shows that with their informal origins and collaborative spirit geared towards achieving like-minded goals, TLCs have the agility that other change agents such as states or intergovernmental institutions often lack.

5.2 Forms of Change

The form of change matters not only for calibrating the ambition of change attempts but also for creating hurdles or opportunities for the successful pursuit of change. In particular, as several contributions show, interpretive change construed incrementally over time will often provoke more limited contestation and have higher chances of success. Tonya Putnam's Chapter 5 traces common dynamics behind such incremental change processes in the revised understanding of the obligation to prevent in the 1948 Genocide Convention. The reconceptualization of atrocity prevention without a formal amendment to the treaty text was possible through the work of many hands such as governments, international organizations, and non-state actors. It did not come as a response to a single event or as a result of a single strategy, but rather through the winding paths of multiple agendas that came together in a non-linear fashion, and through discursive openings that were created by 'actions and glaring inactions'. Yet the impact of norm adjustment was significant since it fundamentally changed the meaning of genocide prevention, shifting the emphasis from non-interference to positive obligations to protect vulnerable populations in countries whose governments are unwilling or unable to do so.

In Chapter 6, Wouter Werner explores the dynamics behind restatements and codifications of existing law through his study of the International Law Commission (ILC) draft conclusions on the identification of customary law. Werner argues that change in this mode, often effectuated by experts with the authority to restate, is governed by the dialectics of repetition; the restated transforms into something new and different. This exercise is highly political, especially because it entails the delineation of relevant materials from irrelevant ones. Yet such restatements cannot appear as new creations, solely as the results of recursive exercises—they simply restate what is already out there. Repetition breeds change but also conceals the political dynamics driving it, Werner maintains.

Jaye Ellis takes us in Chapter 7 into the world of metrics, a form of governance that deviates from and sidelines the typical modalities of change in international law. As Ellis shows, the turn to metrics, which culminated in the adoption of the Sustainable Development Goals and the Paris Agreement in 2015, was in part a response to frustrated multilateral rulemaking. Once performance-oriented metrics became the main propellers of dynamism in environmental governance, bureaucrats, technocrats, and experts moved change processes outside of the law's normative realm. However, the logics of metrics and of legal normativity need not be mutually exclusive, argues Ellis, drawing our attention to the fact that they often operate in parallel, for example within the architecture of the Paris Agreement.

5.3 Forces of Change

Broader forces that drive change—shifts in power, ideas, or actor configurations—stand at the centre of the three next chapters. In Chapter 8, Wayne Sandholtz focuses on the impact of the rising authoritarian challenge to human rights law. Emphasizing that international legal change does not always need to be progressive or liberal, Sandholtz analyses non-liberal forces of change. He observes that authoritarian regimes attempt to hollow out international human rights institutions and tarnish their credibility. Their effect on the national level is more forceful, affirms Sandholtz. Authoritarians aim at curtailing domestic accountability mechanisms and suppressing related norms such as court independence and freedom of expression, press, and association. Sandholtz maintains that as the number and the strength of authoritarian regimes increase, so does their adverse impact on human rights norms and institutions. While cautioning against the challenges posed by the authoritarian resurgence, Sandholtz also points to countervailing dynamics, including the resilience of international human rights courts in the face of backlash or domestic mobilization against authoritarian regimes.

The broader effects of the rise of human rights and environmentalism are the subject of Chapter 9. Seline Trevisanut traces here how the law of the sea transformed in its interaction with both trends. After the adoption of the UN Convention of the Law of the Sea four decades ago, the law of the sea may have appeared as relatively static, but as Trevisanut shows, change has been driven through adjacent fields of international law, especially through the activation of multilateral, bureaucratic, and private authority pathways which channel signals of change from human rights and environmental law. Facilitating this transformation is, in her account, the involvement of several alternative authorities such as international organizations, expert authorities pushing for renewed understandings in guidelines and handbooks, and private actors (eg the oil and gas sector and professional associations).

Nina Kiderlin's Chapter 10 focuses on the effects of major power shifts in what appears as an arcane example only at first sight—the definition of 'public body' in the WTO rules on subsidies. This definition was important to China because of the prominence of state-owned enterprises and banks in its economic system, but it realized soon after its accession to the WTO that the negotiation-driven multilateral path was unlikely to lead to a significant change in its favour. It therefore actively shifted its efforts to the judicial pathway, the WTO dispute settlement system. Kiderlin explains that this required a long-term strategy, involving in particular investments in strong legal expertise. In the subsidies case, this led to a shift in China's direction on the part of the WTO AB, very much against the wishes of the US which, however, was unable to prevent the change. Yet, the episode contributed to growing US frustration, eventually resulting in the blockade of the AB (and a certain realignment of the public body jurisprudence once institutional risks had become clear). For some time, despite increased great-power rivalry, change had continued on the judicial pathway, only to be cut off by backlash when tensions became too strong.

5.4 Situating Change

The contributions to this volume give us a rich picture of the paths along which change travels in international law and the factors and dynamics behind change processes. This last section takes a step back to reflect more broadly on those processes, their doctrinal reconstruction, their sociological frame, and their political context. This begins, in Chapter 11, with a focus on the institutions involved in international legal change. Jeff Kucik and Sergio Puig's analysis focuses on the way in which the WTO AB operates and effectuates change, and in particular on the AB's treatment of 'precedent' in response to political challenges. While the AB generally has a strong tendency to follow its previous jurisprudence, Kucik and Puig ask whether this picture changes when its previous decisions resulted in non-compliance by states. Based on a broad quantitative analysis of the AB record, they conclude that the AB is indeed far more likely to adjust its jurisprudence in the face of such challenges—a very significant finding that sheds light on the political dynamics of the judicial pathway on which states are no longer in the driver's seat but still exert significant influence. Responsive institutions are thus able to calibrate change in a far more flexible way than traditional, state-driven processes of legal change.

In Chapter 12, Dorothea Endres explores the sociological frames through which change in international law is constructed. Endres observes that appraising incremental change is particularly challenging when it is processed in different communities of practice, which might come to diverging conclusions on whether change has occurred and who has the authority to identify it. In the absence of a focal authority that can bring about a convergence of understandings, different positions might persist, reducing the chances of straightforward consolidation, as Endres argues. 'Change' then often lies in the eye of the beholder, conditioned by the specific community of practice they are situated in.

Fuad Zarbiyev's Chapter 13 presents a process-oriented analysis of changing interpretive authority in international law. Zarbiyev skilfully traces how the ILC called into question the state's ultimate authority in treaty interpretation through its draft conclusions on subsequent practice. He argues that although that state authority did not have a formal or jurisprudential grounding, it has been an obvious point of reference for a long time. This began to change, cautiously, with the creation of an official treaty interpretation regime as well as the proliferation of alternative interpretative authorities and treaties with third-party beneficiaries. Yet the ILC has taken this further—surprisingly without challenge from states themselves—to hold that the joint interpretation of a treaty by its parties is not necessarily determinative of its meaning. As the 'conclusions' are likely to have serious implications in practice, Zarbiyev suggests that, even as a matter of doctrine, the central role of states in (interpretive) change in international law is relativized.

The penultimate Chapter 14 by Ingo Venzke continues on this theme and explores whether legal change can exist independently of the changes in its surrounding context. He argues that reducing law to its context denies its relative autonomy and overlooks the internal reasons for change. Venzke asks, if we were to control for the changes in external circumstances, which alternative pathways of change would we observe? The answers to this question reveal the law's contingency, 'the field of possibility, bordering on necessity on one side and chance on the other'. It is through such lenses that we can situate change processes and understand why the law changed in the way it did—which requires investigating also the paths 'not taken'—argues Venzke.

In his epilogue (Chapter 15), BS Chimni reflects on the insights gained in the volume and on the promise and limitations of its frame. For Chimni, the focus on gradual and informal change is important as it has become the dominant form of change due to prevailing treaty saturation. The relative autonomy of the legal order and its decentralized nature create a wide space for gradual or informal change processes. Yet Chimni calls for more attention to the directionality and cumulative impact of such change. Although incremental change may not be revolutionary, it still often amounts to meaningful transformations—though all too often in the interests of powerful states and non-state actors. For Chimni, the pathways of gradual change potentially also open up space for counter-hegemonic movements and ideals, but only a better understanding of the politics of those pathways will enable their use for emancipatory purposes.

6. Conclusion

How, why, and under what conditions change attempts in international law are successful is so far not well understood. This chapter seeks to take us closer to such an understanding by presenting an instrumentarium to help study informal legal change, and by offering a set of conjectures about the factors that explain the success of a given change attempt. To capture the dynamics of change in international law, we argue, we need to focus primarily on the 'paths' along which such change can travel, and which condition the modes, speed, and ease of change in a given field.

Our conjectures point to a picture of international legal change in which states continue to play an important role—but one in which other factors can outweigh a lack of state support for a given change attempt. The picture is a more 'social' one than others that have been advanced in that it seeks to take seriously the practices and authority structures as they exist in different fields and institutional contexts of international law. It is through such practices—which tend to involve state representatives, but also other actors—that the many pathways of change are charted out. The 'secondary rules' of international law, often portrayed as uniform throughout the international legal order, are produced through such practices and appear in fact to vary heavily across time and issue-areas.

This chapter presents a frame, what factors can determine the relevant pathways and account for the speed and success of change attempts in international law is first and foremost an empirical question. We cannot provide conclusive answers to this question here, but the different chapters in this volume present rich material to take us closer to a fuller account, and they provide many entry points for refining (and sometimes challenging) the picture we have presented here. They also urge caution against seeing this more dynamic picture as necessarily being positive—BS Chimni is most open about the risks of the pathways of change being of use primarily to the powerful,[99] but others too sound warnings. Wayne Sandholtz, for example, emphasizes that they might also be employed for non-liberal purposes, in particular by authoritarians to roll back human rights protections.[100] Many of the change processes traced in this volume pursue progressive directions, but this is likely a function of a particular political and ideational context. Many change processes in the past have strengthened rather than countered structures of domination and this is likely to continue as the political context darkens. As we continue exploring 'the many paths of change' in international law, their politics and distributional consequences will have to be at the centre of attention.

[99] Chimni, this volume.
[100] Sandholtz, this volume.

PART II
STRATEGIES OF CHANGE

2
Trump as a Change Agent in International Law
Ends, Means, and Legacies

*Mark A Pollack**

1. Introduction

The administration of United States (US) President Donald Trump is the most significant 'change agent' in the international legal order in recent decades. Representing a declining hegemon that had pioneered the creation and management of the leading institutions of the international legal order, Trump reversed US policy towards a wide variety of agreements and institutions, from trade and arms control to climate change and public health, withdrawing from or attacking these pillars of the American-led legal order. Any account of the paths of change in international law must therefore come to terms with the nature of the Trump administration as a change agent and with the lasting legacies, if any, that his presidency left behind after his replacement by the multilateralist Biden administration. In this chapter, I grapple with the Trump administration as a change agent, analysing the ends and means of Trump's policies as well as the ease (or difficulty) with which those policies were (or were not) overturned in the first year of the Biden administration.

With respect to *ends and means*, I present two theoretical ideal-types. In the first, a 'traditional' change agent seeks change to existing norms of international law, utilizing established methods such as treaty-making, legal argumentation, and adjudication. A 'hostile' change agent, by contrast, seeks to change, not the *rules* of law, but rather the *rule* of law, replacing multilateral rules and institutions with power-based bargaining or coercion; in terms of means, such agents select a 'state-based' path, engaging in unilateral tactics such as withdrawal, delegitimation, or paralysis of international legal agreements and institutions.

With respect to the *legacies* of Trump's actions, I again put forward two ideal-types. In the first, influenced by early historical institutionalism (HI), past legal

* Professor of Political Science and Law, Temple University, Philadelphia, PA, USA.

Mark A Pollack, *Trump as a Change Agent in International Law* In: *The Many Paths of Change in International Law*. Edited by: Nico Krisch and Ezgi Yildiz, Oxford University Press. © Mark A Pollack 2023.
DOI: 10.1093/oso/9780198877844.003.0002

agreements and institutions are both change-resistant and path-dependent, posing high barriers to any efforts to undermine them, and the few successful challenges by a hostile change agent are easily reversible by his successors. In the second view, influenced by more recent HI developments, change to international institutions is costly but possible, and the acts of a hostile change agent may *themselves* be path-dependent, reversible only at a cost by that agent's successors.

In an effort to adjudicate among these theoretical alternatives, I undertake a comparative case study analysing the ends, means, and legacies of Trump administration policies in four areas of international trade law: (a) *renegotiation* of North American Free Trade Agreement (NAFTA) as the United States Mexico Canada Agreement (USMCA); (b) *withdrawal* from the signed but unratified Trans Pacific Partnership (TPP); (c) *non-compliance* with the rules of the World Trade Organization (WTO) in the form of across-the-board tariffs against China; and (d) *paralysis* of the WTO Appellate Body (AB). International trade law is not fully representative of all issue-areas in international law, requiring us to generalize to other issue-areas with caution, but it has the advantage of featuring the full panoply of Trump's tactics, allowing us to parse the impacts of four distinct tactics within a single issue-area.

In terms of ends and means, I find that, in trade as in other areas, Trump's foreign policy features elements of both a traditional and a hostile change agent. The NAFTA case most closely approximates the traditional change agent seeking a change in international law through a combination of threats and negotiations. Trump's withdrawal from the TPP represents an effort to exempt the US from the requirements of an international agreement, and might therefore suggest hostility to international law, yet the withdrawal was carried out legally, and represents a long tradition of US failure to ratify international treaties. By contrast, the launching of a massive trade war through unauthorized tariffs together with the paralysis of the AB demonstrate a clear intent to weaken or destroy international rules and institutions, associated with a hostile change agent.

In terms of legacies, I show that Trump's actions, in all four cases, generated substantial costs of reversal for the Biden administration, which either embraced or failed to fully overturn Trump's policies during its first year in office. Taken alongside evidence from other issue-areas, this study therefore suggests that the Trump administration sought, with variable success, to undermine the international rule of law as such, and that at least some of its efforts have left lasting legacies in the form of weakened international laws and institutions.

2. Change Agents in International Law: Ends, Means, and Legacies

The theoretical framework of the PATHS project is, in the first instance, fundamentally agentic. To be sure, project leaders Nico Krisch and Ezgi Yildiz incorporate structural elements in their five basic paths of change—yet each of those paths begins, explicitly, with a *change agent.*[1] Concretely, the first stage of the process is the selection stage, 'where change agents choose and activate a pathway to realize their vision of change'. The success or failure of these efforts is determined in the construction and reception stages, in which other actors accept or reject the proposed change.

Reflecting this approach, the theoretical analysis in this section proceeds in two stages. In the first, I theorize about the nature of change agents, the ends that they pursue, and the means they use to effect change. I sketch out two ideal-typical change agents, 'traditional' and 'hostile'. Both of these types of change agents are by definition revisionist, but they differ in the ends they seek and the means they bring to bear. The traditional change agent seeks changes in the rules of international law, acting through a well-established repertoire of actions such as treaty-making, legal interpretation and argument, and adjudication. The hostile change agent, seeking to undermine the international rule of law as such, is likely to adopt more coercive tactics such as withdrawals from, and attacks upon, existing agreements. Taking a 'first-cut' survey of the Trump administration's policies across a range of issue-areas, I suggest that Trump, to a far greater extent than his predecessors, fell into the 'hostile' category.

The second stage of the analysis then focuses on the legacies that result from such hostile actions. Here I begin by summarizing dominant views of HI scholars who attribute change resistance and path dependence to existing international institutions, suggesting that challenges are likely to fail in the short term and be easily overturned in the long term. I then contrast these views with a revised HI perspective which considers that international institutions may be less robust than expected, and that a hostile change agent's attacks can *themselves* generate path-dependent legacies that limit the choices of the agent's successors.

2.1 Ends and Means: Traditional versus Hostile Change Agents

Running throughout the literature on the Trump administration is an often inchoate view that Trump was a different *kind* of change agent than previous US presidents—that Trump sought not only to change but to attack international law as such.[2] To get at this distinction, I theorize two ideal-types of change

[1] Nico Krisch and Ezgi Yildiz, 'The Many Paths of Change in International Law: A Frame' in Nico Krisch and Ezgi Yildiz (eds), *The Many Paths of Change in International Law* (Oxford University Press 2023).

[2] Jack Goldsmith, 'The Trump Onslaught on International Law and Institutions' (*Lawfare*, 17 March 2017) <https://lawfareblog.com/trump-onslaught-international-law-and-institutions> accessed 20 October 2022; Harold Hongju Koh, *The Trump Administration and International* Law (OUP 2018); Andrea Birdsall and Rebecca Sanders, 'Trumping International Law?' (2020) 21 International Studies Perspectives 275.

agents, traditional and hostile, distinguished by the ends they seek and the means they adopt.

2.1.1 Traditional change agents: normative change, 'normal science'

Reflected in the PATHS framework is a widely shared set of assumptions about the nature of change agents. All change agents, in this view, seek to change the content of international law, or, more finely, the 'burden of argument' regarding the interpretation of a norm of international law. In pursuit of this aim, change agents select among five discrete pathways: the state action path (unilateral action by a single state), the multilateral path (collective statements by a multilateral institution), the bureaucratic path (actions of international organization bureaucracies), the judicial path (decisions of international courts), and the private authority path (statements of authoritative private actors). Different kinds of change agents, Krisch and Yildiz hypothesize, are likely to select different paths, but all change agents seek to shift international law towards their own values and interests. Put differently, the *end* is normative change, and the *means* is persuading other actors to accept a change to, or reinterpretation of, existing norms.

To illustrate this ideal-type of a 'traditional' change agent, consider Jack Goldsmith's analysis of the Obama administration.[3] As Goldsmith notes, Obama came to the presidency with a 'cosmopolitan outlook and an informed commitment to international law' and sought to move the content of international law in the direction of US interests using 'the two mechanisms through which a president and his team can influence international law', namely executive-branch interpretations of existing international law and new treaty-making—an almost perfect empirical manifestation of Krisch and Yildiz's traditional change agent. With respect to interpretation, the Obama administration 'practiced "normal science" in exercising its interpretive powers to reshape the U.S. view of its international law commitments in light of its view of U.S. interests', and to persuade other actors to accept its interpretations.[4] With respect to treaty-making, Obama's contribution was 'cobbling together tools that significantly expanded the President's power to make international agreements without Congress' consent', as in the case of the Paris climate accord and the Iran-nuclear deal.[5] Goldsmith expresses reservations about these innovations, but concludes that, 'whatever one's view of the substance, the administration and its creative lawyers deserve credit for persistence, innovation, and leadership' and for their 'moderately successful efforts to get more countries than before to accept the U.S. view' of contested legal issues.[6]

[3] Jack Goldsmith, 'The Contributions of the Obama Administration to the Practice and Theory of International Law' (2016) 57 Harvard International Law Journal 455.
[4] ibid 456.
[5] ibid 456.
[6] ibid 473.

Traditional change agents, it should be noted, can sometimes resort to more 'muscular' means, including taking actions of questionable legality to assert new legal precedents, 'forum-shopping' for groups that are more receptive to their views, and threatening to withdraw from agreements to increase their bargaining leverage. For a traditional change agent, however, these means are used selectively, since the aim is not to destroy the legal order but to persuade others to accept changes to it.

Pivoting to the Trump administration, a minority of observers have suggested that Trump, for all his bluster, was a traditional change agent, using disruptive-but-legal tactics as leverage for the renegotiation of long-standing agreements. Goldsmith and Mercer, for example, noted that Trump limited his attacks to a small number of high-profile agreements, exited through lawful means, and left most US commitments unchanged.[7] Indeed, Trump's record may compare favourably with the George W Bush administration, which withdrew from several international agreements *and* violated the Geneva Conventions, the Convention Against Torture, and the UN Charter in its war on terror and invasion of Iraq.[8] Trump's greatest impact on international law, in this view, lay not in his 'bite' but in his 'bark'—in his 'harsh, disdainful rhetoric' suggesting that international institutions were 'corrupt, out of touch, elitist, self-serving or harmful to United States interests'.[9]

Perhaps the strongest presentation of Trump as a traditional change agent was articulated by Daniel Deudney and John Ikenberry. In their account, Trump appears as the leader of a declining hegemon determined to shift the *terms* of international law towards, and the *burdens* of global governance away from, the US, rather than to undermine international law as such:

> The Trump administration's initiatives on trade and alliance politics have generated a great deal of anxiety and uncertainty, but their actual effect is less threatening—more a revisiting of bargains than a pulling down of the order itself. Setting aside Trump's threats of complete withdrawal and his chaotic and impulsive style, his renegotiations of trade deals and security alliances can be seen as part an ongoing and necessary, if sometimes ugly, equilibration of the arrangements underlying the institutions of the liberal world order.[10]

[7] Jack Goldsmith and Shannon Mercer, 'International Law and Institutions in the Trump Era' (2019) 61 German Yearbook of International Law 11 <https://ssrn.com/abstract=3324582> accessed 20 October 2022.

[8] ibid 20.

[9] ibid 24.

[10] Daniel Deudney and G John Ikenberry, 'Liberal World: The Resilient Order' (2018) 97 Foreign Affairs 16, 23.

In this view, Trump's *ends* were traditional, even if his *means* pushed the envelope of legality and decorum. This benign interpretation, however, requires a highly selective reading of the evidence, assuming that Trump's tactics would lead to more sustainable bargains, and not undermine collective action in the meantime.

Time has not been kind to this interpretation. Looking back at the four-year record of the administration, we see only a few instances of Trump's threats and withdrawals producing re-equilibrated agreements, such as the USMCA and the token renegotiations of KORUS and Universal Postal Union rules. By contrast, in most of the areas in which Trump attacked or withdrew from existing agreements—including the WTO, the Paris climate agreement, the Joint Comprehensive Plan of Action (JCPOA, or 'the Iran-nuclear deal'), the Intermediate-Range Nuclear Forces (INF) Treaty, the Open Skies Treaty, the UN Human Rights Council, and the World Health Organization (WHO)—these attacks were *not* followed by any good-faith effort to renegotiate the agreements, most of which were killed or suffered lasting damage. We would therefore do well to consider a different kind of change agent—one that seeks to undermine international law as such and chooses appropriate means to that end.

2.1.2 Hostile change agents: targeting the rule of law, escaping and weakening institutions

The 'hostile' change agent is, like his traditional counterpart, revisionist. But the hostile change agent seeks to attack the rule of international law as such, gaining freedom from legal constraints and, at the extreme, replacing a law-based system with a power-based system predicated on threats and promises rather than legal rules and processes. By definition, such a hostile change agent is likely to eschew most of Krisch and Yildiz's paths in favour of a state-based path, taking unilateral actions to escape from, weaken, or destroy international norms and institutions.

Why might a government, particularly one that represented a founding member of many legal agreements, seek to escape, weaken, or destroy them? At the risk of oversimplification, we can imagine two ideal-type motivations, namely a *realist* change agent who, focusing on the *national* interest, believes that interest will be better served in a power-based order; and a *populist* change agent who, focusing on his *domestic* political interest, believes that he can maximize domestic support by scapegoating international laws and institutions.

The realist change agent is more straightforward—a statesman who decides that his national interests will be served more effectively though power-based bargaining than through international law. This option is most likely to appeal to great powers—either rising powers unhappy with laws drafted by the powers of the past, or declining powers that can no longer control outcomes but are still paying the lion's share of public goods provision. Either way, and consistent with hegemonic stability theory, the expectation is that shifts in the balance of power will destabilize existing agreements, leading dissatisfied powers to reform existing institutions and, failing that, to withdraw from or undermine them.[11]

The populist change agent, by contrast, is a domestic leader motivated by his own political interests, repudiating existing agreements insofar as doing so might secure support from domestic constituencies. Populist leaders, in this view, may find it convenient to scapegoat international agreements and institutions, and to mobilize public opinion against them.[12] Populist leaders are particularly likely to engage in backlash against international courts, whose rulings can be depicted as foreign impositions on 'the will of the people'.[13]

Whatever their motivations, hostile change agents seek to escape the constraints of international laws, whether through systematic non-compliance or unilateral withdrawal (which might leave the institution intact, though weakened by free-riding) or else through active efforts to delegitimate, paralyse, or destroy those laws and institutions. In the language of the PATHS framework, hostile change agents are most likely to choose the state-based path, working against, rather than through, existing legal fora.

Numerous observers have depicted the Trump administration as a hostile change agent. In an early assessment, Goldsmith wrote: 'we are witnessing the beginnings of the greatest presidential onslaught on international law and international institutions in American history.'[14] This onslaught, he argued, took multiple forms, including a slowdown in new international legal agreements, threatened or actual termination of US participation in international agreements, 'disengagement' from international institutions, and backlashes against international courts. Similarly, Harold Koh depicted Trump undertaking an effort to undermine international law in favour of a power-based unilateralism that rejects liberal values such as democracy, human rights, and the rule of law.[15]

We should not, to be sure, overstate the nature of Trump's threat to international law. As noted above, Trump continued with business as usual with respect to many international legal agreements, and his treaty withdrawals generally observed the letter of the law. Nevertheless, the combination of his tactics and the breadth of his assaults suggest that Trump can be considered a hostile change agent who sought to escape from, weaken, or destroy the core agreements and institutions of the international legal order across *multiple* issue-areas:

[11] Robert O Keohane, *After Hegemony* (Princeton University Press 1984) 31–39.

[12] Mark Copelovitch and Jon CW Pevehouse, 'International Organizations in a New Era of Populist Nationalism' (2019) 14 Review of International Organizations 169.

[13] Erik Voeten, 'Populism and Backlashes against International Courts' (2020) 18 Perspectives on Politics 407.

[14] Goldsmith, 'The Trump Onslaught' (n 2).

[15] Koh, *The Trump Administration* (n 2).

- In the area of climate change, Trump withdrew from the Paris climate-change agreement, on factually dubious grounds, making no effort to renegotiate its terms.[16]
- In the area of international criminal law, Trump went beyond previous US non-participation in the International Criminal Court, seeking to delegitimate the Court and threaten its personnel with sanctions.[17]
- In the area of global public health, Trump abruptly withdrew from the WHO in the midst of the Covid-19 pandemic.[18]
- In the area of trade (discussed below), Trump threatened withdrawal from NAFTA and the Korea Free Trade Agreement (KORUS), withdrew from the TPP, violated WTO law, and paralysed the AB.
- In the area of security, Trump attacked the NATO alliance as irrelevant, refused to endorse its Article 5 collective security commitment, and threatened repeatedly to withdraw.[19]
- In the area of arms control, Trump withdrew from the Intermediate-range Nuclear Forces (INF) Treaty, the Open Skies Treaty, and the JCPOA, making no effort to renegotiate any of them, and he failed to engage in any serious effort to renegotiate the soon-to-expire New Strategic Arms Reduction (START) Treaty.[20]
- With regard to the use of force, Trump authorized military actions that pushed the boundaries of international law, including cruise missile attacks against Syria and the assassination of Iranian General Qasem Soleimani, yet the administration offered only vague and belated justifications for these acts.[21]

Many of these actions appear to have been taken with domestic political considerations in mind, reflecting the populist ideal-type, although some, particularly in the security sphere, can be interpreted as realist. Regardless of their motivation, this incomplete list of Trump's policies reveals a fundamental assault on international

[16] Frank Jotzo, Joanna Depledge, and Harald Winkler, 'US and International Climate Policy under President Trump' (2018) 18 Climate Policy 813.

[17] William Burke-White, 'The Danger of Trump's New Sanctions on the International Criminal Court and Human Rights Defenders' (*The Brookings Institution*, 11 June 2020) <www.brookings.edu/blog/order-from-chaos/2020/06/11/the-danger-of-trumps-new-sanctions-on-the-international-criminal-court-and-human-rights-defenders/> accessed 20 October 2022.

[18] Gian Luca Burci, 'The USA and the World Health Organization: What Has President Trump Actually Decided and What Are Its Consequences?' (*EJIL: Talk!*, 5 June 2020) <www.ejiltalk.org/the-usa-and-the-world-health-organization-what-has-president-trump-actually-decided-and-what-are-its-consequences/> accessed 20 October 2022.

[19] Jorge Benitez, 'U.S. NATO Policy in the Age of Trump: Controversy and Consistency' (2019) 43 The Fletcher Forum of World Affairs 179.

[20] Darryl G Kimball, 'Nuclear Arms Control, or a New Arms Race? Trump Seems Bent on the Latter' (*Just Security*, 27 May 2020) <www.justsecurity.org/70407/nuclear-arms-control-or-a-new-arms-race-trump-seems-bent-on-the-latter/> accessed 20 October 2022.

[21] Mary Ellen O'Connell, 'The Killing of Soleimani and International Law' (*EJIL: Talk!*, 6 January 2020) <www.ejiltalk.org/the-killing-of-soleimani-and-international-law/> accessed 20 October 2022.

treaties and institutions, which the US sought not only to escape through withdrawal, but to undermine or destroy through systematic non-compliance, rhetorical attacks, and other extra-legal measures.

2.2 Legacies: Why Attacks on International Law May be Path-Dependent

Whether we imagine a traditional change agent seeking a shift in international legal norms, or a hostile agent undermining the rule of law, most analyses of legal change presuppose some legal status quo ante—a set of customary norms, treaty rules, and institutions purporting to set down rights and obligations in a given issue-area. In that context, a central analytical question has to do with the robustness or resilience of existing norms, rules, and institutions in the face of agents who seek to undermine them. Here again, I distinguish two ideal-typical views. In the first view, influenced by HI and regime theory, international legal agreements are change-resistant and path-dependent, generating obstacles to efforts to undermine them. This view is highly optimistic about the resilience of international law, suggesting that most challenges will either fail or be channelled along existing paths, resulting in at most incremental change. There is, however, a second, more nuanced, and less optimistic view, influenced by more recent HI developments, in which changes to international law and institutions are difficult but hardly impossible—and in which a hostile change agent's successful attacks may *themselves* be path-dependent, reversible only at a cost to his successors. Put simply, it may be that not only the founders of international laws and institutions but also their would-be destroyers can leave legacies for those who come later.

2.2.1 International law is change-resistant (and hostile acts are easily reversed)

The general approach of international relations and international law theorists has been to argue that existing international norms, rules, and institutions are likely to be not only *effective* but also *robust* in the face of changes and challenges.[22] In *After Hegemony*, for example, Robert Keohane sought to refute the hegemonic stability theory according to which international institutions are established by hegemonic powers but likely to weaken and collapse when the balance of power shifts and the hegemon declines. Keohane acknowledged the role of hegemonic powers in establishing international regimes but argued that 'regimes are easier to maintain

[22] Mark A Pollack, 'The Eternal Sunshine of the Theorist's Mind: How Dominant IR Theories Prime Scholars to See a Fragile Legal Order as Robust' (Paper presented at the PATHS Workshop: The Paths of Change in International Law, Graduate Institute, Geneva, 6–7 June 2019).

than they are to create' and that the functional benefits of existing institutions would lend them 'inertia' in the face of geopolitical change.[23]

Historical institutionalist scholars built on this core insight, developing temporal theories of institutional persistence in domestic and international politics. Historical institutionalists agreed that institutional choices can persist, or become 'locked in', but they went beyond rational-choice institutionalism in building increasingly sophisticated temporal theories of continuity and change.[24] In the most influential presentation of this strand of thinking, Paul Pierson argued that political institutions are frequently characterized by 'positive feedbacks', generating incentives for actors to stick with existing institutions, adapting them only incrementally to changing political environments.[25] Other schools of thought, moreover, bolstered these views about the resilience of international institutions. Constructivists argued that institutions had the power to 'socialize' actors into norms that would persist in the face of change.[26] Liberal international relations (IR) scholars explored how domestic 'compliance constituencies' could promote compliance and defend international institutions in the face of challenges.[27] Within the legal academy, Koh's Transnational Legal Process approach theorized the ways in which international law could set in motion processes of internalization into states' domestic legal orders. 'These internalized rules, in turn, create default patterns of international law-observant behavior for all participants in the process. Those default patterns become routinized and "sticky" and thus difficult to deviate from without sustained effort.'[28]

Applying this account to our question about the impacts of hostile change agents, we find a widespread view that the institutions of the liberal international order were likely to prove robust in the face of challenges from Trump's America. For example, Ikenberry acknowledged in 2018 that, for the first time, the US had elected a president hostile to core tenets of the liberal international order, yet he suggested that this order would persist because of its clear superiority in managing economic, security, and environmental interdependence.[29] A similar analysis was put forward in Koh's *The Trump Administration and International Law*. Koh has no illusions about Trump, whom he depicts as undertaking an effort to undermine the international rule of law. And yet Koh's book radiates optimism that international law would remain robust in the face of challenges, due to the internalization of

[23] Keohane (n 11) 100.

[24] Orfeo Fioretos, Tulia G. Falletti, and Adam Sheingate (eds), *Oxford Handbook of Historical Institutionalism* (OUP 2016).

[25] Paul Pierson, 'Increasing Returns, Path Dependence, and the Study of Politics' (2000) 94 American Political Science Review 251.

[26] Alexander Wendt, *Social Theory of International Politics* (CUP 1999).

[27] Miles Kahler, 'Conclusion: The Causes and Consequences of Legalization' (2000) 54 International Organization 661.

[28] Koh, *The Trump Administration* (n 2) 7.

[29] G John Ikenberry, 'The End of the Liberal International Order?' (2018) 94 International Affairs 7.

international law and the compliance constituencies who employ 'outside' and 'inside' strategies to defend international law. Taken together, Koh argues, 'these two strategies can lead a nation into a pattern of sustained default compliance with international law that makes quick deviation from these rules far more difficult than casual observers might predict'.[30]

Not only *can* transnational legal process limit the prospect for 'quick deviation', Koh argues that it had already done so in the early years of the administration:

> To be sure, the United States of America—and its president in particular—are powerful players in the making and unmaking of international law. But upon inspection, the wide-ranging counterstrategy of damage control surveyed in the chapters that follow has spawned a de facto path of least resistance. Under that default, the United States under Trump rarely exits, but rather *stays in and underperforms* in existing international regimes . . . While that may be a suboptimal state of affairs, it has the virtue of being curable, at a future time when Trump no longer controls the two houses of Congress or has been supplanted by a more enlightened successor U.S. administration.[31]

In the area of international trade, for example, Koh focuses primarily on regional trade agreements like the TPP (where Koh argues that US withdrawal is reversible in the future) and the twin cases of NAFTA and KORUS (where Trump backtracked on threats to withdraw, settling instead for renegotiations). With respect to the WTO, Koh notes Trump's hostility to the organization and his imposition of WTO-illegal tariffs, but he concludes optimistically that the 'likely default will be to stay in and underperform'.[32] Underperformance, however, is hardly an adequate term for the Trump administration's instigation of trade wars, or his paralysis of the AB.

I shall return to Trump's impact on international trade law below, but the point here is that, in the dominant view of most IR and legal scholars, international institutions enjoy substantial robustness, thanks to their functional utility, domestic internalization, and the defensive mobilization of domestic and transnational civil society. Furthermore, to the extent that such scholars acknowledge Trump's attacks on international law, they frequently fall back on the idea that his assaults would be reversed by a future, more enlightened successor. Yet this expectation raises a second question: whether the attacks of a hostile change agent might not only succeed, but also become change-resistant and path-dependent after that agent has passed from the scene.

30 Koh, *The Trump Administration* (n 2) 12–13.
31 ibid 14.
32 ibid 60.

2.2.2 Hostile acts are possible and path-dependent

Contrasting with the first-generation HI view sketched out above, a more recent, second-generation strand of HI has emerged over the past two decades, generating new insights into the sources and the nature of institutional change. Consider, for example, the question of 'feedbacks' from existing institutions. While early studies focused almost exclusively on positive feedbacks that lent stability to existing institutions, more recent work has acknowledged that institutions can also produce *negative* feedbacks, which generate resistance and create pressures for change.[33] *Self-reinforcing* institutions, in this view, are those that generate positive feedbacks and make institutions more stable in the face of exogenous shocks. *Self-undermining* institutions, by contrast, 'can cultivate the seeds of their own demise' by producing negative feedbacks and increasing demands for change over time.[34] Applying the same logic to the international legal sphere, Laurence Helfer suggested that international institutions, particularly those with independent dispute settlement, can become 'overlegalized', leading states to withdraw from agreements whose unexpected costs come to outweigh their benefits.[35]

Generalizing from these insights, Mahoney and Thelen put forward a theory of endogenous institutional change, driven not by exogenous shocks such as geopolitical shifts or economic recessions, but by the operations of the institutions themselves over time. Mahoney and Thelen focus on what they call the 'power-distributive' effects of institutions, which they define as '*distributional instruments* laden with power implications'.[36] Institutions, in this view, lock in advantages for winners, who might be expected to support existing institutions—but also disadvantages for losers, who might be expected to challenge them. Hence all institutions contain within them a dynamic, endogenous source of contestation, with dissatisfied actors constantly pressing for changes that will favour them.

Taken together, these theoretical innovations inform a revisionist view of international legal change. In this view, pressure for change is endemic within any institution, since institutions can produce negative feedbacks that turn formerly satisfied supporters into dissatisfied change agents. Just as importantly, the logic of path dependence does not suggest that change is impossible, simply that it is *costly*—leaving open the possibility that strong, or strongly motivated, change

[33] Wolfgang Streeck and Kathleen Thelen, 'Introduction: Institutional Change in Advanced Political Economies', in Streeck and Thelen (eds), *Beyond Continuity: Institutional Change in Advanced Political Economies* (OUP 2005).

[34] Avner Greif and David D Laitin, 'A Theory of Endogenous Institutional Change' (2004) 98 American Political Science Review 633, 634.

[35] Laurence R Helfer, 'Overlegalizing Human Rights: International Relations Theory and the Commonwealth Caribbean Backlash against Human Rights Regimes' (2002) 102 Columbia Law Review 1832.

[36] James Mahoney and Kathleen Thelen, 'A Theory of Gradual Institutional Change' in Mahoney and Thelen (eds), *Explaining Institutional Change* (CUP 2010).

agents might be willing to pay the necessary costs to escape, undermine, or destroy existing institutions.

Furthermore, the logic of HI can be used to understand the path-dependent effects, not only of law-creating moments such as the founding of new institutions, but also of actions undertaken to withdraw from or undermine such institutions. Put simply, I hypothesize, the actions of hostile change agents can create new 'facts on the ground', either domestically or internationally, that make their law-destructive actions difficult or costly to reverse.

Domestically, withdrawal from or non-compliance with an international legal agreement may generate societal adaptations 'from below' and engage change-resistant constitutional constraints 'from above', both of which make a return to the status quo ante costly. From below, hostile acts like non-compliance or withdrawal may mobilize 'non-compliance constituencies' who benefit from violating or escaping international agreements, and lobby to maintain the new status quo.[37] From above, meanwhile, a hostile agent's actions may become institutionally 'locked-in', with high institutional barriers to returning to the status quo ante. Take, for example, a hostile agent's withdrawal from an international treaty. In the US, treaty withdrawal can be undertaken by the unilateral action of the president but overturned only through the re-ratification of the agreement by Congressional ratification, an extraordinarily high hurdle. Withdrawal from executive agreements, by contrast, is institutionally easier to reverse through subsequent executive action, suggesting that treaty withdrawals will generate greater path-dependence, all else being equal, than withdrawals from executive agreements. These differences, in turn, may explain *variations* in the path-dependence of Trump's withdrawals: hence, whereas Biden was able to reengage quickly with the Paris climate accord, which had been concluded and could be rejoined as an executive agreement, the barriers to reengagement are higher with respect to rejoining arms control treaties requiring Senate ratification.

Internationally, meanwhile, the acts of a hostile change agent, including non-compliance, withdrawal, delegitimation, and paralysis, may undermine either (a) the credibility of the change agent's state, or (b) the broader cooperative equilibrium of an international agreement or institution. In terms of the credibility of the change agent's state, consider that the state in question has at some point in the past committed to be bound by an international agreement. If a hostile agent reneges on that agreement through non-compliance or withdrawal, the future credibility of that state will be undermined among its partners—particularly if other states believe that future governments may repeat these actions. Rachel Myrick, for example, has argued that the polarization of US politics and the weakening of a bipartisan foreign policy consensus has been deeply damaging to US credibility,

[37] Zoltan Buzas, *Evading International Norms: Race and Rights in the Shadow of Legality* (University of Pennsylvania Press 2021).

with each successive president increasingly likely to walk away from the commitments of his predecessors. In such circumstances, foreign leaders may rationally conclude that they can no longer have confidence in US commitments, leading to an unravelling of international cooperation.[38] The culprit in Myrick's story is American political polarization, but Trump's record of non-compliance and withdrawals, and the prospect of a Trumpist future president, make it difficult for any American president to reassure other states that the US will honour its international commitments.

The international impact of a hostile change agent may, moreover, extend beyond the reduced credibility of a single state. As Allison Carnegie and Austin Carson have argued, leaders who seek 'to modify or upend existing norms and laws' can promote 'compliance pessimism' within a given normative order by communicating the message that cheating is already rampant. The impact of such compliance pessimism can be profound, they argue, leading to 'cascades' of reciprocal non-compliance, even where most states retain a preference for continued cooperation.[39]

To illustrate the potentially path-dependent nature of actions by a hostile change agent, consider the possible effects of four common tactics of hostile change agents:

- *Renegotiation of existing agreements.* In this first tactic, a revisionist state threatens to withdraw from an existing agreement in order to secure cooperation on more generous terms or to weaken the agreement by, for example, watering down enforcement mechanisms. If a change agent succeeds in renegotiating an agreement, it is likely to demonstrate considerable path-dependence. Because the new agreement is legally binding for all parties, any return to the status quo ante would require *both* a costly international renegotiation *and* domestic ratification. Such actions are not impossible, but a return to the status quo ante is both costly and unlikely.
- *Withdrawal.* A second tactic, withdrawal from a ratified treaty, would render the country in question a non-party, requiring a fresh act of ratification to rejoin—in the US case, typically by a two-thirds Senate majority. Withdrawal from an executive agreement can be overturned more easily from an institutional perspective, although withdrawal may have led to adaptation by interest groups which resist returning to the status quo ante. At the international level, meanwhile, withdrawal and free-riding may have weakened the institution, such that the rejoined institution is weaker than it had been before. Alternatively, if the withdrawal is lasting, the remaining members of

[38] Rachel Myrick, 'America Is Back—but for How Long? Political Polarization and the End of U.S. Credibility' (*Foreign Affairs*, 14 June 2021) <https://www.foreignaffairs.com/articles/world/2021-06-14/america-back-how-long> accessed 20 October 2022.

[39] Allison Carnegie and Austin Carson, 'Reckless Rhetoric? Compliance Pessimism and International Order in the Age of Trump' (2019) 81 Journal of Politics 739.

the agreement may take it off in new directions that further increase the costs of re-entry for the departed member.

- *Systematic non-compliance.* Thirdly, suppose that a hostile change agent, rather than withdrawing, remains within an agreement but 'underperforms' through systematic non-compliance. The primary source of path-dependence here is domestic: any act of non-compliance is likely to have benefited particular constituencies, who are likely to resist coming back into compliance, imposing domestic political costs on any government that seeks to do so. Furthermore, a new government proposing to come into belated compliance may face domestic pressures to use resumption of compliance as a 'bargaining chip', demanding concessions from other members in exchange and increasing the international negotiation costs of returning to compliance. Once again, moreover, protracted non-compliance may have weakened the institution, resulting in lasting damage.
- *Undermining the institution.* Fourthly and finally, imagine that a change agent has undermined an institution from within—by paralysing its internal workings, attacking its legitimacy, etc. Such a weakened or paralysed institution may require substantial diplomatic effort and political capital to rebuild. Whether future governments will be willing to expend such capital to restore international cooperation is uncertain.

In short, there are good reasons to be believe that all of the most common tactics of a hostile change agent are likely to generate lasting, path-dependent legacies. In the next part of the chapter, we examine four case studies of Trump-induced challenges to international trade law, illustrating these four tactics and assessing the ease or difficulty with which the Biden administration has, or has not, returned to the status quo ante.

3. The Trump Administration and International Trade Law: Four Case Studies

In the previous section, I suggested that the Trump administration demonstrated features of a hostile change agent across multiple issue-areas, from climate change and arms control to trade and public health. A thorough analysis of all these issue-areas is beyond the scope of this chapter, and so, in this section, I engage in an empirical study of Trump's international trade policies. I focus on trade because doing so allows us to hold the issue-area constant while at the same time generating variation across the various tactics utilized by hostile change agents. Doing so yields four distinct case studies, distinguished by the dominant Trump administration tactic; (1) *renegotiation* of NAFTA; (2) *withdrawal* from the recently negotiated TPP; (3) *systematic non-compliance* through the imposition of unilateral tariffs on

China; and (4) *institutional attacks* in the paralysis of the WTO AB. In each case, I assess whether the Trump administration's means and ends correspond most closely to traditional or hostile change agents. As we shall see, the US renegotiation of NAFTA most closely resembles the traditional change agent (albeit with a 'hostile' effort to eliminate legalized dispute settlement); TPP withdrawal represents a fairly traditional US effort to escape an international legal commitment; and the final two cases represent clear instances of a hostile change agent seeking to undermine the rule of international law.

Within each case, moreover, I also explore the path-dependent legacy from the end of the Trump presidency into the first year of the Biden presidency. If the more optimistic analyses are to be believed, Trump's actions should be easily overturned by the multilateralist Biden administration; by contrast, if the Biden administration leaves Trump's policies in place, this might be prima facie evidence of path-dependent legacies.

We must, however, be cautious in attributing continuity from Trump to Biden to path-dependence, since it is at least conceivable that Biden might have adopted such policies independently, reflecting, for example, growing scepticism about free trade among Democrats. Within each case study, therefore, I undertake an explicit *counterfactual analysis*, asking *whether the Biden administration would have adopted such policies independently, had Trump not done so*. In such counterfactual thought experiments, to ascertain the effect of a given action, we imagine an alternate world which was identical except for the action in question (the so-called 'minimum rewrite of history' rule) and use our knowledge of history to consider how that scenario might have played out.[40] In keeping with this approach, each case study posits a counterfactual world in which Trump *was* elected president in 2016 but did *not* undertake the policy at the heart of each case: thus, we imagine that Trump, behaving more like previous presidents, adopted occasional protectionist measures and complained about unwelcome WTO rulings, but did *not* (a) coerce Canada and Mexico into renegotiating NAFTA, (b) forcefully denounce the TPP, (c) issue unauthorized tariffs on Chinese imports, or (d) paralyse the AB. We will then ask whether, in this alternate world, the Biden administration would have adopted those (or similar) policies independently, drawing on publicly available knowledge of prior Obama-Biden administration policies, Biden's own preferences, and the preferences of his domestic constituents. To the extent that Biden continued Trump policies that he would *not* have adopted independently, we will attribute those policies, however tentatively, to the legacy of the Trump administration.

To anticipate the findings of these four counterfactual thought experiments, I argue that while Biden might have quietly abandoned the TPP, which had

[40] Jack Levy, 'Counterfactuals and Case Studies' in Janet Box-Steffensmeier, Henry Brady, and David Collier (eds), *The Oxford Handbook of Political Methodology* (OUP 2008) 635.

uncertain prospects of Congressional ratification, he was unlikely to have forced a NAFTA renegotiation, and he almost certainly would have resisted starting a trade war with China or paralysing the AB. As we shall see, however, in all four areas the Biden administration, constrained by substantial domestic and international costs of change, moved slowly, if at all, to reverse Trump's policies. Taken together, these cases suggest that Trump has indeed left a legacy of continued US exceptionalism, non-compliance, and undermining of international trade law.

3.1 Threats and Renegotiation: From NAFTA to USMCA

Among the cases examined here, the renegotiation of NAFTA comes closest to Goldsmith's 'normal science' of securing international legal change by renegotiating existing agreements. One might therefore associate this case with the traditional change agent, although two elements of the case recall the hostile change agent, namely (1) Trump's 'hardball' tactics of repeatedly threatening to abrogate NAFTA if the US failed to get its way, and (2) the effort to weaken the rule of law by eliminating NAFTA's dispute-settlement provisions. With respect to legacies, the USMCA, as a newly ratified treaty, is likely to be path-dependent in the future, remaining in force for decades after Trump's departure.

As noted earlier, Trump campaigned on his opposition to many US trade agreements, including NAFTA, which he called 'a total disaster' and 'one of the worst deals ever'.[41] To carry out his 'America first' mandate, Trump appointed as his head of the Office of the US Trade Representative (USTR) Robert Lighthizer, an experienced trade lawyer with a history of representing the US in losing WTO litigation, who was famously quoted telling a group of business executives that 'the only fucking arbitrator I trust is me'.[42] Over the next four years, Trump and Lighthizer would upend US trade policy, renegotiating NAFTA, denouncing the TPP, and wreaking havoc on the WTO.[43]

Upon taking office, Trump considered unilateral withdrawal from NAFTA, but, under pressure from advisors and interest groups, agreed instead to call for a renegotiation of the agreement, using the leverage of his threat to extract more favourable terms.[44] In the contentious negotiations that followed, Lighthizer directed a variety of demands at his partners, combining some market-opening efforts (particularly with respect to Canadian dairy) with various protectionist

[41] Ashley Parker and others, '"I Was All Set To Terminate": Inside Trump's Sudden Shift on NAFTA' *The New York Times* (27 April 2017).

[42] Aime Williams, 'Superpower Showdown—Trading Blows in a New Cold War' *Financial Times* (3 July 2020).

[43] Gregory C Shaffer, 'A Tragedy in the Making? The Decline of Law and the Return of Power in International Trade Relations' (2018) 44 Yale Journal of International Law Online 37.

[44] Parker and others (n 41).

efforts (particularly with respect to automobile manufacturing) as well as two demands that, if successful, would change not only the contents but also the enforceability of the agreement. First, in an effort to maximize US leverage in the future, Lighthizer proposed a sunset clause whereby the agreement would expire every five years barring a unanimous agreement to extend, generating considerable uncertainty for North American businesses. Secondly, the US sought to remove both investor-state dispute settlement (Chapter 11) and the interstate arbitration procedure (Chapter 19) from the revised agreement, which would create a legally binding but non-justiciable agreement.[45]

The negotiations dragged on for over a year, with Mexico and Canada pushing back against many US demands. During this period, Trump repeatedly threatened to walk away from negotiations, and in the final weeks the administration negotiated bilaterally with Mexico in an effort to put pressure on Canada, while threatening to impose punitive automobile tariffs if negotiations failed.[46] Finally, in September 2018, the three sides agreed to a revision of NAFTA with much the same structure, but with a series of significant changes.[47] First, the new treaty modernized the provisions of the three decades-old NAFTA agreement with respect to intellectual property and digital trade, drawing largely from the TPP agreement that Trump had rejected. Secondly, in keeping with Trump's promise to reinvigorate American manufacturing, the new agreement altered the rules of origin for automobiles, raising the North American content requirement from 62 per cent to 75 per cent and requiring that at least 40 per cent of the parts from any tariff-free vehicle come from a factory in which production workers make an average salary at least $16 an hour—a provision widely seen as driving auto production from Mexico to the US. Thirdly, the US won Canada's agreement to a significant opening of the Canadian dairy market. Fourthly and finally, with respect to dispute settlement, the US secured agreement on the partial abandonment of Chapter 11 investor-state dispute settlement, though Canada held firm in resisting the American demand to abandon Chapter 19 arbitration.[48] The result was an ambiguous agreement, which liberalized and modernized parts of NAFTA while engaging in greater protectionism in other areas and weakening enforcement. Although Trump lauded his political victory, trade-law experts expressed fears that the treaty represented a move towards a more protectionist and power-based

[45] 'Draft NAFTA Notice Targets Dispute Settlement and Other Core Complaints' *Inside U.S. Trade* (31 March 2017).

[46] Adrian Morrow, Barrie McKenna, and Stephanie Nolen, 'How The Deal Was Done' *The Globe and Mail* (6 October 2018).

[47] Jim Tankersley, 'Trump Just Ripped Up Nafta: Here's What's in the New Deal' *The New York Times* (1 October 2018).

[48] 'Trudeau: Chapter 19, Cultural Exemptions Are NAFTA Red Lines for Canada' *Inside U.S. Trade's Daily Report* (5 September 2018).

world,[49] while Daniel Ikenson memorably dubbed the agreement 'the protectionist love child of the labor left and the nationalist right'.[50]

Congressional ratification of free trade agreements is always challenging in the US, where most agreements since NAFTA have been ratified as Congressional-executive agreements, with particularly narrow margins in the House of Representatives. In the case of the USMCA, Republicans generally fell in line behind Trump's signature foreign policy accomplishment, while Democrats demanded changes with respect to labour rights, environmental protection, pharmaceuticals, and enforcement.[51] Having secured such concessions, the House voted to ratify the amended USMCA by a remarkably lopsided 385 to 41, with 193 Democrats joining 192 Republicans in favour of the bill.[52]

Counterfactually, it is unlikely that the Biden administration would have pressured Canada and Mexico into renegotiating NAFTA. Having been successfully negotiated and ratified, however, the USMCA is likely to remain highly stable over time, with Democrats joining Republicans in supporting the new treaty and moving assertively to enforce its labour provisions. Hence, regardless of whether we consider the negotiation of USMCA to be a traditional treaty renegotiation, or a hostile act of coercion using threats to weaken the enforcement provisions of an existing treaty, it is clear that the USMCA will represent an important legacy of the administration for decades to come.

3.2 Exit: Leaving the TPP

The Trump administration's decision to withdraw from the recently concluded TPP represents a commonplace, and legal, action for American presidents, who have often failed to submit signed treaties for Congressional ratification, either because of policy concerns or due to political difficulties in securing the requisite majorities.[53] Indeed, the George W Bush administration went further in 2001, removing the US signature from the 1997 Kyoto Protocol and pronouncing the treaty to be 'dead'.[54] This 'unsigning' of Kyoto represents the best analogy to Trump's

[49] Sergio Puig, 'The United States-Mexico-Canada Agreement: A Glimpse into the Geoeconomic World Order' (2019) 113 AJIL Unbound 56.

[50] Daniel J Ikenson, 'The Protectionist Love Child of the Labor Left and the Nationalist Right' (*CATO at Liberty*, 13 December 2019) <www.cato.org/blog/protectionist-love-child-labor-left-nationalist-right> accessed 20 October 2022.

[51] Emily Cochrane, Ana Swanson, and Jim Tankersley, 'How a Trump Trade Pact Won Over Democrats' *The New York Times* (19 December 2019).

[52] Emily Cochrane and Ana Swanson, 'Revised North American Trade Pact Passes House' *The New York Times* (19 December 2019).

[53] Mark A Pollack. 'Who Supports International Law, and Why? The United States, the European Union, and the International Legal Order' (2015) 13 International Journal of Constitutional Law 873, 878–79.

[54] R Daniel Kelemen and Tim Knievel, 'The United States, the European Union, and International Environmental Law' (2015) 13 International Journal of Constitutional Law 945, 953–54.

withdrawal from the TPP, in that the finality of each president's denunciation led the remaining parties to proceed without the US.

The TPP had been negotiated among twelve Pacific-rim countries during the Obama administration, resulting in the February 2016 signature of an agreement that was designed to write new trade and regulatory standards for a bloc of states comprising 40 per cent of global GDP, *and* conspicuously leave China outside of the agreement.[55] Domestically, however, the TPP proved controversial, with many Americans attributing rising inequality to international trade agreements. Once again, candidate Trump denounced the TPP, angrily depicting it as a 'continuing rape' of the US;[56] Hillary Clinton, meanwhile, also disavowed the agreement, saying that it had failed to guarantee good jobs for Americans.[57] Thus, it must be acknowledged, the TPP faced significant obstacles to ratification under a president of *either* party, although counterfactually a different type of president might have attempted to either reopen negotiations on the treaty to secure amendments (as Bill Clinton did upon inheriting the unpopular NAFTA in 1993), or quietly shelve the treaty (as Clinton did with even more unpopular Kyoto Protocol in 1997) in the hopes of bringing it up for ratification at a more opportune moment.[58]

On his first full day in office, however, Trump fulfilled his campaign promise by signing an executive order withdrawing from the TPP.[59] Trump's very public denunciation made it clear to the other eleven signatories that the US had no intention of returning to the agreement, leading the other parties to renegotiate the treaty, suspending twenty-two provisions that had been inserted at US insistence. The awkwardly renamed Comprehensive and Progressive Agreement for Trans-Pacific Partnership (CPTPP) was signed in March 2018 and entered into force that December, proceeding without the US but leaving the door open for a future US accession.[60]

In terms of our framework, Trump's withdrawal from the TPP falls somewhere between the traditional and hostile ends of the spectrum, illustrating a commonplace US failure to ratify domestically unpopular international agreements. Nevertheless, the decisiveness of Trump's repudiation was unusual, and would leave a legacy for the next administration, making the already difficult prospect of TPP accession *more* difficult for his successor.

[55] Cathleen Cimino-Isaacs and Jeffrey J Schott (eds), Trans-Pacific Partnership: An Assessment (Peterson Institute for International Economics 2016).

[56] Cristiano Lima, 'Trump Calls Trade Deal "a Rape of Our Country"' *Politico* (28 June 2016).

[57] Anne Gearan and David Nakamura, 'Hillary Clinton Comes Out Against Obama's Pacific Trade Deal' *The Washington Post* (7 October 2015).

[58] Pollack, 'Who Supports International Law?' (n 53) 878–79.

[59] Peter Baker, 'Trump Abandons Trans-Pacific Partnership, Obama's Signature Trade Deal' *The New York Times* (23 January 2017).

[60] Matthew P Goodman, 'From TPP to CPTPP' (*Center for Strategic and International Studies*, 8 March 2018) <https://www.csis.org/analysis/tpp-cptpp> accessed 20 October 2022.

Counterfactually, if Trump had followed Obama's 2016 precedent of simply declining to send it forward for Congressional ratification, the incoming Biden administration—with its eagerness to join with allies to stand up to China—might have attempted to revive the TPP by negotiating side agreements as a prelude to ratification. Indeed, as a candidate, Biden initially indicated that his intent was to renegotiate the treaty,[61] and numerous business interests and trade experts urged him to do precisely that, arguing that the geopolitical and economic arguments for the TPP remained as strong as during the Obama years.[62]

However, Trump's denunciation clearly increased the domestic and international costs of reengagement for the incoming Biden administration. Domestically, Democratic presidents have relied historically upon across-the-aisle support from Republicans to secure support for international trade agreements.[63] Trump's frequent denunciations of the TPP, however, had increased the unpopularity of the treaty, making it difficult for Republicans to defy the leader of their own party to ratify a revived TPP. Perhaps reflecting these considerations, Biden announced in Spring 2020 that he would 'not enter into any new trade agreements until we have invested in Americans and equipped them to succeed in the global economy'.[64]

Internationally, the CPTPP had been renegotiated and entered into force by early 2021.[65] This development, together with the November 2020 conclusion of a new Regional Comprehensive Economic Partnership (RCEP) including China, left the US outside two mega-regional trade agreements, at the margins of writing trade rules for the region. Yet it also meant that, in order to reverse Trump's decision and reengage in the region, the US would need to renegotiate the terms of the agreement and reassure allies who worried that future US presidents would once again renege on American commitments.[66]

In light of the challenges posed by Trump's TPP denunciation, former Obama administration trade negotiator Wendy Cutler suggested that the new administration could pursue any one of four paths: returning to the original TPP (no longer realistic); formally acceding to the CPTPP (unlikely, given the changes implemented by the eleven remaining members); 'seeking a broader renegotiation

[61] William Reinsch and others, 'Trade Policy on the 2020 Trail: The Second Debate' (*CSIS Brief*, 6 August 2019) <www.csis.org/analysis/trade-policy-2020-trail-second-debate> accessed 20 October 2022.

[62] See eg Wendy Cutler, *Reengaging the Asia-Pacific on Trade: A TPP Roadmap for the Next U.S. Administration* (Asia Society Policy Institute 2020); Jeffrey J Schott, 'Rebuild the Trans-Pacific Partnership Back Better' (*Peterson Institute for International Economics*, 30 November 2020) <www.piie.com/blogs/trade-and-investment-policy-watch/rebuild-trans-pacific-partnership-back-better> accessed 20 October 2022.

[63] See eg Obama's trade agreements with South Korea, Panama, and Colombia, all of which were ratified only with Republican support in the face of widespread Democratic opposition; Doug Palmer, 'Congress Oks Korea, Panama, Colombia Trade Deals' *Reuters* (12 October 2011).

[64] Joseph R Biden, 'Why America Must Lead Again' (2020) 99 Foreign Affairs 64, 70.

[65] Cutler (n 62) 11–12.

[66] Aime Williams, 'US Will Not Be as Quick into CPTPP as UK' *Financial Times* (3 February 2021).

with the CPTPP' (plausible but still 'a heavy lift'); and 'working on a narrower sectoral deal as an immediate, interim step'.[67] In practice, Biden moved slowly in his first year, opting for none of Cutler's four options. Although Biden's US Trade Representative, Katherine Tai, spoke frequently about reengaging with US partners in the Asia-Pacific region,[68] the administration took no steps in its first year to initiate negotiations and allowed Trade Promotion Authority to lapse in July 2017.[69] White House spokeswoman Jen Psaki, asked in September 2021 about China's recently lodged application for CPTPP membership, left the door open to possible US negotiations, suggesting that 'if there's an opportunity to negotiate, then that could be a discussion we could be a part of', although she added that the US was 'obviously not there at this point'.[70]

None of this is to say that a US return to a renegotiated TPP is impossible, but it will be diplomatically and politically costly to renegotiate and ratify such an agreement, and those costs increased as a result of Trump's actions. Whether the Biden administration will be willing to incur these political costs and risks remains uncertain, but in the meantime Trump's rejection of the TPP represents another important legacy.

3.3 Systematic Non-compliance: The US-China Trade War

Beyond renegotiation and withdrawal, a third change strategy—and one specific to a hostile change agent—is *systematic non-compliance* with international legal agreements, designed either to escape the discipline of legal rules or to weaken them by undermining interstate reciprocity. The emphasis here is not on isolated incidents of non-compliance, or even on specific cases in which a state engages in arguably non-compliant activity in an effort to influence the interpretation of an existing norm, but rather on prolonged, material breaches of international legal obligations, accompanied by weak or non-existent legal justifications.

During the Trump years, two specific policies appear to fit this characterization, namely the adoption of punitive tariffs on Chinese goods from 2018 without WTO authorization, and the imposition of across-the-board tariffs on steel and aluminium imports on questionable 'national security' grounds. Both sets of tariffs were challenged on legal grounds at the WTO, and in the in the first case found to violate US commitments, but both sets of tariffs were popular with domestic constituencies, and the Trump administration retained them until it left office

[67] Cutler (n 62) 6.

[68] 'Eyes on Asia, Tai Says U.S. Must "Fully Engage" in the Indo-Pacific' *Inside U.S. Trade* (8 October 2021).

[69] Doug Palmer, 'Say Goodbye to Trade Promotion Authority' *Politico* (28 June 2021).

[70] 'USTR: China's "Economic Coercion" Likely to Weigh on CPTPP Members' *Inside U.S. Trade's Daily Report* (20 September 2021).

in January 2021. Counterfactually, it seems unlikely that a Biden administration would have adopted such aggressive, and arguably illegal, tariffs, which had no precedent in the Obama-Biden administration. Here again, however, path-dependent processes set in, leading the administration to prolong and even defend Trump's tariffs once in office. Domestically, both sets of tariffs became a fait accompli, presenting the administration with potentially significant political costs of alienating important constituencies if it withdrew them. Internationally, moreover, the Trump tariffs had, whether legal or not, become bargaining chips for the incoming administration, which was under pressure to leverage these inherited tariffs to secure foreign concessions in new international agreements. Such agreements, however, involved difficult negotiations with US counterparts, and the result was the continuation of the China tariffs, and only a partial lifting of the steel and aluminium tariffs, during Biden's first year in office. For reasons of space, I focus here on the China tariffs, and return briefly to the steel and aluminium tariffs at the end of the section.

As we have seen, candidate Trump frequently denounced China's trade practices, and these complaints found support within Lighthizer's USTR. Upon taking office, the administration undertook a Section 301 investigation into Chinese trade practices, concluding in March 2018 that China had engaged in discriminatory or unreasonable practices in multiple areas, including technology transfer, intellectual property, and investment.[71] While past administrations might have pursued these complaints through WTO adjudication, Trump took a more direct approach, issuing unilateral tariffs against hundreds of billions of dollars of Chinese exports to the US. In July 2018, the administration imposed tariffs of 25 per cent on Chinese imports with an annual trade value of $34 billion, later increased to $50 billion. In September, the US increased the pressure on China, adopting 10 per cent tariffs on a further $200 billion worth of Chinese imports, rising to 25 per cent in 2019.[72] China, for its part, responded with retaliatory tariffs, also without WTO authorization, escalating the dispute into a full-blown trade war. Within the US, interest groups were divided, with import-competing industries generally supporting the tariffs, while export-oriented firms objected, filing a record number of complaints before the US Court of International Trade.[73]

Throughout the conflict, Trump sought to use the tariffs to pressure China to make concessions, and the Chinese, for their part, agreed to such negotiations, resulting in the so-called phase 1 agreement in January 2020. In the agreement,

[71] Office of the United States Trade Representative, *Findings of the Investigation into China's Acts, Policies, and Practices Related to Technology Transfer, Intellectual Property, and Innovation under Section 301 of the Trade Act of 1974*, 22 March 2018.

[72] *United States—Tariff Measures on Certain Goods from China*: Panel Report, WT/D543/R <www.wto.org/english/tratop_e/dispu_e/cases_e/ds543_e.htm> accessed 20 October 2022, at 13–14.

[73] Nina M Hart and Brandon J Murrill, 'Section 301 Tariffs on Goods from China: International and Domestic Legal Challenges' (*Congressional Research Service*, updated 5 April 2022).

China pledged to undertake a series of commitments with respect to intellectual property protection and market access for US firms, as well as a managed-trade commitment to purchase an additional $200 billion worth of US goods during each of the two following years.[74] Presented by Trump as a significant victory for the US, the agreement represented not so much a settlement as a ceasefire in the ongoing trade war. In return for Chinese commitments, the US agreed to reduce tariffs on $120 billion worth of Chinese goods, and not to impose further tariffs, but it would keep in place tariffs on approximately $360 billion of Chinese imports. Reflecting its status as a first-stage agreement, the document failed to address a number of important structural issues in the US-China trade relationship, including Chinese domestic subsidies and state-owned industries, which remained to be addressed in a future, phase 2, agreement, which never materialized.

China, meanwhile, challenged the US tariffs before the WTO, claiming that the US had violated the Most Favoured Nation clause and its agreed-upon tariff bindings. The US acknowledged the increased tariffs, but offered two (dubious) legal justifications: first that the tariffs were justified under General Agreement on Tariffs and Trade (GATT) Article XX provisions allowing member states to 'take measures necessary to protect public morals'—a provision that had hitherto been interpreted narrowly by WTO members and by the DSB—and secondly that the dispute had been the subject of a mutual settlement.[75] In September 2020, however, a WTO panel ruled against the US, rejecting its public morals claim on the grounds that the US had failed to demonstrate the link between its specific tariffs and the public morals in question, and holding that there had been no 'mutually satisfactory solution' between the US and China, which had not relinquished its WTO rights.[76] The US rejected the panel's reasoning and appealed the panel decision 'into the void' of the paralysed AB, postponing indefinitely a final ruling in the dispute.[77] As Geraldo Vidigal aptly summarized, '[t]hese developments undermine the core bargain underlying the WTO regime: the commitment by sovereign entities to entrust decisions regarding permissible and impermissible conduct to

[74] 'Economic and Trade Agreement Between the Government of the United States of America and the Government of the People's Republic of China Text' <https://ustr.gov/countries-regions/china-mongolia-taiwan/peoples-republic-china/phase-one-trade-agreement/text> accessed 20 October 2022; David A Gantz, Sergio Puig, and Jingyuan Zhou, 'The Scorecard of the Phase One Trade Agreement' (*EJIL Talk!*, 14 February 2020) <www.ejiltalk.org/the-scorecard-of-the-phase-one-trade-agreement/> accessed 20 October 2022.

[75] *United States—Tariff Measures on Certain Goods from China* (n 72) 16. For an excellent discussion, see Jingyuan (Joey) Zhou, 'No Unilateral Action—WTO Panel Ruled U.S. Section 301 Tariffs on Chinese Imports Inconsistent with WTO Obligations' (2020) 24(26) *ASIL Insights*.

[76] ibid.

[77] *United States—Tariff Measures on Certain Goods from China: Notification of an Appeal by the United States under Article 16 of the Understanding on Rules and Procedures Governing the Settlement of Disputes ('DSU')*, WT/DS543/10, 27 October 2020.

authoritative decision-making and to react to other Members' conduct only following an institutional authorization to do so.'[78]

Counterfactually, it is highly unlikely that the Biden administration would have initiated a trade war with China without WTO authorization. As Vice President, Biden had supported Obama's policy of engaging with China through the WTO dispute-settlement system, and candidate Biden criticized Trump's trade war as counterproductive, increasing prices for American consumers and reducing exports for American farmers while alienating allies and producing no meaningful changes to Chinese trade practices.[79] Supporters of free trade and multilateralism therefore hoped and expected Biden to reverse course.[80]

Nevertheless, it soon became clear that the Biden administration would be in no hurry to remove the Trump-era tariffs.[81] Here, as in other areas, Trump's actions had changed the status quo for the incoming administration, imposing substantial domestic and international costs to withdrawing the tariffs. Domestically, Biden appeared to share the view that 'rushing to remove the tariffs could prove risky ahead of the 2022 congressional midterm elections, when any sign of softness on China could weaken Democrats at the ballot box'.[82] Any tariff reduction, it was widely understood, would likely come only as part of a broader trade agreement with China.[83] Internationally, however, it became clear that Chinese leaders were unwilling to contemplate the prospect of reducing subsidies to state-owned industries, preferring to endure punitive US tariffs indefinitely.[84]

Faced with these constraints, US trade policy towards China remained in a holding pattern during the administration's first year in office. Despite increasing criticism of the tariffs and pressure for reengagement with China from the US Chamber of Commerce and other interest groups, Tai refused to speculate on the fate of the tariffs, pending a 'top-to-bottom' review of its China policy.[85] Biden's Justice Department lawyers, meanwhile, appeared before the Court of International Trade to *defend* Trump's tariffs, arguing that the tariffs had been

[78] Geraldo Vidigal, 'Westphalia Strikes Back: The 2018 Trade Wars and the Threat to the WTO Regime' (2 October 2018). Amsterdam Law School Research Paper No 2018-31, Amsterdam Center for International Law No 2018-13, <http://dx.doi.org/10.2139/ssrn.3259127> accessed 20 October 2022.

[79] Stuart Anderson, 'Biden Says He Will End Trump's Tariffs On Chinese-Made Goods, Aide Walks Back Statement' *Fortune* (6 August 2020).

[80] Tommy Koh, 'The Biden Administration: The Road Ahead for Asia' *The Straits Times* (21 January 2021).

[81] Gavin Bade, 'Trump's Final Trade Battles Create an Early Test for Biden' *Politico* (11 January 2021) (noting that 'if Biden eventually moves to decrease many of those tariffs, he will face backlash—not only from Republicans, but from companies and unions that welcomed them').

[82] Aime Williams, 'US Business Frustrated by Lingering Effect of Trump China Tariffs' *Financial Times* (4 June 2021).

[83] Bob Davis and Yuka Hayashi, 'New Trade Representative Says U.S. Isn't Ready to Lift China Tariffs' *The Wall Street Journal* (28 March 2021) (quoting Tai: 'No negotiator walks away from leverage, right?').

[84] Keith Bradsher, 'A Temporary U.S.-China Trade Truce Starts to Look Durable' *The New York Times* (27 May 2021).

[85] Ana Swanson and Keith Bradsher, 'U.S. Suggests It Will Not Ease Tough Line on Chinese Trade' *The New York Times* (5 October 2021).

legally authorized and that the Biden administration's efforts to negotiate with China should not be 'impaired' by domestic litigation.[86] One unintended effect of these developments was to entrench the 'temporary' phase 1 agreement. Indeed, despite concerns about Chinese compliance and about the important issues left unaddressed, the phase 1 agreement remained in place well into the new administration, with no sign of willingness on either side to move beyond it.[87]

These impressions were confirmed in October 2021, when Tai presented the results of the USTR's top-to-bottom China policy review. In a widely reported address, she suggested that Beijing had 'doubled down on its state-centered economic system', and did not intend to adopt meaningful reforms to address US concerns.[88] Faced with such Chinese intransigence, however, Tai indicated that the US did not intend to engage in new negotiations with China over a 'phase 2' agreement, which were unlikely to succeed, but would instead continue the status quo by retaining the Trump-era tariffs and pressing China to honour its phase 1 commitments.[89]

The following January, in a press conference to mark the end of his first year in office, Biden was asked whether the US intended to withdraw Trump's China tariffs, responding: 'I'd like to be able to be in a position where I can say they're meeting more of their commitments and be able to lift some of them, but we're not there yet.'[90] In short, although a multilateralist Biden administration would have been unlikely to initiate the largest trade war of the post-war era, it ultimately opted—in the face of domestic political opposition and difficult international negotiating challenges—to retain the Trump administration's basic approach to US-China trade.

Finally, although space precludes a full analysis of the case, we see a very similar pattern with respect to the Trump administration's tariffs on imported steel and aluminium. Adopted in 2018 on allies and adversaries alike, the tariffs were justified by the administration on dubious 'national security' grounds, citing Section 232 of the 1962 Trade Expansion Act and GATT Article XXI, which allows member states to restrict trade flows that might constitute a threat to national security. Whereas previous US presidents had interpreted these provisions narrowly and invoked them rarely during times of armed conflict, the Trump administration argued that reliance on imports of these metals, even from allied countries, constituted a national security threat justifying the imposition of across-the-board tariffs. Widely

[86] 'Biden Administration Asks CIT To Dismiss Section 301 Lawsuits' *Inside U.S. Trade's Daily Report* (3 June 2021).

[87] Alan Rappeport and Keith Bradsher, 'Yellen Says China Trade Deal Has "Hurt American Consumers"' *The New York Times* (16 July 2021).

[88] 'Tai: China Has No Plans for Meaningful Reforms to Address U.S. Concerns' *Inside U.S. Trade's Daily Report* (5 October 2021).

[89] 'Tai Seen as Keeping Options Open as She Pins Hope for Progress on Renewed Talks with China' *Inside U.S. Trade's Daily Report* (6 October 2021).

[90] 'Biden Says He Wants to Be Able to Lift China Tariffs, "But We're Not There Yet"' *Inside U.S. Trade's Daily Report* (20 January 2022).

seen as a bad-faith abuse of the national security provision, Trump's tariffs were met with both retaliatory tariffs and WTO legal challenges from multiple US trading partners.[91] Once in office, the Biden administration negotiated a bilateral steel and aluminium settlement with the European Union,[92] but Biden's USTR never abandoned Trump's dubious national security arguments, maintaining that the tariffs were an 'effective' and 'legitimate tool';[93] nor did it remove the tariffs with respect to other trading partners, reportedly under pressure from interest groups in the swing states of the upper Midwest.[94] Here again, as with the China tariffs, it seems counterfactually unlikely that a Biden administration would have imposed tariffs on its allies on dubious legal grounds—but having inherited the tariffs, it kept them in place, another destructive legacy of Trump's systematic non-compliance.

3.4 Attacking International Legal Institutions: The WTO Appellate Body

As noted above, one of the hallmarks of a hostile change agent is the effort, not simply to change international legal norms, but to weaken the rule of law as such, and one of the central means of doing so has been 'backlash' against international courts. While 'pushback' against unwelcome judicial decisions is commonplace in international politics, backlash goes further, attacking the fundamental legitimacy of a court and triggering 'significant institutional reform or even the dismantling of tribunals'.[95] During his four years in office, Trump engaged in backlash against the International Criminal Court by withdrawing visa privileges from its lead prosecutor and threatening those who cooperated with it, and most spectacularly against the WTO AB, which it not only criticized but paralysed from 2019 onwards.[96]

[91] Ana Swanson and Paul Mozur, 'Trump Mixes Economic and National Security, Plunging the U.S. Into Multiple Fights' *The New York Times* (8 June 2019); Tania Voon, 'The Security Exception in WTO Law: Entering a New Era' (2019) 113 AJIL Unbound 45; and J Benton Heath, 'Trade and Security Among the Ruins' (2020) 30 Duke Journal of Comparative & International Law 223.

[92] Franco Ordoñez, 'Biden and the EU Call a Truce in a 17-Year Trade Fight to Focus on Threats from China' *NPR* (15 June 2021).

[93] 'Tai Calls for New Trade "Tools" to Better Compete with China' *Inside U.S. Trade's Daily Report* (13 May 2021).

[94] Steven Overly, 'Why Trump's Steel Tariffs Are Now Biden's Political Headache' *Politico* (6 September 2021).

[95] Mikael Rask Madsen, Pola Cebulak, and Micha Wiebusch, 'Backlash Against International Courts: Explaining the Forms and Patterns of Resistance to International Courts' (2018) 14 International Journal of Law in Context 197, 198.

[96] This section draws on the more extensive analysis in Mark A Pollack, 'Court-Curbing in Geneva: Lessons from the Paralysis of the WTO Appellate Body' (2022) 36(1) Governance 23–39 <https://doi.org/10.1111/gove.12686> accessed 20 October 2022.

Trump, it must be acknowledged, was not the first president to express their dissatisfaction with the rulings, and the purported judicial activism, of the AB.[97] Indeed, both the Bush and Obama administrations had used the US veto in the consensus-based WTO to block the reappointments of three judges considered to have ruled in an activist fashion against US interests.[98] Trump, however, dramatically escalated both rhetorical attacks on the legitimacy of the AB and institutional attacks on its very existence.

Trump's campaign to delegitimize the AB was a two-pronged operation, with Lighthizer's USTR offering critiques of AB procedures and jurisprudence in official trade circles, while Trump emitted a stream of wildly inaccurate accusations before a wider public. Lighthizer's USTR criticized the AB's 'chronic violations' of WTO procedural rules and its 'erroneous' interpretations of WTO legal provisions, arguing that '[t]here is no legitimacy under our democratic, constitutional system for the nation to submit to a rule imposed by three individuals sitting in Geneva, with neither agreement by the United States nor approval by the United States Congress'.[99] Trump, meanwhile, amplified US attacks on the AB, falsely claiming that 'we lose the lawsuits, almost all of the lawsuits at the WTO', and that the WTO Dispute Settlement Mechanism was rigged: 'Because we have fewer judges than other countries. It's set up as you can't win. In other words, the panels are set up so that we don't have majorities. It was set up for the benefit of taking advantage of the United States.'[100]

Against that backdrop, the Trump administration's institutional tactic at the WTO was both simple and consistent across four years—using its veto to prevent the appointment of any new AB members as existing members ended their respective four-year terms, eventually depleting the body until, from December 2019, it no longer enjoyed a quorum of three members and was forced to suspend operations.

The effect of the shutdown was dramatic. All existing appeals were frozen, leaving eight disputes in limbo. Just as importantly, parties to future disputes could, if unsatisfied with the panel ruling in their case, appeal the panel's decision 'into the void', freezing the outcome of those cases indefinitely as well. By the start of 2021, the number of frozen appeals stood at eighteen.[101] Moreover, the paralysis of the

[97] Cosette D Creamer and Zuzanna Godzimirska, '(De)Legitimation at the WTO Dispute Settlement Mechanism' (2016) 49 Vanderbilt Journal of Transnational Law 275.

[98] Manfred Elsig and Mark A Pollack, 'Agents, Trustees, and International Courts: The Politics of Judicial Appointment at the World Trade Organization' (2014) 20 European Journal of International Relations 391; Jeffrey L Dunoff and Mark A Pollack, 'The Judicial Trilemma' (2017) 111 American Journal of International Law 225.

[99] Office of the United States Trade Representative, *Report on the Appellate Body of the World Trade Organization*, February 2020.

[100] 'In Four Years, President Trump Made 30,573 False or Misleading Claims' *Washington Post* (?? 2021) <www.washingtonpost.com/graphics/politics/trump-claims-database/?itid=lk_inline_manual_11> accessed 20 October 2022 [search for WTO].

[101] 'U.S. Appeals WTO Decision in South Korea Trade Dispute, Official Says' *Reuters* (19 March 2021).

AB appeared to have had a knock-on effect on the use of the DSM more generally, resulting in a dramatic decline in new cases, which dropped from thirty-eight new legal proceedings in 2018, to twenty in 2019, to just five in 2020.[102]

Throughout this period, other WTO members called repeatedly for the US to put forward concrete proposals for reform. In 2019, the WTO members appointed New Zealand's WTO Ambassador David Walker to compile a 'Draft General Council Decision on the Functioning of the Appellate Body', addressing US and other concerns about the AB. Walker's proposal called for a legally binding decision that would constrain the AB to respect treaty-imposed timelines for its work, limit the AB's ability to rule on issues not raised by the parties, and explicitly rule out any binding precedent for AB judgments.[103] Walker's proposals, however, did not go far enough for the US, which rejected them out of hand. As former AB member Jennifer Hillman commented, '[i]f the goal was to kill the Appellate Body, OK, they've succeeded ... It's so easy to burn down the barn—now comes the hard work of what do you build in its place.'[104]

Facing this outcome, the EU and fifteen other WTO members agreed in April 2020 to a Multiparty Interim Appeal-Arbitration Arrangement (MPIA), which would institute an alternative procedure whereby any two WTO members could agree to binding appeal of a panel decision by a three-member appeals panel.[105] Yet, as its creators acknowledged, the MPIA was a stopgap arrangement, which did not restore the AB, and which allowed non-participating WTO members to continue appealing panel reports into the void.[106]

By the end of Trump's single term of office, it was clear that, notwithstanding US claims that it sought only reforms of the WTO, the administration's real aim had been to kill the AB. Following the November elections that made Trump a one-term president, Lighthizer spoke bluntly, telling a forum: 'We have taken these steps at the WTO to stop the Appellate Body. And by the way, it's been a year—no one's really missed it. No one's missed it at all. It's like, "Oh, the Appellate Body"—nobody cares.'[107] A week later, Lighthizer again disparaged the AB, concluding

[102] World Trade Organization Dispute Settlement Gateway, Chronological List of Disputes Cases <www.wto.org/english/tratop_e/dispu_e/dispu_status_e.htm> accessed 20 October 2022.

[103] 'Informal Process on Matters Related to the Functioning of the Appellate Body—Report by the Facilitator, H.E. Dr. David Walker (New Zealand), World Trade Organization' General Council, JOB/GC/222, 15 October 2019.

[104] 'Hillman: Big Tests Ahead for the Rules-Based Trading System' *Inside U.S. Trade's Daily Report* (31 December 2019).

[105] 'Multi-Party Interim Appeal Arbitration Arrangement Pursuant to Article 25 of the DSU' World Trade Organization, JOB/DSB/1/Add.12, 30 April 2020.

[106] Holger Hestermeyer, 'Saving Appeals in WTO Dispute Settlement: The Multi-Party Interim Appeal Arbitration Arrangement Pursuant to Article 25 of the DSU' (*EU Law Live*, 2 April 2020) <https://eulawlive.com/op-ed-saving-appeals-in-wto-dispute-settlement-the-multi-party-interim-appeal-arbitration-arrangement-pursuant-to-article-25-of-the-dsu-by-holger-hestermeyer/> accessed 20 October 2022.

[107] 'Lighthizer: "No One's Really Missed" the Appellate Body' *Inside U.S. Trade's Daily Report* (11 December 2020).

that, 'it's almost like there's nothing you can do about it, other than what we did, which is to say: get rid of it. We don't need an Appellate Body like this. We don't need jurisprudence made by bureaucrats.' He concluded by urging the Biden administration not to 'roll over' on the issue.[108]

Clearly, the Trump administration was operating in this case as a hostile change agent, dealing a fundamental blow to the dispute-settlement system at the heart of the global trade regime. This leaves only the question of the legacy of Trump's policies, and whether the multilaterally inclined Biden administration might remove the US block and restore the AB. One year into the Biden administration, it was clear that this optimistic scenario had not come to pass. Instead, Biden continued Trump's block on AB appointments, with Tai telling Congressional legislators that '[t]he Appellate Body has overstepped its authority and erred in interpreting WTO agreements in a number of cases, to the detriment of the United States and other WTO members'.[109]

In October, Tai made her first trip to Geneva as US Trade Representative, assuring the assembled delegates of continued US support for the WTO, yet she reiterated US concerns about the dispute-settlement system, which she said had become synonymous with 'prolonged, expensive, and contentious' litigation. 'Reforming dispute settlement', she argued, 'is not about restoring the Appellate Body for its own sake, or going back to the way it used to be', but rather engaging in a long process of negotiation in which the fate of the AB would be 'intimately linked' to a global reform of the WTO.[110] Tai later confirmed that the US, while bringing its 'best game' to the scheduled WTO ministerial conference in November 2021, would not be presenting any proposals for a resolution to the AB stand-off.[111] In any event, the scheduled ministerial conference was indefinitely postponed due to the outbreak of the omicron variant of Covid-19, leaving the fate of the AB in limbo, unlikely to be decided for months or years.

Counterfactually, it is unlikely that the Biden administration would have taken the extreme step of paralysing the AB, as the Trump administration did. Having inherited a paralysed AB, however, Biden was unwilling, in the words of Robert Hudec, to 'throw any capital into the renewal of the WTO'.[112] For our purposes here, it was clear, by the end of Biden's first year in office, that the paralysis of the AB was certain to outlast Trump, and that any restoration would likely take years,

[108] 'Rewind: Lighthizer Reflects on Some Unfinished Business' *Inside U.S. Trade's Daily Report* (30 December 2020).

[109] David Lynch, 'Tai Confirmed as Top U.S. Trade Negotiator' *Washington Post* (17 March 2021).

[110] 'Ambassador Katherine Tai's Remarks as Prepared for Delivery on the World Trade Organization' <https://ustr.gov/about-us/policy-offices/press-office/speeches-and-remarks/2021/october/ambassador-katherine-tais-remarks-prepared-delivery-world-trade-organization> accessed 20 October 2022.

[111] 'Tai: U.S. Bringing "Best Game" to MC12, Seeking "Honest" Talk to Drive Reform' *Inside U.S. Trade's Daily Report* (11 November 2021).

[112] Michael Goldhaber, 'Headless in Geneva' *FDI Intelligence* (15 October 2021). See also Sarah Anne Aarup, '"All Talk and No Walk": America Ain't Back at the WTO' *Politico* (23 November 2021).

resulting, at best, in a chastened body whose independence would be substantially reduced. This state of affairs is likely Trump's most profound legacy with respect to the rule of international trade law.

4. Conclusion

In this chapter, I have attempted to advance the PATHS project of understanding change in international law by focusing on the nature of change agents and the legacies they leave for the international legal order. In the first, theoretical, section of the chapter, I distinguished between two ideal-types of change agents, traditional and hostile, with the first using means such as negotiation, interpretation, and adjudication to influence the content of international legal norms, while the second uses more aggressive means to escape or undermine the rule of international law as such. In the second, empirical, section, I explored Trump administration policies, and the Biden administration's responses to those policies, with respect to the renegotiation of NAFTA, the withdrawal from the TPP, the US-China trade war, and the paralysis of the AB. The findings of the case studies, and their implications for international legal change during and after the Trump administration, are twofold.

First, with respect to the ends and means of the Trump administration as a change agent, the evidence is mixed, but points primarily to Trump as a genuinely disruptive or hostile change agent, targeting not only the content of specific international norms but also the international rule of law as such. As we have seen, Trump's renegotiation of NAFTA could be argued to fall under the rubric of a traditional change agent, since the administration was essentially pursuing legal change through the negotiation of a new treaty; yet that new treaty, if the administration had gotten its way, would have eviscerated the NAFTA dispute-settlement system, a classic aim of a hostile change agent. Similarly, Trump's denunciation of the TPP arguably fits into a pattern of US presidents walking away from unpopular treaties with questionable chances of Congressional ratification. The remaining two policies, however, clearly bear the hallmarks of the hostile change agent, targeting and weakening the rule of law as such. With respect to Trump's China and steel and aluminium tariffs, Trump adopted historically unprecedented tariffs without WTO authorization, and on dubious legal grounds that threatened to create enormous loopholes using 'public morals' and 'national security' as thinly veiled means to weaken established legal norms. Finally, in paralysing the AB, Trump attacked one of the central pillars of the WTO, weakening enforcement and generating fundamental uncertainty about the future of the global trading system.

Secondly, with respect to the legacy of the Trump administration's hostile actions, we need to proceed carefully, asking counterfactually what a Biden administration might have done in the absence of Trump's prior acts of renegotiation, withdrawal, non-compliance, and attack. Faced with rising

US scepticism, it is likely that Biden, a long-time supporter of international trade, would have moderated that support, taking a more sceptical line towards China, trade agreements, and the WTO dispute-settlement system. Nevertheless, it is highly unlikely that a Biden administration would have undertaken Trump's most extreme actions, including the instigation of a trade war and the paralysis of the AB. Yet in each case, Trump's policies changed the status quo for the incoming Biden administration, creating domestic and international impediments to change. In the case of NAFTA, Lighthizer skilfully renegotiated NAFTA in a more protectionist direction, securing bipartisan ratification of the USCMA and enshrining the agreement in US law. With respect to the TPP, Trump not only declined to ratify the agreement, but did so in a way that prompted the other eleven members to move on without the US, raising the costs of rejoining for any future administration. In adopting the China and steel and aluminium tariffs, Trump created a new political fait accompli, mobilizing protectionist interests that would resist the removal of tariffs, and increasing the diplomatic costs of a return to the status quo ante. Finally, and most strikingly, the Trump strategy of paralysing the AB generated domestic support in the US, and once again served as a potential bargaining chip, but one that could be used only in global agreement that would be extraordinarily difficult and costly to negotiate; in the meantime, Biden and Tai continued, albeit politely, the hostage-taking attack on the rule of WTO law that they had inherited from their predecessors. In all four areas, therefore, Trump left behind important, and destructive, legacies for the rule of international law.

This conclusion, however, does not constitute a counsel of despair. Path-dependent policies of the sort we have examined in this chapter *do* increase the cost of reversion to policies more in line with the rule of international law. But path-dependence does not mean an irrevocable 'lock-in' of Trump-era policies, and it does not remove all agency from subsequent administrations seeking to restore the rule of international law. In some areas, such as the US/EU agreement on steel and aluminium tariffs, the Biden administration proved able to steer between the Scylla of domestic political opposition and the Charybdis of difficult international negotiations to remove a Trump-era irritant in transatlantic trade relations, and the administration appeared ready in its second year to negotiate similar agreements with others. Just as importantly, these preliminary agreements demonstrate that a determined, intelligent administration can, within limits, minimize and manage the costs of change, overturning or at least limiting the impacts of law-destructive acts by its predecessors.

The Trump administration, through its rhetoric and actions, set US trade policy (and other policies) down a particular path, but a determined Biden administration can, albeit at some cost in political and diplomatic effort, walk back along that path towards a more international law-supportive strategy, for example by walking back its dubious public-morals or national-security arguments for protectionist tariffs. Perhaps most importantly, the administration can also work with its WTO partners to negotiate a mutually beneficial reform of the AB—one that would use the ill-gotten leverage of American hostage-taking to address US concerns and restore the essence of a rules-based global trading system.

Whatever the ultimate outcome of the Biden administration's efforts in the trade realm, we can reflect in closing on the generalizability of this chapter's arguments and evidence, first with respect to Trump's broader impact, and secondly with respect to other change agents. With respect to Trump, I have suggested above that he sought either to escape or to undermine the rule of international law across multiple issue-areas, including the use of force, arms control, the environment, climate, and human rights. I have not had space in this chapter to explore the legacy of Trump's policies in each of these areas, but even a brief survey suggests that it has been quite substantial, although also highly variable. In the area of arms control, for example, Trump dragged his feet on the extension of the New START Treaty, denounced the JCPOA executive agreement, and formally withdrew from the INF and Open Skies treaties. During his first year in office, Biden was able to reach agreement with Russia on a New START extension, but negotiations to renew the JCPOA remained difficult, and the costs of re-ratifying the INF and Open Skies treaties seemed prohibitively high.[113] In other areas, like the Paris accord and WHO membership, Trump's actions were less entrenched in US and international law and politics and have been more easily reversed by the Biden administration.

Finally, this chapter invites us to ask a similar set of questions about *other* change agents, namely whether they seek to secure a change in the normative content of international law, or to escape, weaken, or destroy the rule of international law as such. As with Trump, the answers may be nuanced, with change agents like Xi Jinping's China or Vladimir Putin's Russia pursuing traditional ends and means in some issue-areas, while wielding a wrecking ball in others.[114] In any event, since hostile change agents seem likely to persist and even proliferate in this age of geopolitical change, rising authoritarianism, and populism, we would do well to face directly the problem of hostile change agents' legacies, and the strategies and tactics that defenders of international law might use—imperfectly, and at a cost—to walk them back.

[113] Amy Woolf, 'Nuclear Arms Control After the Biden-Putin Summit', *Congressional Research Service* (3 January 2022).

[114] See eg Alastair Iain Johnston, 'China in a World of Orders: Rethinking Compliance and Challenge in Beijing's International Relations' (2019) 44 International Security 9; Tom Ginsburg, 'Authoritarian International Law?' (2020) 144 American Journal of International Law 221.

3

Norm-instability as a Strategy in International Lawmaking

The Case of Self-defence against Non-state Actors

*Pedro Martínez Esponda**

1. Introduction

Is self-defence under Article 51 of the UN Charter available against non-state actors? Over three-quarters of a century after its entry into force, this question remains disputed. States, the International Court of Justice (ICJ), the UN Security Council, and scholars have all approached it in different and at times contradictory ways. The fact of the matter remains, though, that no treaty, resolution, judgment, or pronouncement of any type has to date settled the matter in a final and authoritative way. Thus, confronted with the question, no international lawyer can present in all honesty any solution as uncontroversial, even if certain reference points do exist. How can such pervasive uncertainty be accounted for?

One might begin to answer this question by saying that law is an open-ended discursive practice. Normative meaning in legal rules is not pre-fixed but rather built through practices of argumentation and authority.[1] In international law, moreover, this open-endedness is deeper.[2] Several structural reasons account for this. On the one hand, international legal texts generally have a low level of specificity, which leaves vast room for interpretation. On the other hand, non-textual legal norms are pervasive in international law, making argumentation a systemic precondition. More generally, though, international law lacks constitutionally established authorities that centralize lawmaking and adjudication in the way parliaments and judicial systems do in domestic contexts. This means that in practice

* Professor of International Law at Universidad Iberoamericana in Mexico City, Mexico.

[1] Manuel Atienza, 'Argumentación Jurídica' in Ernesto Garzón Valdés and Francisco Laporta (eds), *El derecho y la justicia*, vol II (Trotta 2000) 231–37.

[2] For an overview of classic thinking on the matter, see Herbert L Hart, *The Concept of Law* (Clarendon Press 1961) 209, 210; Georges Abi-Saab, 'Interprétation et auto-interprétation. Quelques réflexions sur leur rôle dans la formation et la résolution du différend international' in Ulrich Beyerlin and others (eds), *Recht zwischen Umbruch und Bewahrung: Völkerrecht, Europarrecht, Staatsrecht: Festschrift für Rudolf Bernhardt* (Springer Verlag 1995) 13, 15.

Pedro Martínez Esponda, *Norm-instability as a Strategy in International Lawmaking* In: *The Many Paths of Change in International Law*. Edited by: Nico Krisch and Ezgi Yildiz, Oxford University Press. © Pedro Martínez Esponda 2023.
DOI: 10.1093/oso/9780198877844.003.0003

most international legal questions cannot be formally and conclusively settled—and the question of self-defence against non-state actors is a very telling example of this.[3]

But there is more than this structural open-endedness to account for the uncertainty surrounding Article 51. In international law, what actors do—their arguments, silences, unilateral acts, etc—has a substantial effect in shaping international legal norms. One sentence in a judgment of an international court, a seemingly innocuous paragraph in a resolution by an international organization, or the conspicuous silence of a minister of foreign affairs on a key issue all have the potential of becoming weighty elements in the interpretation of an international rule or in establishing their customary existence. Aware of this, international actors tend to conduct their international relations calculating the potential effect of their actions or omissions on their own legal position, and to some extent on the broader normative structure of international law.[4] Agency, therefore—and not only the systemic open-endedness of international law—is a key element in the often ambivalent evolution of international norms. Yet, agency does not necessarily mean that actors conduct themselves in unequivocal ways all the time. Sometimes actors may stay silent, and sometimes they may say one thing but do another. Sometimes they may even say things that are manifestly intended to create confusion. It is thus a mistake to think that there are only entrepreneurs or antipreneurs when it comes to the making of international rules.

This chapter approaches a rather understudied form of engagement with international law that goes beyond pursuance and opposition: the deliberate perpetuation of instability in international legal rules. Standing somewhere between full advocacy for a clear-cut rule and manifest opposition to the existence of a rule, norm-destabilization as a form of agency in international lawmaking is the reluctance by an international actor to concretize an argument about the meaning, scope, bindingness, or existence of a rule to an extent that would provide a straightforward answer to a given legal question. Normative instability is therefore understood here as a situation where an international rule fails to provide an unambiguous answer to a legal problem, either because its terms remain significantly unclear, or because the scope of its bindingness is very disputed.

Somewhat more narrowly—focusing mostly on diplomatic negotiation—scholars of international relations (IR) have sometimes approached the subject through the notion of *constructive ambiguity*, which has been defined as 'the

[3] David Kennedy, 'A New Stream of International Law Scholarship' (1988) 7 Wisconsin International Law Journal 28, 44; Martti Koskenniemi, 'The Politics of International Law' (1990) 1 European Journal of International Law 8.

[4] Wayne Sandholtz, 'Dynamics of International Norm Change: Rules against Wartime Plunder' (2008) 14 European Journal of International Relations 102; Kenneth W Abbott and Duncan Snidal, 'Hard and Soft Law in International Governance' (2000) 54 International Organization 421, 422–24; Stephen D Krasner, 'Realist Views of International Law' (2002) 96 Proceedings of the Annual Meeting (American Society of International Law) 265, 265–68.

deliberate use of ambiguous language on a sensitive issue in order to advance some political purpose'.[5] The focus in this chapter, however, is different in that norm-instability looks specifically at the content of a rule, and not only at the transactional, political, or diplomatic elements of ambiguity. Similarly, the notion of norm-instability, contrary to constructive ambiguity, is not limited to the use of language in the context of formal negotiation, but can include silences, equivocal attitudes, or overtly formalistic approaches in any setting of IR. What matters analytically for norm-instability, as understood here, is that the meaning, scope, bindingness, or existence of a legal rule is destabilized through the attitudes of international actors. Constructive ambiguity as used in IR would certainly fall into the category of norm-instability, but norm-instability would also encompass other types of destabilizing attitudes.

This chapter therefore seeks to bring an additional element into the discussion of how political change translates into change in international law—the question with which Nico Krisch and Ezgi Yildiz open this edited volume.[6] Norm-instability, it is argued here, works as a fender between political and legal change, allowing actors to pursue different courses of action without having to face the hurdles of changing international rules. In this sense, the notion of norm-instability helps account for the initial observation in the introduction of this work that not everything that happens in international politics is registered by international law or is registered unevenly in different sites. Particularly in the construction stage—to use the project's terminology—a strategy of norm-destabilization can have the effect of stalling a norm change attempt by creating legal uncertainty around it. The aim of this chapter is to better understand how this happens and explore some of the main paths of action through which norm-instability is pursued. In order to do that, focus is set here on the rule of self-defence against non-state actors (SD-NSA). This case is particularly telling because SD-NSA, much more than any other shifting rule in international law, has been both equivocally advocated for and equivocally contested since it started to be claimed in the late 1960s and to this day. It is therefore a case in point of norm-instability.

A clarification is pertinent before setting off, however. The term 'strategy', as used in this work, does not necessarily imply a planned, coherent, or continuous attitude by an actor. It includes these, of course, but it extends to much less articulated and less mindful forms of agency. What is central, in any case, is that the norm-destabilizing outcome is the product of a preference—whatever its motivation—for a legal formulation that does not clarify a crucial issue nor set a clear precedent, in contexts in which an actor could theoretically opt for a less ambiguous course of

[5] GR Berridge and Lorna Lloyd, 'Constructive Ambiguity' in *The Palgrave Macmillan Dictionary of Diplomacy* (3rd edn, Palgrave Macmillan 2012).

[6] Nico Krisch and Ezgi Yildiz, 'The Many Paths of Change in International Law: A Frame' in Nico Krisch and Ezgi Yildiz (eds), *The Many Paths of Change in International Law* (Oxford University Press 2023).

action.[7] That is to say, the relevant element of analysis here is the acceptance by an actor of a destabilizing normative result, regardless of whether its intention is to actually destabilize or not. For example, diplomatic compromise could be the reason for supporting an unstable outcome, without instability being itself the primary objective. What would make such an instance relevant for the purposes of this work is that the unstable outcome is preferrable to a stable one for certain actors, and thus they passively or actively orient their behaviour towards perpetuating the instability of a rule. Distilling the exact reasons for these preferences is, nevertheless, beyond the scope of this work.

The chapter is structured as follows. After this introduction, the second section briefly provides an account of the historical trajectory of the rule of SD-NSA, going from the enactment of the UN Charter in 1945 to recent times. The third section then jumps into the core of the matter and analyses different strategies of norm-instability as observed in the case of SD-NSA. The fourth section zooms out of SD-NSA to reflect on the extent to which norm-destabilization strategies are a broader phenomenon in international law. The conclusion brings the main findings together.

2. The Historical Trajectory of Self-defence against Non-state Actors

For analytical purposes, the history of SD-NSA can be neatly summarized along three main chronological phases. The first one runs from the entry into force of the UN Charter in 1945 until roughly 1969.[8] During this period, self-defence seems to have been generally understood as operating exclusively between states—the hypothesis of a non-state actor launching a full-blown armed attack not really having been conceivable for most international lawyers and diplomats at the time. Evidence of this is the fact that, while the final text of Article 51 of the Charter did not define who the author of an armed attack triggering the right to self-defence had to be, the *travaux préparatoires* of 1945 indicate that the matter was in fact

[7] See, in this regard, Byers' approach to strategic ambiguity: Michael Byers, 'Still Agreeing to Disagree: International Security and Constructive Ambiguity' [2020] Journal on the Use of Force and International Law 1, 23, 24.

[8] 1945 is taken to be the point of departure in this historical account despite the fact that the right to self-defence as part of *ius ad bellum* came into being well before the foundation of the UN. This is because the advent of the UN Charter in that year in many ways reset *ius ad bellum*, inter alia by outlawing the unilateral use of force and placing self-defence as the only narrow exception to it. Whether SD-NSA was outlawed before 1945 seems difficult to determine considering the contradicting practice. For insights into this issue, see Ian Brownlie, 'International Law and the Activities of Armed Bands' (1958) 7 The International and Comparative Law Quarterly 712, 732. For a more detailed review of the pre-1945 practice, see Ian Brownlie, *International Law and the Use of Force by States* (Clarendon Press 1963) ch XII.

never discussed during the negotiations in San Francisco.[9] Moreover, state practice and the records of debates at the UN Security Council (UNSC) evidence that self-defence was invoked exclusively in the context of armed activities among states. This was strictly the case in the conflicts between Israel and its Arab neighbours, Tunisia and France, the UK and Yemen, and North Vietnam and the US, where no argument was made involving non-state actors in the invocation of self-defence.[10] Only two cases departed from this narrow interstate setting during this period, one relating to the early Indo-Pakistani conflict and the other to Lebanon and Jordan's struggle to control internal anti-government movements in 1958.[11] However, in both cases the reference to non-state actors was only made with the purpose of denouncing the use of non-state proxies by foreign governments attacking the countries concerned, thus confirming that SD-NSA per se was not thought to be covered by Article 51. This assessment is further confirmed by the academic debates on *ius ad bellum* of this period. Most academics simply did not include SD-NSA in their accounts of the laws of war, and the few that did rejected the idea.[12]

The second phase of the history of SD-NSA covers the period from 1969 to 2001. During these years, in contrast to the previous period, some states started to invoke SD-NSA without resorting to any element of attribution to a state. Israel was the first and most consistent state to do so, mainly in relation to its periodical military operations against Hezbollah and the Palestine Liberation Organization (PLO) in Lebanese territory—claiming that the inability and unwillingness of the Lebanese government to prevent the use of its territory for attacks against Israel entitled it to resort to self-defence directly against the non-state aggressors.[13] This argument would come to be known thereafter as the *unwilling or unable doctrine*. In addition to Israel in Lebanon, other instances in which SD-NSA was invoked include by Southern Rhodesia—although its status as a state was not recognized—targeting anti-apartheid Zimbabwean liberation forces in Mozambican territory; by Israel pursuing alleged terrorists in Tunisia; by South Africa against the African National

[9] Kimberley Trapp, 'Can Non-State Actors Mount an Armed Attack?' in Marc Weller (ed), *The Oxford Handbook of the Use of Force in International Law* (1st edn, OUP 2015) 685.

[10] See Repertoire of the Practice of the UNSC, supplements of 1946–51, 1956–58, 1964–65, and 1966–68.

[11] See Repertoire of the Practice of the UNSC, supplements of 1946–51, at 448 and 1956–58, at 174–76.

[12] See eg Hans Kelsen, 'Collective Security and Collective Self-Defense Under the Charter of the United Nations' (1948) 42 The American Journal of International Law 783, 783, 791, 792; Myres McDougal and Florentino Feliciano, 'Legal Regulation of Resort to International Coercion: Aggression and Self-Defense in Policy Perspective' (1959) 68 Yale Law Journal 1134; 'Panel on "Force, Intervention and Neutrality in Contemporary International Law"' (1963) 57 Proceedings of the American Society of International Law at Its Annual Meeting (1921–1969) 147, 147; Josef L Kunz, 'Individual and Collective Self-Defense in Article 51 of the Charter of the United Nations' (1947) 41 The American Journal of International Law 872, 872,878; Brownlie, 'International Law and the Activities of Armed Bands' (n 7) 731; Brownlie, *International Law and the Use of Force by States* (n 7) 278–79, 379, 380.

[13] See Repertoire of the Practice of the UNSC, supplements of 1969–71, at 206; 1972–74, at 223; 1975–80, at 402; 1981–84, at 326; 1985–88, at 427; 1989–92, at 942; and 1996–99, at 1172.

Congress forces in Botswana, Zimbabwe, and Zambia; by Iran against terrorists groups sheltering in Iraqi territory; by Angola against Cabindan separatists in the territory of the Democratic Republic of the Congo (DRC); by Tajikistan against armed opposition groups operating from Afghanistan; by the USA against terrorists operating from Sudan and Afghanistan; by the DRC against anti-governmental forces taking shelter in Rwanda, and by Liberia against rebel groups operating from Guinea.[14]

What is remarkable about the practice in this period, however, is that while these cases did trigger thorough debates at the UNSC on the interpretation of Article 51—mainly regarding the claim of preventive self-defence and the issue of proportionality—no state ever objected to them on the basis of the argument that self-defence could not be invoked against non-state actors. In fact, not only did the point go uncontested, but it was not even mentioned in these discussions. Interestingly, something similar can be said about academic work of the time. As in the first phase, a clear majority of *ius ad bellum* scholars continued wholly to ignore SD-NSA, though sometimes referring to the related topic of indirect aggression.[15] Just a few considered it openly, though always in passing and ultimately rejecting it or expressing perplexity about it.[16] The only clear exception seems to have been Israeli author Yoram Dinstein, who unambiguously wrote about and endorsed SD-NSA in 1988.[17] However, it is fair to say that, despite the fact that SD-NSA was already taking place on the ground, it largely passed unnoticed in discussions on *ius ad bellum* among both diplomats and scholars, as it had done before 1969.

This radically changed in the third and last phase of the trajectory, which began with the terrorist attacks of 9/11 in 2001. From this point on, the practice of SD-NSA expanded considerably, and this time the topic became explicitly and extensively debated in both institutional and academic fora. In the aftermath of 9/11, the US formally communicated to the UNSC that it was exercising its right to self-defence against Al-Qaeda and the Afghan Taliban regime separately, by taking forcible actions 'designed to prevent and deter further attacks on the United States'.[18] A vast coalition formed by Western allies followed suit informing the

[14] See Repertoire of the Practice of the UNSC, supplements of 1975–80; 1985–88, at 430–31; 1993–95, at 1150; 1996–99, at 1176, 1178; and 2000–03, at 1007, 1016.

[15] Thomas M Franck, 'Who Killed Article 2(4) or: Changing Norms Governing the Use of Force by States' (1970) 64 American Journal of International Law 809, 809, 817, 821; Quincy Wright, 'The Middle East Problem' (1970) 64 American Journal of International Law 270, 270, 274; Oscar Schachter, 'Self-Defense and the Rule of Law' (1989) 83 The American Journal of International Law 259, 259, 271; Linos-Alexandre Sicilianos, 'L'invocation de la légitime défense face aux activités d'entités non-étatiques' (1989) 2 Hague Yearbook of International Law 147, 147, 161; Albrecht Randelzhofer, 'Article 51' in *The Charter of the United Nations: A Commentary* (OUP, CH Beck 1995).

[16] Pierluigi Lamberti Zanardi, 'Indirect Military Aggression' in Antonio Cassese (ed), *The Current Legal Regulation of the Use of Force* (Martinus Nijhoff 1986) 112, 113; Jean Combacau, 'The Exception of Self-Defense in UN Practice' in ibid 22, 23.

[17] Yoram Dinstein, *War, Aggression and Self-Defence* (Grotius 1988) 200, 221–23.

[18] UNSC, 'Letter Dated 7 October 2001 from the Permanent Representative of the United States of America to the United Nations Addressed to the President of the Security Council (S/2001/946)'.

UNSC of its actions of collective SD under Article 51 directly against Al-Qaeda. This included the UK, Canada, France, Germany, Australia, the Netherlands, New Zealand, Poland, and Belgium.[19] In the years that followed, several states claimed SD-NSA in other contexts. Unsurprisingly, Israel was one of them, continuing to pursue its unwilling/unable doctrine against Hamas, PLO groups operating from Syria, and again Hezbollah in Lebanese territory.[20] Another state that followed a similar path was Russia, which invoked SD-NSA in the context of the conflicts in South Ossetia and Northern Abkhazia.[21] Uganda, Kenya, and Turkey did so too in different regional contexts.[22] Then, another major breakthrough came towards the end of 2014, when a coalition of mainly Western allies was formed to fight the advance of ISIS in the territories of Syria and Iraq, using SD-NSA as their main legal basis.[23] The US, Australia, and Canada joined under the unwilling/unable argument, while France, Germany, the UK, Denmark, the Netherlands, Norway, Belgium, and Turkey also undertook military action under SD-NSA, yet without resorting to the unwilling/unable criteria. However, for the first time in history, the invocation of SD-NSA as a legal basis awoke a minor degree of explicit opposition within some states, namely Brazil[24] and Mexico.[25] In terms of academic voices, 9/11 marked a turning point as well. From 2001 on, SD-NSA became a hotly debated and somewhat unavoidable element of any discussion on self-defence, in contrast to its almost complete concealment in academic circles in the previous phases. Against this background, it seems that today a majority of scholars is of the opinion that SD-NSA could be covered by Article 51, although the feeling that the matter is rather obscure is still widespread.[26]

[19] See Repertoire of the Practice of the UNSC, supplement of 2000–03, 1013.

[20] ibid 1010–12; supplement of 2004–07, 1024, 1026.

[21] See Repertoire of the Practice of the UNSC, supplement of 2000–03, 1015.

[22] See Repertoire of the Practice of the UNSC, supplements of 2004–07, 1025; 2010–11, 571; and 2014–15, 353.

[23] See Repertoire of the Practice of the UNSC, supplement of 2014–15, 352.

[24] UNSC, '8262nd Meeting (S/PV.8262)' para 44; UNSC, '8395th Meeting (S/PV.8395)' para 62.

[25] UNSC, '8262nd Meeting (S/PV.8262)' (n 23) para 47.

[26] For an idea of the different positions in the academic debate on SD-NSA, see the following. In favour of SD-NSA: Thomas M Franck, 'Terrorism and the Right of Self-Defense' (2001) 95 The American Journal of International Law 839, 839; Christian J Tams, 'The Use of Force against Terrorists' (2009) 20 European Journal of International Law 359, 359; Amin Ghanbari Amirhandeh, 'Examination of the Plea of Self-Defence vis a vis Non-State Actors' (2009) 15 Asian Yearbook of International Law 125, 125; Terry D Gill and Dieter Fleck, 'Part III Military Operations within the Context of the Right of Self-Defence and Other Possible Legal Bases for the Use of Force, Ch.8 Legal Basis of the Right of Self-Defence under the UN Charter and under Customary International Law' in *The Handbook of the International Law of Military Operations* (1st edn, OUP 2010); Daniel Bethlehem, 'Principles Relevant to the Scope of a State's Right of Self-Defense Against an Imminent or Actual Armed Attack by Non-State Actors" (2012) 106 American Journal of International Law 106; Raphaël Van Steenberghe, 'Self-Defence in Response to Attacks by Non-State Actors in the Light of Recent State Practice: A Step Forward?' (2010) 23 Leiden Journal of International Law 183, 183; Trapp (n 8); Pemmaraju Rao, 'Non-State Actors and Self-Defence: A Relook at the UN Charter Article 51' (2016) 56 Indian Journal of International Law 127, 127; Nicholas Tsagourias, 'Self-Defence against Non-State Actors: The Interaction between Self-Defence as a Primary Rule and Self-Defence as a Secondary Rule International Law and Practice: Symposium on the Fight against ISIL and International Law' (2016) 29 Leiden Journal of International Law 801, 801; Christian Henderson, *The Use of Force and International Law*

On the whole, therefore, the evolution of state practice and the debate in academic settings around SD-NSA show that, from being basically a non-issue in 1945, it has evolved into a legal argument that is recurrently used by states nowadays, and an unavoidable topic for scholars dealing with *ius ad bellum*. Nevertheless, uncertainty as to its validity under Article 51 of the UN Charter persists.

3. Strategies of Norm-destabilization

The trajectory just described is plagued with discontinuities, ambiguities, and conspicuous silences that are perhaps not evident at first sight, but that have played a big role in determining the development of SD-NSA. Crucially, they evidence the extent to which strategies of norm-destabilization have been operating in the background at least since Israel started using the argument of SD-NSA in 1969. As will be seen, these range from arrangements in multilateral settings, to erratic judicial decisions and sporadic displays of individual opposition. Whatever form they take, it is contended here that these strategies reflect a certain reluctance by different actors to acknowledge manifestly their position in favour of or against the rule, purposefully obstructing a transparent debate on the matter, and thus blocking the consolidation—or stabilization—of SD-NSA in one way or another. This section describes and analyses these strategies as seen in the case of SD-NSA.

(CUP 2018); Jutta Brunnée and Stephen J Toope, 'Self-Defense against Non-State Actors: Are Powerful States Willing but Unable to Change International Law?' (2018) 67 International & Comparative Law Quarterly 263, 263. For positions expressing uncertainty or ambiguity: Marcelo Gustavo Kohen, 'The Use of Force by the United States after the End of the Cold War, and Its Impact on International Law' in Georg Nolte and Michel Byers (eds), *United States Hegemony and the Foundations of International Law* (CUP 2003) 206, 207; Tom Ruys, *'Armed Attack' and Article 51 of the UN Charter: Evolutions in Customary Law and Practice* (CUP 2010) 529, 530; Georg Nolte and Albrecht Randelzhofer, 'Ch.VII Action with Respect to Threats to the Peace, Breaches of the Peace, and Acts of Aggression: Article 51' in Bruno Simma and others (eds), *Oxford Commentaries on International Law* (OUP 2012) 38, 41; André De Hoogh, 'Restrictivist Reasoning on the Ratione Personae Dimension of Armed Attacks in the Post 9/11 World' (2016) 29 Leiden Journal of International Law 19, 19; Robert Kolb, *International Law on the Maintenance of Peace: Jus Contra Bellum* (Edward Elgar 2018) 385; Marja Lehto, 'The Fight against Isil in Syria. Comments on the Recent Discussion of the Right of Self-Defence against Non-State Actors' (2018) 87 Nordic Journal of International Law 1, 1; Anne Peters and others, 'Self-Defence Against Non-State Actors: Impulses from the Max Planck Trialogues on the Law of Peace and War' [2017] Max Planck Institute for Comparative Public Law & International Law (MPIL) Research Paper No 2017-07 <https://papers.ssrn.com/abstract=2941640> accessed 16 October 2022; For positions expressly rejecting SD-NSA: Olivier Corten, *The Law Against War: The Prohibition on the Use of Force in Contemporary International Law* (Hart 2010); Mary Ellen O'Connell, Christian J Tams, and Dire Tladi, *Max Planck Trialogues on the Law of Peace and War, Vol. I, Self-Defence against Non-State Actors* (Anne Peters and Christian Marxsen eds, CUP 2019).

3.1 Multilateral Ambiguity

Multilateral ambiguity is the endorsement by multilateral institutions—ie international institutions in which decisions are taken by membership vote—of legal positions that touch upon a certain issue, but without resolving or addressing important related legal questions that could reasonably be expected to be solved or addressed. More often than not, this type of ambiguity is the result of compromise. States might have conflicting views on a given matter but be constrained by circumstances to act in concert. The avoidance of an issue in these contexts is therefore a technique of negotiation that seeks to divert attention from meaningful disagreements by focusing on finding solutions to the immediate, pressing issue on the table, where the disagreement might be more tenuous or irrelevant. In these cases, diplomatic pragmatism is the reason behind ambiguous formulations or selective silences in multilateral settings, much in the sense of the notion of constructive ambiguity, referred to above.

The history of SD-NSA has very telling examples of this strategy. The clearest one is the role played by the UNSC in the last twenty years. Most authors point to its rare pronouncements on the matter as an authoritative indication of the consolidation of SD-NSA in international law. However, only under extreme conditions has the UNSC come close to openly endorsing it—never actually crossing the line of explicit recognition. In fact, only in three resolutions has the UNSC moved in this direction, and in each of them it left a door open for counterargument and counterinterpretation. The first two were resolutions 1368 and 1373, adopted in the aftermath of 9/11. To put it briefly, in both instances, the Council recognized in preambular paragraphs the 'inherent right of individual or collective self-defence in accordance with the Charter' and condemned 'the horrifying terrorist attacks' in New York, qualifying them as a 'threat to international peace and security'.[27] Yet, neither referred explicitly to the use of force against Al-Qaeda, went beyond mentioning self-defence only in the pCreamble, nor gave any express indication that the terrorist attacks of 9/11 were to be understood on their own as an armed attack for the purpose of Article 51. Rather, the UNSC qualified the attacks as a threat to the peace under Article 39 and emphasized the duty of all states to 'refrain from organizing, instigating, assisting or participating in terrorist acts'—a point placing the focus of the resolutions on states as sponsors of terrorists rather than on terrorists themselves. As a result, while the resolutions certainly provided a very plausible basis for the US and its allies to consider their claims to SD-NSA backed by the UNSC, a plausible argument could also be made that the UNSC's focus and intention were elsewhere, and that its reference to self-defence was not at all meant to endorse SD-NSA.[28]

[27] UNSC, 'S/RES/1368 (2001)'; UNS, 'S/RES/1373 (2001)'.

[28] Eric Rosand, 'Security Council Resolution 1373, the Counter-Terrorism Committee, and the Fight against Terrorism' (2003) 97 The American Journal of International Law 333, 334.

The third example is even more telling of this ambiguity: resolution 2249 of 2015. Adopted unanimously in the wake of the coalition against ISIS, it made a call for 'Member States that have the capacity to do so' to 'take all necessary measures, in compliance with international law [...] on the territory under the control of ISIL [...] to redouble and coordinate their efforts to prevent and suppress terrorist acts'.[29] A masterpiece of multilateral ambiguity, it clearly gave a green light to the states intervening in Syria based on the argument of SD-NSA, without even mentioning self-defence in the resolution—let alone SD-NSA.

What does it mean to say that there was a strategy of norm-instability behind these resolutions and how do we know this was the case? The first element to note is that, as seen in the previous section, a host of Western countries notified the UNSC of their use of force against Al-Qaeda and ISIS explicitly on the basis of SD-NSA. One could thus reasonably think that they would have ideally opted for a resolution at the UNSC unambiguously endorsing SD-NSA—as they actually did in other multilateral fora.[30] Doing this, however, would have made little difference in practice: it sufficed for their objectives to have some loose language interpretable as authorizing military operations in Afghanistan and Syria. Expediency in getting troops on the ground outweighed the potential value of a solid precedent. On the side of the non-Western permanent members, while in 2001 all diplomats in the UNSC had clear instructions from their capitals to collaborate with the US, it seems very unlikely that Russia, and more so China, would have been so easy-going about an express endorsement of SD-NSA in resolutions 1368 and 1373.[31] That was even more clearly the case with resolution 2249 of 2015, where Russia had direct interests in the Syrian civil war and China had a much more hardened foreign policy of non-intervention.[32] For both, establishing a precedent on SD-NSA seems to have been off the table. Yet, it was a reasonable compromise to pass watery resolutions giving Western countries their way without conceding on a point that could have compromised their positions in the future. Consequently, resolutions 1368, 1373, and 2249, ambiguous as they were on the point of SD-NSA, provided a pragmatic solution suiting all the main stakeholders.

As these examples reflect, when it comes to norm strategizing in multilateral institutions, the underlying decisive element is the capacity of institutions to set authoritative precedents.[33] Avoiding the adoption of authoritative statements, resolutions, or any other form of decision that might become an unavoidable legal standard in the future can be of utmost importance when a state's strategic interests are at stake. The resolutions of the UNSC, to take the case at hand, are of major

[29] UNSC, 'S/RES/2249 (2015)'.

[30] NATO, 'Statement by the North Atlantic Council (Press Release (2001) 124)', 12 September 2001.

[31] Kent Roach, *The 9/11 Effect: Comparative Counter-Terrorism* (CUP 2011) 32.

[32] Sebastian von Einsiedel, David N Malone, and Bruno Stagno Ugarte, 'The UN Security Council in an Age of Great Power Rivalry' (2015) 04 United Nations University Working Paper Series 3.

[33] Nico Krisch, 'Liquid Authority in Global Governance' (2017) 9 International Theory 237, 240–41.

precedential value, among other things because of the constitutional hierarchy of the Council and their potential irreversibility in practice. In international law, furthermore, this dynamic is reinforced precisely by the legal value that institutional precedent and practice have both for treaty interpretation and for customary law. As such, the norm-consolidating capacity of a resolution of a UN organ—and particularly of the UNSC—is high.[34] In these conditions, it is only reasonable for states to think twice before they support the multilateral endorsement of a rule, even when they use it on occasion. Keeping a multilateral institution quiet or evasive, and thus avoiding limiting their scope of manoeuvre in the future, is in many cases a safer bet.

3.2 Selective Protest

A second strategy of norm-destabilization often used in international law is selective protest. Selective protest is the silence by an actor with regard to a given normative development, coupled with its active opposition to other normative developments surrounding or related to—yet distinct from—the first one. The purpose of this strategy is usually to oppose legally and politically the actions of the actor wielding the norm in question, without taking a final stance on its legality. In these cases, the reactionary actor often truly opposes the related normative development and thus is willing to be vocal against it but is uncertain about the main norm invoked by its adversary, and therefore has an incentive not to compromise its position by explicitly denouncing it. In this sense, there is usually less of an element of compromise than there is in multilateral ambiguity, and more of a somewhat calculated hypocrisy. The outcome in legal terms is in any event destabilizing for the norm because the opposition to the related normative developments creates an aura of disapproval that impacts the main norm indirectly, leaving nevertheless a discursive avenue open for eventual endorsement.

The case of SD-NSA is, again, a very telling example of this strategy. The first element to note is the attitude of states individually at the UNSC for nearly five decades. As explained in the historical overview above, a stunning feature of the trajectory of SD-NSA is that no state explicitly challenged SD-NSA qua legal rule until Brazil and Mexico decided to do so in recent years. Indeed, from 1969 to 2001, a multitude of states did denounce Israel time and again for its use of force against Hezbollah and Hamas, and the same happened with regard to the operations of Southern Rhodesia, South Africa, and the US against non-state actors in foreign territories. However, the legal arguments used against them did not mention at all the point that self-defence might not be available against NSA under Article

[34] Ingo Venzke, *How Interpretation Makes International Law: On Semantic Change and Normative Twists* (OUP 2012) 7, 8.

51 of the Charter. The recurring legal arguments were, rather, the baselessness of the claim of pre-emptive self-defence, and the disproportionality of the military reprisals.[35] Unsurprisingly, there was also no open endorsement of SD-NSA by these opposing states. A neutral observer would therefore not have been able to tell whether these states actually opposed SD-NSA—the general impression would have been that they disagreed with what was happening on the ground. The attitude therefore cast a shadow of doubt over SD-NSA, without truly objecting to it.

The same can be said of states acting in diplomatic clusters. The clearest example is the stance taken by the Non-Aligned Movement (NAM) since at least 2004. Their interventions at the UNSC debates and in the final documents of their summits usually included the following statement: '[. . .] consistent with the practice of the UN and international law, as pronounced by the International Court of Justice, Article 51 of the UN Charter is restrictive and should not be re-written or re-interpreted' without adding anything further.[36] Clearly, the scope of this claim is very vast and ambiguous, and could be reasonably read as discarding everything beyond the hypothesis of interstate self-defence from the scope of Article 51—including of course SD-NSA. Such has been the reading by several scholars and diplomats, who often take it as an example of consistent opposition to SD-NSA, mainly because the statement has been made in contexts where non-state actors were involved.[37] Yet, there is no indication whether the NAM actually opposes SD-NSA or not. In fact, many states that participate in the NAM have in other settings endorsed SD-NSA. That is the case of Iran—a leading member of the NAM—which has itself resorted to SD-NSA to justify military action in Iraq. It is also the case of African states—over 40 per cent of the NAM's membership—which in 2005 adopted a formal definition of aggression including hostile acts by non-state actors, under Article 1(C) of the African Union's Non-Aggression and Common Defence Pact. Hence, it appears that the NAM members, when acting through the NAM, have an interest in projecting an anti-interventionist attitude that suggests opposition to SD-NSA, but that does not in fact compromise their individual positions on the topic.[38]

Selective protest is therefore a way of amplifying the discursive effect of a statement of disapproval. By expressing legal opposition in a general way, states achieve the political goal of delegitimizing—before other states and before public opinion—a situation that they disagree with or that is prejudicial to their interests. But by formulating it in an ambiguous way, states simultaneously eschew any commitment to

[35] See section 2.

[36] '17th Summit of Heads of State and Government of the Non-Aligned Movement, Final Document (NAM 2016/CoB/DOC.1. Corr.1)' para 25.2.

[37] See eg Corten (n 25) 432; Peters and others (n 25) 20; O'Connell, Tams, and Tladi (n 25) 78.

[38] A similar thing can be said of a statement by CELAC of 2018. See CELAC, 'Measures to Eliminate International Terrorism. Statement by the Permanent Mission of El Salvador to the UN on Behalf of the Community of Latin American and Caribbean States (CELAC)' 3 <https://celac.rree.gob.sv/wp-content/uploads/2018/10/Measures-to-Eliminate-International-Terrorism.pdf> accessed 16 October 2022.

the concrete implications of their opposition, stay free to use the norm opposed in the future, and liberate themselves from the burden of justification in case allies resort to it. On the whole, the strategy has a clear norm-destabilizing effect in that the norm will remain widely unendorsed. Crucially, though, the destabilization will not take the change attempt to the point of failure.

3.3 Compromised Support

A third type of strategy with norm-destabilizing effects is compromised support. For the purpose of this chapter, compromised support is understood as the partial display of approval for a certain normative development, yet refraining from articulating this support in a clear and unambiguous way. Compromised support usually takes the form of silence on a crucial point. This can happen, for example, by hinting the normative endorsement of a given rule but not clarifying the necessary details to make the endorsement unequivocal, or by explicitly claiming to endorse a rule, but then omitting a key element in the formulation. In these cases—in contrast to the previous strategies—there is usually no active intention to destabilize the normative development in question, but rather an element of caution or self-restraint seeking not to compromise one's position. The result, nevertheless, is destabilizing because these attitudes block the establishment of a precedent and withhold the discursive authority that comes with endorsement, invariably leaving room for counterinterpretation of the actor's sayings or doings.

Compromised support can be seen in the case of SD-NSA in the attitude adopted by the UN Secretary General (SG) in the aftermath of 9/11 and in the following years. Kofi Annan, SG at the time, condemned on many occasions and in different fora the terrorist attacks against the US, usually commending the international community for acting with determination and cohesion through the UNSC.[39] In these documents he usually did not address the legal dimension of the claim under which the coalition of Western countries was intervening in Afghanistan—SD-NSA—nor could one reasonably have expected him to do so.[40] Yet, it is apparent that he supported the claim. In one of these speeches, for example, he spoke in an approving tone of the solidarity with the US shown by many governments in cooperating in the UNSC and acknowledging its right to self-defence under Article 51 of the UN Charter.[41] This cannot but be read as a timid endorsement of SD-NSA. More telling than these speeches, though, is the landmark report of 2004 *A More Secure*

[39] See eg UN Secretary General, 'Address to the General Assembly on Terrorism (Press Release G/SM/7977-GA/9920) (1/10/2001)'; 'Address to the General Assembly (23/09/2003)'; UN Secretary General, 'Address to the Los Angeles World Affairs Council (3/12/2003)'.

[40] Jayantha Dhanapala, 'The United Nations' Response to 9/11' (2005) 17 Terrorism and Political Violence 17, 20, 21.

[41] UN Secretary General, 'Address to the Los Angeles World Affairs Council' (n 38).

World: Our Shared Responsibility, commissioned by the SG to a panel of sixteen prominent former diplomats and experts.[42] The report allocated a section to the issue of preventive self-defence, ultimately rejecting it in concluding with the categorical statement: 'we do not favour the rewriting or reinterpretation of Article 51.'[43] This view reflected a strong personal stance taken by the SG—repeated in many other documents—against the legal grounds invoked by the US for its intervention in Iraq. In passing, however, the section tacitly endorsed SD-NSA in that it spoke of terrorism as a ground that would not justify a claim of preventive self-defence but hinting that an *imminent* terrorist threat would indeed trigger Article 51.[44] In other words, the SG's panel had a problem with invoking self-defence against the possibility of terrorist attacks in the future, but not per se with invoking self-defence against terrorist groups. It seems valid to assume that, in a time and context in which SD-NSA was a hot topic, the panel would have expressed its doubts about it, had it had any, just as it did with preventive self-defence. But it did not. At the same time, however, the panel refrained from making any open endorsement of SD-NSA, something that could seem appropriate in a report discussing the legal meaning of Article 51. One can only venture to suggest that this was because doing so would have provoked discomfort in some diplomatic circles. In any case, what is certain is that this dance of silence around SD-NSA did more to destabilize it than to concretize it.

A second example of clear compromised support regarding SD-NSA is provided by the Institut de droit international's resolution 'Present Problems of the Use of Armed Force in International Law' of 2007. In addressing the topic of SD-NSA, the resolution recognized in its tenth paragraph that, '[i]n the event of an armed attack against a State by non-State actors, Article 51 of the Charter as supplemented by customary international law applies as a matter of principle.'[45] The relative clarity of this statement, though, is eroded by its subparagraphs, which only mention two rather uncontroversial scenarios as 'preliminary responses to the complex problems arising' out of the topic: the case where an attack by a non-state actor is instructed, directed, or controlled by a state; and the case where an attack by a non-state actor is 'launched from an area beyond the jurisdiction of any State.'[46] The fact that the resolution does not address the most discussed and relevant hypothesis, namely the launching of an attack by a non-state actor without the sponsorship of a state but from within the territory of a state, certainly shows that the Institut attempted in good faith to address the topic but could not manage to get its members to agree on anything useful. This did more to destabilize and fuel doubts than to bring SD-NSA forward.

42 For the composition of the Panel, see <www.un.org/en/events/pastevents/a_more_secure_world.shtml> accessed 16 October 2022.

43 UN Secretary General, 'A More Secured World: Our Shared Responsibility, Report of the Secretary-General's High Level Panel on Threats, Challenges and Change' (2004) A/59/565, para 192.

44 ibid 188–94.

45 Institut de droit international (IDI), 'Present Problems of the Use of Armed Force in International Law (A. Self-Defence)' (2007) Session de Santiago, para 10.

46 ibid.

Compromised support, therefore, is in a way the other side of the coin of selective protest. Whereas selective protest has the purpose of destabilizing a norm by objecting to the normative developments surrounding the main norm, compromised support destabilizes it by timidly supporting the main norm but doing it in an ambiguous way. The common element is silence. What hinders the main norm here is thus leaving it unaddressed and disavowed; missing the chance of openly discussing it and withholding any authoritative endorsement that could contribute to its consolidation. The result is, of course, instability: the perpetuation of a situation in which arguing for and against a norm are both legally plausible.

3.4 Cryptic Precedent

A last possible form of norm-destabilizing strategy is the use of cryptic precedent. A cryptic precedent consists of a bald authoritative statement—usually by an international court—seemingly disfavouring a given normative development, but without fully engaging with it, basing it on a very narrow factual base, or leaving its implications for other cases unclear. Cryptic precedents usually come in the form of *obiter dicta* or are presented as such, and they are formulated in a downplaying and simplifying tone. Through them, courts or other authorities actively refrain from endorsing the normative development in question, but also seek to evade dealing head-on with any of the hurdles implicated by this position. This can be in order to dodge the potential compromising implications it could have on the institution, or because internal disagreements among the bench or the members of the decision-making body block less ambiguous formulations. Yet, cryptic precedents have a fateful potential on a given normative development. They tend to become consequential ammunition for legal argument and they commit the body issuing it and other bodies to follow the precedent in future cases. Therefore, cryptic precedents can have long-lasting consequences in destabilizing an international legal rule.

The case of SD-NSA is paradigmatic of cryptic precedent. The International Court of Justice (ICJ), in three decisions spanning over two decades, has played a remarkably reactionary and destabilizing role vis-à-vis SD-NSA, sometimes willingly and sometimes unwillingly. The first crucial cryptic precedent—unwilling this time—was the *Nicaragua* case of 1986. In it, the Court held that the application of self-defence under the Charter and customary international law was not limited to cases of 'action by regular [state] armed forces across an international border', but that it also applied to cases where an attack by a non-state armed band would be somehow attributable to a state under the rules of state responsibility.[47] The ICJ here did nothing more than endorse the doctrine of indirect

[47] *Military and Paramilitary Activities in and against Nicaragua (Nicaragua v United States of America). Merits, Judgment. ICJ Reports 1986, p 14, para* [195].

aggression—something that was not particularly ground-breaking at the time. It did not, at any rate, pronounce itself on the hypothesis of SD-NSA—an issue that was not on the table and which arguably no one involved in the proceedings had in mind. Yet, this precedent became after several years—especially after 9/11—one of the main argumentative bulwarks of the opposition to SD-NSA, who chose to read the judgment as *requiring* that an armed attack be attributable to a state in order for self-defence to become available.[48]

This understanding of the *Nicaragua* decision was then confirmed, cryptically, in two cases after the critical juncture of 2001—though unrelated to 9/11. The first of these was the *Wall* Advisory Opinion of 2004. In it, the Court discarded, with an appalling lack of discussion, Israel's argument that the construction of a wall in occupied territories had been done under the legal entitlement of Article 51. Rather than discussing the legal absurdity of a permanent wall in occupied territory as a means of self-defence, as Israel contended, the Court determined, in four arid lines, that Article 51 was not relevant since it only 'recognizes the existence of an inherent right of self-defence in the case of armed attack by one State against another State', and 'Israel [had not claimed] that the attacks against it [were] imputable to a foreign State'.[49] Then, the third decision relevant for SD-NSA, only one year later, was *Armed Activities (DRC v Uganda)*. Here, again, the ICJ assessed Uganda's claim of self-defence against the Lord Resistance Army (LRA) in Congolese territory under the logic of attributability. As if self-evident—and in line with *Nicaragua* and the *Wall* Advisory Opinion—this meant for the Court that self-defence was unavailable for Uganda because the LRA's acts were not attributable to the other state involved— namely the DRC. This notwithstanding, a paragraph later, in a seldom-matched display of cryptic reasoning, the Court rejected explicitly the need to pronounce itself on the matter of SD-NSA, as if it had not precisely just ruled against it.[50]

The reasons why the Court decided in this way are uncertain and should not be over-interpreted. Both the *Wall* Advisory Opinion and *Armed Activities* were adopted by highly divided benches on the point of the interpretation of Article 51, which makes it likely that the arcane outcomes were the product of compromises among the judges, rather than well-thought elements of case theory. What is certain, however, is that the three cases did much to convince a good portion of the international legal community that SD-NSA was a groundless legal subterfuge, rather than a widely followed and virtually uncontested practice among states. These precedents therefore became crucial elements in any argument against SD-NSA in

[48] See eg Corten (n 25) 188, 191.

[49] *Legal Consequences of the Construction of a Wall in the Occupied Palestinian Territory, Advisory Opinion*, ICJ Reports 2004, p 136, para 139.

[50] *Armed Activities on the Territory of the Congo (Democratic Republic of the Congo v Uganda)*, Judgment, ICJ Reports 2005, p 168, paras 146, 147..

the following years.[51] There is good reason to think that, had the Court decided the *Wall* Advisory Opinion differently, not conceding to Israel's extravagant argument, but at least taking seriously both the old and more recent state practice on Article 51, the trajectory of SD-NSA would have been different. As it happened, the ICJ's precedents destabilized the rule enormously by making it a taboo in certain circles; a claim that only apologists of interventionism could make.

It is therefore fundamental to this strategy that the reasoning of the precedent being created is obscure. Not putting the facts out on the open and not discussing thoroughly the legal merits of a claim can be decisive because it conceals any disagreement, portraying the issue as straightforward when it actually is not. As a precedent, therefore, a cryptic statement substitutes the burden of argument: instead of having to argue why a legal claim is invalid on its own merits, an actor has only to point to the authoritative precedent barring the argument. In the case of SD-NSA this is clear. After the ICJ's intervention, arguing against SD-NSA became a matter of citing *Nicaragua*, the *Wall* Advisory Opinion, or *Armed Activities*, instead of, for instance, explaining the lack of legal value of the whole 9/11 practice—a much more cumbersome exercise to pull off. Cryptic precedent, therefore, has a huge norm-destabilizing potential.

4. Norm-destabilization in International Politics

To what extent are the four strategies just described generalized patterns of behaviour in international lawmaking or, conversely, peculiar to SD-NSA? In the case in focus, it was crucial that both supporters and opponents of SD-NSA were in tacit agreement that the absence of a clear precedent was desirable under the circumstances. On the one hand, this might have been related to the high salience of the matter, which made the creation of a precedent hugely consequential—more likely to constrain states eventually than to yield any tangible benefit. On the other hand, the individual nature of the legal entitlement implied by self-defence made it possible for states to act unilaterally, without there being a practical need for external endorsement of their legal basis. Hence, overall, it seems that a stable, unambiguous rule of SD-NSA was too difficult to accomplish, too compromising, and in fact unnecessary. But do all of these conditions have to be met in order for actors to pursue norm-destabilization strategies in international law? The answer is a straightforward no. Three examples concerning very contrasting subfields of international law are used here to put the observations regarding SD-NSA into perspective.

[51] See eg the argument of the Brazilian representative: UNSC, '8262nd Meeting (S/PV.8262)' (n 23) 44.

The first one, from international trade law, concerns the bargaining that took place between developing and developed states around the Generalized System of Preferences in the GATT regime during the 1960s and 1970s. During this time, developing states found themselves empowered by their growing numbers and by the threat posed to GATT by the creation of the UN Conference on Trade and Development under the sponsorship of the Eastern bloc.[52] Emboldened by this, they challenged the foundational principle of reciprocity and demanded, as a bloc, the adoption within GATT of an exception to the Most-Favoured-Nation (MFN) rule allowing them to have privileged access to the markets of developed countries. The outcome was the Enabling Clause, adopted in 1979 by the GATT contracting parties, which authorized developed countries to grant preferential treatment to developing countries if they so wished.[53] The rule, however, was a far cry from the stable, unambiguous rule sought by the group of developing states. It merely enabled developed countries to graciously adopt preferential measures, but it did not at any rate establish clear criteria under which this should be done, nor any binding obligation to do so.[54] Instability here—achieved through multilateral ambiguity—appears therefore as half-hearted concession by the powerful, meant to appease and preserve the status quo.

The second example concerns the effects doctrine under the laws of jurisdiction in general international law. Here the story began with the US Court of Appeals for the Second Circuit ruling in 1945 that it was legitimate for US courts to exercise antitrust jurisdiction in cases where the relevant conduct had taken place abroad and had been undertaken only by foreigners, as long as it had had a negative effect in US markets.[55] This inaugurated unilaterally an exception to the long-standing principle of territoriality in jurisdiction.[56] During the following fifty years, US judges and policymakers continued to implement the effects doctrine in antitrust matters, despite the loud protests of the country's Western allies.[57] No effort was undertaken by the US during this time to bring clarity to the rule by discussing it in a multilateral setting or by seeking the endorsement of international institutions. Moreover, when the tides of global economy eased the confrontation in the 1990s, and most countries adopted the effects doctrine through legislation, it was precisely the US who sought to keep the topic from being addressed in fora such as the

[52] Robert E Hudec, *Developing Countries in the GATT Legal System* (CUP 2010) 39, 51.

[53] Mitsuo Matsushita (ed), *The World Trade Organization: Law, Practice, and Policy* (3rd edn, OUP 2015) 699.

[54] George A Bermann and Petros C Mavroidis, 'Introduction' in George A Bermann and Petros C Mavroidis (eds), *WTO Law and Developing Countries* (CUP 2007) 2.

[55] *United States v Aluminum Co of America*, US Court of Appeals for the Second Circuit, 148 F2d 416 (2d Cir 1945) [444]; Maher M Dabbah, *International and Comparative Competition Law* (CUP 2010) 434.

[56] Cedric Ryngaert, *Jurisdiction in International Law* (2nd edn, OUP 2015) 49.

[57] AV Lowe, 'The Problems of Extraterritorial Jurisdiction: Economic Sovereignty and the Search for a Solution' (1985) 34 International and Comparative Law Quarterly 724, 727.

World Trade Organization.[58] Thus the effects doctrine has been, for over seventy years, deliberately kept in the shadowy realm of unilateral state action, despite its ever-broadening endorsement. Instability, it appears, has been the product of the self-sufficiency of the powerful state making use of the effects doctrine.

The third and last example regards the rules for continental shelf-delimitation. Towards the end of the 1950s, the equidistance principle seemed to be the leading emerging rule for continental-shelf delimitation—especially since its codification in the 1958 Geneva Convention on the Continental Shelf. At face value, this was a stable norm inasmuch as it determined clearly how delimitation ought to be carried out. Yet, several countries, disfavoured by the equidistance principle in view of the configuration of their littoral, argued that international law demanded not a 'one size fits all' method, but rather the general principle that a boundary ought to be 'fair and equitable'—a rather instable rule.[59] The matter eventually reached the ICJ, which decided, in the *North Sea Continental Shelf Cases* of 1969, that the equidistance principle had not yet crystallized into customary international law, and that custom required delimitation to be undertaken 'in accordance with equitable principles, and taking account of all the relevant circumstances'—a precedent that is in hindsight remarkably cryptical.[60] This left the law of continental shelf-delimitation extremely instable, as reflected in the outcome of the UN Convention on the Law of the Sea in 1982. Only much latter would the *North Sea* precedent be adjusted, the competing rules merged, and the matter restabilized to a certain extent.[61]

These instances show how norm-instability can be present in vastly different contexts. In the case of the Enabling Clause in GATT, there were radically opposed interests regarding the establishment of an unambiguous norm: the less powerful states needed a clear rule, while the most powerful saw it as harmful. The unstable normative outcome thus came as a veiled imposition from the latter through the means of multilateral ambiguity—seeking to appear as a substantial concession but preserving the asymmetric nature of the system in force. The effects doctrine, in contrast, has to this day remained unstable because its main proponent—the US—has never seen a meaningful added value in seeking external endorsement. As in SD-NSA, the individual-entitlement nature of the rule in question made this possible. The opponents of the effects doctrine, who suffered harm from this instability over many decades, could not do much about it. Thus, instability was for the most part an individual game of the US. Lastly, in the case of the rules for

[58] Henning Klodt, 'Conflicts and Conflict Resolution in International Anti-Trust: Do We Need International Competition Rules?' (2001) 24 The World Economy 877, 877, 886; Matsushita (n 52) 819.

[59] Malcolm Evans, 'Maritime Boundary Delimitation' in Donald R Rothwell and others (eds), *The Oxford Handbook of the Law of the Sea* (OUP 2015) 257.

[60] *North Sea Continental Shelf, Judgment*, ICJ Reports 1969, p 3, para [101]..

[61] Ezgi Yildiz and Umut Yüksel, 'Understanding the Limitations of Behavioralism: Lessons from the Field of Maritime Delimitation' (2022) 23 German Law Journal 413. <https://pathsofinternationallaw.files.wordpress.com/2020/05/working-paper-23.pdf> accessed 16 October 2022.

continental-shelf delimitation, instability was the result of a successful strategy of cryptic precedent by the countries resisting the consolidation of the equidistance principle. Here, the authority of the *North Sea* judgment was the crucial stronghold of the minority against the majority, who relied on it to erode the solidity of the emerging equidistance rule. Instability was a means of keeping an undesired norm at bay and allowing a rival norm to emerge.

These instances show that destabilization strategies can be observed in contexts that are far less exceptional than the one seen in SD-NSA. What seems to be the common denominator is the incentive for most stakeholders in each case—or for the most powerful ones—to avoid the consolidation of a clear-cut, unambiguous rule. The value of instability, one might speculate, is that it preserves the freedom of action of the stakeholders involved. While stable rules leave little doubt as to what is prohibited, norm-instability maximizes the spectrum of possible courses of behaviour andpreserves an appearance of legality and—crucial in a discursive environment governed by the idea of the rule of law—legitimacy. Thus, in many contexts, preserving normative instability by avoiding the consolidation of an unfavourable rule will be a rational course of action to follow for actors in international law.

5. Conclusion

This chapter has given an overview of the phenomenon of norm-destabilization in international law. Focusing on the example of the case of SD-NSA, it has analysed four possible strategies of destabilization: multilateral ambiguity, selective protest, compromised support, and cryptic precedent. Although the case of SD-NSA seems exceptionally prone to normative instability, the chapter has also sought to take the issue into different legal contexts in order to show that strategies of norm-destabilization are not at all exceptional in international law. Norm-instability, it is suggested, will be pursued whenever actors in international law—for whatever reason—seek to preserve a wide margin of manoeuvre with regard to an issue in which a clearly constraining rule might be emerging. The added value of norm-destabilization, in contrast to bald opposition, is that it conducts the challenge within the boundaries of legal discourse and the rule of law, preserving for the opposing states the appearance of legitimacy, while at the same time eroding the stability of the norm in question.

4
Transnational Lawmaking Coalitions as Change Agents in International Law

*Nina Reiners**

1. Introduction

International human rights law and its institutions are under pressure. The workload of the treaty-monitoring bodies increased rapidly without accompanying funding or personnel, and to strengthen the treaty bodies, states initiated a year-long reform process which did not bring the relief needed for the United Nations (UN) human rights system.[1] At the same time, the adoption of new treaties stagnates, and challenges for human rights and their defenders increase around the globe and also within multilateral institutions. The members of the UN human rights treaty bodies, elected in their personal capacity as independent experts, are confronted with various social, economic, and political challenges for human rights when monitoring states compliance with the obligations in the treaties. Examples for such challenges range from threats to human rights by climate change or growing social inequalities to a decline of democratic institutions in many countries once at the forefront of human rights protection.

To address such challenges for human rights, treaty bodies increasingly make use of their instrument which allows them to interpret the human right treaties, the so-called 'general comments'.[2] They are general in the sense that they address all states parties to the covenants but require no further act of consent by those states for their adoption. Governments regularly reject general comments as non-binding when confronted with obligations arising from such a document, often accusing the treaty bodies to overstep their mandate. Yet, general comments can play an important role for domestic policy change, for example through their 'persuasive authority' among several stakeholders,[3] by being referenced in domestic court rulings, or because

* Associate Professor for Human Rights and Social Sciences at the Centre for Human Rights, University of Oslo, Norway; Associated Researcher, Graduate Institute of International and Development Studies, Geneva, Switzerland.

1 <www.ohchr.org/en/treaty-bodies/treaty-body-strengthening> accessed 27 October 2022.

2 Nina Reiners, *Transnational Lawmaking Coalitions for Human Rights* (CUP 2022).

3 Laurence R Helfer and Erik Voeten, 'International Courts as Agents of Legal Change: Evidence from LGBT rights in Europe' (2014) 68(1) International Organization 77–110, 81ff.

Nina Reiners, *Transnational Lawmaking Coalitions as Change Agents in International Law* In: *The Many Paths of Change in International Law*. Edited by: Nico Krisch and Ezgi Yildiz, Oxford University Press. © Nina Reiners 2023.
DOI: 10.1093/oso/9780198877844.003.0004

their content requires national policymakers to react to them.[4] Some general comments can also impact the development of international law. The Human Rights Committee, for example, has, in its General Comment No 36, substantially expanded the right to life in relation to issues such as environment and abortion. In 2013, the Committee on the Elimination of All Forms of Racial Discrimination (CERD) adopted a general recommendation aimed at combatting racist hate speech, creating far-reaching obligations for states parties to adopt measures preventing racist hate speech. And the Committee on Economic, Social and Cultural Rights in 2002 established the first normative framework in human rights law for a human right to water. General comments sit somewhere between two maximalist positions defining its boundaries in international law: some scholars praise general comments as influential tools in human rights law[5] and as 'authoritative interpretation[s]'[6] of the human rights treaties, while others are more hesitant to attribute legal value to general comments for the development of soft law.[7]

This chapter focuses on the agents behind the drafting of such instruments for international legal change, so called transnational lawmaking coalitions (TLC).[8] They are transnational in the sense that they are not coalitions between states or state delegates (thus not international) but are formed by experts in international monitoring bodies with professionals working in various professions relevant to human rights across borders, thus transnational. Transnational lawmaking coalitions are temporary and informal collaborations between one or more professionals and one or more member(s) of a treaty-monitoring body. Within a TLC, all involved actors coalesce around a like-minded goal of action: to develop, apply, or interpret a legal norm. Their interactive structure is thus temporary—in contrast to alliances, which operate long-term—maintained simply until the desired outcome is achieved.[9] The type of actor we seek to describe as a TLC shows two characteristics which distinguish it from other actors in global governance

[4] Beth A Simmons, *Mobilizing for Human Rights. International Law in Domestic Politics* (CUP 2009).

[5] Max Lesch and Nina Reiners, 'Informal human rights law-making: How treaty bodies use "General Comments" to develop international law' (2023) 12(2) Global Constitutionalism, 378–401.

[6] Kasey L McCall-Smith, 'Interpreting International Human Rights Standards. Treaty Body General Comments as a Chisel or a Hammer' in Stephanie Lagoutte, Thomas Gammeltoft-Hansen, and John Cerone (eds), *Tracing the Roles of Soft Law in Human Rights* (OUP 2016) 27–46, also P Alston, 'The Historical Origins of the Concept of 'General Comments' in Human Rights Law' in Laurence Boisson de Chazournes and Vera Gowlland-Debbas (eds), *The International Legal System in Quest of Equity and Universality/L'Ordre Juridique International, un Système en Quête d'Equité et d'Universalité: Liber Amicorum Georges Abi-Saab* (Martinus Nijhoff Publishers 2001) 763–76.

[7] Stephen Tully, 'A Human Right to Access Water-A Critique of General Comment No 15' (2005) 23(1) *Netherlands Quarterly of Human Rights* 35–63; Conway Blake 'Normative Instruments in International Human Rights Law: Locating the General Comment' (2008) NYU Center for Human Rights and Global Justice Working Paper 17, 2–38.

[8] Reiners, *Transnational Lawmaking Coalitions* (n 2).

[9] Achieving a goal can, however, result in mission expansion, as Haddad analysed in the case of the NGO Coalition for an International Criminal Court. After achieving their advocacy goal of the establishment of the ICC, they became service providers to the ICC: 'mission expansion was not originally intended, but evolved with the perceived needs of the court so that the ICC could become the fair, effective court that the CICC envisioned' Heidi Nichols Haddad, 'After the Norm Cascade: NGO Mission

literature: first, TLCs form around experts. Its members do not need to pressure, socialize, or persuade governments; rather, the targets of their activities are expert bodies. Secondly, their mode of operation is determined by the interpersonal relationships among the members of a TLC. This shift to their personal interactions comes at the cost of reaching the limits of common explanations for transnational actors' influence—which are of lesser importance in lawmaking (eg the size of a non-governmental organization (NGO) or network or strategies employed to publicly reach a wide audience). So far, TLCs have been fruitfully applied to explain single drafting processes in the UN human rights treaty bodies.[10] Yet, their significance for broader change processes in international law remains to be explored. I argue that UN experts and professionals act on legal change by influencing the development of international human rights law through TLCs. To illustrate TLCs and the conditions of their influence, the chapter discusses two interpretation processes within the UN. The interpretation of the right to decent working conditions by the Committee on Economic, Social and Cultural Rights and the inclusion of right to abortion under the right to life by the UN Human Rights Committee.

2. Interpretation and Change Agents in International Law

The framework for this volume identifies different ideal-typical paths which may contribute to change in international law.[11] As Krisch and Yildiz note, such pathways in reality often overlap and some become more central to change than others. I want to explore agents and agency of legal change with a focus on expert bodies on the bureaucratic path. Expert bodies are often authorized to monitor the law but have the potential to change international law through their treaty interpretations. While fewer multilateral treaties are concluded in international law, which is said to symbolize 'treaty fatigue'[12] among states, international law remains the common language of global governance,[13] and normative change increasingly happens through interpretation. States strategically use interpretive tactics to influence how other states interpret legal obligations.[14] In addition, the literature on international

Expansion and the Coalition for the International Criminal Court' (2013) 19(2) Global Governance: A Review of Multilateralism and International Organizations 187–206, 200.

[10] Reiners, *Transnational Lawmaking Coalitions* (n 2); Max Lesch, *Dynamics of Deviance: Torture and Its Prohibition in World Politics* (Johann-Wolfgang-Goethe-Universität 2020).

[11] See Nico Krisch and Ezgi Yildiz, "The Many Paths of Change in International Law: A Frame," in *The Many Paths of Change in International Law*, ed. Nico Krisch and Ezgi Yildiz (Oxford University Press, 2023).

[12] Joost Pauwelyn, Ramses A Wessel, and Jan Wouters, 'When Structures Become Shackles: Stagnation and Dynamics in International Lawmaking' (2014) 25(3) European Journal of International Law 733–63.

[13] Hannah Birkenkötter, 'International Law as a Common Language Across Spheres of Authority?' (2020) 9(2) Global Constitutionalism 318–42.

[14] Tonya L Putnam, 'Mingling and Strategic Augmentation of International Legal Obligations' (2020) 74(1) International Organization 31–64.

courts has demonstrated how judges and communities of legal practice are able to develop and change legal norms through interpretation.[15]

Analytical inquiries usually reveal states' interests and power dynamics as creators and blockers of international law but may also point to other pathways for legal change. Within these alternative pathways, international legal scholarship has emphasized the sizeable role formal legal institutions, such as international and domestic courts, potentially play as change agents.[16] Scholarship in this field has helped us to understand that international courts' judgments change domestic policies beyond the parties to the case,[17] how the design of these institutions constrains judicial practices,[18] and how despite these constraints judicial activities can at least invoke incremental norm change.[19] Of further importance to assess agency are interactions with other institutions and inter-organizational relationships.

For example, the literature provides a rich account of the important role that NGOs play for the operation of courts,[20] how regulatory intermediaries influence the rulemaking by third parties.[21]

Although the field of human rights shows no dearth of models for norm change through non-state actors, these models remain largely state-centric. The boomerang and the spiral models,[22] as well as the justice cascade,[23] all theorize

[15] Nora Stappert, 'Practice Theory and Change in International Law: Theorizing the Development of Legal Meaning Through the Interpretive Practices of International Criminal Courts' (2019) 12(1) International Theory 1–26; Armin von Bogdandy and Ingo Venzke, *In Whose Name? A Public Law Theory of International Adjudication* (OUP 2014).

[16] Oumar Ba, *Agents of Change: How International Courts Alter International Politics* (OUP 2017); Anthea Roberts, 'Comparative International Law? The Role of National Courts in Creating and Enforcing International Law' (2011) 60(1) International and Comparative Law Quarterly 57–92.

[17] Helfer and Voeten (n 3).

[18] Jeffrey L Dunoff and Mark A Pollack, 'The Judicial Trilemma' (2017) 111(2) American Journal of International Law 225–76.

[19] Ezgi Yildiz, 'A Court with Many Faces: Judicial Characters and Modes of Norm Development in the European Court of Human Rights' (2020) 31(1) European Journal of International Law 73–99.

[20] Heidi Nichols Haddad, *The Hidden Hands of Justice: NGOs, Human Rights, and International Courts* (CUP 2018); Heidi Nichols Haddad, 'Judicial Institution Builders: NGOs and International Human Rights Courts' (2012) 11(1) Journal of Human Rights 126–49; Theresa Squatrito, 'The Democratizing Effects of Transnational Actors' Access to International Courts' (2018) 24(4) Global Governance: A Review of Multilateralism and International Organizations 595–613.

[21] Luc Brès, Sébastien Mena, and Marie-Laure Salles-Djelic, 'Exploring the Formal and Informal Roles of Regulatory Intermediaries in Transnational Multistakeholder Regulation' (2019) 13(2) Regulation & Governance 127–40; Kenneth W Abbott, David Levi-Faur, and Duncan Snidal, 'Theorizing Regulatory Intermediaries: The RIT Model' (2017) 670(1) The Annals of the American Academy of Political and Social Science 14–35; Tom Pegram, 'Regulatory Stewardship and Intermediation: Lessons from Human Rights Governance' (2017) 670(1) The Annals of the American Academy of Political and Social Science 225–44.

[22] Thomas Risse, Stephen C Ropp, and Kathryn Sikkink (eds), *The Persistent Power of Human Rights: From Commitment to Compliance* (CUP 2013); Thomas Risse, Stephen C Ropp, and Kathryn Sikkink (eds), *The Power of Human Rights: International Norms and Domestic Change* (CUP 1999); Martha Finnemore and Kathryn Sikkink, 'International Norm Dynamics and Political Change' (1998) 52(4) International Organization 887–917; Margaret E Keck and Kathryn Sikkink, *Activists Beyond Borders: Advocacy Networks in International Politics* (Cornell University Press 1998).

[23] Kathryn Sikkink, *The Justice Cascade: How Human Rights Prosecutions are Changing World Politics* (WW Norton & Company 2011).

influential non-state actions to bring about human rights change vis-à-vis governments. This state-centrism owes itself largely to the models' approach of norm change as change in commitment or compliance with human rights, thus when a norm already exists as a right but is not yet (fully) implemented. I thus distinguish between human rights as law and as norms.[24] Norm emergence models in international relations that account for different stages and actors were recently introduced to the discipline,[25] but do not fully take into account the specifics of *legal* norm change. Scholars of international legal change, on the other hand, are interested in why some norms still remain to be codified as independent rights into human rights law, and how co-dependent rights finally became independent human rights.

Several motives explain the interest of non-state actors, especially those claiming to represent civil society, in the making of international human rights law. In general, domestic and transnational advocacy groups and networks need the international legal framework to hold governments accountable.[26] Human rights defenders and lawyers use strategic litigation,[27] both through national and regional courts but also through individual complaints to the treaty bodies, to get clarification on what constitutes a human rights violation and can point to international human rights law when domestic law is ambiguous or silent about a violation. This clarity, rendered tangible, is crucial for awareness-raising: as grassroots or local actors *need* people to know that a certain government behaviour is unlawful and that they have the right to defend themselves, international human rights law may be cast as an instrument to overcome injustice,[28] speak 'Rights to Power',[29] and empower individuals in international politics.[30] While this assumption deserves critical examination regarding just representation, civil society actors' interest in the change of human rights law and the long-standing success of NGOs and

[24] Arguments about the meaning and application of laws in-use (Antje Wiener, 'Enacting Meaning-in-Use: Qualitative Research on Norms and International Relations' (2009) 35(1) Review of International Studies 175–93) are thus inbuilt features of human rights law, itself providing for the possibility of norm change (Wayne Sandholtz, *Prohibiting Plunder: How Norms Change* (OUP 2007). Hence, when norms become validated as law, that does not mean that human rights are ready for implementation in all places or immediately achieve acceptable levels of compliance (Abram Chayes and Antonia H Chayes, 'On Compliance' (1993) 47(2) International Organization 175–205).

[25] Elvira Rosert, 'Norm Emergence as Agenda Diffusion: Failure and Success in the Regulation of Cluster Munitions' (2019) 25(4) European Journal of International Relations 1103–31.

[26] Risse, Ropp, and Sikkink, *The Persistent Power of Human Rights* (n 21); Risse, Ropp and Sikkink, *The Power of Human Rights* (n 21).

[27] Helen Duffy, *Strategic Human Rights Litigation: Understanding and Maximising Impact* (Bloomsbury Publishing 2018).

[28] Kathryn Sikkink, *Evidence for Hope: Making Human Rights Work in the 21st Century* (Princeton University Press 2019); Sikkink, *The Justice Cascade* (n 22).

[29] Alison Brysk, *Speaking Rights to Power: Constructing Political Will* (OUP 2013).

[30] Gita Sen and Avanti Mukherjee, 'No Empowerment without Rights, No Rights without Politics: Gender-Equality, MDGs and the Post-2015 Development Agenda' (2014) 15(2–3) Journal of Human Development and Capabilities 188–202.

transnational advocacy networks in bringing about domestic policy change highlight their role as potential change agents in international law.

Krisch and Yildiz assume that paths other than state-led ones are likely to emerge when alternative authorities exist in a given context—authorities that, like courts, international bureaucracies, and public or private expert bodies, are recognized as having significant weight in the ascertainment of international law, even if they do not enjoy acceptance as formal lawmakers.[31] United Nations human rights treaty bodies are widely regarded as authorities for the monitoring of human rights law,[32] best described as state-empowered entities.[33] Actors who want to see change enacted are likely to turn to such authorities when state-led paths are blocked. The coalition created to develop treaty interpretations together with external professionals—which is this chapter's main focus—is a powerful change agent for international law.

3. Transnational Lawmaking Coalitions and Change

The UN human rights treaty system is monitored by committees composed of independent experts. They consider state reports and individual complaints and are further authorized to interpret the treaty norms. Their outputs sometimes lead to the development and specification of human rights.[34] They have limited resources available for this task, which encourages the involvement of other actors such as NGOs or academics, and a resource exchange takes place, whereby knowledge is traded for access.[35] These external actors provide material and ideal resources to the treaty bodies in both formal and informal ways. If the treaty body requires external resources to work on a treaty interpretation, such drafting coalitions are mainly constituted through personal relationships. Such relationships enable individuals to influence the interpretation of the treaty, through which the respective committee can in turn influence the further development of

[31] Nico Krisch and Ezgi Yildiz, 'From Drivers to Bystanders: The Varying Roles of States in International Legal Change' (LCIL Lecture, 2021).

[32] Machiko Kanetake, 'UN Human Rights Treaty Monitoring Bodies Before Domestic Courts' (2018) 67(1) International & Comparative Law Quarterly 201–32; Helen Keller and Geir Ulfstein (eds), *UN Human Rights Treaty Bodies. Law and Legitimacy, Studies on Human Rights Conventions* (CUP 2012); Eckart Klein, 'Impact of Treaty Bodies on the International Legal Order' in Rüdiger Wolfrum and Volker Röben (eds), *Developments of International Law in Treaty Making* (Springer 2005) 571–79.

[33] Sandesh Sivakumaran, 'Beyond States and Non-State Actors: The Role of State-Empowered Entities in the Making and Shaping of International Law' (2017) 55(2) Columbia Journal of Transnational Law 343–94.

[34] Çalı Başak, Cathryn Costello, and Stewart Cunningham, 'Hard Protection through Soft Courts? Non-Refoulement before the United Nations Treaty Bodies' (2020) 21(3) German Law Journal 355–84 .

[35] Jonas Tallberg and others, 'NGO Influence in International Organizations: Information, Access and Exchange' (2015) 48(1) British Journal of Political Science 1–26; Michele M Betsill and Elisabeth Corell, 'NGO Influence in International Environmental Negotiations: A Framework for Analysis' (2001) 1(4) Global Environmental Politics 65–85.

human rights norms—without further involvement of state actors being needed. Individual members of the TLC may belong to distinct epistemic communities[36] or professional[37] or advocacy networks.[38] The emphasis on personal relationships as an entry requirement provides a pathway to understand transnational actors' influence at the individual level, which is different from organizational level explanations that usually revolve around the internal structure of an NGO[39] or the purpose of an organization.

The role of civil society actors in the UN human rights system has been extensively researched, highlighting their potential power.[40] The influence of NGOs on international legal developments is often summed up as difficult to depict due to the lack of formal access rules with reference to methodological difficulties.[41] Typically, their influence on legal developments is seen to flow through intermediaries such as states and international courts.[42]

Transnational lawmaking coalitions are understood as an informal collaboration in pursuit of a like-minded goal of action, occurring between one or more non-state actors and one or more members of an expert committee, for the purpose of elaborating an interpretation of one (or more) human rights norms. The concept of coalition is often used to describe temporary cooperation between two or more states,[43] or collaboration among civil society actors. Like civil society coalitions, such as the International Campaign to Ban Landmines, TLCs are characterized by in-depth expertise and the ability 'to reach outside their comfort zone'.[44]

[36] Mai'a K Davis Cross, 'Rethinking Epistemic Communities Twenty Years Later' (2013) 39(1) Review of International Studies 137–60; Peter Haas, 'Introduction: Epistemic Communities and International Policy Coordination' (1992) 46(1) International Organization 1–35.

[37] Leonard Seabrooke and Lasse Folke Henriksen, *Professional Networks in Transnational Governance* (CUP 2017).

[38] Keck and Sikkink (n 21).

[39] Wendy H Wong, *Internal Affairs: How the Structure of NGOs Transforms Human Rights* (Cornell University Press 2012); Stephen Hopgood, *Keepers of the Flame: Understanding Amnesty International* (Cornell University Press 2006).

[40] Ann M Clark, Elisabeth Friedman, and Kathryn Hochstetler, 'The Sovereign Limits of Global Civil Society—A Comparison of NGO Participation in UN World Conferences on the Environment, Human Rights, and Women' (1998) 51(1) World Politics 1–35; Anna Holzscheiter, 'Representation as Power and Performative Practice: Global Civil Society Advocacy for Working Children' (2016) 42(2) Review of International Studies 205–26; Fiona McGaughey, 'From Gatekeepers to GONGOs: A Taxonomy of Non-governmental Organisations Engaging with United Nations Human Rights Mechanisms' (2018) 36(2) Netherlands Quarterly of Human Rights 111–32.

[41] Gamze Erdem Türkelli, Wouter Vandenhole, and Arne Vandenbogaerde, 'NGO Impact on Law-Making: The Case of a Complaints Procedure under the International Covenant on Economic, Social and Cultural Rights and the Convention on the Rights of the Child' (2013) 5(1) Journal of Human Rights Practice 1–45.

[42] Charlotte Dany, *Global Governance and NGO Participation: Shaping the Information Society in the United Nations* (Routledge 2012); Cynthia Price Cohen, 'The Role of NGOs in the Drafting of the Convention on the Rights of the Child' (1990) 12(1) Human Rights Quarterly 137–47; Haddad, *The Hidden Hands of Justice* (n 19); Nicole Deitelhoff, 'The Discursive Process of Legalization: Charting Islands of Persuasion in the ICC Case' (2009) 63(1) International Organization 33–65.

[43] eg Amrita Narlikar, *International Trade and Developing Countries: Bargaining Coalitions in the GATT & WTO* (Taylor & Francis 2003).

[44] George E Mitchell, Hans-Peter Schmitz, and Tosca Bruno-van Vijfeijken, *Between Power and Irrelevance: The Future of Transnational NGOs* (OUP 2020) 69.

Drafting an interpretation of a human right requires knowledge of international and domestic case law on the one hand and technical knowledge about the legal norm to be interpreted on the other. The functional demands on members are twofold. First, external members must possess expertise on the applicability which the expert committee member does not have. This knowledge can be of a purely technical nature—for example, basic scientific knowledge—or stem from professional practice, such as the knowledge of an NGO member about implementation gaps in a local context. An example of this is the interpretation of the right to water by the UN Committee for Economic, Social and Cultural Rights (CESCR),[45] where knowledge of the global status of such a right was as important as knowledge of implementation in local contexts and technical expertise on water provision.[46] Ideally, these areas of knowledge are combined and complemented by a member with a broader view on international relations to facilitate the implementation of the interpretation by states. This makes the staff of international institutions valuable members of a TLC: they have expert knowledge, have often gained experience in local contexts—or are at least informed about it—and are familiar with government positions on the subject. Secondly, at least one member should have legal expertise and be familiar with the terminology of international law. This member ensures that the formulation of state obligations is based on international standards, thereby facilitating implementation. Without being embedded in state practice and case law, the coalition runs the risk of only formulating political goals instead of working towards a legally convincing framework.

How can this collaboration be explained? Principal-agent approaches explain the delegation of certain tasks by states to international organizations to reduce the transaction costs of policymaking.[47] This also explains why treaty monitoring and interpretation were delegated to expert bodies.[48] The delegation leads to a loss of control, which over time affords the expert committees greater autonomy in their decision-making processes than originally intended by the principals. Resources, such as special knowledge, have long been recognized as an important access requirement for cooperation in global law.[49] From a rationalist point of view, TLCs

[45] Madeline Baer, 'Beyond Consensus: Contesting the Human Rights to Water and Sanitation at the United Nations' (2022) Human Rights Review 1–23; Eibe Riedel, 'The Human Right to Water and General Comment No 15 of the CESCR' in Eibe Riedel and Peter Rothen (eds), *The Human Right to Water* (BWV 2006) 19–36. For an in-depth study of the drafting process of General Comment No 15 see ch 4 in Reiners, *Transnational Lawmaking Coalitions* (n 2).

[46] Malcolm Langford and Anna FS Russell, *The Human Right to Water: Theory, Practice and Prospects* (CUP 2017).

[47] Darren G Hawkins and others, *Delegation and Agency in International Organizations* (CUP 2006).

[48] Liliana Andonova and Manfred Elsig, 'Informal International Law-Making: A Conceptual View from International Relations' in Joost Pauwelyn, Ramses Wessel, and Jan Wouters (eds), *Informal International Law-Making* (OUP 2012) 63–80.

[49] Susan Block-Lieb and Terence C Halliday, *Global Lawmakers: International Organizations in the Crafting of World Markets* (CUP 2017); Sigrid Quack, 'Law, Expertise and Legitimacy in Transnational Economic Governance: An Introduction' (2010) 8(1) Socio-Economic Review 3–16.

and their individual members are goal-oriented, mindful of their individual preferences for the content of treaty interpretation, and their relationships within the TLC initially provide mutual benefits due to the sharing of resources. This exchange is manifested in the information or activities that a committee member needs and that they receive from professionals outside the UN. However, the committee member bears personal risks if they or the committee are unable to carry out the tasks delegated by states parties or go beyond the mandate by imposing excessive human rights obligations.[50] On the external member side, the benefit of sharing resources within informal coalitions is more difficult to explain. Non-governmental organizations have always played a central role in the human rights field, including in the development of standards.[51] The interpretations by the human rights treaty bodies are no exception and have long since become the focus of legal and political science research as a contribution to legal developments in international law.[52] Yet, professionals often invest a lot of time in preparing the interpretation, for which they are not officially recognized or compensated. Close and trusting interpersonal relationships enable effective collective action even in situations that feature uncertainty.[53] While this may not support the establishment and maintenance of large networks and movements,[54] personal relationships are a central feature of the TLC and enable individual influence on the interpretation of the treaty.

4. Change Agents in Action: Two Case Studies of Human Rights Treaty Interpretation

All nine international human rights treaties are overseen by committees composed of independent experts who are appointed and elected by the states parties for a

[50] Stephen Tully, 'A Human Right to Access Water—A Critique of General Comment No 15' (2005) 23(1) Netherlands Quarterly of Human Rights 35–63.

[51] Andrea Liese, *Staaten am Pranger: Zur Wirkung internationaler Regime auf innerstaatliche Menschenrechtspolitik* (Verlag für Sozialwissenschaften 2006); Jutta M Joachim, 'Framing Issues and Seizing Opportunities: The UN, NGOs, and Women's Rights' (2003) 47(2) International Studies Quarterly 247–74; Holzscheiter (n 39); Nina Reiners and Andrea Liese, 'Nichtstaatliche Akteure in der Menschenrechtspolitik: von Normanwälten über Komplizen zu Infragestellern und Herausforderern' (2015) 8(2) Zeitschrift für Außen- und Sicherheitspolitik 651–76.

[52] David Roth-Isigkeit, 'Die General Comments des Menschenrechtsausschusses der Vereinten Nationen: ein Beitrag zur Rechtsentwicklung im Völkerrecht' (2012) 17(2) MenschenRechtsMagazin 196–210; Nina Reiners, 'Die Interpretation von Menschenrechtsnormen durch die Vertragsausschüsse der Vereinten Nationen' (2018) 23(1) MenschenRechtsMagazin 5–14; Max Lesch, *Dynamics of Deviance: Torture and Its Prohibition in World Politics* (Johann-Wolfgang-Goethe-Universität zu Frankfurt am Main 2020).

[53] Nina Reiners, 'The Power of Interpersonal Relationships: A Socio-Legal Approach to International Institutions and Human Rights Advocacy' (2023), Review of International Studies, online first.

[54] Hans-Peter Schmitz and Kathryn Sikkink, 'International Human Rights' in Walter Carlsnaes, Thomas Risse, and Beth A Simmons (eds), *Handbook of International Relations* (SAGE 2013) 827–52, 839.

fixed, renewable, four-year term primarily based on their human rights expertise.[55] For all committees, there initially was no regulation as to the committees' task to develop general comments. This raises the question of how the committees decide on the interpretation of human rights. The following illustrates the formation and operation of TLCs in two cases of norm development and specification: first, the interpretation of the right to decent working conditions by the CESCR, and secondly, the extension of the right to life towards abortion by the UN Human Rights Committee (CCPR). In both cases, using primary and secondary sources as well as interviews, I outline how the experts in the committees fulfil their assigned task of interpreting the treaty. The two covenants, entered into force in 1976, have roughly the same number of states parties, and, together with the Universal Declaration of Human Rights, are regarded as the international charter of human rights.[56] It shows that it is not the committee as a collective, but individual committee members, who work with non-state actors to develop treaty interpretations and use their knowledge to further develop global human rights norms.

4.1 General Comment No 23, CESCR

The UN Committee for Economic, Social and Cultural Rights is the committee charged with overseeing compliance with the International Covenant on Economic, Social and Cultural Rights (ICESCR). It has eighteen members and is one of the oldest treaty committees in the UN human rights system.[57] The ICESCR includes a wide range of norms, which in turn are considered vague and open to interpretation. This explains why the instrument of treaty interpretation in the form of general comments is used particularly frequently.[58] Collectively, the members of the committee have broad expertise in economic, social, and cultural rights. Some experts specialize in the norms of individual articles of the covenant, while others have expertise in human rights in general.

General Comment No 23 was adopted by the committee at its 57th meeting in March 2016.[59] It specifies the state obligations resulting from Article 7 ICESCR, the

[55] Valentina Carraro, 'Electing the Experts: Expertise and Independence in the UN Human Rights Treaty Bodies' (2019) 25(3) European Journal of International Relations 826–51.

[56] Christopher NJ Roberts, *The Contentious History of the International Bill of Human Rights* (CUP 2014).

[57] OHCHR, United Nations Human Rights—Office of the High Commissioner for Human Rights, 'United Nations Human Rights Appeal 2020'.

[58] Matyas Bodig, 'Soft Law, Doctrinal Development, and the General Comments of the UN Committee on Economic, Social and Cultural Rights' in Stephanie Lagoutte, Thomas Gammeltoft-Hansen, and John Cerone (eds), *Tracing the Roles of Soft Law in Human Rights* (OUP 2016) 69–88.

[59] UN Committee on Economic, Social and Cultural Rights (CESCR), General Comment No 23 (2016) on the right to just and favourable conditions of work (art 7 of the International Covenant on Economic, Social and Cultural Rights), 7 April 2016, E/C.12/GC/23 <www.refworld.org/docid/5550a0b14.html> accessed 27 October 2022.

right to just and favourable working conditions. In its opening remarks, the comment also refers to General Comment No 18, in which the committee interpreted the right to work enshrined in Article 6 ICESCR.[60] The need for this general comment arose from the government measures taken after the 2008 financial crisis. In May 2012, the committee addressed the states parties in writing and emphasized that 'any proposed policy change or adjustment made to deal with the negative impact of the austerity measures […] must identify the minimum core content of rights or a social protection floor […] and ensure the protection of this core content at all times'.[61] This letter also repeatedly emphasized the importance of the International Labour Organization's (ILO) agreements for this purpose.

A first draft of the general comment was presented by the two rapporteurs Virginia Bras Gomes and Renato Ribeiro Leao in the 54th session of the committee in 2015.[62] At the same meeting, the committee adopted a statement in which minimum social standards, the so-called social protection floors of the ILO, were emphasized as an fundamental part of the agreement and agreed that these must also be guaranteed in view of austerity measures.[63] Just three months after this meeting, the draft was discussed in Geneva, based on more than thirty written comments.[64] The short time between the public presentation of the draft and its discussion, as well as the fact that the comments received deal in detail with certain aspects of the draft, points to the common practice that the draft had already been made available to selected stakeholders in advance.

Given the short time available, only three countries (Australia, Greece, and Mexico) submitted written statements on the draft, and only one representative, namely from Greece, came to discuss the draft. As a country particularly affected by the financial crisis, Greece explicitly supported the committee's view that workers' rights are a prerequisite for economic growth.[65] In this discussion, the International Commission of Jurists (ICJ), an NGO based in Geneva, insisted on clearer wording of the general comment and criticized the draft as still too vague,

[60] UN Committee on Economic, Social and Cultural Rights (CESCR), General Comment No 18: The Right to Work (art 6 of the Covenant), 6 February 2006, E/C.12/GC/18 <www.refworld.org/docid/4415453b4.html> accessed 27 October 2022.

[61] CESCR, 'Social Protection Floors: An Essential Element of the Right to Social Security and of the sustainable Development Goals', E/C.12/2015/1; OHCHR [website], 15 April 2015 <http://docstore.ohchr.org/SelfServices/FilesHandler.ashx?enc=4slQ6QSmlBEDzFEovLCuW1AVC1NkPsgUedPlF1vfPMJvHEXEU4Khj3y6yINSyq8u5n%2ba%2bgVU%2fQRd1%2bntxmQe%2beWynffCas%2fNSBp%2bf2U0tNs0CiwKxDPx8dBbFO50SIXs> accessed 27 October 2022, 1.

[62] CESCR, 'Report on the Fifty-fourth, Fifty-fifth and Fifty-sixth Sessions', E/C.12/2015/3, OHCHR [website], 2016 <http://daccess-ods.un.org/access.nsf/Get?Open&DS=E/2016/22&Lang=E> accessed 27 October 2022.

[63] CESCR, 'Social Protection Floors' (n 59).

[64] See United Nations Office of the High Commissioner for Human Rights <www.ohchr.org/en/events/days-general-discussion-dgd/2015/general-discussion-draft-general-comment-article-7-icescr> accessed 27 October 2022; CESCR, 'Fifty-fifth session. Summary record of the first part (public) of the 44th meeting', E/C.12/2015/SR.44, United Nations [website], 6 July 2015 <https://undocs.org/E/C.12/2015/SR.44> accessed 27 October 2022.

[65] CESCR, 'Fifty-fifth session. Summary record' (n 62) para 10.

especially with regard to state obligations. The ICJ's chief legal adviser had been working on such a general comment for years with committee member Philippe Texier, who left the CESCR in 2012.[66] This was not just an NGO lawyer's attempt to lobby an independent committee member to support and provide information about a standard-setting process. Philippe Texier and the legal adviser were colleagues in the ICJ, as Philippe Texier had worked for the NGO since 2008 and held the office of committee member at the same time.[67] Both had a common goal and access to the instrument of choice and prepared this general comment together. After Philippe Texier left the CESCR, plans for such a general comment initially stalled. In order to revive this plan, the ICJ advocate had to find other members to support the draft, even though this decision had consequences for the relationship with the CESCR member.. The first draft was finally presented and publicly discussed in 2015. At the next meeting of the CESCR, in March 2016, General Comment No 23 was then adopted by the committee.

The interpretation of Article 7 as a reaction to the impact of the global financial and economic crisis required external input, as the broad expertise within the committee was not specialized enough regarding workers' rights and austerity measures. Several non-state actors feared that austerity policies and state measures to contain the effects of the financial crisis would lead to weakened workers' rights. To counter such developments, they argued for an increased specificity of a state's obligations under the ICESCR. In particular, the personal connection of committee member Texier to the ICJ enabled the close and early involvement of a colleague from civil society in the development of a general comment about workers' rights under the impact of economic, financial, and tax crises.

4.2 General Comment No 36, Human Rights Committee

The Human Rights Committee stands out among the UN human rights treaty committees, as membership consists almost exclusively of lawyers. The ICCPR only states that the eighteen members of the committee must be 'persons of high moral character and recognized competence in the field of human rights' and 'consideration [is to be given] given to the usefulness of the participation of some persons having legal experience'.[68] The interpretations of the CCPR are considered particularly authoritative for the development of international human rights.[69] The committee has a high level of expertise regarding the legal interpretation of the treaty.

[66] Interview with Senior Legal Officer of NGO ICJ, 8 November 2013.

[67] See International Commission of Jurists, <www.icj.org/commission/commissioners-from-europe-and-cis/> accessed 27 October 2022.

[68] Art 28 ICCPR.

[69] Helen Keller and Leena Grover, 'General Comments of the Human Rights Committee and their Legitimacy' in Keller and Ulfstein (eds) (n 31) 116–98; Roth-Isigkeit (n 51).

In view of the openness of the norms in the covenant and the particularity that human rights treaties are considered 'living instruments',[70] the committee must, when interpreting the norms, also consider political, social, and economic developments. Consultation with external actors is an important part of the working processes of the CCPR. The committee regularly invites interested stakeholders to submit written and oral comments on the various drafts.[71] How the committee evaluates and considers those inputs, given the increasing workload and other activities of its members, is left to the internal decision-making process.

After more than three years of drafting, the committee adopted General Comment No 36 in October 2018. It provides a comprehensive interpretation of the substantive provisions of Article 6 ICCPR, the right to life.[72] These provisions include the right to life in the face of environmental threats, defending the right to life in times of war, and addressing threats to the right to life in the face of extreme poverty and homelessness.[73] The document was approved unanimously and reflects the CCPR consensus on the scope of the right to life. Surprisingly for many observers, the general comment also contained obligations arising for states for guaranteeing the right to life and its compatibility with abortion. In this commentary, the committee goes further than in previous views by recognizing a human right to abortion.

The two rapporteurs for the general comment were Yuval Shany and Sir Nigel Rodley. Nigel Rodley died during the drafting process, so Yuval Shany took over the sole continuation of the draft, Nigel Rodley having been the initiator of this interpretation.[74] The committee began the formal drafting process with a half-day of general discussion during the 114th session on 14 July 2015. The committee invited interested members of the National Human Rights Institutions (NHRIs), civil society, and academia to the event. After two years, a first draft was ready and the CCPR invited all interested stakeholders to comment on the committee's draft. Comments were submitted by various stakeholders, including states parties, other UN and regional human rights mechanisms, UN agencies or specialized agencies, NHRIs, NGOs, research institutions, and academics. The wording of the draft was subsequently amended. At the outset, the draft contained a declaration excluding the unborn child from the scope of application of the right to life under Article 1

[70] Daniel Moeckli and Nigel D White, 'Treaties as "Living Instruments"' in Dino Kritsiotis and Michael Bowman (eds), *Conceptual and Contextual Perspectives on the Modern Law of Treaties* (CUP 2016) 136–71.

[71] Keller and Grover (n 67).

[72] Sarah Joseph, 'Extending the Right to Life Under the International Covenant on Civil and Political Rights: General Comment 36' (2019) 19(2) Human Rights Law Review 347–68.

[73] United Nations Human Rights Committee, 'General Comment 36' (2018) UN Doc CCPR/C/GC/36.

[74] OHCHR, United Nations Human Rights—Office of the High Commissioner for Human Rights, 'Human Rights Committee Adopts General Comment on the Right to Life' <www.ohchr.org/EN/NewsEvents/Pages/DisplayNews.aspx?NewsID=23797&LangID=E≥ accessed 27 October 2022.

ICCPR.[75] Accordingly, the potential right to life of the unborn child does not take precedence over the right to life of pregnant mothers.

Then, in October 2018, the CCPR adopted General Comment No 36, including paragraph 8 on abortion. The article links the denial of access to abortion to the violation of women's and girls' right to life. It calls for legal access to abortion when the pregnancy endangers the mother's life or health, completion of the pregnancy would cause significant pain or suffering, particularly in cases of rape or incest, and calls on states to decriminalize abortion and promote confidential healthcare in this regard.

In view of the internal controversies within the committee and critical conservative legal voices,[76] the progressiveness of the general comment regarding abortion is linked to Nigel Rodley's driving role.[77] His clear views on abortion had been noticeable in many state reporting procedures before the CCPR. Nigel Rodley was not only a professor of human rights and published many key works in this field, he also worked for Amnesty International for almost twenty years, was the UN Special Rapporteur on torture, and a member of numerous NGOs. His close relationships with non-state actors are also reflected in the #NotAVessel campaign organized by the NGO Abortion Rights Campaign, which can be traced back to a statement by Rodley to the Irish government.[78]

For the general comment, Nigel Rodley needed the expertise of his former NGO colleagues to push through progressive content during the public discussions of the draft, even against the numerous anti-abortion organizations. It required the formation of an advocacy network[79] to support the committee in its progressive endeavour.[80] At the same time, the revision of the draft was made possible by research work on worldwide state practice in the academic environment of the two rapporteurs.[81] The work of advocacy networks was important for the committee members to generate support for their own interests in the public debate. However, the drafting work itself took place outside of the committee meetings and favoured the involvement of a few individuals in the personal environment of committee

[75] CCPR/C/GC/R.36/Rev.2, Human Rights Committee. 'Draft General Comment No 36: Article 6, Right to Life: International Covenant on Civil and Political Rights: Draft/Prepared by Yuval Shany and Nigel Rodley, Rapporteurs', 2015, para 2.

[76] Andrea Stevens, 'Pushing a Right to Abortion through the Back Door: The Need for Integrity in the UN Treaty Monitoring System, and Perhaps a Treaty Amendment' (2018) 6(1) Pennsylvania State Journal of Law & International Affairs 71–141.

[77] See United Nations Human Rights Committee, 'Concluding Observations on the Fourth Periodic Report of Ireland' (2014) UN Doc CCPR/C/IRL/CO/4.

[78] Fiona De Londras and Mairead Enright, *Repealing the 8th: Reforming Irish Abortion Law* (Bristol University Press 2018) 50.

[79] Keck and Sikkink (n 21).

[80] Livio Zilli, 'The UN Human Rights Committee's General Comment 36 on the Right to Life and the Right to Abortion' (*Opinio Juris*, 6 March 2019) <http://opiniojuris.org/2019/03/06/the-un-human-rights-committees-general-comment-36-on-the-right-to-life-and-the-right-to-abortion/> accessed 27 October 2022.

[81] Interview with Yuval Shany, 7 January 2021.

members, in this case, the doctoral students of the two rapporteurs at their universities in Tel Aviv and Essex.

5. Conclusion

As a joint path of international expert institutions and individual experts from academia, NGOs, or other international institutions, TLCs can foster change processes in international human rights law. The chapter demonstrates that NGOs working towards change in international human rights law likely 'select' the path on which they already have connections—a fact that makes that path appear more receptive to their claims than others. Transnational lawmaking coalitions aid in the 'construction' of change, especially on bureaucratic or private-authority paths—a construction that will often not be entirely conclusive but pave the way for further construction efforts by others and an eventual broader 'reception' of the respective interpretive community.[82]

The state path runs largely in parallel to a TLC path. The possibility for experts on the human rights treaty bodies to closely collaborate with legal and technical experts on treaty interpretations to shape the development of human rights law is a powerful strategy to meet backlash and human rights contestation by states. States are certainly the creators and primary addressees of the human rights treaty regime, but they have delegated the monitoring and interpretation of these norms to independent expert committees, who are expected to act as international intermediaries.[83] Yet, the treaty bodies as intermediaries do not always act in the spirit of their principals, with some exceeding their mandates with progressive general comments, as the above cases attest, by means of exemplification of the TLC workings. The important roles that individual professionals in TLCs in connection with the expert body play [84] change 'the bilateral and formal nature of the interstate monitoring regime in significant ways'..[85] In human rights, the multitude of actors—rather than fixed institutions—further manifests in the implementation of decisions by treaty bodies.[86] While this might lead to area-specific 'human rights experimentalism',[87] the observation that state-empowered entities step in as authorities for legal change can be extended to such entities in other fields.[88]

[82] Krisch and Yildiz, this volume.
[83] Pegram (n 20).
[84] Reiners, *Transnational Lawmaking Coalitions* (n 2).
[85] Gráinne De Búrca, 'Human Rights Experimentalism' (2017) 111(2) American Journal of International Law 277–316, 310.
[86] Gráinne De Búrca, *Reframing Human Rights in a Turbulent Era* (OUP 2021).
[87] De Búrca, 'Human Rights Experimentalism' (n 83).
[88] Sivakumaran (n 32); Anthea Roberts and Sandesh Sivakumaran, 'Lawmaking by Nonstate Actors: Engaging Armed Groups in the Creation of International Humanitarian Law' (2012) 37(1) Yale Journal of International Law 107–52.

Nevertheless, states technically hold the power to end the practice of the treaty bodies, as well as numerous ways to shape its bounds. For one, they can elect the members of the expert committees at their discretion, and thereby can choose candidates who are less progressive or with more or less expertise in a given legal field. For another, they can exercise their particularly powerful thumb on budgetary support in contexts where the authority and decisions of a committee exceed their tolerance.

Considering the discourse on the stagnation of treaty-making and a growing range and types of challenges to international law, TLCs remind future International Relations and International Law scholarship to take the varying roles of states in legal change processes seriously. More attention needs to be devoted to how such coalitions impact the values and structure of international law,[89] and specifically, how human rights change could otherwise take place in an increasingly under-financed and contested regime.

[89] Heike Krieger, Georg Nolte, and Andreas Zimmermann (eds), *The International Rule of Law: Rise or Decline?* (OUP 2019); Heike Krieger and Andrea Liese, 'A Metamorphosis of International Law? Value Changes in the International Legal Order From the Perspectives of Legal and Political Science' (2019) KFG Working Paper Series No 27 <https://papers.ssrn.com/sol3/papers.cfm?abstract_id=3322745> accessed 27 October 2022.

PART III

FORMS OF CHANGE

5
Tracing International Legal Change in Genocide Prevention

Tonya Putnam[*]

1. Introduction

In 1949, Australia, Ecuador, Ethiopia, Iceland, and Norway became the first members of the United Nations Convention on the Prevention and Punishment of the Crime of Genocide (the Genocide Convention). Within five years, nearly forty more countries joined, and others have continued to do so over subsequent decades. On 20 April 2022, Zambia deposited its accession at the United Nations, thereby becoming the 153rd member of the Convention. In the more than seventy years since its adoption, not a single comma has changed in the text. Nevertheless, in practical terms the package of obligations to which Mauritius acceded is quite different from that to which the early joiners initially consented.

In what ways is it different? First, in the intervening decades key definitional changes have occurred. The set of protected groups has expanded as theories of 'ethnicity' (a protected category) have blended with ideas about 'culture' (an excluded category).[1] Sexual violence in the form of systematic rape has been recognized as a mode of genocide[2] and 'command responsibility' is now broadly acknowledged as a basis for criminal culpability.[3] There are also ongoing debates about the character of the 'intent' element of the crime of genocide under the Convention with direct implications for the breadth of its applicability.[4] Secondly, the punishment aspects of the Genocide Convention have greater immediacy following the creation of international and hybrid tribunals and a standing International Criminal Court

* Research Scholar, Columbia University, New York, NY, USA.

[1] See eg *Prosecutor v Krstic* (Judgment) [2001] IT-98-33-T, para 580.

[2] Sherrie Russell-Brown, 'Rape as an Act of Genocide' (2003) 21 Berkeley Journal International Law, 350.

[3] Tahlia Petrosian, 'Secondary Forms of Genocide and Command Responsibility under the Statutes of the ICTY, ICTR and ICC.' [2010] Australian International Law Journal 17, 29.

[4] Yuval Shany, 'The Road to the Genocide Convention and Beyond' in Paola Gaeta (ed), *The UN Genocide Convention: A Commentary. Oxford Commentaries on International Law* (OUP 2009); Katherine Goldsmith, 'The Issue of Intent in the Genocide Convention and its Effect on the Prevention and Punishment of the Crime of Genocide: Toward a Knowledge-Based Approach' (2010) 5(3) Genocide Studies and Prevention 238; Hannibal Travis, 'On the Original Understanding of the Crime of Genocide' (2012) 7(1) Genocide Studies and Prevention 30.

Tonya Putnam, *Tracing International Legal Change in Genocide Prevention* In: *The Many Paths of Change in International Law.* Edited by: Nico Krisch and Ezgi Yildiz, Oxford University Press. © Tonya Putnam 2023.
DOI: 10.1093/oso/9780198877844.003.0005

with jurisdiction over genocide crimes. Many countries now have domestic anti-genocide legislation, and some have adopted anti-genocide laws that include universal jurisdiction.[5] Thirdly, and perhaps most strikingly, the prevention element of the Genocide Convention has become a plausible basis for insisting that states have obligations toward vulnerable populations *in other (foreign) states* that require affirmative measures to thwart impending atrocities.[6]

This third development is particularly noteworthy in that it entails collective acceptance of a limited qualification to long-standing international rules and norms concerning territorial sovereignty and non-interference in states' domestic affairs.[7] At the Genocide Convention's inception in the late 1940s—which coincided with the beginnings of a wave of decolonization movements in Africa and Asia, and a deepening security rivalry between the US and the Soviet Union—such a qualification was all but unimaginable in the absence of interstate aggression. Indeed, a state's decision to ratify the Convention in this early period was far more likely to be understood as a safeguard against foreign intervention than as a legal justification for it. Only decades later did governments begin to consider, and to partially coalesce around, the idea that states that commit, or allow, genocidal acts against their own populations *are themselves violating a core principle of state sovereignty*.[8] In turn, this shift enabled additional (and more contentious) claims that, in situations where authorities with effective control over territory are unwilling, or unable, to avert genocide and related mass atrocities, states with the capacity to do so have an affirmative obligation to intercede.

Nothing in the scope or character of these changes was prefigured, and much is still contested. Their emergence involved multiple developments brought about by diverse agents and interactions along several pathways. Although many of the most visible developments have occurred since the end of the Cold War on the multilateral and judicial pathways, these developments were enabled by decades of prior and contemporaneous work on the part of activists, journalists, scholars, and human rights and humanitarian organizations, along with engagement and support from concerned states and officials, and from government and international organization (IO)

[5] A. Hays Butler, 'The Doctrine of Universal Jurisdiction: A Review of the Literature' (2000) 11(3) Criminal Law Forum 353; but see Máximo Langer, 'Universal Jurisdiction is not Disappearing: The Shift from "Global Enforcer" to "No Safe Haven" Universal Jurisdiction' (2015) 13(2) Journal of International Criminal Justice 245–56.

[6] Louise Arbour, 'The Responsibility to Protect as a Duty of Care in International Law and Practice' (2008) 34(3) Review of International Studies 445; Jose E Alvarez, 'The Schizophrenia of R2P' in Philip Alston and Euan Macdonald (eds), *Human Rights, Intervention, and the Use of Force* (OUP 2008); Alex J Bellamy, and Ruben Reike, 'The Responsibility to Protect and International Law' (2010) 2(3) Global Responsibility to Protect 267.

[7] Art 2(7) of the UN Charter underscores its lack of authority in the domestic affairs of high contracting parties, albeit with a loophole for Chapter VII enforcement measures. The critically important change thus concerns what qualifies as grounds for invoking Chapter VII.

[8] Francis Deng, 'From "Sovereignty as Responsibility" to the "Responsibility to Protect"' (2010) 2(4) Global Responsibility to Protect 353.

bureaucrats. Some of this work entailed directed efforts to advocate for more robust institutions and mechanisms in response to specific events. Others involved changing the more general legal and political context in which the Genocide Convention operates. This includes, notably, a sustained surge of international and regional treaty-making on human rights and humanitarian issues starting in the 1960s, some of which include prohibitions on genocide,[9] and the proliferation of governmental and non-governmental roles and institutions that followed. The end of the Cold War also brought greater opportunities for multilateral cooperation on conflict resolution, which, in turn, prompted growing intergovernmental and scholarly attention to understanding the nexus between conditions conducive to mass atrocities inside states, and larger regional and global security threats.

To be sure, the shift in dominant understandings of what the international legal obligation to prevent genocide entails toward requiring that those capable of averting atrocities take affirmative measures to do so has not brought an end to genocidal violence. However, there are some grounds to believe that this shift—which is both a cause and a consequence of efforts to institutionalize early warning mechanisms, and to develop a slate of de-escalatory interventions in line with prevention imperatives—has helped to avert, or quell, some genocidal violence, even as new situations continue to emerge.

In the next section, I lay out some parameters for theorizing pathways of legal change. From there I proceed to trace in greater detail how collective interpretations of the Genocide Convention and, in particular, its prevention element, have changed over time as leading states have come to view the threat of genocide and other mass violence as legitimate grounds for intervening in the security affairs of other states. I conclude with some thoughts about the merits of focusing on specific pathways of engagement with international law in efforts to account for change over time.

2. A Few Theoretical Parameters

Rationalist international relations scholars have long theorized treaties and conventions as bargains among states aimed at formalizing rights, or at addressing collective action problems related to shared policy goals.[10] This emphasis on the

[9] Christian Tams, Lars Berster, and Björn Schiffbauer (eds), *Convention on the Prevention and Punishment of the Crime of Genocide: A Commentary* (Bloomsbury Publishing 2014) 16; ICCPR art 6.

[10] George Downs, David Rocke, and Peter Barsoom, 'Is the Good News about Compliance Good News about Cooperation?' (1996) 50(3) International Organization 379–406; Robert Keohane, 'International Relations and International Law: Two Optics' (1997) 38 Harvard International Law Jorunal 487; B Peter Rosendorff and Helen Milner, 'The Optimal Design of International Trade Institutions: Uncertainty and Escape' (2001) 55(4) International Organization 829; Barbara Koremenos, Charles Lipson, and Duncan Snidal, 'The Rational Design of International Institutions' (2001) 55(4) International Organization 761; Beth A Simmons, *Mobilizing for Human Rights: International Law in Domestic Politics* (CUP 2009); Paul

bargained-over character of legal texts underwrites widely shared disciplinary expectations that international legal instruments may be altered only though formal amendment, or by being superseded by other agreements.[11] However, this is sharply at odds with how legal scholars and practitioners view international law and mechanisms of legal change. From this perspective, law is a dynamic corpus of source-based claims and modes of claiming a medium of describing and ordering social relations. Using law, for example, to guide or assess behaviour, to assert rights, to create new legal relationships, or to justify and regulate state coercion creates bodies of practice that, in turn, may influence how written texts may subsequently be invoked, interpreted, and applied.[12]

None of these elements is trivial in political terms, and all have normative and distributive consequences.[13] Complicating matters further, it is rare to encounter legal rules and obligations 'in the wild' in isolation from other rules and obligations. Skilled users of law and legal argumentation, therefore, try to frame, or configure, obligations of special interest within, or alongside, other rules in ways that complement, or reinforce, the goals of interpreters (or, more typically, of the institutions or organizations through, or on behalf of, which they act), or to de-emphasize, or place limiting conditions on, features that detract from those goals.[14]

When thinking about processes of change, it is likewise important to recall that multiple interpretations of legal rules may be in active circulation at any given time within and across specific domains. Not only may individual rules be invoked, interpreted, and applied by multiple agents simultaneously in different settings involving different actors and substantive elements, these interpretations may reflect different efforts to order and configure the laws and obligations at issue. This variance, in turn, may be tied to different policy objectives and priorities, as well as different stakes in the outcomes.[15] Stated simply, savvy researchers

Huth, Sarah Croco, and Benjamin Appel, 'Bringing Law to the Table: Legal Claims, Focal Points, and the Settlement of Territorial Disputes Since 1945' (2013) 57(1) American Journal of Political Science 90; Yonatan Lupu, 'The Informative Power of Treaty Commitment: Using the Spatial Model to Address Selection Effects' (2013) 57(4) American Journal of Political Science 912.

[11] Joseph Jupille, Walter Mattli, and Duncan Snidal, *Institutional Choice and Global Commerce* (CUP 2013). Note, in standard IR accounts, courts 'clarify' or 'enforce' law; their decisions do not 'make' law.

[12] I define legal 'usage' broadly to encompass official pronouncements and applications by governments, courts, or other official bodies, but also those of non-state actors whose engagement on specific issues as protagonists, victims, or interested third parties makes them part of relevant communities of practice.

[13] Tonya L Putnam, 'Mingling and Strategic Augmentation of International Legal Obligations' (2020) 74(1) International Organization 31; Ingo Venzke, *How Interpretation Makes International Law: on Semantic Change and Normative Twists* (OUP 2012). Such invocations may be direct or indirect, for contentious or cooperative purposes, and undertaken in good faith or bad.

[14] Putnam 'Mingling and Strategic Augmentation' (n 13). This way of thinking about the strategic uses of law resonates with Riker's (1986) theory of 'herestetics', which explores efforts to manipulate issue dimensions actors must consider in decision-making. See Iain McLean, 'William H. Riker and the Invention of Heresthetic(s)' (2002) 32(3) British Journal of Political Science 535.

[15] Eyal Benvenisti and George Downs, 'The Emperor's New Clothes: Political Economy and the Fragmentation of International Law' (2007) 60 Stanford Law Review 595; Nico Krisch, 'The Decay

and advocates should not expect experts in the US State Department to hold views on any given international application of human rights law that are identical to those of the United Nations Human Rights Council, or to Human Rights Watch.[16] Furthermore, it is through encounters among competing applied interpretations of specific laws, each of which purports to be authoritative, that underlying beliefs about what is feasible, or appropriate, in legal terms may shift—albeit still without necessarily producing anything approaching a consensus view.

To be clear, this scope for variance does not imply that international law is wholly malleable. Processes of legal interpretation and analysis are *themselves* heavily mediated by other substantive and procedural rules that restrict the range of meanings that users can reasonably attribute to particular instruments or provisions.[17] In addition, there is a general expectation that parties' assertions about what a given law permits or requires will be checked against prior practice,[18] and also vetted by wider interpretative communities whose members may call out usages they deem to be wrong or improper, and urge the adoption of different legal framings.[19] Still, a relative lack of institutional resources and attention, combined with underlying power relations, means that some interpreters carry more sway than others.[20]

It is helpful to recall that not all interpretations of legal rules carry equal legal or political weight in every context, and that underlying resources to push preferred understandings also vary widely among interpreters. Moreover, legal interpretations that align with broadly endorsed patterns of prior practice are often less noteworthy to peripheral observers than usages that challenge contextually

of Consent: International Law in an Age of Global Public Goods' (2014) 108(1) American Journal of International Law 1.

[16] Different agents have different formal and informal grants of authority and standing. For many—eg IO officials, judges and arbitrators in specialized courts, state functionaries, and even civil society groups—their interpretative authority and practical scope of action are limited to particular laws or mandates.

[17] Rosalyn Higgins, *Problems and Process: International Law and How We Use It* (OUP 1995). Legal instruments also include express or implied provisions specifying to whom its rules are intended to apply, under what circumstances, who has standing to invoke them formally, and in which venues.

[18] Irina Buga, *Modification of Treaties by Subsequent Practice* (OUP 2018), 18–19; Georg Nolte (ed), *Treaties and Subsequent Practice* (OUP 2013); Myers S McDougal, 'The International Law Commission's Draft Articles Upon Interpretation: Textuality Redivivus' (1967) 61(4) American Journal of International Law 992; Gerald G Fitzmaurice, 'Law and Procedure of the International Court of Justice: Treaty Interpretation and Certain Other Treaty Points' (1951) 28 British Yearbook of International Law 1. Functionally, subsequent practice is akin to state practice in customary international law in that it directs agents to consider how states purporting to act in accordance with the law behave, and when they encounter legal pushback. It is also related to broad definitions of legal 'precedent', albeit with less doctrinal baggage.

[19] Ian Johnstone, 'Treaty Interpretation: The Authority of Interpretative Communities' (1991) 12 Michigan Journal of International Law 371. Examples of interpretative authorities that may have this capacity in some settings include UN-level institutions and mechanisms, regional or international courts, and the high courts of influential states.

[20] Tonya L Putnam, *Courts Without Borders: Law, Politics, and US Extraterritoriality* (CUP 2016); Putnam, 'Mingling and Strategic Augmentation' (n 13).

dominant understandings of a rule's applicability, scope, or meaning. In situations where embedded agents seeking particular outcomes mount such challenges, whether rhetorically or via practice, they may look to additional rules, principles, and institutions—including those on multiple pathways.[21] Without diverse nodes of interpretative activity, ideas, and oversight, it is difficult to imagine how, or on what basis, legal change would occur, or indeed how law could function as an effective medium for structuring and administering social orders.[22]

2.1 Research Design and Case Selection

Understanding change in how the prevention-related obligations of the Genocide Convention have changed since the 1940s requires attention to their origins, and also to broader political, institutional, and normative developments in human rights and humanitarian law and policy, together with changes in the dominance of different actors and approaches to international security policy. My approach shows how those obligations were understood by most governments at the time of the Convention's enactment in the early Cold War period, and traces how and why modal interpretations of state obligations associated with genocide prevention became open to reinterpretation in the late and post-Cold War era. I use a combination of historical documents, contemporary legal commentaries, secondary sources, and author interviews with direct participants in some of these efforts. I also track the creation of other features of international human rights law and regional human rights conventions that relate to the prevention of genocide and other crimes against humanity.

Why focus on the Genocide Convention? First, it governs a topic of obvious gravity at the nexus of international human rights, humanitarian law, and international criminal law. Secondly, the Genocide Convention provides a hard case for shared understandings of treaty obligations to change over time through interpretative means. Not only has the text not been amended, but states have also adopted no optional protocols extending or tightening its provisions. Unlike other key multilateral human rights conventions, the Genocide Convention has no specialized body to oversee its implementation, or to provide authoritative interpretations of its provisions.[23] Thirdly, the Genocide Convention has long been dismissed by many policymakers, social scientists, and legal scholars as ineffective, thus making it an unlikely anchor for efforts to design and implement more robust international mechanisms for preventing mass atrocities.

[21] ibid.

[22] Monica Hakimi, 'The Work of International Law' (2017) 58 Harvard International Law Journal 1.

[23] Indeed, the first UN appointment to specifically oversee matters related to genocide prevention did not take place until 2004, see Alex J Bellamy and Edward C Luck, *The Responsibility to Protect: From Promise to Practice* (John Wiley & Sons 2018).

3. 'Prevention' and the Genocide Convention

The substantive elements of the Convention are laid out in eight articles. Article I establishes genocide as an international crime in both peace and war, and pledges signatories to undertake its prevention and punishment. Article II enumerates acts that constitute genocide under the Convention when undertaken with intent to destroy, in whole or in part, a national, ethnical, racial, or religious group. These include:

> (a) killing members of [a protected] group; (b) causing serious bodily or mental harm to members of the group; (c) deliberately inflicting on the group conditions of life calculated to bring about its physical destruction in whole or in part; (d) imposing measures intended to prevent births within the group; [or] (e) forcibly transferring children of the group to another group.

Article III criminalizes not just the commission of these acts, but also their attempt and incitement, along with complicity. Article IV provides that the Convention applies not only to 'rulers' but also to public officials and private individuals.

In comparison, the prevention and punishment aspects of the Convention lack detail. Article V obligates signatories to pass supporting legislation. Article VI requires those accused of covered acts to be tried in a competent domestic body or international penal tribunal with appropriate jurisdiction, and Article VII prohibits restrictions on extradition. With regard to 'prevention and suppression', Article VIII provides only that contracting members *may call upon* competent organs of the United Nations to take actions under the UN Charter. Article IX offers a weak check on use of these mechanisms by allowing disputes among states over the interpretation of the Convention to be referred to the International Court of Justice.[24] This vagueness on state obligations regarding prevention reflects the Convention's overall emphasis on establishing *individual* criminal responsibility, together with sharp disagreements among enacting states concerning the legal status of preparatory acts.[25]

[24] This mechanism was used only once in the Cold War era in a case questioning the permissibility of reservations to the Genocide Convention. Since 1990, thirteen additional cases have been filed in the ICJ, but to date only one has survived the jurisdictional phase: *The Case Concerning Application of the Convention of the Prevention and Punishment of Genocide* (*Bosnia and Herzegovina v Serbia and Montenegro)* (Merits), *see* Judgment, I.C.J. Reports 2007, [2007] ICJ 2 (hereafter *Bosnia and Herzegovina v Serbia and Montenegro*).

[25] Shany (n 4) 14 notes that several contemporary critics of the Convention found its focus on establishing individual criminal liability at the expense of fleshing out elements of state responsibility 'seriously misconceived'.

3.1 Getting to a Legal Prohibition on Genocide

The Genocide Convention was created in 1948 in the aftermath of atrocities committed during World War II, most notably Germany's efforts to rid territories under its control of Jews and other 'undesirable' minorities using mass extermination. International condemnation of these policies was a central feature of the war crimes trials of Axis leaders at Nuremberg (1945–49). Still, the immediate international legal response might have ended with these trials but for the work of Dr Raphael Lemkin, a Jewish jurist and specialist in historical war crimes and atrocities, who fled to the US from Poland in 1941. Lemkin coined the term 'genocide' to describe coordinated efforts to annihilate entire peoples to address what he insisted was an intolerable gap in international law. Lemkin worked tirelessly to have genocide formalized as an international crime distinct from atrocity crimes against individuals, and independent of prior acts of international military aggression.[26]

An important hurdle in this quest was cleared in December 1946 when the UN General Assembly (UNGA) recognized genocide as an international crime and requested the Economic and Social Council (ECOSOC) to prepare an international convention.[27] Two years and several drafts later, on 9 December 1948, the Convention on the Prevention and Punishment of the Crime of Genocide was unanimously adopted by the UNGA.

The initial (Secretariat) draft proposed an expansive definition of genocide that covered acts undertaken with intent to destroy any ethnic, cultural, or political group. It provided for universal jurisdiction, and a standing international court,[28] and categorized acts 'preparatory' to genocide as independent offences.[29] In addition, this draft authorized high contracting parties to call upon UN bodies to take measures to suppress or prevent genocide, and obligated member states to give their full support to such efforts. This intentionally ambitious draft was winnowed down substantially, however—first by an Ad Hoc Committee of state representatives,[30] and then by the 'Sixth Committee' (the UNGA's legal arm).

[26] Matthew Lippman, 'The Drafting of the 1948 Convention on the Prevention and Punishment of the Crime of Genocide' (1985) 3 Boston University International Law Journal 1, 4; A Dirk Moses, 'Raphael Lemkin, Culture, and the Concept of Genocide' in Donald Bloxham and A Dirk Moses (eds), *The Oxford Handbook of Genocide Studies* (OUP 2010) 19–41; Philippe Sands, *East West Street: On the Origins of Genocide and Crimes Against Humanity* (Vintage 2017).

[27] UN Doc A/C.6/96 (1946). The Ad Hoc Committee consisted of representatives from China, France, Lebanon, Poland, the US, the USSR, and Venezuela.

[28] Debates around the question of general ('universal') jurisdiction reflected awareness that genocide originates in states' domestic affairs, and that those who initiate, or allow, genocidal acts are unlikely to be effective prosecutors. Even so, few states supported this feature of the Secretariat draft.

[29] Acts proposed for prohibition included gathering or creating military or other materials with intent for use in genocidal acts, issuing orders or instructions to commit genocide or ancillary tasks, and propaganda aimed at inciting national, racial, or religious hatreds. These ideas were strongly supported by Soviet representatives. See Lippman (n 26) 32–33, citing Ad Hoc Committee Report, UN Doc E/794 (1948) 30.

[30] The represented states were China, France, Lebanon, Poland, the US, the USSR, and Venezuela.

The final Convention draft retained protections for national, racial, and religious groups, but discarded those for political and cultural groups.[31] At the same time, the Sixth Committee added the phrase 'in whole or in part' to the much-debated 'intent to destroy' clause, thus broadening the scope of Article II considerably. Although Article VI retained a reference to an international penal tribunal, it provided no mechanism for its establishment. Also gone was any reference to universal jurisdiction. Draft provisions concerning prevention were likewise diluted due to sharp disagreements over the legal status of acts preparatory to genocide. The Soviet Union, Netherlands, and Yugoslavia had strongly favoured provisions that would have criminalized preparatory acts. However, the US, Venezuela, and the U.K. insisted that the difficulty of proving that acts preceding the onset of mass violence were motivated by genocidal intent would make such provisions useless for prevention, and redundant once violence had commenced.[32] A key concern about criminalizing preparatory acts was that authoritarian governments might use those provisions as international legal cover for the repression of domestic opposition groups.[33] Even the weak mechanism in Article VIII—which permits (but not does not require) contracting members to refer situations alleged to involve genocide to competent organs of the UN—involved a compromise among negotiating parties. Whereas some insisted that specifying a right of referral would be superfluous under the U.N. Charter, others argued that including such a right would entail an impermissible expansion of Security Council powers.[34]

In the end, the Convention text retained a general obligation to prevent genocide but encompassed no definition of its content or mechanisms for implementation. Under then-prevailing understandings of issues presumptively within the exclusive purview of member states, the Genocide Convention thus served largely to reaffirm the priority of territorial sovereignty and the norm of non-interference.[35]

[31] Lippman (n 26) 42. Those opposed argued that political affiliations are associations of choice and thus differ from racial, ethnic, and religious affiliations.

[32] According to Greenawalt, the character of the 'intent' provision and its relationship to motive was extensively debated during drafting, but 'remained alarmingly unresolved at the time of the Convention's adoption', Alexander Greenawalt, 'Rethinking Genocidal Intent: the Case for a Knowledge-Based Interpretation' [1999] Columbia Law Review 2259–94, 2266

[33] William A Schabas, *Genocide in International Law: the Crimes of Crimes* (CUP 2009) 589–92.

[34] In Sixth Committee deliberations, Great Britain and Belgium objected that what became art VIII was superfluous, since art 39 of the UN Charter gives the UNSC competence to address threats to international peace and security. The Soviet Union and Poland objected that the option to refer would expand UNSC powers beyond those envisioned under the Charter, Shabas (n 33) 536–37, citing UN Doc A/C.6/217 and UN Doc A/C.6/SR.101.

[35] Lippman (n 26). This outcome reflects a deal in which the Soviet Union dropped its opposition to an international court in exchange for the US agreeing to exclude protections for political groups, Beth Van Schaack, 'The Crime of Political Genocide: Repairing the Genocide Convention's Blind Spot' (1997) 106(7) *The* Yale Law Journal 2259–91, 2268.

3.2 Developing Authority and Expertise to Address Threats

The adoption of the Genocide Convention coincided with a period of rapid deterioration in US-Soviet relations. The ensuing rivalry ripened into a Cold War that severely hobbled Security Council operations from the 1950s to the early 1990s, and also generated deep rifts in the General Assembly. Under these conditions, invoking Article VIII became all but impossible despite continued incidences of mass violence.[36] By one fairly conservative estimate, there were more than sixty episodes during the Cold War era involving the intentional killing of more than a thousand non-combatants from discrete groups, with some claiming hundreds of thousands of lives.[37] Although far from every such incident involved 'genocide' under the Convention definition, according to numerous scholars and advocacy groups several plausibly fit that definition, and could have been identified as such as they were occurring.[38] As a clear pattern of multilateral inaction began to emerge, in which neither prevention nor punishment was forthcoming, the Genocide Convention came increasingly to be viewed as a 'dead letter' and a mere 'paper promise'.[39]

Still, some developments on the multilateral pathway during this period helped to lay groundwork for later progress on prevention. Orford (2011) argues that, under the leadership of Dag Hammarskjöld, several early UN operations established a legal and administrative foundation for asserting international 'executive authority' in situations of actual or impending violence due to government incapacity to assert effective control. These include the rapid formation and dispatch of an armed stabilization force during the 1956 Suez Crisis to prevent escalation, and the establishment of a 'peace force' to forestall Belgian intervention during the 1960 Congo Crisis.[40] Although this authority gathered dust under Security

[36] During the Cold War the Security Council issued no resolutions using the term 'genocide'. The UNGA issued only one such resolution condemning the 1982 massacre of Palestinian civilians in Lebanon by Israeli security forces—albeit without the support of several prominent members (UN Doc A/37/L.52). The Security Council condemned that incident as a 'criminal massacre' (UNSC Res 521 (1982)).

[37] Jay Ulfelder and Benjamin Valentino, 'Assessing Risks of State-Sponsored Mass Killing' [2008] Available at SSRN 1703426. To be included in this tally, counted deaths must be from 'a period of sustained violence' and directly involve state agents. https://papers.ssrn.com/sol3/papers.cfm?abstract_id=1703426.

[38] Which mass violence events constitute 'genocide' (or its attempt) is hotly debated among victims' groups, scholars, and activists. Whereas some insist only a few episodes satisfy the Convention definition, others argue for more inclusiveness based on multiplicities of characteristics among targeted groups, less stringent thresholds for intent, broadening categories of perpetrators, or on de-emphasizing the scale of attempts and perpetrators' degrees of success. Travis (n 4) 31–40; Goldsmith (n 4) 241–42.

[39] See eg Barry M Schiller, 'Life in a Symbolic Universe: Comments on the Genocide Convention and International Law' (1977) 9 Southwestern University Law Review 47, 67 (although the Genocide Convention 'should represent the *sine qua non* of human rights legislation, its role is more that of a poor-relation').

[40] Anne Orford, *International Authority and the Responsibility to Protect* (CUP 2011) 10 and 28–31.

Council deadlock from the mid-1960s through the mid-1980s, it was later recovered and revitalized.[41]

Also of considerable importance at the multilateral level was the advent of numerous treaty-based mechanisms for human rights engagement, along with so-called 'special mechanisms' under ECOSOC and the (then) Human Rights Commission. Beginning in the 1960s, a raft of multilateral human rights Conventions came into force, several of which created standing bodies to monitor and assist member states with implementation through self-reporting. A few such instruments specifically reinforce prohibitions against genocide[42] and many further formalized rights directly or indirectly relevant to protecting individuals and groups from violence and other debilitating forms of abuse or discrimination. Also in this period, the UN Human Rights Commission evolved a set of Special Procedures in the form of working groups and special rapporteurs for situations of concern in specific countries.[43] In 1980, the Commission created its first 'thematic' mandate to investigate enforced involuntary disappearances in multiple countries. Other mandates for extrajudicial, summary, or arbitrary executions (1982) and torture (1986) soon followed. The use of special procedures continued to expand, and by the late 1990s there was a peak of more than thirty country and thematic procedures in simultaneous operation. Although limited to information gathering and recommendations, these mechanisms helped to lay groundwork for understanding precursors to genocide and mass violence, while also serving as points of access for actors and activities on other pathways.

Indeed, as opportunities for Security Council-based actions on genocide prevention narrowed during the Cold War, the relative importance of activities on other pathways grew. On the private authority pathway, numerous non-state actors emerged to pressure governments and national and international bureaucracies to address mass violence and its consequences by documenting and publicizing information about such occurrences. These included victims and diaspora-based organizations and activists, along with journalists and networks of scholars, religious groups, anti-war activists, and humanitarian organizations such as the Oxford Committee on Famine Relief (later Oxfam), and the International Rescue Committee. This period also brought the creation and expansive growth of several key international human rights non-governmental organizations (NGOs) based in western democracies, such as Amnesty International, Helsinki (later Human Rights Watch), and the Lawyers' Committee for Human Rights (now Human

[41] ibid 90–92.

[42] See art 6 of the 1966 International Covenant on Civil and Political Rights, and art I of the Convention on the Non-Applicability of Statutes of Limitations to War Crimes and Crimes Against Humanity.

[43] Marc Limon and Hilary Power, *History of the United Nations Special Procedures Mechanism, Origins, Evolution and Reform* (Universal Rights Group 2014). These procedures were first used in South Africa (1967), Palestine (1969), Chile (1975), and Equatorial Guinea (1979).

Rights First) with support from private foundations and members.[44] Beginning in the 1980s, growing rights awareness tied to new treaties and associated institutions likewise prompted the emergence across the Global South and in the former Eastern Bloc of a wide range of NGOs focused on human rights, humanitarian issues, and crossover development issues.

A symbiotic relationship thus developed between international and national officials, bureaucrats, and jurists subject to expanding international human rights and humanitarian obligations via treaty ratifications, and a growing array of NGOs willing and able to gather and report information about those practices. This generated still greater public awareness of these issues which, in turn, ramped up pressure on governments and IOs to devise more effective ways to address a range of problems up to and including threats of genocide and other mass atrocities.[45]

3.3 Taking on Genocide Prevention

In the late 1980s, a combination of domestic economic malaise and internal political shifts prompted the Soviet Union to seek greater engagement with rival capitalist countries. As a sign of warming relations, in 1988 the Security Council authorized a handful of military observer and verification missions to conflict sites in Asia, Africa, and Latin America.[46] Following the August 1990 military incursion of Iraq (a Soviet client) into Kuwait, the Security Council responded with a series of condemnatory resolutions, and ultimately authorized a multinational military operation to restore the international status quo.[47] After this mission was completed in early 1991, the Security Council also condemned Iraq's treatment of its Kurdish populations and demanded that international humanitarian organizations be allowed to access to affected areas.[48]

Shortly thereafter, in late 1991, the Soviet leadership took the extraordinary decision to peacefully disband the Union of Soviet Socialist Republics (USSR). The Russian Federation government—the successor to the USSR's seat on the Security Council—was eager to reconfigure relations with Western powers. This opened a new era of possibility for multilateral cooperation on issues of international conflict mitigation and prevention. At the same time, scaling back Cold War-era economic, political, and military support for client regimes prompted crises in many developing states, and allowed

[44] Schiller (n 39); William Korey, *NGOs and the Universal Declaration of Human Rights: A Curious Grapevine* (Springer Press 1998).

[45] Felice Gaer, 'Implementing International Human Rights Norms: U.N. Human Rights Treaty Bodies and NGOs' (2003) 2(3) Human Rights Quarterly 339–57; Korey (n 44).

[46] These missions were UNGOMAP (Afghanistan and Pakistan), UNIIMOG (Iran and Iraq), UNAVEM I (Angola), UNTAG (Namibia,) and ONUCA (Central America), <https://peacekeeping.un.org/sites/default/files/unpeacekeeping-operationlist_1.pdf> accessed 3 November 2022.

[47] See especially S/RES/660 and S/RES/678.

[48] S/RES/688.

the reinvigoration of long-simmering internal and secessionist conflicts. Within two years, the Security Council had authorized ten additional missions—among them several with peacekeeping and peacebuilding mandates. This included a peacekeeping force for the growing conflict among successor states to the former Yugoslavia that by the spring of 1993 would include formal allegations of genocide.[49]

Inside the US, anti-internationalist political elements were critical of this multilateral engagement and its burden on US taxpayers. After eight US Marines on a UN peace enforcement mission in Mogadishu, Somalia, were killed and publicly mutilated in October 1993, domestic demands to scale back US involvement increased. Other governments began to express similar reticence. Consequently, when in early 1994 UN peacekeeping officials in Rwanda began to report on what appeared to be preparations for a large-scale massacre of the Tutsi minority at the urging of the country's Hutu leadership, the international response was tepid.[50] In April, the killing of Tutsis and their sympathizers began on a large scale. Instead of using the peacekeeping forces already on the ground to halt the bloodshed (much of which involved machetes and other low-tech implements), the UN command infamously ordered their withdrawal—after first evacuating foreign nationals.[51] Roughly 800,000 Rwandans were slaughtered over the subsequent ten weeks.

Glaring defects in mechanisms for atrocity prevention were also clearly evident in July 1995, when Dutch troops under UN command opted not to defend a UN-declared 'safe area' in Srebrenica, Bosnia-Herzegovina, as it was overrun by Bosnian Serb troops intent on slaying fleeing Bosnian Muslims. The proffered justification (later rejected by Dutch courts) was that attempts at armed defence would have exceeded the force's UN mandate and might not have succeeded.[52] Roughly 8,000 presumptive non-combatants were killed in the ensuing massacre.[53]

Prior to the outbreak of widespread killing in Rwanda and at numerous sties in the former Yugoslavia, international officials, human rights groups, and journalists on the ground had issued warnings of impending mass violence with genocidal characteristics. Moreover, in both situations as violence was occurring, official pronouncements by UN bodies and influential governments resisted using the 'genocide' label.[54] As the newly elected UN Secretary General, Kofi Annan sought to

[49] Application of Bosnia Herzegovina to Institute Proceedings Against Serbia and Montenegro before the International Court of Justice (20 March 1993) <www.icj-cij.org/public/files/case-related/91/7199.pdf> accessed 3 November 2022.

[50] Roméo Dallaire, *Shake Hands with the Devil: The Failure of Humanity in Rwanda* (Vintage Canada 2004). UNAMIR was authorized on 5 October 1993 (S/RES/872), immediately before the Mogadishu incident, to assist the implementation of the 1993 Arusha Accords ostensibly ending the Rwandan civil war.

[51] Human Rights Watch Report, *Ignoring Genocide* (1999).

[52] Stephanie van den Berg, 'Dutch State Accepts Partial Responsibility for Srebrenica Deaths' *Reuters* (19 July 2019).

[53] Peter Romijn, *Srebrenica: Reconstruction, Background, Consequences, and Analysis of the Fall of a 'Safe' Area* (NIOD 2002). http://publications.niod.knaw.nl/publications/srebrenicareportniod_en.pdf.

[54] Michael Barnett, *Eyewitness to a Genocide* (Cornell University Press 2012).

derive official 'lessons learned' from these failures. This produced sobering indictments of UN oversight, the underfunding of missions, and Security Council risk averseness in the face of impending disasters.[55] The deep divide between the legal rhetoric of prevention and associated state and IO practices that had long prioritized the principle of sovereign non-interference over the basic rights of individuals was thus laid bare in official terms.[56]

Concurrently, the state of social science knowledge about the precursors to genocide and other mass atrocities also was growing. The post-Cold War spike in both armed conflicts and multilateral engagement prompted a wave of new academic and policy attention to the origins, dynamics, and prospects for resolving civil wars and related humanitarian crises. One influential branch of this work explored modes by which civil wars, separatist movements, and so-called 'failed states' could metastasize into international crises.[57] Others encompassed efforts to identify general preconditions for genocidal campaigns, along with efforts to devise frameworks for detection and early warning.[58] These efforts provided policymakers and entrepreneurial government and IO officials with new policy ideas and prototypes.

Also of note, during the 1990s there were several remarkable institutional advances toward prosecuting high-level perpetrators of genocide under international criminal law. In 1993, the Security Council established an ad hoc tribunal to investigate and prosecute alleged international crimes tied to the armed conflict in the former Yugoslavia after UN officials, NGOs, and journalists amassed overwhelming evidence of atrocities. A similar tribunal was created for Rwanda in 1995. In parallel, multiple governments worked to pass a statute establishing a standing International Criminal Court in 1998.[59] The mandates for each of these bodies identified genocide as an international crime within their specific jurisdiction. And yet, even as these institutions were entering into operation, mass atrocities continued in the former Yugoslavia and elsewhere, thus revealing stark limits to prosecution as a deterrent.[60]

[55] See eg Independent Inquiry into the Actions of the United Nations During the 1994 Genocide in Rwanda, UN Doc S/1999/1257 (15 December 1999); Report of the Secretary-General on The Fall of Srebrenica, UN Doc A/54/549 (15 November 1999); UN Department of Peacekeeping Operations Comprehensive Report on Lessons Learned from UNAMIR (31 October 1997); Romijn (n 53).

[56] Bellamy and Reike (n 6).

[57] See eg Michael Edward Brown, *The International Dimensions of Internal Conflict* (MIT Press 1996); David A Lake and Donald Rothchild (eds), *The International Spread of Ethnic Conflict: Fear, Diffusion, and Escalation.* (Princeton University Press 1998); Kristian Gleditsch and others, 'Fighting at Home, Fighting Abroad: How Civil Wars Lead to International Disputes' (2008) 52(4) Journal of Conflict Resolution 479.

[58] Barbara Harff and Ted Robert Gurr, 'Systematic Early Warning of Humanitarian Emergencies' (1998) 35(5) Journal of Peace Research 551; Klaas Van Walraven (ed), *Early Warning and Conflict Prevention: Limitations and Possibilities* (Martinus Nijhoff 1998).

[59] The ICC first began to function in July 2002 after its founding statute entered into force.

[60] Prior to the 1990s, Bangladesh was the only state to move to prosecute foreign (Pakistani) nationals for alleged acts of genocide during its 1971 war of independence. Ultimately the matter was subsumed under a broader repatriation deal between Bangladesh, Pakistan, and India; Richard Edwards,

In the midst of this reckoning, yet another test of international resolve on genocide prevention arose in the form of violence between Serbs and Kosovar Albanian separatists in the (then) autonomous enclave of Kosovo. In 1998, episodes of deadly violence became common as Serbian forces displaced hundreds of thousands of Kosovars in efforts to reassert territorial control. In marked contrast to earlier events, US, British, and other leaders did not hesitate to use the term 'genocide'.[61] Still, although the UN Security Council invoked Article 39 and demanded that Serbian forces engage in peacemaking, it was clear to all that Chapter VII initiatives encompassing military intervention to halt the violence would be vetoed by Russia and China.

Faced with this impasse, the US, UK, France, and Italy opted to act through the North Atlantic Treaty Organization (NATO). After several failed attempts to broker peace, in March 1999 NATO's Governing Council authorized an aerial bombing campaign as a matter of 'humanitarian necessity' to protect Kosovo's non-Serb populations from further brutalization and ethnic cleansing.[62] The UK asserted further that NATO's actions reflected an emerging exception to Article 2(4) of the Charter, permitting states to respond militarily to humanitarian emergencies where such action is necessary, proportionate to the threat, and 'strictly limited in time and scope' to the humanitarian aim.[63] Russia, China, and several other states denounced the NATO operation as an 'illegal military action' and 'unprovoked aggression'.[64] In only partial contrast, numerous US and Europe-based international lawyers assessed NATO's actions as 'illegal but legitimate'.[65] At the same time, experts cautioned that recognizing a humanitarian exception could be abused as a ready pretext for other types of military action, and that it could generate perverse incentives within conflicts.[66] The Kosovo campaign was halted after three months when the parties on the ground agreed to allow a UN peacekeeping mission to be established.[67]

Jr, 'Contributions of the Genocide Convention to the Development of International Law' (1981) 8 Ohio Northern University Law Review 300, 304.

61 Mike Hanna and others, 'NATO, British Leaders Allege "Genocide" in Kosovo' (29 March 1999).

62 Adam Roberts, 'NATO's "Humanitarian War" Over Kosovo' (1999) 41(3) Survival 102, 106.

63 Roberts (n 62) 106, citing UK Foreign & Commonwealth Office, FRY/Kosovo: The Way Ahead; UK View on the Legal Base for Use of Force (7 October 1998).

64 BBC News, 'Russia Condemns NATO at UN' (25 March 1999).

65 See Independent Commission on Kosovo, 'The Kosovo Report: Conflict, International Response, Lessons Learned' (October 2000) cf John C Yoo, 'Kosovo, War Powers, and the Multilateral Future' (2000) 148(5) University of Pennsylvania Law Review 1673.

66 Louis Henkin, 'Kosovo and the Law of "Humanitarian Intervention"' (1999) 93(4) American Journal of International Law 824; Roberto Belloni, 'The Tragedy of Darfur and the Limits of the "Responsibility to Protect"' (2006) 5(4) Ethnopolitics 327.

67 Shabas (n 33) 531.

3.4 Reframing (and Re-taming) Genocide Prevention

NATO's armed intervention in Kosovo, along with the justifications advanced by some of its core protagonists, prompted a crisis at the UN. From one side, the intervention had been undertaken in support of international legal and humanitarian principles, and with the stated aim of enforcing prior UNSC resolutions. From the other, the absence of Security Council authorization made NATO's actions a clear violation of Article 2(4) of the Charter. Recognizing this dilemma, Kofi Annan challenged member states to find ways to uphold the core principles of the UN Charter, and also to act 'in defense of our common humanity'.[68] The government of Canada took up this charge and established an International Commission on Intervention and State Sovereignty (ICISS) to explore these issues. A central idea of the resulting ICISS Report is that states have a 'responsibility to protect' vulnerable populations from genocide and other mass atrocities, and further that it overrides traditional notions of sovereign non-interference in situations where governments are unable or unwilling to prevent those atrocities in their own territories. This phrase was soon shortened to 'R2P'.[69]

The ICISS Report, which was issued three months after the 11 September 2001 terrorist attacks against the US, did little to create international consensus on humanitarian intervention. In particular, its efforts to identify conditions under which military intervention to quell internal violence might be justified generated pushback from several directions. The governments of countries most likely to be *targets of such interventions* resisted any effort to spell out justifications for violating their territorial sovereignty. The governments of countries most likely to *lead such operations* also bristled at potential loss of autonomy to decide when and where to intervene.[70] Still, for the first time in decades, the legal and policy underpinnings of genocide prevention were being seriously debated at the highest levels in state and multilateral settings.

Supporters of multilateralism grew more concerned after the US partnered with the UK and an uneven coalition of other states to launch yet another armed intervention without clear Security Council authorization in March 2003—this time against Iraq on classic threat preemption grounds.[71] To address this danger head on, in late 2003 Kofi Annan convened a High-Level Panel to catalogue and analyse the range of threats and challenges on which the UN might be called to act going

[68] 'Secretary General Presents His Annual Report to General Assembly' (20 September 1999) SG/SM/7136.

[69] 'The Responsibility to Protect', Report of the International Commission on Intervention and State Sovereignty (IDRC December 2001) para 2.28 describes R2P as a purposeful reframing away from the rights of states to intervene toward the responsibilities embodied in state sovereignty.

[70] Edward C Luck 'The Responsibility to Protect: Growing Pains or Early Promise?' (2010) 24(4) Ethics & International Affairs 349–65; Bellamy and Luck (n 23)

[71] Michael Glennon, 'Why the Security Council Failed' [2003] Foreign Affairs 16.

forward, and to issue recommendations for how it might do so more effectively under the Charter.[72]

The December 2004 Report of the High-Level Panel identified genocide prevention as one of ten critical issues for the UN. Unsurprisingly, it reaffirmed the UNSC's exclusive authority to authorize the use of force. However, the Report also endorsed R2P as a basis for future UN engagement on humanitarian issues. According to Stephen Stedman, the fact that Panel members ultimately agreed on R2P as an orienting principle is 'quite astounding' since it involved a diverse set of entities—from sceptical members the Africa Group, to non-aligned states, to the US—endorsing the idea that 'sovereignty isn't sacrosanct'.[73] The General Assembly formally adopted many of the Panel's recommendations, including those on R2P and its role in preventing genocide and other atrocities, at the 2005 World Summit;[74] R2P was further reaffirmed by the Security Council in resolution 1674 on protecting civilians from armed conflict.[75] As would soon become evident, however, underlying these institutional endorsements was a spectrum of legal and operational understandings concerning what R2P encompasses.

On the heels of these developments, activity on the judicial pathway offered additional evidence in the form of the ICJ's 2007 judgment in the long-running case of *Bosnia and Herzegovina v Serbia and Montenegro* that baseline interpretations of the nature and scope of states' legal obligations under the Genocide Convention had shifted. The Court decided that Serbia had breached its duties toward Bosnia and Herzegovina under the Genocide Convention by failing to take adequate actions to prevent the 1995 Srebrenica massacre.[76] In justifying its decision, the Court held that state responsibility is triggered whenever a state has 'manifestly failed to take all measures to prevent genocide which were within its power, and which might have contributed to preventing the genocide',[77] and that these obligations 'are not on their face limited by territory'.[78] This contrasts sharply with

[72] 'Secretary General Names High Level Panel to Study Global Security Threats, and Recommend Necessary Changes' (4 November 2003).

[73] Author interview with Stephen J Stedman, Research Director for the High-Level Panel (16 March 2021).

[74] Resolution Adopted by the General Assembly on 16 September 2005. A/RES/60/1, paras 138–40.

[75] Contemporaneously and in the years since 2005, there have been many sharp critics of R2P, including Alex De Waal, 'Darfur and the Failure of the Responsibility to Protect' (2007) 83(6) International Affairs 1039–54; Roland Paris, 'The "Responsibility to Protect" and the Structural Problems of Preventive Humanitarian Intervention' (2014) 21(5) International Peacekeeping 569; Christopher Hobson, 'Responding to Failure: The Responsibility to Protect after Libya' (2016) 44(3) Millennium 433. See below for additional discussion.

[76] *Bosnia and Herzegovina v Serbia and Montenegro* (Judgment). Note, however, that the Court found no breach of responsibility in other incidents of mass violence carried out by Respublika Srpska-controlled forces.

[77] ibid para 183. The Court's 'purposive' construction of the Convention found this obligation on grounds that commitments to 'prevention' are not logically necessary to states' primary commitment to not engage in genocide within their own territories, and thus must be interpreted as implying broader obligations, Tams, Berster, and Schiffbauer (n 9) 48.

[78] *Bosnia and Herzegovina v Serbia and Montenegro* (Judgment) para 430.

the assessment of Elihu Lauterpacht—a notably progressive jurist—only fourteen years before in his role as an ICJ Judge (Ad Hoc) in an early phase of proceedings on Bosnia. Writing in 1993, Lauterpacht had argued that, although the plain meaning of the words in the Genocide Convention appeared to oblige states to prevent the crime of genocide wherever it occurs, the accompanying record of state practice appeared to suggest 'the permissibility of inactivity' when genocide takes place in another state with which the considering state is not already involved in armed conflict.[79]

The ICJ decision in *Bosnia* further intensified debate among lawyers and policymakers over the existence and nature of states' obligations to act extraterritorially to prevent mass atrocities, and how to square any such obligations with the political and institutional limitations of R2P.[80] These issues were hardly academic in light of an evolving situation of disputed genocide in the Darfur region of Sudan, together with multiple other ongoing armed conflicts on several continents.[81]

Additional evidence that the legal and rhetorical ground had shifted away from an uncritically sovereigntist default in situations involving impending mass atrocities was seen in, and reinforced by, several initiatives undertaken by Annan's successor as Secretary General, Ban Ki-Moon (2007–16). Early in his tenure as Secretary General, Ban created a permanent Special Advisor for Genocide and another for Responsibility to Protect. In 2009, Ban issued the first Report on Implementing the Responsibility to Protect. The Report—which lays out three mutually reinforcing pillars of responsibility—underscores that, although R2P is grounded in 'well-established principles' of international law obliging states to prevent and punish genocide, war crimes, and crimes against humanity, it is not itself a legal instrument.[82] Instead, the 2009 Report explains that the version of R2P

[79] Application of the Convention on the Prevention and Punishment of Genocide (*Bosnia and Herzegovina v Yugoslavia (Serbia and Montenegro)*) [1993] Order of 13 September 1993, Separate Opinion of Judge Lauterpacht, paras 113–15; Shabas (n 33) 527–28.

[80] See eg Stedman, Stephen John, 'UN Transformation in an Era of Soft Balancing' (2007) 83(5) International Affairs 933; Alvarez (n 6); Gareth Evans, *The Responsibility to Protect: Ending Mass Atrocity Crimes Once and for All* (Brookings Institution Press 2009); Alex J Bellamy, 'The Responsibility to Protect and the Problem of Military Intervention' (2008) 84(4) International Affairs 615; Jennifer Welsh, 'Implementing the Responsibility to Protect' (2009) 1 Policy Brief 1–9; Ekkehard Strauss, 'A Bird in the Hand is Worth Two in the Bush—on the Assumed Legal Nature of the Responsibility to Protect' (2009) 1(3) Global Responsibility to Protect 291; Bellamy and Reike (n 6); Orford (n 40); Michael Byers, 'International Law and the Responsibility to Protect' in Ramesh Thakur and William Maley (eds), *Theorising the Responsibility to Protect* (CUP 2015) 101; Harold Hongju Koh, 'The War Powers and Humanitarian Intervention' (2016) 53(4) Houston Law Review 971, 1007–09.

[81] In September 2004, US Secretary of State Colin Powell called atrocities in Sudan 'genocide' in testimony before the US Senate Foreign Relations Committee, 'The Crisis in Darfur' US Senate Foreign Relations Committee Testimony (9 September 2004). However, the Report of a Special Commission of Inquiry created by the UNSC (Res 1574) immediately thereafter determined that the government was not carrying out a policy of genocide. In 2005 the UNSC voted to refer the situation in Sudan to the ICC under its Chapter VII powers, with one member (Benin) expressly invoking R2P as a reason for the referral, 'Security Council Refers Situation in Darfur, Sudan to Prosecutor of International Criminal Court' (Press Release, 31 March 2005) SC/8351.

[82] The first of these pillars encompasses states' responsibilities to protect populations inside their own territories from four high international crimes: genocide, war crimes, crimes against humanity,

endorsed by various governments and UN bodies in 2005 is a *policy framework only*, albeit one that aims to avoid many of the limitations and blind spots of existing legal instruments.[83]

These protestations regarding R2P notwithstanding, baseline expectations around engagement with atrocity prevention continued to develop—although patterns of practice remain highly uneven. For example, after the 2005 World Summit, Security Council resolutions began to reference R2P and related documents frequently. As of May 2021, the UNSC had invoked R2P in ninety-two separate resolutions—or roughly 10 per cent of those issued since 2005.[84] Many of these references are limited to recalling states' first pillar obligations to protect civilians inside their own territories.[85] Even so, R2P-based considerations have also become a standard element of Security Council processes for authorizing or updating mandates for non-military and military operations under pillars two and three.[86]

These changes in the work of the Security Council have been buttressed by those in other UN bodies and agencies involved in conflict stabilization, humanitarian response, human rights, and economic development—often with inputs from the UN Offices of the Special Advisors for Genocide and the Responsibility to Protect. There have also been many capacity-building efforts at the regional, sub-regional, and state (and therefore also bureaucratic) level to anticipate and respond to impending human rights and humanitarian crises. These include, notably, initiatives from the African Union and the Economic Community of West African States (ECOWAS) to maintain early warning and conflict prevention systems. Numerous countries also have established, or augmented, state-level mechanisms for anticipating and preventing conflict. These changes have been further consolidated by a growing range of intergovernmental organizations (IGOs), such as the World Bank

and ethnic cleansing. The second encompasses responsibilities to 'encourage and assist' other states in fulfilling their pillar one obligations. The third comprises collective responsibilities to protect vulnerable populations in other states using UN Charter mechanisms if territorial governments are unwilling or unable to act. The Report states further that R2P's legal underpinnings are strongest under the first pillar, and that only a state's 'manifest failure' to fulfil its pillar one obligations can validate Security Council actions under pillar three, 'Implementing Responsibility to Protect' Report of the Secretary General (12 January 2009) A/63/677, paras 11(a) and 13.

[83] ibid para 3. For example, R2P—unlike the Genocide Convention—does not require ascertaining the intentions of authorities inside states in crisis, see Edward C Luck, 'Getting There, Being There: The Dual Roles of the Special Advisor' in Alex Bellamy and Tim Dunne (eds), *The Oxford Handbook of the Responsibility to Protect* (OUP 2016) 288, 296.

[84] 'R2P References in United Nations Human Rights Council Resolutions' Global Centre for the Responsibility to Protect.

[85] As expected with any system of staged conflict prevention, most uses have involved pillars one and two only, including in situations where the Security Council has taken no other action, as is the case with the situations in Yemen and with violence against the Rohingya minority in Myanmar, both of which involve widespread killings, displacements, and allegations of genocide.

[86] This encompasses missions for Sudan (Darfur) (2006), Kenya (2007), Democratic Republic of the Congo (2010), Libya (2011), Côte d'Ivoire (2013), South Sudan (2013), Central African Republic (2014), and Mali (2014).

and the Organisation for Economic Co-operation and Development (OECD).[87] As always, these developments have been heavily influenced by the work of local and international NGOs and civil society organizations (CSOs).[88]

Of course, the shift to more proactive interpretations of state obligations on prevention has not meant an end to genocide, or to the politics that have long complicated UNSC operations.[89] Although there have been some full and partial successes,[90] P-5 members have continued to suppress or veto resolutions involving themselves or their close strategic partners, including in situations where experts have alleged that ethnic cleansing and genocide are occurring.[91] This is the case with Russia's defence of Syria's regime in that country's (now) ten-year-old conflict; the unwillingness of the US and the UK to press Saudi Arabia on its role in Yemen's civil war; China's protection of Myanmar's actions toward its Rohingya minority; and its own actions vis-à-vis Tibetans, Uighurs, and other minorities.[92] However, whatever the perceived shortcomings of R2P as a policy process, its core importance to this argument is as a sign that baseline understandings of states' legal obligations around atrocity prevention had shifted in ways that placed a presumptive asterisk on the international legal principle of sovereign non-interference.

4. Conclusion

Tracing decades of developments involving governments, IO officials, and non-state actors shows unequivocally that baseline understandings of what the prevention obligations contained in the Genocide Convention entail have changed over

[87] See eg 'Preventing Violence, War, and State Collapse: The Future of Conflict Early Warning and Response' (OECD 2009) and related publications on crisis and state fragility.

[88] 'Advancing Atrocity Prevention: Work of the Office of Genocide Prevention and the Responsibility to Protect' Report of the Secretary General (3 May 2021) A/75/863.

[89] As of May 2021, the Global Center for the Responsibility to Protect lists eleven active crises in which genocide is known to be occurring or is at high risk of occurring.

[90] Gareth Evans (2020) cites initiatives in Kenya, Côte d'Ivoire, Liberia, Guinea, The Gambia, Sierra Leone, and Kyrgyzstan as R2P successes; and Democratic Republic of the Congo, South Sudan, and the Central African Republic as partial successes (due mainly to slowness of international responses). There have also been serious failures in genocide prevention and response beyond those mentioned, such as in Darfur and in Sri Lanka. Gareth Evans, 'R2P: The Dream and the Reality' (Speech at Leeds University, 26 November 2020).

[91] Russia, which abstained from the UNSC vote authorizing an initial humanitarian operation in Libya, was highly displeased when the US and UK extended the operation to the decapitation of Libya's ruling regime, and the channelling of arms and supplies to rebel groups. Louis Charbonneau, 'Russia UN Veto Aimed at Crushing West's Crusade' *Reuters* (8 February 2012).

[92] Nor have efforts to reassert UNSC control over international use of force for 'humanitarian' purposes been entirely successful. In 2008, France's military entered Myanmar to provide emergency aid to victims of cyclone Nargis without government or UNSC consent, and Russia intervened militarily in Georgia ostensibly to protect its South Ossetian minority. In 2017 and 2018, the US conducted military attacks against Syria with mixed international support in retaliation for chemical attacks against Syrian civilians, see BBC News, 'Syria War; World Reacts to US Missile Attack' (7 April 2017) and Zachary Cohen and Kevin Liptak, 'US, UK and France Launch Syria Strikes Targeting Assad's Chemical Weapons' *CNN Politics* (14 April 2018).

time without the text having been modified or supplemented. From initially reinforcing the principle of sovereign non-interference in the absence of external aggression, interpretative practices around prevention have come to incorporate a narrow exception to that principle when other governments manifestly fail in their humanitarian duties to protect populations inside their borders from genocide and similar mass atrocities. A minority of authoritative interpreters insist, in addition, that states have affirmative duties to act in situations outside their borders where they have the capacity to prevent genocide and other mass atrocities from occurring. This is far from what the Convention's enacting governments had envisioned, or what the 100+ states that signed on prior to the mid-1990s could reasonably have foreseen.

This case illustrates that indirect (or informal) modes of legal change may be contingent, non-linear, and subject to influence from multiple agendas within and across different pathways.[93] Various state, IO, and non-state actors and actions that have sought to promote, or enact, different constructions of genocide law have not produced consensus on the details of states' legal obligations to act to prevent genocide outside their own territories. Nevertheless, they contributed to a reconceptualization of atrocity prevention as integral to larger goals of promoting international peace and security. Three features of this account may be of particular use in efforts to identify and further theorize the dynamics of interpretative forms of change in international law.

First, the collective shift toward more expansive interpretations of prevention obligations was not the result of any one decision or event. To the contrary, it involved decades of cumulative work from actors on multiple pathways—some directly engaged with the prevention or punishment of genocide, and others focused more broadly on strengthening human rights and humanitarian protections, conflict prevention and mitigation, or countering general threats to international peace and security. Notably, much of the activity that led to widespread support for conditioning the right to sovereign non-interference on non-engagement in, and effective prevention of, mass atrocities on a state's territory under the guise of R2P occurred outside courts and other paradigmatically 'legal' institutions and processes. Instead, discursive openings for legal change and (re)interpretation emerged through a combination of practice (actions and glaring inactions) and subsequent legal and policy evaluations by broader communities of engaged stakeholders.

Secondly, actions on individual pathways often proceeded in reaction to, or in interaction with, activities on others. Cold War-era multilateral treaty-making

[93] Putnam, 'Mingling and Strategic Augmentation' (n 13); Harold Hongju Koh, 'The Legal Adviser's Duty to Explain' (2016) 41 Yale Journal of International Law 189; Korey (n 44). See also James Mahoney and Kathleen Thelen (eds), *Explaining Institutional Change: Ambiguity, Agency, and Power* (CUP 2009); Orfeo Fioretos (ed), *International Politics and Institutions in Time* (OUP 2017).

formally expanded states' legal responsibilities for ensuring the basic rights of individuals and groups—a process that began with the Genocide Convention and the Universal Declaration of Human Rights. In turn, this necessitated growing bureaucratic oversight of human rights and humanitarian practices by state- and IO-based agents. It also underwrote the emergence of a wide array of non-state monitoring and advocacy organizations, thereby gradually increasing the visibility of collective failures to prevent mass atrocities. A spike in multilateral engagement in conflict prevention following the end of the Cold War created additional demand for expertise on the origins and dynamics of armed conflicts, and for developing policy tools for early warning and mitigation in politically fragile settings. By increasing the capacity for states and IOs to detect impending mass atrocities, these international legal and policy developments coalesced to alter the operational feasibility of preventive actions, thereby opening the practical meaning of obligations embodied in the Genocide Convention to interpretative debate.

A third aspect of this case with broader resonance involves the character of efforts to contain, or redirect, changes in dominant understandings of the law when those changes begin to threaten the legal or political priorities of powerful actors. Here, interpretative flux concerning legal imperatives around genocide prevention was forced into the foreground of legal and political debate in the late 1990s, when a small but influential minority of states began to insist, both rhetorically and through concrete actions, that states' legal and moral obligations to protect vulnerable groups trumped both the principle of sovereign non-interference *and* the necessity of securing UNSC authorization for international uses of military force. Broad endorsement of, and engagement with, R2P thus served a dual purpose—as acknowledgement that the rhetorical and legal ground around atrocity prevention had shifted toward recognizing affirmative obligations to prevent mass atrocities, and also as a brake on further legal experimentation with any 'humanitarian exception' to Article 2(4) of the Charter. Indeed, for US officials and for many governments and regional allies of fragile states, collective reaffirmation of the Security Council's authority over the international use of military force was an important objective—not despite what this foreshadowed for limiting R2P, *but because of it.*

6

The Making of Lawmaking

The ILC Draft Conclusions on the Identification of Customary Law

Wouter Werner[*]

1. Introduction

On 20 December 2018, the General Assembly of the United Nations 'took note' of the Draft Conclusions on the Identification of Customary Law, as formulated by the International Law Commission (ILC). In addition, the General Assembly (GA) 'encouraged their widest possible dissemination'.[1] At first sight, this seems to have little to do with the central topic of this volume, pathways of legal change. After all, taking note and recommending dissemination are not quite the same as creating new rules of treaty or customary law. Neither do they amount to a binding decision by an international organization or the adoption of new, informal guidelines. Instead, the GA took note of conclusions that aim to restate what is already out there: the methods used by states and courts when they identify rules of customary international law. In that sense, the Draft Conclusions are more about continuity than about change. Their aim is not to set out novel criteria specifying how to identify rules of customary international law. Instead, the ILC 'finds' such criteria in past practices.

However, the Draft Conclusions do not restate the past merely for the sake of it. Just like the Roman God Janus, they face past and future at the same time. Their aim is to instruct future law-appliers how to identify rules of customary international law. Yet, they do so by looking back, through role modelling: if you want to find 'only such rules as actually exist',[2] do as others have done in the past. This implies that the Draft Conclusions not only face past and future at the same time. They also combine truth claims ('this is what others have done') with normative claims ('and so should you'). Like other restatement reports in international law, they go beyond setting out what is already out there. They are 're-presentations': presentations-again of

* Professor in International Law, Vrije Universiteit Amsterdam, Amsterdam, The Netherlands.

1 Draft Conclusions on the Identification of Customary International Law, as adopted by the International Law Commission at its seventieth session, in 2018, and submitted to the General Assembly as a part of the Commission's report covering the work of that session, A/RES/73/203, para 4.

2 ibid 125.

Wouter Werner, *The Making of Lawmaking* In: *The Many Paths of Change in International Law*. Edited by: Nico Krisch and Ezgi Yildiz, Oxford University Press. © Wouter Werner 2023. DOI: 10.1093/oso/9780198877844.003.0006

what has been, in order to steer what is yet to come. Restatements therefore facilitate new understandings of law—or they do the opposite: they delegitimize attempts to renew the law. They may also confirm authoritatively that law is undecided on certain issues or lay bare disagreements on the proper interpretation of law.[3] In any case, restatements have a potential impact on the development of law, especially if carried out by authoritative bodies such as the ILC. The transformative potential of restatements does not exist *despite* the claim that they only represent what is already out there. It exists precisely *because* of this claim and its subsequent adoption or rejection.

In terms of the volume as a whole, my main focus is on the so-called 'bureaucratic path' towards change. The ILC, as the editors of this book rightly observe, 'derives its weight from both its mandate and the recognized expertise of its members'.[4] At the same time, as I will argue below, the ILC is different from almost all other legal expert bodies because of its special institutional position. It is embedded in a state-dominated structure and partly dependent on the input and reception by them. When it comes to the work of the ILC, the bureaucratic path and the state action path tend to cross ways. The main concern of my chapter is the construction of norms by the ILC, the stage where 'actors and authorities associated with a particular pathway process the change and generate statements about the status of the norm in question'.[5] In this context, I focus on a specific kind of norm (or 'instructions'): the criteria that are to be used to identify rules of customary law. The status of these criteria remains somewhat ambiguous, as I hope to show in the sections which follow. Still, these criteria are crucial to understand the construction of norms, as they instruct agents how to determine the existence of rules of international customary law. They are meant to discipline the way in which statements about the status and validity of norms can be made. To specify the focus of my chapter even further, I zoom in on the specific technique used by the ILC to construct the criteria for the identification of customary law. The ILC presents the criteria in the form of 'restatements', as if the Commission only 'presents again' what is already out there. However, since repetition requires selection and since it tends to breed transformation, the Draft Conclusions on the Identification of Customary Law are also an attempt to delineate the paths for change in international law.

I will develop this argument further in the two sections below. In section 1, I will start out by discussing the rise of restatements and codifications by groups of international legal experts in contemporary international law. In response to

[3] For this argument, see also Oliver Kessler and Wouter Werner, 'Expertise, Uncertainty, and International Law: A Study of the Tallinn Manual on Cyberwarfare' (2003) 26(4) Leiden Journal of International Law 793.

[4] Nico Krisch and Ezgi Yildiz, 'The Many Paths of Change in International Law: A Frame' in Nico Krisch and Ezgi Yildiz (eds), *The Many Paths of Change in International Law* (Oxford University Press 2023).

[5] ibid.

deadlocks in formal lawmaking, expert bodies have sought to pave alternative paths of legal adaptation by restating the law 'as it is'. This discussion is followed by a more focused analysis of the impact of restatements on the development of customary international law. In section 2, I zoom in on the ILC Draft Conclusions on the Identification of Customary Law. The Draft Conclusions, I argue, are different from most other work of the ILC, as they seek to discipline the way in which international law is found. This makes the Draft Conclusions, quite literally, 'foundational', and thus also more openly political than most of its other projects. The Draft Conclusions are not just registrations of past practices. They construct certain practices as relevant and exemplary, while they ignore or delegitimize others. They instruct the reader *where* to look and *how* to look for role models, thus making the past 'present again' as a guide for the future.

2. Codification as Pathway of Change

2.1 From Progressive Development to Codification

The first task assigned to the ILC is the 'promotion of the progressive development of international law'.[6] This task echoes the ambition, already voiced in the League of Nations, to have a standing group of legal experts to prepare topics 'the regulation of which by international agreement [was] desired and realizable'.[7] In close co-operation with states, legal experts were called upon to identify topics and to set the stage for further negotiations on international agreements. In a similar spirit, the ILC brings together 'persons of recognized competence in international law',[8] all of different nationalities. The close relationship with states is expressed in Article 1, which speaks of the promotion of progressive development. It is not up to the ILC to progressively develop international law on its own, its function is to *promote* such development. This takes the form, as Article 15 of the ILC Statute sets out, of drafting conventions on subjects not yet sufficiently regulated by international law. When it comes to the selection of such subjects, the discussion of draft texts, or the adoption of final texts, the role of states (within the General Assembly) remains pivotal. Moreover, at the end of the day, it is up to states to transform draft conventions into valid treaties through negotiations and their expressed consent to be bound. Not surprisingly, the institutional position of the ILC has affected its mode of operation. As Morton has argued: 'The commission generally seeks to ascertain rules which are likely to be useful to states in the conduct of their relations, bears in

[6] United Nations General Assembly, Statute of the International Law Commission and Other Resolutions of the General Assembly Relating to the International Law Commission (1949), art 1 <un.org> accessed 3 November 2022.

[7] ILC, 'About the Commission' <https://legal.un.org/ilc/league.shtml> accessed 3 November 2022.

[8] Statute of the International Law Commission (n 6) art 2.

mind what rules and formulations states are likely to agree to and, on the basis of its assessment of these two questions, proceeds to examine and deal with each topic.'[9]

In line with this approach, the ILC has gradually moved away from the promotion of progressive development towards its second main task, codification. In this context, codification stands for 'the more precise formulation and systematization of rules of international law in fields where there already has been extensive State practice, precedent and doctrine'.[10] In the first two decades of its existence, the ILC mostly focused on drafting and recommending conventions. What is more, the vast majority of its proposals were approved by the GA and eventually turned into formal treaties.[11] From the 1970s onwards, the number of recommended conventions went down, as did the percentage of recommended texts that resulted in formal treaties.[12] In the twenty-first century, most projects undertaken by the ILC have not resulted in recommended conventions. According to Helfer and Meyer, this is a direct consequence of stalemates in the GA and the diverging opinions of states on many topics.[13] Under such conditions, the ILC may reasonably expect that its attempts to promote progressive development may fail, with the risk of what Crawford has called the 'decodifying effect': the exposure of diverging opinions, which makes it more difficult to claim that rules of customary law exist or that they are crystallizing.[14] In this context, it is not surprising to see the ILC moving to other kinds of instruments, which leave the Commission and states more leeway. Where 'progressive development' is supposed to result in a recommended convention, 'codification' can take a variety of forms, including 'draft articles', 'draft principles', 'draft conclusions', 'draft guidelines', and 'draft declarations'.[15] When the ILC opts for 'codification', it enjoys more discretion in terms of topic selection, and it is not dependent on affirmative approval by the GA. The latter can, if it prefers, simply 'take note' of the work by the ILC, as was done in the case of the Draft Conclusions on the Identification of Customary Law. This still leaves open the possibility that other agents, such as individual states, courts, and scholars, will treat the ILC products as expressive of customary law. In this way, the ILC can leave quite an important imprint on the development of international law, as the adoption of its Draft Articles on State Responsibility attest.[16]

9 Jeffrey S Morton, *The International Law Commission of the United Nations* (University of South Carolina Press 2000) 2–3. Quoted in Lawrence R Helfer and Timothy Meyer, 'The Evolution of Codification; A Principal-Agent Theory of the International Law's Commission's Influence' in Curtis A Bradley (ed), *Custom's Future, International Law in a Changing World* (CUP 2016) 305.

10 Statute of the International Law Commission (n 6) art 15.

11 Helfer and Meyer (n 9) 314–18.

12 ibid 314–18.

13 ibid 313.

14 James Crawford (2001), Fourth Report on State Responsibility, UN Doc A/CN.4/517, para 23.

15 For an overview, see Laurence Boisson de Chazournes, 'The International Law Commission in a Mirror—Forms, Impact and Authority in United Nations' in *Seventy Years of the International Law Commission* (Brill Publishers 2020) 4.

16 For an overview, see Simon Olleson, The Impact of the ILC's Articles on Responsibility of States for Internationally Wrongful Acts (British Institute of International and Comparative Law 2007).

Of course, the distinction between progressive development and codification does not mean that codification reports are restricted to a recital of established rules of international law. As the ILC has expressed on several occasions, it is often difficult to make neat separations between restatements of the law as it is and statements about how law should develop. Already in the 1970s, it argued that some reports 'contain elements of both progressive development as well as of codification of the law and, as in the case of several previous drafts, it is not practicable to determine into which category each provision falls'.[17] However, this does not mean the distinction has lost its value altogether. Codification reports still come with the claim that, by and large, the report in question reflects existing rules. This is why, for example, courts and tribunals have been willing to rely on several of the ILC Articles on State Responsibility as shorthand for rules of customary international law.[18] This is also why the ILC sometimes explicitly sets out which provisions go beyond existing law, such as Article 48(2) of the Articles on State Responsibility, and it is why many have called upon the ILC to specify, where possible, which provisions codify and which ones go beyond existing law.[19] The ILC thus has to maintain a distinction that it knows to be difficult to sustain in practice. The complex relation between codification and progressive development was summed up concisely by the Special Rapporteur on the Identification of Customary International Law, Sir Michael Wood: 'Somewhat paradoxically, then, differentiating between codification and progressive development has been both difficult (if not undesirable) and useful for the Commission.'[20]

2.2 The Turn to Restatements More Broadly: The Example of IHL Manuals

The move from the promotion of progressive development to codification fits a broader trend in international law. As several sociologists have pointed out, contemporary societies undergo self-propelling processes of change.[21] While the speed of social and technological change has accelerated, processes of formal

[17] [1974] II(1) ILC Ybk 174.

[18] Olleson (n 16).

[19] See eg Boisson de Chazournes (n 15).

[20] Lecture by Sir Michael Wood, *The UN International Law Commission and Customary International Law*, 13 <www.scienzegiuridiche.uniroma1.it/sites/default/files/varie/GML/2017/GML_2017-Wood.pdf> accessed 3 November 2022.

[21] Harmu Rosa, *Social Acceleration, A New Theory of Modernity* (Columbia University Press 2015); Harmut Rosa and William Scheuerman (eds), *High-Speed Society, Social Acceleration, Power, and Modernity* (Penn State University Press 2008); Thomas Eriksen, *Tyranny of the Moment* (Pluto Press 2001); William Scheuerman, *Liberal Democracy and the Social Acceleration of Time* (Johns Hopkins University Press 2004).

international lawmaking have slowed down in the last decades.[22] A good example is the field of cyberwarfare, where technological changes spurred new military strategies and tactics, which in turn led to the call for new cyber technologies. At the same time, the field of cyber war is characterized by a lack of formal lawmaking. So far, the field is not regulated by specific treaties and states have been very reluctant to express their formal legal position in response to concrete attacks.[23] As a result, there is neither treaty law nor fully developed customary law specifically dealing with issues of cyber war. The absence of specific formal law, together with the rapid developments in the field of cyber war formed the basis for the so-called *Tallinn Manual*, initially published in 2013. Four years later, the Manual was updated and extended to a larger area of topics related to cyber space more generally.[24] The *Tallinn Manual* consists of 'restatements' of existing international law, as applicable to cyber. The meaning of the term 'restatement' in this context is not fundamentally different from the meaning of the 'codification' as used in the ILC Statute. It refers to the representation of existing rules, in order to clarify and systematize (sub)fields of law.

There is a longer tradition of such 'restatements' in the field of international humanitarian law (IHL), published as so-called 'manuals'. The *Tallinn Manual* self-consciously positions itself in this tradition by stating that the Manual 'followed in the footsteps of earlier efforts, such as those resulting in the 1880 *Oxford Manual*, the International Institute of Humanitarian Law's 1994 *San Remo Manual on International Law Applicable to Armed Conflicts at Sea*, and the Harvard Program on Humanitarian Policy and Conflict Research's 2009 *Manual Applicable to Air and Missile Warfare*.[25] The *Tallinn Manual* will not be the last in line either. As I write this chapter, preparations are made to update and expand the *Tallinn Manual* once more (Tallinn 3.0),[26] while other experts are busy preparing a 'Manual on International Law Applicable to Military Uses of Outer Space'. The expressed rationale of the latter project, founded by McGill University, is worth citing in detail. It not only recalls, once more, the tradition of manual writing in humanitarian law, but also explains why it is necessary for legal experts to restate the law:

> Recent history suggests that non-governmental efforts to clarify the application of the law of armed conflict to new domains and means and methods of warfare are

[22] For an analysis, see Wouter Werner, 'Regulating Speed; Social Acceleration and International Law' in Andrew Lang and Moshe Hirsch, *Handbook on the Sociology of International Law* (Edward Elgar 2020).

[23] For an analysis, see Dan Effrony and Yuval Shany, 'A Rule Book on the Shelf? Tallinn Manual 2.0 in Cyberoperations and Subsequent State Practice' (2018) 112(4) American Journal of International Law 583.

[24] Michael Schmitt (ed), *Tallinn Manual on the International Law Applicable to Cyberwarfare* (CUP 2013); *Tallinn Manual on the International Law Applicable to Cyber Operations* (2nd edn, CUP 2017).

[25] Schmitt, *Tallinn Manual* (2nd edn) (n 24) 1.

[26] See CCDCOE, 'CCDCOE to Host the Tallinn Manual 3.0 Process' <https://ccdcoe.org/news/2020/ccdcoe-to-host-the-tallinn-manual-3-0-process/> accessed 3 November 2022.

> more successful than attempts to influence State behaviour. An international and independent group of experts working together to agree upon a set of rules is able to place constraints on State behaviour and shape the legality of State action. The process and success of the San Remo Manual on International Law Applicable to Armed Conflict at Sea, the Harvard Manual on International Law Applicable to Air and Missile Warfare, and the Tallinn Manual on International Law Applicable to Cyber Warfare demonstrate how international experts and engagement with governments have managed to produce quasi-legal documents that enjoy widespread recognition and authoritativeness.[27]

However, while the invocation of tradition is understandable, it glosses over an important transformation in manual writing since the late nineteenth century. This transformation foreshadows the ILC's move from progressive development to codification. The oldest Manual in IHL, the 1880 *Oxford Manual*, was meant as input for states to adopt new legislation: 'The Institute, […] believes it is fulfilling a duty in offering to the governments a "Manual" suitable as the basis for national legislation in each State, and in accord with both the progress of juridical science and the needs of civilized armies'.[28] The Manual saw this as part of its task of 'giving assistance to the gradual and progressive codification of international law'.[29] As can be inferred from the wording of the preamble, the 1880 Manual explicated the 'progress of juridical science' as the basis for the adoption of new laws. Manuals drafted since the 1990s may also have the ambition to lead to adoption of national legislation or to be adopted in national military manuals. However, they do so by restating rules of international law as they are validated by states beforehand, by codifying law that is supposedly to be already 'out there'. The *Harvard Manual*, for example, presents itself as an 'accurate mirror-image of existing international law', with no ambition to present the law as more coherent that it actually is.[30] While the metaphor of the mirror does not recur in other Manuals, the *Tallinn Manual* shares the spirit of its predecessor. It presents itself most of all as 'an objective restatement of the *lex lata*'.[31]

Manuals in the field of IHL thus seek to address the lack of formal lawmaking by restating rules that are already in existence. This bears resemblance to the ILC's move from progressive development to codification. Faced with an absence or unlikelihood of formal lawmaking by states, experts set out those rules which are in place already.

[27] McGill, 'About MILAMOS' <www.mcgill.ca/milamos/about> accessed 3 November 2022.

[28] *Oxford Manual on the Laws of War on Land* (1880) Preface <https://ihl-databases.icrc.org/en/ihl-treaties/oxford-manual-1880/preface?activeTab=historical> accessed 3 November 2022.

[29] Introductory Note to the Manual < https://ihl-databases.icrc.org/pt/ihl-treaties/oxford-manual-1880?activeTab=historical> accessed 3 November 2022.

[30] *HCPR Manual on International Law Applicable to Air and Missile Warfare* (CUP 2013) 2.

[31] Schmitt, *Tallinn Manual* (2nd edn) (n 24) 3.

2.3 The Transformative Power of Restatements

2.3.1 Dialectics of repetition

Of course, one can always pose the question whether codification reports 'really' restate existing rules of law or whether they propose new rules or interpretations. More fundamentally, however, one may wonder what it means to 'restate' in the first place. At first sight, restatements appear as knowledge claims: anyone who follows the accepted sources and methods of interpretation will come to the same conclusion: this or that rule 'really exists'. The possibility of restating '*lex lata*' (and setting it apart from proposing '*de lege ferenda*') is predicated upon the distinction between acts of cognition and acts of will.[32] However, this distinction does not capture what happens when experts restate, and others accept or reject their claims. Codification reports are not so much about cognition; they are about re-cognition, in the dual meaning of the term. They 'cognize again' what they claim to be already there. At the same time, they 'acknowledge' the rule as operating in the present and the future, thereby adding new layers of meaning. The difference between codification and progressive development thus lies in the way they seek confirmation. Proposals for progressive development seek confirmation through acts of will; codification seeks confirmation through further acts of recognition. If states or courts do not recognize restatements as reflecting pre-existing rules, they challenge them in two ways: they take issue with the knowledge claim implicit in the restatement and they refuse to acknowledge the restated rule as already valid. In that sense, the validity of restatements is always yet to be seen. It cannot be determined by only looking at the past, by asking whether they 'really' reflect pre-existing rules. They require further recognition by others. In terms of Derrida, one may say that they are re-petitions: they petition, they solicit, to be validated by others. If that happens, the question whether they really restate what was already there loses its relevance: what is recognized as already there will be treated as such. Restatements thus illustrate what Kierkegaard has called the 'dialectics of repetition': 'The dialectics of repetition is easy, for that which is repeated has been—otherwise it could not be repeated—but the fact it has been makes repetition into something new.'[33]

2.3.2 Restatements and customary law

The dialectics of repetition not only occurs at the level of individual rules that are restated. It also occurs at the level of a codification report as a whole, especially if it seeks to restate rules of customary law. After all, to restate rules in a particular form or genre does not leave their meaning unattached. Restatements take the form of,

[32] In his recent study on expert reports in IHL, Petrov uses this distinction to critique several reports for overstepping their mandate, see Anton Orlinov Petrov, *Experts Law of War, Restating and Making Law in Expert Processes* (Edward Elgar 2020).

[33] Søren Kierkegaard, *Fear and Trembling and Repetition* (first published 1843, Princeton University Press 1983) 146.

for example, 'articles', 'rules', or 'conclusions'. They are numbered, often printed in black, or they appear centred on the page (or both). In case of manuals in the field of IHL, the restatements are even called 'black letter rules', thus echoing the idea of straightforward 'black letter law'. If anything, the codification report looks like the text of a treaty or resolution.

Such 'rules', 'articles', or 'conclusions' are a far cry from the original meaning of customary law, as it developed in small tight-knit communities. As Kadens has argued, the idea that 'custom' is a formal source of law, to be identified through pre-given criteria, is an invention of European lawyers since the twelfth century. Before that, custom worked in quite different ways, as it probably still does in many (sub-) communities today: 'historical and anthropological evidence suggests that custom, before the medieval lawyers got hold of it, functioned as a relatively flexible and malleable set of social norms ostensibly held in the memory of the community, but in many instances more likely invented or reinvented on the spot to solve a problem.'[34]

Kadens' argument explains some of the recurring tensions and paradoxes in contemporary understandings of customary law.[35] By contrast with legislation and treaty law, custom is understood as a set of rules that develops out of practices and beliefs in a legal community. At the same time, lawyers seek to mould rules of customary law in formal categories, which should make it possible to identify them in a relatively predictable way. Restatements or codifications only deepen the tension between the informal nature of customary rules and the formal categories used to present them again. What emerges spontaneously in social interaction is represented in the form of a 'code' or '(black letter) rules'. The rules, articles, or conclusions are subsequently submitted for 'approval', as if customary law is a matter of formal decision-making after all. What is more, the practices and beliefs are not restated in the form of a random set of propositions. They are presented as a set of interrelated rules, held together by an internal logic. Take, for example, the first thing the reader notices when they take up a codification report by the ILC: the title. The title suggests that all restatements revolve around a single topic, which secures the internal coherence of the report and establishes boundaries to what is excluded. The logic of the report is further explicated in the commentaries that accompany the rules, articles, or conclusions. The commentaries not only explain individual

[34] Emily Kadens, 'Custom's Past' in Bradley (ed), Custom's Future: International Law in a Changing World (n 9) 11–33.

[35] The most famous (or notorious) being the chronological paradox. As Watson has summarized the paradox: for a new customary rule to develop it

> should arise first through custom, but at the time of the first behavior the law was, of course, not in existence. But the first relevant behavior should be accompanied by the *opinio necessitatis*. Consequently the first behavior rested on an error and should not be counted for the creation of the customary law. But this also applies to the second act of behavior, which now becomes the first, and so on through all subsequent acts.

Alan Watson, *The Evolution of Western Private Law* (The Johns Hopkins University Press 2001) 94–95.

restatements, but also the *rationale* of the report as a whole. The commentary to the ILC Articles on State Responsibility, for example, starts out by explaining the role of Article 1, which reads as follows: 'Every internationally wrongful act of a State entails the international responsibility of that State.' According to the commentary, Article 1 reflects the organizing principle 'underlying the articles as a whole'.[36]

The metaphor of the mirror is therefore misleading when it comes to restatements or codifications. A restatement report is more like a photoshop: a representation of practices and beliefs in clean and mean form. If it were otherwise, the codification effort would be close to pointless. Experts are called in precisely because rules of customary law are seldom uncontested, seldom crystal-clear, seldom completely coherent. Their job is not to copy-paste the contingencies of socio-political life, but rather to re-present them, to present them anew, in a different form and format. Restatements, therefore, are future-oriented, as they seek recognition by other agents. As I said earlier, their validity cannot be determined by only looking at the past, by asking whether they 'really' represent customary law. In a way, they never do—and that's exactly why they matter. They present rules *anew* by claiming they are in existence already, and by presenting them as part of a coherent set of rules. The novelty of the representation, however, has to be undone by other agents. If they accept the codification report as reflecting customary law, they turn it into 'nothing new', into a correct restatement of law that was already out there. Therefore, as I hinted at in the previous section, codification should not be viewed as a stand-alone activity, carried out in a particular moment in time. Rather, it is an ongoing process of recognition and revalidation. In the case of the ILC, this process is relatively pre-structured, with GA involvement in the selection of topics, annual reports, informal consultations, and the adoption or 'taking notice' of reports. Of course, this does not mean that states or the GA are the only audiences for the ILC. Courts, both international and domestic, also frequently use ILC products, as I will examine in more detail below. Still, institutionally the ILC is very much embedded in a state-dominated structure. For other groups of experts, obtaining support from other actors may be more difficult. The Tallinn Group of Experts, for example, did not have pre-arranged pathways to solicit support for its restatements of international law applicable to cyber. Instead, it had to rely on alternative mechanisms such as publications by its chair, claiming congruence between the Manual and subsequent speeches by states,[37] or conferences where legal advisors from different states could comment on draft texts.[38]

[36] Responsibility of States for Internationally Wrongful Acts, *Yearbook of the International Law Commission*, vol II (pt two) (2001); Annex to UNGA Res 56/83 of 12 December 2001, and corrected by Doc A/56/49(Vol I)/Corr.4.

[37] Michael Schmitt, 'International Law in Cyberspace: The Koh Speech and Tallinn Manual Juxtaposed' (2012) 54 Harvard International Law Journal 13

[38] For a discussion, see Paul Rosenzweig, 'Tallinn 2.0' (*Lawfare*, 27 April 2015) <www.lawfareblog.com/tallinn-20> accessed 3 November 2022.

3. The Draft Conclusions on the Identification of Customary Law

3.1 The Special Nature of the Draft Conclusions

The Draft Conclusions on the Identification of Customary Law are different from most other ILC final products. Most of the time, the ILC deals with the question of how a specific field is—or ought to be—regulated by international law. Examples are the succession of states, the immunities for states and their officials, statelessness, law of the sea, or crimes against humanity.[39] These are typical examples of the ILC acting as a body codifying existing rules or promoting the progressive development of international law. Not all reports are like this, though. A somewhat different question and approach could be found, for example, in the conclusions on the fragmentation of international law.[40] These conclusions do not cover a specific field or specific sources of international law, but a general problem arising across fields and sources: the specialization, diversification, or fragmentation of international law. The core maxim of the conclusions seems meta-legal: 'International law is a legal system […] As a legal system, international law is not a random collection of such norms. There are meaningful relationships between them.'[41] However, the conclusions and their commentaries subsequently set out how this maxim can be rooted in existing sources of international law, such as general principles, the law of treaties, and the United Nations Charter.

In this sense, the Draft Articles on the Identification of Customary Law are more radical. They do not set out how existing sources can be *applied*, but how one of the main sources of international law can be *identified*. Although the ILC explains that the conclusions do not deal with the question of how rules of customary law emerge, in practice the two are not that easy to distinguish. After all, for a rule of customary law to emerge, it is necessary that states express their *opinio iuris*, the belief that a rule actually exists as legally valid. In other words, for a rule of customary law to emerge, it has to be identified. Conclusions on the identification of customary law thus also contain statements on the emergence and development of those rules.

The Draft Conclusions on the Identification of Customary Law present a method or methodology for the identification of rules of customary law. This methodology itself cannot be treated as part of customary law, as this would only beg the

[39] For an overview, see <https://legal.un.org/ilc/texts/texts.shtml> accessed 3 November 2022.

[40] Conclusions of the Work of the Study Group on the Fragmentation of International Law: Difficulties Arising from the Diversification and Expansion of International Law, Adopted by the International Law Commission at its Fifty-eighth Session, in 2006, *Yearbook of the International Law Commission*, vol II (pt two) (2006).

[41] ibid Conclusion 1.

question: how to identify the customary rules on the identification of customary law?[42] So, where does the ILC look for guidance? Although the Draft Conclusions do not invoke the work of HLA Hart as such, they do seem to follow the logic of his legal theory. In *The Concept of Law*, Hart argues that legal orders rest on a 'rule of recognition' that officials and the legal community at large use to identify other rules of law. This raises the question of how the highest rule of recognition of the legal system can be said to exist. By definition, Hart argues, this question cannot be answered within the legal system itself. Its existence is a matter of (professional) practice: the rule exists because it is used. As Hart puts it: 'No question can arise as to the validity of the very rule of recognition which provides the criteria; it can neither be valid nor invalid but is simply accepted as appropriate for use in this way.'[43] More recently, d'Aspremont has applied Hart's approach to international law, arguing that the sources of international law are ultimately rooted in social practices of law-applying agents.[44] In similar fashion, the ILC Draft Articles move beyond existing sources, into the professional practices in which the rules of recognition are shown. This, however, means that the ILC had to decide which professional practices count as evidence, which practices do not count as such, and which ones should be regarded as the mistaken application of rules of recognition.[45]

3.2 Method, Authority, and the Development of Customary Law

3.2.1 Where to look

As I stated above, the Draft Conclusions have an ambivalent position vis-à-vis the officials that are called to identify rules of customary international law. On the one hand, the Draft Conclusions were written in order to prevent mistakes. Law-appliers should follow the criteria set out in the Draft Conclusions to ensure they only identify rules that 'actually exist'. On the other hand, the criteria for the correct identification of rules of customary law are derived from the practices of those

[42] Of course, theoretically speaking similar questions may arise in relation to the other major source of international law, treaties. The criteria for how to identify a treaty cannot be grounded in a treaty without begging the same question. However, when the ILC presented its 'Draft Articles on the Law of Treaties' it could argue that most of its provisions were already part of customary law, and thus defer the question.

[43] Herbert Hart, *The Concept of Law* (Clarendon Press 1961) 107. I have also used this brief section on Hart in Wouter Werner, *Repetition and International Law* (CUP 2022).

[44] Jean d'Aspremont, *Formalism and the Sources of International Law: A Theory of the Ascertainment of Legal Rules* (OUP 2012) 201.

[45] Although the Draft Conclusions are special because of their foundational nature, they are not unique in this respect. The ILC also had to operate at or beyond the boundaries of existing sources when it took up the topic of unilateral declarations of states. Unilateral acts were not included in the canon of sources and much controversy existed around their status as an independent source of international law. Perhaps not surprisingly, the ILC eventually opted for the adoption of 'guidelines', which emphasized the crucial importance of 'context' in the determination of the legal effect of unilateral declarations.

that identified rules of customary international law in the past. In other words, the Draft Conclusions advise officials to follow the example set by some other officials. In this context, it is interesting to see who is singled out as the primary example by the ILC. The Draft Conclusions rely heavily on the way in which the ICJ has identified rules of customary law. All the main findings of the report are backed up primarily by examples from the case law of the ICJ.[46] The very definition of customary law as consisting of state practice and *opinio iuris*, for example, is justified by reference to Article 38 as well as to the *Nicaragua* case, the *North Sea Continental Shelf* case, the 2012 *Jurisdictional Immunities* case, the 1985 *Continental Shelf* case, the *Colombian-Peruvian Asylum* case, the *Rights of Passage* case, the *Nuclear Weapons* Advisory Opinion, the *Pulp Mills* case and the *Nicaragua v Colombia Territorial and Maritime Dispute* case.[47] The only other source mentioned in this context is the *Norman* case before the Special Court for Sierra Leone.[48] A similar trend is visible when it comes to conclusions such as those pertaining to the assessment of evidence for customary law,[49] the forms of state practice that matter for the identification of customary law,[50] the assessment of state practice,[51] the general nature of state practice,[52] *opinio iuris* and evidence thereof,[53] or the status of resolutions of international organizations.[54]

This is not a politically innocent move, as can be inferred from the discussion between the ILC Special Rapporteur, Sir Michael Wood, and the Informal Expert Group of the Asian-African Legal Consultative Organization (AALCO).[55] The Informal Expert Group formally responded to the work of the ILC regarding the identification of customary law. Given the colonial heritage of international law, the topic of customary law is of course sensitive for an organization such as AALCO. In this context, the Informal Expert Group emphasized the importance of state sovereignty and the need to rely on practices of states when reconstructing a method for the identification of customary law. In order to 'ensure the respect for the exercise of State power', the AALCO Expert Group took issue with the ILC's strong reliance on the jurisprudence of the ICJ:

46 The examples of references to the case law of the ICJ are taken from Werner (n 43) ch 2.
47 Draft Conclusions on the Identification of Customary International Law (n 1) 82–84.
48 ibid 84.
49 ibid 84–87.
50 ibid 91–92.
51 ibid 92–93.
52 ibid 93–96.
53 ibid 96–101.
54 ibid 106–09.
55 By now, AALCO comprises forty-eight states from Asia and Africa. The Expert Group was established in 2014 as 'working group', to formulate responses to the work of the ILC. For the work of AALCO in general, see <www.aalco.int/> accessed 3 November 2022. The report of the Expert Group was published by Sienho Yee, 'Report on the ILC Project on Identification of Customary Law' (2015) 14 Chinese Journal of International Law 375.

> Placing the decisions of international courts and tribunals and the work of the ILC on such a high pedestal is alarming, because these are really secondary materials under Article 38 of the ICJ Statute. Since paragraph 1(b) of this article defines 'international custom' as 'international custom, as evidence of a general practice accepted as law', only State materials are primary materials in the true sense of the term in the identification of customary international law. International courts and tribunals are not agents of any State.[56]

In response, the Special Rapporteur downplayed the critique by the Expert Group. At the general level, he agreed with the importance of state sovereignty as the core principle in international law. As a consequence, he argued, the opinions of the Asian and African states matter, not because they represent a specific region or perspective, but because they represent so many states. The comments on the work of the ILC, he argued, 'are welcome more because they may be seen as reflecting, to some degree at least, the views of a considerable number of States, rather than because they necessarily reflect a particular regional view on the matter'.[57] However, while acknowledging the importance of state sovereignty, the Special Rapporteur denied that this should affect the approach used by the ILC. It was perfectly sound, he argued, to develop criteria for the identification of customary international law from the practice of the ICJ. In this context, he distinguished between two matters: 'First, the materials that need to be looked at in order to ascertain the methodology for identifying rules of customary international law. Second the materials (evidence) needed to be examined in order to determine whether a rule of customary international law exists'.[58] The Draft Conclusions only concern the first question, and in order to answer this question 'decisions of the International Court of Justice are in my view invaluable'.[59] To answer the second question, Wood held, the practices of states come first, and the work of the ICJ is indeed only 'subsidiary but often in practice very important'.[60]

In line with this position, later versions of the Draft Conclusions maintained their strong focus on the practice of the ICJ. The comments by AALCO were formally acknowledged, but this did not affect the ILC's orientation on the ICJ. In subsequent GA discussions, the ICJ bias was not brought up frequently and only in general terms. China, for example, referred to the AALCO comments as such,[61]

56 AALCO Informal Working Group Report, para 31. Reprinted in Yee (n 55) 383–84.

57 Sir Michael Wood, 'The Present Position within the ILC on the Topic "Identification of customary international law" in Partial Response to Sienho Yee', Report on the ILC Project on 'Identification of Customary International Law' (2016) 15(1) Chinese Journal of International Law 3, 5.

58 ibid 5.

59 ibid 5.

60 ibid 5.

61 See, however, China's remarks on the importance of the AALCO report more generally: 'The AALCO report could help the Commission appreciate the concerns and views of many Asian and African States on the topic.' Summary record of the 22nd meeting: 6th Committee, 6 November 2015, 70th session (para 68); A/C.6/70/SR.22.

whereas Israel emphasized in more general terms the need to base the Draft Conclusions on state practice: 'In accordance with the Statute of the International Court of Justice and the International Law Commission's conclusions on identification of customary international law, the identification and development of customary law should be based on State practice.'[62] These comments did not change the end product and the Draft Conclusions kept their focus on the ICJ. The position of the ILC can thus be summarized as follows: rules of customary international law are primarily made by states, yet in order to know what counts as rules of customary international law it is best to follow the examples set by the ICJ.

3.2.2 How to look

The Draft Conclusions prescribe a so-called 'inductive approach' to the identification of customary law.[63] Rules of customary international law, it argues, should be ascertained on the basis of empirical evidence, not on the basis of logical inferences from pre-given axioms. The latter method, 'deduction', is not ruled out altogether by the ILC. It can be used to spell out the consequences of an existing rule or regime of customary law. However, it should be used merely as an 'aid' and 'employed with caution'.[64] The default position is induction: the inference of general rules of customary international law from individual observations. Although it is not spelled out as such, the Draft Conclusions themselves are also the result of inductive reasoning. The ILC did not develop them deductively out of abstract categories or axioms. They are taken from what the ILC observes: the ways in which others, and in particular the ICJ, have identified rules of customary international law in the past.

Or are they? After all, pure induction is impossible. This is not only because it is problematic to generalize from individual observations, as Popper's famous 'black swan example' has shown. (No matter how many white swans one may observe, the general conclusion that all swans are white is unfounded. However, one black swan suffices to arrive at a solid negative conclusion: apparently not all swans are white.)[65] More fundamentally, pure induction is a myth because evidence does not reveal itself as such. What counts as evidence, to put it another way, is not self-evident. Observations only appear as relevant evidence (or as irrelevant) in light of an idea, concept, or theory. This also applies to the identification of a rule of customary international law. Identifying rules of customary law is not just a matter of registering what goes on in practice. To be able to identify a rule of customary international law, it is necessary to have a concept of what counts as customary international law to begin with. Depending on the concept of customary international

[62] Summary record of the 8th meeting: 6th Committee, held at Headquarters, New York, on Tuesday, 20 October 2020, General Assembly, 75th session (p 7, para 43).
[63] Draft Conclusions on the Identification of Customary International Law (n 1) 126.
[64] ibid 126.
[65] Karl Popper, *The Logic of Scientific Discovery* (2nd edn, Taylor & Francis 2002)

law, different observations count as relevant or irrelevant. This point can be illustrated by comparing the concept of customary law used by the ILC to two alternative conceptions: (a) the 'public conscience' approach adopted by the ICTY in the *Kupreškić* case, or (b) the treaty-based approach advocated by D'Amato. To be sure, the point of these comparisons is not to assess which approach is better or more correct. The point is to show how different conceptions of customary law lead to different readings of what counts as relevant practice, and thus to different readings of how induction should be carried out. This, I argue, is why the Draft Conclusions matter as a form of legal change: they attempt to steer how customary law is found and developed. What is more, this attempt is subsequently restated and reaffirmed by states. States referred to the Draft Conclusions as 'important to bear in mind',[66] endorsed the ILC's use of the report as showing 'good judgment',[67] and called it 'a comprehensive examination'.[68] Somewhat ironically, Germany called upon the ICJ to stick closely to the 'excellent' Draft Conclusions: 'The Court should continue to be rigorous in its use of the Commission's excellent work on the identification of customary international law, as it had done in the Jurisdictional Immunities case.'[69]

3.2.2.1 The two elements test and public conscience

The basic approach of the ILC is set out in Draft Conclusion 2: 'To determine the existence and content of a rule of customary international law, it is necessary to ascertain whether there is a general practice that is accepted as law (*opinio juris*).' According to the ILC, the 'two elements approach' is widely supported by case law, state practice, and scholarly writing. Moreover, the ILC argues that the two elements test applies across the board. Citing its report on the fragmentation of international law, the ILC once more emphasizes the unity of international law: irrespective of the field of law, the two elements test applies. For the ILC, a general practice only

[66] Summary record: 24th meeting: 6th Committee, held at Headquarters, New York, on Tuesday, 29 October 2019, General Assembly, 74th session, Mr Oyarzábal (Argentina): 'For the identification of a jus cogens norm in customary international law, it was important to bear in mind the Commission's work on the topic "Identification of customary international law"' (p 3, para 7) <https://digitallibrary.un.org/record/3841582?ln=en> accessed 3 November 2022.

[67] Summary record of the 26th meeting: 6th Committee, held at Headquarters, New York, on Thursday, 31 October 2019, General Assembly, 74th session, Mr Jiménez Piernas (Spain): 'The Commission had shown good judgment by basing that work on the 1969 Vienna Convention on the Law of Treaties and on its own work on other topics, such as international responsibility of States, reservations to treaties and identification of customary international law, and more generally on international judicial and treaty practice and doctrine' (p 3, para 11) <https://digitallibrary.un.org/record/3841146?ln=en> accessed 3 November 2022.

[68] Summary record of the 33rd meeting: 6th Committee, held at Headquarters, New York, on Wednesday, 6 November 2019, General Assembly, 74th session, Ms Green (Australia): 'Just as in the case of the work on identification of customary international law, a comprehensive examination of the development of the topic "General principles of law" would help States to draw on all sources of international law and thereby better understand their obligations and resolve their disputes peacefully' (p 3, para 10) <https://digitallibrary.un.org/record/3856205?ln=en> accessed 3 November 2022.

[69] Summary record of the 28th meeting: 6th Committee, held at Headquarters, New York, on Friday, 1 November 2019, General Assembly, 74th session (p 18, para 104) <https://digitallibrary.un.org/record/3847218?ln=en> accessed 3 November 2022.

counts as relevant if it is accompanied by *opinio iuris*: 'Practice without acceptance as law (*opinio juris*), even if widespread and consistent, can be no more than a non-binding usage.'[70] Interestingly, the ILC here deviates from the formulation of customary law in Article 38 of the ICJ Statute, which speaks of 'international custom, as evidence of a general practice accepted as law', a formulation that echoes the German Historical School conception of customary law. According to the text of Article 38, practices themselves can be treated as 'evidence'. The ILC, however, follows the by now dominant interpretation of customary law, which downplays practice as mere 'usage' if it is not accompanied by *opinio iuris*. However, *opinio iuris* as such is not recognized as evidence either: 'a belief that something is (or ought to be) the law unsupported by practice is mere aspiration.'[71]

A different conception of customary law was formulated by the Trial Chamber of the ICTY in *Kupreškić*.[72] In this case, the Chamber carved out IHL as a special regime, different from other branches of international law since it is regulated by the so-called 'Martens Clause'. This clause made its first appearance in the preamble to the 1899 Hague Convention and has subsequently been recalled in the Geneva Conventions and the 1977 Additional Protocols. According to the Clause, the absence of treaty law on a specific topic does not lift the protection offered by the laws of armed conflict, as 'populations and belligerents remain under the protection and empire of the principles of international law, as they result from the usages established between civilized nations, from the laws of humanity and the requirements of the public conscience'. As a result, the Chamber held, the concept of customary law obtains a different meaning. Where the ILC emphasized the two elements test, the Chamber argues that in the sub-regime of humanitarian law state practice may matter less (or may even be discarded altogether). Because of the Martens Clause, the Chamber argues, this is 'an area where *opinio iuris sive necessitatis* may play a much greater role than *usus*'.[73] Paradoxically, however, the Chamber grounds this proposition in the practices of states and courts: 'In the light of the way States and courts have implemented it, this Clause clearly shows that principles of international humanitarian law may emerge through a customary process under the pressure of the demands of humanity or the dictates of public conscience, even where State practice is scant or inconsistent.'[74] In other words, state (and court) practice shows that state practice matters less because of the imperatives of humanity and public conscience. As a result, the Chamber concludes, *opinio iuris*, this time emerging out of humanity and public conscience, 'may turn out to be the decisive element heralding the emergence of a general rule or principle of humanitarian law'.[75]

[70] Draft Conclusions on the Identification of Customary International Law (n 1) 126.
[71] ibid 126.
[72] *Kupreškić et al*; Case No: IT-95-16-T, 14 January 2000.
[73] ibid para 527.
[74] ibid.
[75] ibid.

If one adopts the two elements approach, together with the maxim of international law's unity, *Kupreškić* can only appear as an aberration. It does not count as 'evidence' for how to identify customary international law, but as a mistake, better ignored or used as an example of how not to go about.[76] On the other hand, if one accepts the game-changing nature of the Martens Clause, sticking to the two elements test means missing out on what makes international humanitarian law so special. My point is not to argue in favour of one or the other concept of customary law. I compare the two approaches to show how the concept of customary law determines what counts as evidence. Both approaches are inductive in their own way, and both would argue that the other leaves out relevant practices. This is what makes the ILC Draft Conclusions so important for the topic of this volume: it is an attempt to discipline the identification of customary international law, and thus to delegitimize possible alternative concepts and approaches. Since the identification of customary law cannot be separated from its emergence and development, the Draft Conclusions are about the making of lawmaking: certain ways of looking are presented as restatements of what is 'actually out there'; other ways of looking are presented as mistaken, not grounded in practices that count.

3.2.2.2 The two elements test and generative treaties

The two elements test also determines the position of the ILC in relation to treaties. According to Draft Conclusion 11:

> A rule set forth in a treaty may reflect a rule of customary international law if it is established that the treaty rule:
> (a) codified a rule of customary international law existing at the time when the treaty was concluded;
> (b) has led to the crystallization of a rule of customary international law that had started to emerge prior to the conclusion of the treaty; or
> (c) has given rise to a general practice that is accepted as law (*opinio juris*), thus generating a new rule of customary international law.

Draft Conclusion 11 is based on a strict distinction between the sources of validity for treaties and for customary law. Treaties exist by virtue of the properly expressed consent to be bound and cannot, as such, create obligations for third parties. Customary law is derived from the two elements (practice and *opinio iuris*) and, once established, in principle binding for all states. Treaty provisions, as Draft Conclusion 11 states, may reflect already existing rules of customary law, but they cannot be their source of validity. Similarly, treaty provisions may spur the

[76] And indeed, the *Kupreškić* case is not mentioned in the ILC Draft Conclusions, although in general terms the idea that customary law can grow out of *opinio iuris* alone is discredited.

formation of a rule of customary law, but again, this does not mean they ground their validity. The latter is solely derived from the elements contained in the concept of customary law that the ILC started out with: a general practice accepted as law. By definition, therefore, treaty provisions cannot be used as evidence for a rule of customary law unless they reflect or transform into something else, a practice accepted as law.

A radically different interpretation of the relation between treaty provisions and customary law can be found in the work of D'Amato. According to D'Amato, the idea that treaty provisions cannot, as such, be generative of customary law fails to do justice to relevant precedents. Most rules of customary law, he contends, found their first expression in treaties.[77] What is more, these rules were identified as customary *not* based on a separate examination of whether they reflected pre-existing rules or whether they had spurred a new, general practice accepted as law. The customary status of the treaty provisions was rather derived from their general (or generalizable) nature, the possibility to turn them into rules binding for all states: 'nothing subsequent to the treaty can be found, or needs to be found, to prove that its generalizable provisions have passed into custom.'[78] All that are required, D'Amato argues, are generalizable provisions and lack of objections by non-party states.[79]

Again, my point is not to assess which conception of customary law is better, let alone 'correct'. The comparison is meant to illustrate the constitutive function of a concept of customary law. What counts as evidence for the identification of a rule of customary law is determined by how customary law is conceptualized in the first place. For the ILC, treaties cannot as such be generative of customary law, as the latter always requires state practice and *opinio iuris*. If courts behave otherwise, this is not counted as a practice that reveals a rule of recognition, but as a deviation from the way in which custom ought to be identified. The mere conclusion of treaties, then, can never count as relevant evidence. What is necessary is what the ILC would call an 'inductive approach', based on what the ILC deems to be the relevant practice and acceptance. For D'Amato, however, this position is the opposite of induction. It is based on the a priori belief that treaties cannot as such generate rules of customary law. Historical precedent, he argues, belies this belief and shows that in fact states and scholars have always used treaty provisions to identify rules of customary law. Followers of D'Amato will see their position confirmed by empirical studies into the case law of international courts and tribunals. As Choi and Gulati have argued, by far the most cited evidence of a rule of customary law by international courts are provisions in international treaties (62.9 per cent). In most

[77] Anthony D'Amato, *The Concept of Custom in International Law* (Cornell University Press 1971).

[78] Anthony D'Amato, 'The Concept of Human Rights in International Law' (1982) 82(6) Columbia Law Review 1110, 1146.

[79] ibid.

of the cases where courts referred to treaties, they did not add a separate analysis of how the cited provisions reflect existing customary law.[80] However, for those that follow the ILC Draft Conclusions, this probably merely indicates that the courts were of the opinion that the pre-existing customary rule was self-evident. Alternatively, they may argue that the courts made a mistake in applying the criteria correctly. In any case, they can point to the numerous instances where international courts have argued that rules of customary law exist by virtue of a general practice accepted as law. How to weigh the different elements, when to treat them as evidence, and when as mistakes—all this cannot be determined on the basis of observation alone. It calls for a different searchlight, different evidence, different forms of induction.

4. Conclusion

In 1995, Diana Deutsch discovered the so-called 'speech-to-song illusion'. Deutsch recorded a spoken sentence on the behaviour of sounds. She had the last part of the sentence, 'sometimes behave so strangely', on a loop. After a number of repetitions, the spoken words transformed into a melody: 'However, when you play the phrase that is embedded in it: "sometimes behave so strangely" over and over again, a curious thing happens. At some point, instead of appearing to be spoken, the words appear to be sung.'[81]

What Deutsch called an illusion is in fact a well-known effect of repetition: it tends to breed change. This is certainly true for the topic of this chapter, restatements of international law and the methods of identifying rules of international law. In the past decades, restatements of international law have grown in importance. Across different fields, expert committees have drafted reports which restate international law 'as it is'. The ILC fits this trend, with a gradual move away from the 'promotion of progressive development' towards 'codification' of international law. Recently, the ILC went even further in an attempt to restate the methods to be used for the identification of customary law. In this chapter, I have shown how the ILC Draft Conclusions on this topic are governed by the dialectics of repetition. Just like the speech-to-song illusion, they necessarily transform what they restate into something else. Inchoate and only partially consistent practices are presented anew in the form of a structured report, with numbered conclusions held together by an internal logic. The Draft Conclusions are based on a series of choices, for example

[80] Stephan Choi and Mitu Gulati, 'Customary International Law: How do Courts do it' in Bradley (ed), Custom's Future: International Law in a Changing World (n 9) 133. Choi and Gulati found evidence of this 'in fewer than 20% of the determinations'.

[81] Diana Deutsch, 'Speech to Song Illusion' <https://deutsch.ucsd.edu/psychology/pages.php?i=212> accessed 3 November 2022. The website contains the recording, as well as references to Deutsch's other works.

on whose practices to include, where to look for examples, and how to look at examples. None of these choices is politically innocent. The Draft Conclusions, therefore, are more than a recital of what is out there already. They constitute an attempt to discipline how customary law is to be identified. As the identification of customary law is difficult to separate from its (re)-creation, the Draft Conclusions also set out pathways of legal development and potential change.

7

The Turn to Metrics in International Environmental Law

Jaye Ellis[*]

1. Introduction

A compelling narrative about international environmental law (IEL) has been making the rounds for several years: IEL is fading into the background as other, more promising governance approaches emerge, focused on the management of states' performance in pursuing largely material environmental goals such as increased habitat protection and reduced emissions of harmful substances. Central to these approaches are sustainability metrics such as indicators, succinctly and clearly defined by Kevin E Davis, Benedict Kingsbury, and Sally Engle Merry as:

> a named collection of rank-ordered data that purports to represent the past or projected performance of different units. The data are generated through a process that simplifies raw data about a complex social phenomenon. The data, in this simplified and processed form, are capable of being used to compare particular units of analysis (such as countries, institutions, or corporations), synchronically or over time, and to evaluate their performance by reference to one or more standards.[1]

In this narrative, the inability of IEL to bring about significant changes in state behaviour and environmental outcomes could be resulted in the adoption in 2015 of the Sustainable Development Goals (SDGs). Frustration is certainly warranted: the failure of states at the Copenhagen Climate Change Conference in 2009 to conclude a binding agreement to replace the Kyoto Protocol, particularly in the face of overwhelming evidence of the seriousness of the climate crisis, is one example among many of missed opportunities, inadequate effort, and failure to meet objectives. By the time of Copenhagen, doubts about international law as the engine of international environmental governance were already sown, and the assumption that

* Associate Professor, McGill University, Montreal, Canada.
[1] Kevin E Davis, Benedict Kingsbury, and Sally Engle Merry, 'Indicators as a Technology of Global Governance' (2012) Law & Society Review 71, 73–74.

Jaye Ellis, *The Turn to Metrics in International Environmental Law* In: *The Many Paths of Change in International Law*. Edited by: Nico Krisch and Ezgi Yildiz, Oxford University Press. © Jaye Ellis 2023. DOI: 10.1093/oso/9780198877844.003.0007

a global climate agreement ought to be seen as the cornerstone of climate law and policy was already being called into question from a variety of perspectives.[2] Other governance approaches, relying heavily on performance standards and review, and intersecting with law without necessarily being reliant on it, have begun to emerge. In fact, the logic of metrics was inscribed in IEL early on: targets and timetables have long been incorporated into international environmental agreements, as they offer both the possibility of measuring progress towards meeting objectives and a degree of flexibility, particularly as regards the selection of means to pursue ends, that functions very well in a horizontal legal system. Increasingly, however, performance metrics are coming to be seen not as a complement to legal obligation and a dimension of the architecture of legal regimes, but as a distinct approach, running parallel to international law and, possibly, operating quite separately from it. National governments, international organizations, and non-state transnational regulatory authorities are among the actors most likely to see the value in metrics, as they are under clear pressure to be seen to produce results. Indeed, the global ecological crisis requires results, and civil society organizations, citizens, and a wide range of economic actors that are acutely aware of their vulnerability to environmental degradation are not wrong to focus attention on the material effectiveness of environmental and sustainability governance. However, the question arises whether law still has a role to play, and if so, what that role should be.

International environmental law has been a highly dynamic, innovative body of law since its inception. At all levels—legal principles, regime-building, construction of legal texts, and the development of processes, structures, and institutions to support the confection and implementation of legal norms and standards—IEL has been a site of experimentation and innovation. The advent of the SDGs is of great interest and importance to IEL, as it appears that this initiative may inaugurate a new approach whereby legal normativity runs in a parallel track alongside the cognitive approach represented by the SDGs. This would be an unfortunate development. As the evolution of the climate regime has demonstrated, there are good reasons for normative and cognitive to relate to one another. The Paris Agreement, adopted in the same year as the SDGs, shows some promise of bringing these two approaches together. Of particular interest is an apparent rediscovery of formal law, namely an obligation of means that may serve to structure and discipline the development and implementation of states' individual commitments to work towards carbon neutrality, and the ongoing emphasis on procedural obligations, the workhorses of the climate regime. The climate regime may indicate a promising pathway to change, namely a more robust engagement between normative and cognitive approaches to environmental and sustainability governance.

[2] Mike Hulme, 'Reducing the Future to Climate: A Story of Climate Determinism and Reductionism' [2011] Osiris 245; Elinor Ostrom, 'Polycentric Systems for Coping with Collective Action and Global Environmental Change' [2010] Global Environmental Change 550.

The analysis presented here reveals how states' inability to deploy international law to make significant and lasting progress towards environmental protection and sustainability goals pushed the change initiatives outside of the normative realm into the world of metrics such as standards and indicators. Put in the language of the PATHS project's theoretical framework, the frustration of the multilateral path and its failure to bring about meaningful environmental protection was notably complemented by the bureaucratic pathway's attempts to provide metrics-based solutions.[3] Relying on expert authority, international institutions contributed to the turn to metrics and performance-oriented cognitive standards, which came to operate in parallel to normative standards. This increasingly visible trend has circumvented the logic of law, as well as having an impact on the form of law, notably through increased reliance within environmental regimes on metrics.

My first task in this chapter is to call into question the narrative of stasis in IEL. I begin by identifying important dynamic dimensions in IEL. I then turn to a discussion of the interplay between metrics and law, pointing out that IEL has incorporated metrics from the fairly early stages. Through a case study of the Paris Agreement on Climate Change, I point to ongoing experimentation in IEL regimes with embedding metrics in a legal framework, thus promoting—or at least creating the potential to promote—important dimensions of rule of law. I argue that it is precisely through the interplay between scientific and technical expertise and legal normativity that environmental regimes develop the capacity to learn and adapt, responding not only to environmental degradation but also to the abiding need in international society for fundamental prestations of law: stability, predictability, fairness and equitableness, and due process.

2. Promoting the Dynamism of IEL

Dynamism seems intuitively to be an important property for a system or body of law to possess. Social change is rapid and accelerating; as for ecosystem degradation, it is both steady and rapid, and subject to negative feedback loops that accelerate the pace of that deterioration. Complexity, uncertainty, and heavy reliance on rapidly evolving scientific knowledge also seem to demand dynamism of international law, both in the form of rapid responses to shifting epistemic inputs and in the form of learning as the impacts of legal, judicial, and policy initiatives come to be observed. It seems clear that IEL ought to display dynamism, but what form should this take? What ends should dynamism serve in IEL? These are crucial questions to ask regarding legal systems, given that key prestations of law include

[3] Nico Krisch and Ezgi Yildiz, 'The Many Paths of Change in International Law: A Frame' in Nico Krisch and Ezgi Yildiz (eds), *The Many Paths of Change in International Law* (Oxford University Press 2023).

the provision of a degree of order, stability, and predictability. Looked at from a non-instrumental point of view, law's crucial contribution to society is stabilization of expectations,[4] which in turn depends on a degree of stasis in law, or at least on a rate and direction of change that are not at odds with this end. How might this balance be struck?

It is often argued, and very often simply assumed, that dynamism is necessary to legal systems in order to keep up with rapid changes in the society that these systems govern. Under conditions of social acceleration,[5] social changes take a variety of forms: technological advances, rapid—and accelerating—rates of ecosystem change, evolution of scientific and other forms of knowledge and insight, and rapid changes in social structures and processes. In the face of these various changes, law must 'keep up', it would seem. What is often meant by this is that the substantive content of legal norms must be subject to ongoing change: the substance of instruction rules that guide the behaviour of subjects of law must be continually updated, and new bodies of law must be developed in response to the emergence of new problems or phenomena or, more likely, new conceptions of such problems. This approach to legal dynamism tends to be predicated on a highly materialistic, instrumental perspective on law. If law is assumed to consist mainly of commands and instruction norms that guide behaviour to bring it in line with policy objectives, then it would stand to reason that when new problems emerge or understandings of them evolve, the appropriate legal response is innovation: new rules, new bodies of law. Within this conception, law is not necessarily conceived of as a system but rather as a collection of rules, of which the most salient are instruction rules. In contrast, a systemic approach reveals the resources available to legal systems to evolve in the face of changes within society, including material changes such as industrialization and environmental degradation, but also extending to social changes such as evolving attitudes towards ecosystems. Legal systems are able to evolve, for example by bringing norms into relation to one another in novel ways, or by pushing the interpretation of norms and legal institutions in new directions. This evolution can be prompted by legislation, but it is mainly driven by myriad processes of norm interpretation and application in contexts of adjudication, management of compliance, ongoing decision-making within administrative bodies, and in many cases input from observers such as scholars and civil society organizations. These contributions do not necessarily take the form of new rules as such, but rather of new ways of conceiving of and interpreting legal rules, and innovative approaches to working with legal normativity.

Martti Koskenniemi's conception of constitutionalism as mindset helps us to observe these capacities and the possibilities to which they give rise. Constitutionalism

[4] Martin Albrow and Niklas Luhmann (eds), *A Sociological Theory of Law* (Routledge 2014).

[5] Hartmut Rosa and William E Scheuerman, *High-Speed Society: Social Acceleration, Power, and Modernity* (Penn State University Press 2009).

as mindset reminds us that law is not an autonomous machine, acting on problems and disputes; instead, legal norms are put in motion by actors that refer to them as guides to behaviour or problem-solving, seek to problematize them, bring them into relation with one another—in short, make use of and interact with them. In the context of interpretation and application of laws, Koskenniemi, drawing on his work with the International Law Commission's Study Group on Fragmentation,[6] makes the important point—one that appears self-evident but which, in IEL in any event, has come to be obscured—that:

> the application of any one rule presumes the presence of principles about how to determine the rule's validity, whom it binds, how to interpret it, and what consequences might follow from its breach. You could not just take one bit and leave the rest aside: *il n'y pas de hors-droit*.[7]

Key to this form of evolution within a system is authoritative, or at least persuasive, interpretation and application of rules, principles, and concepts; that is, the bringing to bear of the resources of a legal system on novel problems or issues in creative ways. International environmental law suffers somewhat from a dearth of adjudication, but processes of interpretation and application take place within implementation and compliance processes, as well as in the day-to-day work of IEL regimes. We will return below to the actual and potential contributions of compliance processes in particular.

2.1 Forms of Dynamism in IEL

Legislative or regulatory processes involving the updating of the content of instruction norms are not the only ways in which the dynamism of IEL can or does manifest itself, but they are important, nonetheless. Social acceleration in general, and rapid ecological change in particular, present good reasons for promoting the ongoing renewal of IEL norms. Also relevant are the complexity of human society and ecosystems, and resulting uncertainty, notably about causation. Proponents of adaptive ecosystem management have long argued that legal rules and standards should be understood not as conclusions but rather as hypotheses.[8] Rational

[6] Martti Koskenniemi, 'Fragmentation of International Law: Difficulties Arising from the Diversification and Expansion of International Law: Report of the Study Group of the International Law Commission' A/CN.4/L.682, 13 April 2006.

[7] Martti Koskenniemi, 'Constitutionalism as Mindset: Reflections on Kantian Themes about International Law and Globalization' [2007] Theoretical Inquiries in Law 9, 19.

[8] JB Ruhl, 'Thinking of Environmental Law as a Complex Adaptive System: How to Clean Up the Environment by Making a Mess of Environmental Law' [1997] Houston Law Review 933; Carl Folke and others, 'Adaptive Governance of Social-Ecological Systems' [2005] Annual Review of Environment and Resources 441.

planning models, which, despite decades of harsh criticism, are still highly influential in thinking about governance, posit a process of information gathering and analysis followed by decision, or, to put it another way, inputs of all available pertinent information and outputs in the form of policy and regulation.[9] However, knowledge gaps make it necessary to decide in the face of considerable uncertainty, while complexity, particularly taking the form of non-linearity, makes it difficult to predict how policy interventions will work out. We cannot predict how effective legal innovations will be in the narrow sense of promoting the stated policy objective. This is largely due to the capacity of regulated actors to behave reflexively in the face of legal innovations, finding ways to accomplish their goals within the constraints that new rules impose, often disrupting the manner in which those rules were meant to operate. Much of the time, the rules are more or less deliberately circumvented through the exploitation of loopholes, for example. But a great deal of the time, regulated actors are not necessarily seeking to undermine the objectives the rules seek to promote; they are simply responding to the changes that the rules make to their environments and their plans in ways that their drafters may not have intended or predicted.

In attending to feedback regarding the effectiveness, and unintended consequences, of legal innovation, it is not only the extent to which legal rules promote material policy objectives that stands to be considered. Other, broader objectives of legal systems are at least equally important: order, predictability, and stability; fairness; respect for human rights and for due process; and so on. One important way in which unintended consequences of environmental law and policy play themselves out, particularly in a society as unequal as international society, is through the inequitable distribution of costs and benefits of policies, with vulnerable groups and communities often made more vulnerable as a result of legal initiatives, even in contexts in which those initiatives were designed specifically to help them.

If the introduction of legal innovation sets in motion an uncertain, non-linear, unpredictable series of events, actions, and reactions, then close attention to the nature and direction of those changes is necessary to inform ongoing adjustments to legal norms and the manner of their application. This is not to suggest that observation of these feedbacks will point in the direction of clear conclusions regarding further rounds of legal change; the non-linear nature of causation in operation between law and the world makes this impossible. It does mean, however, that the process of legal interpretation, application, reform, and generation is one of ongoing observation, reflection, judgement, and decision. In the context of environment and sustainability in particular, these judgements and decisions stand to be informed by data that is collected and analysed through organizations such

[9] The concept of wicked problems, first described in the 1970s, has enjoyed a huge resurgence of interest as a means of describing and analysing global environmental change: Horst WJ Rittel and Melvin M Webber, 'Dilemmas in General Theory of Planning' [1973] Policy Sciences 154.

as the Intergovernmental Panel on Climate Change (IPCC), the scientific and technical bodies of individual regimes, and through the ambitious and wide-ranging—but also deeply flawed—SDGs. Introducing these managerial approaches into a discussion of constitutionalism as mindset may seem misguided, but as discussed below, much is likely to depend on the manner in which sustainability indicators and other metrics are understood, and in particular the extent to which they are seen to interact with legal normativity.

2.2 Alternate Pathways

The increased prominence of metrics in IEL, and the adoption of the SDGs more particularly, are, as noted above, illustrative of a larger trend that can be observed across jurisdictional levels and issue-areas, and within states and international organizations as well as private organizations, towards more cognitive forms of governance, of which metrics such as goals and indicators are a prominent example. This trend is generally assumed to be driven by neoliberalism, understood as a retreat of the state and greater reliance on private entities to implement governance initiatives. This is how the emergence of New Public Management (NPM) is often understood by critics of neoliberalism; NPM involves a partial retreat by governmental agencies that devolve the implementation and delivery of programmes and services to private actors, while retaining responsibility for establishing policy and programme objectives.[10] This division of labour tends to increase reliance on metrics that permit government agencies to evaluate the performance of the organizations to which responsibilities have been delegated.[11] It is true that non-state regulatory authorities are increasingly active in environmental governance, including at the international—or rather transnational—level, operating across jurisdictional boundaries and relying heavily on economic incentive structures. But neither the SDGs nor the Paris Agreement seem to represent neoliberal approaches, however this term may be understood. Moreover, neoliberalism generally and NPM in particular do not shed much light on the long-standing influence of metrics in IEL. Among the background conditions that paved the way for the SDGs, a reaction against the narrowly focused approach taken in their predecessor project, the Millennium Development Goals, and a long-standing turn away from law by the United Nations Environment Program that was clearly underway in the early 2000s, appear to be prominent. While this cannot be the whole explanation, the SDGs seem to be influenced by two factors: the wave of regime-building in the 1980s and 1990s in which law was seen in largely material, instrumental terms; and a later loss of faith in law as an instrument of material and behavioural change.

[10] Christopher Hood, 'A Public Management for All Seasons' (1991) 69 Public Administration 3, 3–5.
[11] Michael Power, *The Audit Society: Rituals of Verification* (OUP 1999) 43.

Just as metrics have long been an important component of IEL, the turn to metrics is part of a broader trend of increased cognitivization of law.[12] A key feature of legal normativity (and normativity in general) is resistance to learning in the face of disappointment. When a legal norm is violated, it does not follow that the norm is invalid; rather, violation generates an expectation of consequences, themselves organized through legal norms. Cognitive standards, on the other hand, stand to be revised when they do not function as intended: for example, if changes to an industrial process do not allow a firm to attain emissions reductions objectives, further changes must be adopted, or a different pollution control approach implemented. There are good reasons to turn to cognitive approaches at the international level. The articulation and ongoing legitimation of normative standards are demanding processes, particularly in a society as heterogeneous and inegalitarian as international society. Norms depend on some degree of consensus regarding collective objectives to be pursued, as well as common notions of how one ought to behave in light of those objectives. They also require acceptance of the authority of institutions and processes through which norms are created, interpreted, and applied. Problem-solving and dispute-resolution through normative frameworks call for judgement, and acceptance of those judgements requires a reasonably high degree of confidence in the judging actors and institutions. Cognitive standards, on the other hand, are much easier to apply in a consistent and objective manner. They do not depend, at least not in transparent ways, on conceptions of what is appropriate, fair, or reasonable in a given context, but rather on the bringing to bear of forms of expertise and processes of reasoning that constrain the influence of the perspectives, priorities, or ideologies of the actor who is making assessments and reaching conclusions. In other words, cognitive standards *appear* to obviate the need for judgement, making them seem extremely well suited to governance contexts in which broad and deep acceptance of the authority of political and legal structures, institutions, and processes cannot be taken for granted.

While there is no doubt that IEL regimes that incorporate metrics are often strongly oriented towards material, instrumental approaches to law, and certain regimes, notably that for climate change, have tended to incorporate market mechanisms and economic incentive structures, once again, the turn to metrics does not here seem to be driven by a preoccupation with shrinking the state or restricting its fields of activity. These moves seem to have much more to do with pragmatic assessments of the limits of international diplomacy, a recognition that instruction rules do not on their own compel states to change their behaviour, and an acknowledgment that international environmental regimes cannot be built around deep consensus on the objectives to be achieved and the means to attain them. However, it also appears that the architects of these regimes have been working

[12] Albrow and Luhmann (eds), *Sociological Theory* (n 4); Niklas Luhmann, 'Die Weltgesellschaft' in *Soziologische Aufklärung 2* (Springer 1975) 51.

with a unidimensional perspective on law, one that pays insufficient attention to the non-instrumental, non-material dimensions of law.

Early initiatives to develop a body of international environmental law focused significant attention on formal rules that have a structure similar to that of private law. Chief among these was the obligation to take reasonable measures to prevent transboundary harm, articulated in the 1972 Stockholm Declaration's Principle 21[13] and the 1992 Rio Declaration's Principle 2,[14] and further developed in the International Law Commission's Draft Articles on Transboundary Harm.[15] Attention soon turned away from formal rules with a wave of regime-building characterized by highly innovative approaches to enhancing incentives to join and remain in regimes; structuring decision-making, with a focus on the incorporation of scientific inputs; and promoting compliance with obligations. Law was rather neglected in processes of constructing regimes and implementing standards.[16] An excellent illustration of this neglect is the approach initially taken within implementation and compliance procedures: decisions about individual states' transgressions and the approaches to be taken to bring them back into compliance tended to be made in an ad hoc, highly pragmatic manner, with little regard for procedural fairness or equitable treatment across cases. The implementation of consequences and compliance plans was often approached without due regard to the principle of non-retroactivity and publicity of legal norms and standards.[17] In short, these processes were generally not regarded as legal processes, or even as processes in which a certain degree of legalization ought to be respected. Anna Huggins has indicated that this situation is gradually changing in some regimes, and that a higher degree of regard for procedural legal norms, standards, and principles can now be observed in some contexts.

This brief discussion has sought to indicate that IEL regimes have been heavily influenced by metrics, and that, although the deployment of metrics has taken place within a legal framework, legal normativity and cognitive metrics have tended to move along parallel tracks. The SDGs represent a departure from this approach: they are avowedly political, not ensconced in a legal framework. Indeed, one could argue that the SDG framework treats bodies of law relevant

[13] Stockholm Declaration (1972).

[14] Rio Declaration (1992).

[15] International Law Commission, 'Draft Articles on Prevention of Transboundary Harm from Hazardous Activities' (2001).

[16] Martti Koskenniemi, 'Breach of Treaty or Non-Compliance? Reflections on the Enforcement of the Montreal Protocol' (1992) 3 Yearbook of International Environmental Law 123; Koskenniemi, 'Constitutionalism as Mindset' (n 7); Martti Koskenniemi, 'Formalism, Fragmentation, Freedom: Kantian Themes in Today's International Law' [2007] No Foundations 7; Anna Huggins, 'The Desirability of Depoliticization: Compliance in the International Climate Regime' [2015] Transnational Environmental Law 101; Anna Huggins, *Multilateral Environmental Agreements and Compliance: The Benefits of Administrative Procedures* (Routledge 2017).

[17] Huggins, 'Desirability of Depoliticization' (n 16); Huggins, *Multilateral Environmental Agreements* (n 16).

to sustainability as additional data points that feed into its cognitive approach. A combination of factors has contributed to this situation. In the first place, the properties of IEL norms have been deemed inappropriate to the projects of environmental protection and sustainability: first formal then instrumental norms have been tried and, if not abandoned, then relegated to less influential roles. There are many indications that cognitive approaches are in the ascendant, and that serious doubts are being harboured about the relevance of legal normativity, with its flexibility and openness to interpretation and resulting need for political legitimation, to international environmental law. Secondly, the influence of NPM approaches has created a discursive opening for serious consideration of a more explicitly cognitive approach.

3. Turn to Metrics

The adoption of the SDGs in 2015 is a high-water mark for the influence of metrics in global sustainability governance, as well as a potential threat to the role and influence of legal normativity in that field. The SDGs, and other metrics, are organized around a series of goals, often phrased in very broad terms, with more specific targets associated with each, as well as a series of indicators for measuring progress towards each target. Reliance on metrics in domestic and international governance has been criticized in literatures in a variety of disciplines. One facet of these critiques is the tension between the logics of metrics and norms, which, due to the strength of expert inputs in public discourse, and more particularly to the influence of quantitative forms of knowledge, tends to play out in favour of metrics. Another facet is the tendency to assume that quantitative inputs are objective, in the specific sense of reflecting reality rather than opinion and belief, derived in a manner independent of judgement or appreciation. Were such a form of knowledge possible, it would clearly be of immense value in a heterogeneous, highly unequal society such as international society whose institutions do not rest on widely and deeply held beliefs in their legitimacy or authority. Claims to objectivity in this sense of the term tend, however, simply to mask the political and normative stakes at work in the design and implementation of metrics.

Some of the criticisms of law, and the arguments in favour of sustainability metrics as key governance tools, stem from certain assumptions about law in general and IEL in particular. International environmental law is often seen as inadequate because insufficiently instrumental. If the most important objective by far of IEL is deemed to be promoting particular material outcomes such as decreased levels of atmospheric carbon or a halt to habitat destruction, then the emphasis in many IEL regimes, notably the climate regime, on process, procedure, and the structure of decision-making, will no doubt seem misplaced. The decentralized structure of international law and the importance that states bestow on their sovereignty and independence place a command-and-control approach out of reach, while setting broad objectives and making states accountable for their progress towards these objectives is a more plausible approach. Given the vital importance of these objectives, devoting resources to assessing the extent to which they are being promoted makes eminent sense. But this turn to metrics does open up a series of questions about the role of law: must legal normativity recede into the background? Do norms and metrics necessarily operate on parallel tracks? What could be achieved through various forms of interaction between these logics, promoted by different paths of international law, and how could robust forms of interaction be structured?

One plausible argument is that the increased influence of metrics in IEL, pushed primarily by the bureaucratic path, is a salutary development, likely to inject some much-needed dynamism into a body of law that has been gravely afflicted by scientific controversies, lack of political will, failure to gain traction regarding both state behaviour and the accelerating environmental crisis, and—yes—stasis. The Kyoto Protocol's timeline for an emissions reduction target, which was widely acknowledged to be utterly inadequate, was initially 2012, but was extended to 2020 by a decision by the Meeting of the Parties (MOP)[18] in the face of repeated failure of states to adopt a successor instrument. Given the overwhelming scientific evidence of grave risks of ecological catastrophe, this result seems more like capitulation than failure. So why not change tracks? Why not conclude that law can no longer be seen as the main vehicle driving environmental protection, and shift to a different strategy and approach? Metrics and other quantitative approaches to governance have much to contribute to governance in contexts in which the legitimacy of political and legal authorities and institutions is not a matter of widespread, deeply held consensus—as in international society. However, the limitations of metrics quickly emerge in turn.

3.1 Metrics and Authority

The central obligations of the climate change regime, namely decreased levels of atmospheric carbon through reduction of sources and removal by sinks, depend heavily on the gathering and reporting of extensive data, and therefore on the panoply of rules regulating these processes, including methodologies to be used to derive this data. This is hardly surprising given the immense importance of methodology; the need for transparency to promote confidence in data; and the presentation of data to facilitate comparisons across time, space, industrial sector, etc. But this emphasis on methodology and procedure, and the development of legal rules for this purpose, do represent important contrasts to the approach taken in the

[18] Doha Amendment to the Kyoto Protocol, Decision 1/CMP.8, 8 December 2012.

SDGs. The climate regime has long displayed awareness, absent in the SDG framework, that rules governing the gathering and reporting of data may, in their way, be almost as important to the regime's operation as rules about carbon emissions and sinks themselves. The rules on data collection and reporting are also of interest in that they constitute a crucial point of intersection between science and law, each serving to reinforce the other, since neither expertise nor legal normativity is adequate on its own to generate the necessary authority to support the system of norms embedded in the climate regime.

The authority of international law, and of international legal and political institutions, rest on fragile foundations, given the heterogeneous, unequal, and decentralized nature of international society and the necessarily horizontal structure of international law. While many international organizations rely at least to some extent on the reputations of their leaders, it is highly unlikely that widespread trust in the capacity of an office-holder to make a judgement will be generated by generally held perceptions of that individual's wisdom, expertise, fair-mindedness, and rigour.[19] An alternative basis for the grounding of authority, particularly useful in contexts in which trust in institutions or individual decision-makers is inadequate to the task, is expertise. However, whether in international or domestic contexts, expertise in the form of specialized knowledge and skill is no longer enough to bestow authority and legitimacy on a decision. As the lessons derived from implementation and compliance procedures have taught us, it is important that expertise be exercised in a particular way, in conformity with a series of rules, standards, and practices that lend it objectivity. The forms of objectivity that are apposite here are disciplinary objectivity anchored in consensus, for example the consensus of a community of experts; and mechanical objectivity, involving adherence to rules and standards that operate as a check on subjectivity, interestedness, and partiality.[20] Neither expertise itself nor rules, processes, and designated methodologies obviate the need for judgement on the part of decision-makers, of course, but, as Theodore M Porter puts it, they may make 'mere judgment, with all its gaps and idiosyncrasies, [seem] almost to disappear'.[21] Porter also notes that the apparent eclipsing of judgement is particularly likely when the expert knowledge being applied involves quantification and calculation: numbers appear non-arbitrary and impartial,[22] especially when they are based on standardized measures and classifications that can come to have a taken-for-granted quality, despite the work, evaluations, and judgements that go into their creation.[23]

[19] Theodore M Porter, *Trust in Numbers: The Pursuit of Objectivity in Science and Public Life* (Princeton University Press 2001) 7.

[20] ibid 3–4.

[21] ibid 7.

[22] ibid 8.

[23] ibid 25.

The heavy reliance of the climate regime on data, and the thicket of rules, procedures, and accepted methodologies that guide the production, reporting, and analysis of that data, could be seen as a double-edged sword. On one hand, the data possess objectivity in the important sense that they are not heavily dependent on personal preference: different individual experts ought to produce similar results working through these procedures regardless of their predilections or biases. In this light, the procedural rules operate to promote the rule of law, in that it is the rules not the personal preferences or perspectives of the agent applying the rules that guide the process. Under these conditions, like cases will tend to be treated alike. On the other hand, the choices that have been made in the design of these methodologies and procedural rules are neither neutral nor free of judgement. Yet the judgements and choices that undergird these procedural rules are screened from view, with the result that they can be easy to forget, and with the further result that their various impacts on the resulting data and influences on conclusions reached cannot readily be rendered visible.

One of the frequently cited results of reliance on governance metrics is a narrowing of political space: decisions are framed as essentially technical, expert-driven matters not requiring the exercise of judgement.[24] As a result, consideration of different perspectives, discussion, and debate are seen as largely beside the point. In this sense, reliance on metrics tends to pull away from democratic principles. At the same time, the use of quantification in political decision-making may also be understood to promote democratic principles. Methodological and procedural rules guiding the collection and presentation of data promote objectivity in a particular sense of the term. Objectivity is often understood as judgement-free knowledge that simply reflects reality rather than consisting of interpretations of the shared world; this is not the meaning intended here. Among many other meanings, the term relates to constraints operating upon decision-makers that compel them to look past personal preferences and prejudices and follow a series of standards and criteria in conducting their analyses. In this sense, objectivity is consonant with the rule of law, promoting an impersonal, impartial approach but not eliminating judgement.[25] Moreover, objectivity in this sense pulls away from elitism by reducing the influence of subjectivity.[26] At the international level, particularly respecting a regime such as climate change, with its major implications for national economies and societies and its high stakes for a wide variety of actors, neither the regime itself nor international law writ large has the capacity to generate the necessary compliance pull.

[24] Wendy Nelson Espeland and Mitchell L Stevens, 'A Sociology of Quantification' [2008] European Journal of Sociology/Archives Européennes de Sociologie 401; Sally Engle Merry, 'Measuring the World: Indicators, Human Rights, and Global Governance' (2011) 52 Current Anthropology S83.

[25] Porter (n 19) 74.

[26] ibid 75.

Metrics are attractive to observers of international environmental governance because they appear to promote a certain type of objectivity, akin to universal validity, and to obviate the need for messy, complex, and highly normative processes of judgement. Metrics have gained a very prominent role in international environmental governance with the 2015 adoption of the SDGs, but they have long constituted important dimensions of IEL regimes. The recent adoption of the Paris Agreement is seen by many to signal a capitulation to the performance-oriented, data-driven logic of New Public Management, notably because that agreement does not contain individualized emissions reductions targets for its parties but rather calls on them to establish their own targets in the form of Nationally Determined Contributions (NDCs). The Paris Agreement is still very much a work in progress, but it is possible to discern in its design a potential for bringing together epistemic and normative forms of authority, and more particularly the logics of law and metrics.

4. The Paris Agreement

The Paris Agreement has disappointed many for a range of reasons, the most dramatic being the projected significant shortfall in the collective commitments, which at present are clearly inadequate to avoid warming of less than 2°C above pre-industrialization levels.[27] While this is a significant and deeply troubling failure, my focus here is not on the effectiveness of the regime as such, but rather on certain features of the regime, and of the Paris Agreement more particularly, that have some capacity to foster a robust and fruitful interaction between science and law. Daniel Bodansky describes the Paris Agreement's structure as a hybrid between bottom-up—notably the NDCs to reduce carbon emissions and promote carbon removal by sinks—and top-down, embedding voluntary commitments in a legal regime that conditions and structures these commitments as well as efforts towards their realization.[28] Bodansky is among the commentators who have, if not praised, then at least acknowledged the appropriateness of this approach, particularly in light of the fact that Paris extends emissions reduction obligations to all parties, while Kyoto's reduction obligations applied only to developed states. The universal applicability of reduction obligations is a significant, and necessary, achievement, increasing the odds that developing states may shift to a low-carbon development path.

[27] United Nations, Conference of the Parties serving as Meeting of the Parties to the Paris Agreement, Decision 1.CMA.2, Madrid, December 2019, para 5. The 2° C commitment is set out in the Paris Agreement (2015), art 2.

[28] Daniel Bodansky, 'The Paris Climate Change Agreement: A New Hope?' [2016] American Journal of International Law 288.

Paris may have moved much further along the spectrum towards NPM, but managerial approaches generally and metrics in particular have been part of the structure of the climate regime since its inception. However, there is reason to doubt that the logic of managerialism has completely taken over the regime, and some reason to hope that the potential of the regime to discipline the logic of metrics and subject it to the rule of law has been strengthened with the advent of the Paris Agreement. Paris pays great attention to transparency, and to the accountability of parties through highly structured reporting requirements; consistency and commensurability of data reported through the imposition of common methodologies; and a structured process for reviewing global and individual progress, and for increasing the ambition of individual commitments. Interestingly, this hybrid approach has the capacity to render the Paris Agreement much more dynamic than the Kyoto Protocol, with its hard-won but ultimately static schedule of reduction obligations. Because a process for ratcheting up the ambition of commitments was not built into the structure of Kyoto, the approach of the deadline for largely unmet emissions reduction obligations may have accomplished the opposite of what a deadline is intended to achieve. Rather than building up pressure on the parties, the deadline seemed to have been viewed as an expiry date, transforming the obligatory emissions reduction targets into a lame-duck arrangement.

4.1 Procedural Obligations

Unlike Kyoto, which had substantive reduction obligations at its core,[29] the Paris Agreement is largely—or perhaps simply more obviously—procedural.[30] The central obligation is the preparation of NDCs and their renewal every five years.[31] In their NDCs, parties are to set a target for peak greenhouse gas (GHG) emissions and subsequent reductions, account being taken of the different positions and resulting differences in expectations for developed and developing states.[32] A series of standards and expectations regarding NDCs is specified. For example, successive NDCs 'will represent a progression beyond the Party's then current nationally determined contribution and reflect its highest possible ambition'.[33] Adjustments to an NDC may be made along the way, but only to 'enhanc[e] its level of ambition'.[34]

[29] An overall emissions reduction target of 5 per cent below 1990 levels was established; in addition, developed country parties negotiated their own emissions reduction obligations, ranging from an 8 per cent reduction to a 10 per cent increase: Kyoto Protocol to the United Nations Framework Convention on Climate Change (UNFCCC) (1997).

[30] Alexander Zahar, 'Collective Obligation and Individual Ambition in the Paris Agreement' [2020] Transnational Environmental Law 168s.

[31] Paris Agreement, art 4.

[32] ibid art 4(1).

[33] ibid art 4(3).

[34] ibid art 4(11).

Naturally enough, there are myriad ways to engage in sleight of hand, appearing to ratchet up ambition while in fact lightening one's load. This has been addressed by providing that the MOP is to provide guidance on the matter,[35] opening up an avenue for standards to measure ambition or, less likely, a review or evaluation of mid-term adjustments to NDCs. Naturally, it remains to be seen how effective these checks will be.

Benoît Mayer's argument that the carbon reduction obligations in the Paris Agreement set out obligations of conduct reveals that these obligations may not be as purely procedural as they appear at first glance: the Agreement specifies standards that are defined in terms of the level of ambition of NDCs.[36] As Alexander Zahar notes, the ambition of the parties' commitments is specified in two ways: first, the need for individual states to set ambitious targets; and secondly, the creation, through the Agreement's overall objective, of what he argues is a collective obligation. The requirement to specify NDCs that collectively bring warming well below the 2^{0} threshold provides further content and structure to parties' individual obligations.[37] Zahar does not conclude that the parties have created an actionable, legally binding collective obligation, as this type of legal innovation would, he argues, require clearer and more explicit language.[38] Nevertheless, to pick up on Mayer's argument, Paris may have prepared the ground for the emergence of something resembling a reasonable person standard: an open-ended and flexible principle whose contents are filled out in particular contexts, often, at the domestic level, by courts in the resolution of disputes. The authoritative interpretation and application of such principles is crucial to their effectiveness, because otherwise plausible arguments about the reasonableness of a wide range of conducts could be proffered with no basis for selecting among them and thereby specifying the contents of the standard that is applicable in a given situation. The Paris Agreement provides three main avenues for such authoritative interpretation, making it possible to evaluate the robustness of individual NDCs: technical expert review,[39] the compliance process,[40] and the global stocktake.[41] These elements will be discussed below, but in order better to understand how they will operate and how they may prove to be effective, another set of procedural obligations falls to be considered, namely reporting obligations.

[35] ibid art 4(11).
[36] Benoît Mayer, 'Obligations of Conduct in the International Law on Climate Change: A Defence' [2018] Review of European, Comparative & International Law 130.
[37] Zahar (n 30).
[38] ibid 179.
[39] The Paris Agreement provides that the parties' progress towards their NDCs falls to be evaluated through a technical expert review, which includes 'identify[ing] areas of improvement for the Party:' Paris Agreement, art 13(12).
[40] ibid art 15.
[41] ibid art 14.

The climate regime, along with other environmental regimes, pushed obligations to report on progress towards meeting the regime's goals well beyond the realm of pro forma compliance, and the Paris Agreement has moved further still in this regard. States' reporting requirements are carefully specified, and the methodologies to be used for the presentation of data make it somewhat more difficult for states, knowingly or unknowingly, to disguise underperformance through data reporting approaches that deviate from the specified standards. Many of the norms that structure the collection and reporting of data are found in the Agreement itself, while others remain to be specified by subsequent decisions of the MOP.[42] The workhorses in this process are methodological standards and other specifications regarding the manner in which data are to be collected, collated, and reported. The process of developing approved methodologies has long been underway, having been a central task of the Subsidiary Body on Scientific and Technical Advice, established in the 1992 UNFCCC. Nor do states have the last word on the data they report: since 2003, the regime provides for a review process of parties' inventories of GHG sources and sinks.[43] The Paris Agreement contains a fairly extensive provision on a transparency framework, including an obligation to prepare the inventory 'using good practice methodologies' accepted by the IPCC and agreed on by the MOP.[44] The inventories, as well as developed countries' pledges of financial, technological, and capacity-building support, are subject to a review process, the technical expert review.[45] There is a good deal of experience within the climate change regime with methodologies for measuring and reporting GHG emissions and their removal by sinks. Due to the complexity of these phenomena and the resulting difficulties associated with their measurement, issues of methodology are of immense importance. Not only is it essential to measure emissions accurately and reliably, but it is perhaps just as essential that the methodologies and modalities for measuring and reporting be sufficiently consistent across time and space to admit of comparison and evaluation against common standards. There is significant potential for promoting transparency and consistency of data—of great importance in a regime that depends heavily on mutual assurance.

It is important to note that common methodologies and approaches would be vital even if there were no reason to fear that states would seek to game the system. Inadequate methodologies, or defensible methodologies that nevertheless produce

[42] eg para 13 of art 4 identifies a series of principles or objectives which parties are to respect in reporting their achievements: 'environmental integrity, transparency, accuracy, completeness, comparability and consistency, and ... the avoidance of double counting:' ibid art 4(13). Parties are to 'take into account ... existing methods and guidance under the Convention', guidance which is to be provided by MOP decisions: ibid art 4(14).

[43] UNFCCC guidelines for the technical review of greenhouse gas inventories from Parties included in Annex I to the Convention, Decision 19/CP.8, November 2002. The decision provides for the guidelines it contains to become applicable in 2003: para 2.

[44] Paris Agreement, art 13(7)(a).

[45] ibid art 13(11).

bodies of data that cannot be reliably compared to one another, would diminish the utility of data reporting. If individual states were able not only to set their targets but also decide for themselves how they were to be measured, the regime's potential effectiveness would be severely, perhaps critically, endangered. This would be the case even in a context in which all parties had every confidence in the good faith and high level of commitment to the regime's objectives on the part of all other parties. In short, this is a vital component of the regime. The presence of third-party verification and validation of national reports does not guarantee the regime's effectiveness, but it does lay a crucial stone on the foundation of the regime's effectiveness.

Two of the important dimensions of the methodologies are robustness and consistency. In addition, different methodologies, even if they are acknowledged to be sound, will have different repercussions for differently situated actors. In other words, the selection among methodologies is not merely a matter of quality; it will also be a question of equity. This is in part because of the need for methodologies to be relatively easy to apply, and to produce results that are reasonably easy to interpret and analyse. But it is also because, as with the establishment of baselines to establish pollution reduction obligations, given approaches will confer advantages on some parties and disadvantages on others, often quite arbitrarily. Therefore, even something as apparently technical as methodologies for compiling and reporting GHG inventories has political dimensions and requires the making of judgements. As a result, confidence in the structures and processes through which these decisions are made is necessary—and, for reasons already discussed, difficult to establish in international society.

Another important feature of the Paris Agreement is the global stocktake provided for in Article 14, which has been aptly described as:

> the central vehicle to create a dynamic towards enhanced ambition by linking the cycles of the Agreement to its purpose and long-term goals. The global stocktake may thus help parties to transcend purely domestic perspectives and adjust their actions to what they need to do to reach their common objectives.[46]

The nature of the legal obligations created by this provision has been the object of some debate, in part because of its fundamental importance to the dynamism of the Agreement, and thus the regime as a whole, and in part because it creates a collective rather than individualized obligation. The main, or at least the stated, purpose of the stocktake is to 'assess the collective progress towards achieving' the Agreement's purpose and goals,[47] notably maintaining global warming well below 2°C. The first exercise is currently being prepared, with a meeting to consider

[46] Daniel Klein and others, *The Paris Climate Agreement: Analysis and Commentary* (OUP 2017) 337.
[47] Paris Agreement, art 14(1).

outputs scheduled for 2023; thereafter, it is to occur every five years. The adequacy of NDCs is addressed indirectly by Article 14: '[t]he outcome of the global stock-take shall inform parties in updating and enhancing . . . their actions and support.'[48] The logic of performance evaluation in particular, and NPM more generally, is strongly inscribed in this provision. Its structure provides no legal recourse and no avenue for the imposition of legal consequences in the event of a failure to meet the Agreement's goals, not least because none of these goals, not even the 2°C goal, can be declined into legally binding obligations for individual states. As frustrating as this may be from the point of view of global climate action, it is not inappropriate, given the very different degrees of responsibility and capacity of individual states and the futility, in a heterogeneous and highly unequal international society, of seeking consensus on the assignment of carbon budgets to individual states on a top-down basis. It is also worth pointing out that simply making a standard legally binding does not in and of itself increase the compliance pull of the standard; in a horizontal system such as international law, compliance pull depends on a range of other factors.

As would be expected of a reasonably skilfully crafted legal text, Article 14 does not stand alone. What potential it possesses may be realized through the interaction between a number of different provisions in the Agreement, as well as norms present in the broader climate change regime.[49] These include the range of provisions, backed by institutional mechanisms and processes, to promote transparency and accountability (including the fairly rigorous reporting obligations) as well as the unidirectional nature of adjustments to NDCs: they may only become more ambitious. The point of this argument is not to demonstrate that the Paris Agreement is bound, or even likely, to reach its ambitious goals. No agreement can generate political will, nor bring about material results through linear causation. The argument made here is, rather, that the hybrid structure of the Paris Agreement holds out some hope that the data-driven, managerial logic clearly on display will be tempered and, possibly, its effectiveness enhanced, through the embedding of this logic in a legally binding agreement that contains many important features conducive to rule of law.

Alexander Zahar argues that the global stocktake provides a potential avenue to make good on what, in form at least, is a collective obligation to keep warming below the 2° threshold; that it is a means to decline the collective obligation into individual obligations. This would not likely occur if the global stocktake focuses only on individual NDCs but could occur if states are compared to one another or if the sufficiency of their individual ambitions is compared in a reasonably serious and rigorous manner to the nature of the contribution that states would have to

48 ibid art 14(3).

49 Lukas Hermwille and others, 'Catalyzing Mitigation Ambition under the Paris Agreement: Elements for an Effective Global Stocktake' [2019] Climate Policy 996.

make in order to meet the collective goal. Zahar argues that this could easily transpire, given the manner in which the global stocktake is structured. In particular, non-party stakeholders are able to participate; furthermore, Zahar notes that the stocktakes are '"high-level events" that are completely unscripted', and that, as a result, the opportunity to focus the spotlight on overall achievements and away from individual ambition will be much slimmer. Zahar argues that '[t]he process, in practice, is likely to resolve itself into a long argument about individual ambition: in other words, a de facto individuation forum'.[50]

The fact that the Paris Agreement's hybrid structure creates conditions appropriate for a reasonably strong interaction between the logics of metrics and legal normativity does not, of course, guarantee that this potential will be realized. The potential for the global stocktake to shine a light on individual as well as collective ambition and performance may result in a highly political process in which shared understandings and common standards have little influence. This is made more likely by the influence on the Paris Agreement of the principle of common but differentiated responsibility: a single, rigid standard is inappropriate in this context. Incorporating appropriate degrees of flexibility and accommodating different levels of responsibility and capacity might nevertheless permit convergence on conceptions of acceptable claims and arguments in their support, perhaps combined with relatively informal groupings of similarly situated states for purposes of comparison and leveraging of peer pressure. As Lukas Hermwille et al have argued, these standards could take the form of benchmarks for emissions reduction targets based on modelling data and projections.[51] Following on Mayer's logic, they could also take a qualitative rather than quantitative form, akin to the reasonable person standard in private law. The light shed on individual performance by comparative analysis could generate an informal set of understandings regarding what is feasible and practical, perhaps taking the form of best practices which states are expected to emulate.[52] It is unlikely that such norms or standards will emerge spontaneously, and powerful states with high current and historical levels of emissions may strongly resist their articulation in a bid to maintain as much flexibility and manoeuvrability as possible. Nevertheless, the transparency promoted by the Agreement and the various forms of accountability fostered as a result may give a range of actors, including researchers, industry associations, and civil society actors, sufficient leverage to develop such standards and promote their influence.

While the global stocktake is bound to remain a highly political event, whose results will depend significantly on rhetorical strategies, capacity to command attention, and political and economic influence, both Mayer and Zahar have shown that the potential to put in place a normative structure is not insignificant. This

[50] Zahar (n 30) 187.
[51] Hermwille (n 49) 991.
[52] ibid 991–92.

structure's main avenue of influence would likely be at the level of evaluating justifications by individual states of their ambition and performance, as well as arguments about the appropriateness and adequacy of individual states' contributions to the collective goal. This type of influence could nevertheless make a modest contribution to disciplining the exercise of political and economic power in the process by holding up argumentation and justification to evaluative standards that could come to possess some constraining and influencing potential.

The importance of subjecting processes such as the global stocktake to the discipline of norms and standards is brought home by analyses of implementation and compliance procedures in IEL regimes. These procedures provide an excellent example of the dynamism of IEL: they were designed for flexibility and adaptability, oriented around a problem-solving approach for which a high degree of structure and formalism is arguably inappropriate.[53] They also represent a managerial approach at work: conformity to legal norms is treated not so much as a question of respect or violation but of performance. A key tool in these procedures is a compliance plan with measurable objectives, subject to periodical progress reports.

4.2 Compliance in the climate change regime

As the compliance procedure created under the Paris Agreement remains a work in progress,[54] our focus here will be on the predecessor procedure under the auspices of the Kyoto Protocol. At the time, this was the most innovative and ambitious such procedure in IEL,[55] and therefore provides many important lessons, notably respecting the role of legal normativity in this process. Kyoto's compliance process centres on three components: first, expert review teams (ERTs) that review the all-important inventory and reporting requirements; secondly, a facilitative branch (FB) oriented toward overcoming obstacles to compliance; and thirdly, a major innovation, an enforcement branch (EB) focused on compliance with emissions reduction targets assumed by developed states. Given its innovative nature, it is hardly surprising that the compliance procedure did not function as designed. In particular, the respective roles of the ERTs and the FB departed in important respects from the original plan. The ERTs were conceived of as an essential component of the process, granted the capacity to trigger the compliance process 'to ensure that all questions of implementation pertaining to emissions-related

[53] Huggins, 'Desirability of Depoliticization' (n 16) 102.

[54] The bare bones of the compliance procedure are set out in art 15 of the Paris Agreement. Modalities and procedures for the effective operation of the committee to facilitate implementation and promote compliance referred to in art 15(2) are set out in Decision 20/CMA.1, in Report of the Conference of the Parties serving as the Meeting of the Parties to the Paris Agreement, Katowice, December 2018: FCCC/PA/CMA/2018/3/Add.2.

[55] Daniel Bodansky, Jutta Brunnée, and Lavanya Rajamani, International Climate Change Law (OUP 2017) 196.

commitments come before the Compliance Committee, a feature that is designed to enhance transparency with respect to parties' performance, as well as the predictability and credibility of the compliance procedure'.[56] In this manner, potential problems with implementation were to be referred virtually automatically to the appropriate branch of the Compliance Committee.[57] This has not happened, however, as ERTs developed the practice of exercising discretion regarding the treatment of compliance issues.[58] Many observers regard this as problematic, since the triggering of the compliance process was designed to strictly limit the role of discretion at that stage. One result has been that the FB 'has been almost entirely dormant'.[59] The expert review process features procedural rules, including rules to foster due process, but it is the FB, and not the ERTs, that were designed to engage in negotiation, the exercise of discretion, flexibility, and problem-solving embedded in political contexts, and as a result a greater investment in due process was made at that level than at the ERT stage.[60] Furthermore, there are indications that ERTs are not well equipped to engage in the more political and diplomatic work of facilitation.[61] As Huggins puts it, the restructuring of the respective roles of ERTs and the FB 'effectively equates to a sanctioned bypassing of the more formal processes and procedural safeguards of the Facilitative Branch in favour of the less transparent and accountable facilitative processes undertaken by ERTs'.[62]

One could conclude that, while this arrangement may not be by design, it is a salutary development. Implementation and compliance processes are not the same as adjudicative processes for several good reasons: the obstacles and difficulties that can arise in environmental (and other) regimes may call for flexible, pragmatic responses rather than highly formalized procedures leading to a binary violation/no violation conclusion. Furthermore, the application of expert knowledge even to technical issues such as compiling and reporting inventories is not a mechanical process: it inevitably involves judgement and the exercise of discretion. Therefore, the evolution of the compliance process could be regarded as a salutary development that involves an open acknowledgment of the impossibility of banishing politics by turning to expertise. Huggins is sensitive to this response, and to the roles of judgement and discretion in the deployment of expertise. However, the climate change regime's compliance process is not designed to be solely, or even mainly, facilitative: the EB not only reaches conclusions on violations of emissions reduction

[56] ibid 196. This third-party trigger is regarded as crucial to the effectiveness of the compliance procedure: René Lefeber and Sebastian Oberthür, 'Key Features of the Kyoto Protocol's Compliance System' in Jutta Brunnée, Meinhard Doelle, and Lavanya Rajamani (eds), *Promoting Compliance in an Evolving Climate Regime* (CUP 2012) 86.

[57] Bodansky and others (n 55) 196.

[58] ibid 196.

[59] ibid 197.

[60] Huggins, 'Desirability of Depoliticization' (n 16) 116.

[61] ibid 115; Alexander Zahar, Jacqueline Peel, and Lee Godden, *Australian Climate Law in Global Context* (CUP 2012).

[62] Huggins, 'Desirability of Depoliticization' (n 16) 116–17.

obligations but metes out legal consequences that include lack of access to the regime's flexibility mechanisms such as emissions trading, as well as penalties in the form of increased emissions reduction obligations. Secondly, there are concrete problems with the ERTs' fulfilling roles not intended for them. For example, members of ERTs are often also involved in the preparation of inventories, meaning in essence that they are reviewing their own work and that of their colleagues, leading to reluctance to challenge that work, possibly arising on occasion from conflicts of interest.[63] Furthermore, the work of facilitation requires capacities and forms of expertise that members of expert review teams do not necessarily possess. The members may face pressure to revise the language of their reports, and may also exert pressure on states to revise their data.[64] Huggins argues that '"the mantle of expertise" appears to mask sensitive political negotiations that occur behind the scenes, and it is doubtful that technical experts are best qualified for this type of role'.[65] Finally, because ERTs were not designed to negotiate with states, they do not have access to the same range of information as the EB, and in particular are heavily dependent on information supplied by the states themselves.

What emerges from this discussion of the climate change regime's compliance process is an attempt to move beyond material, ad hoc approaches and work towards formalizing the process through a carefully designed procedural structure that assigned different roles and responsibilities to different bodies. Huggins argues that the main impetus of this design was to depoliticize the triggering process, while permitting a degree of diplomacy and negotiation within the two branches of the Compliance Committee. That this division of labour has not been maintained means that different incidents, and different states, may be treated differently; that, in particular, differences may be attributable to the influence and negotiating capacities of individual states; and, overall, that the process is not as predictable, consistent, or transparent as it was designed to be. Jan Klabbers, in his discussion of the much longer history of the ozone regime's Implementation Committee, notes a very strong tendency to implicate less wealthy states,[66] with developed states' compliance rarely coming under scrutiny. He also notes the degree to which compliance seems to be a matter of negotiation.[67] A few years after the publication of Klabbers' text, the picture had changed somewhat, with a handful of developed states coming on the carpet.[68] Based on this and other trends and

[63] ibid 110–11.

[64] ibid 112.

[65] ibid 115.

[66] At the time Klabbers' text was published, the only developed state that had appeared before the Committee was Israel; the others were either developing states or CEITs (countries with economies in transition, namely the states of the former Soviet Union and Eastern Bloc: Jan Klabbers, 'Compliance Procedures' in Daniel Bodansky, Jutta Brunnée, and Ellen Hey (eds), *The Oxford Handbook of International Environmental Law* (OUP 2007) 996; Huggins, *Multilateral Environmental Agreements* (n 16) 82.

[67] Klabbers (n 66) 996.

[68] Huggins, *Multilateral Environmental Agreements* (n 16) 82.

tendencies, Huggins' assessment of the ozone regime's compliance process is less critical than Klabbers'; she notes in particular a greater tendency to treat like cases alike, focusing not only on a state's individual circumstances but also on common standards against which compliance is assessed across the board.[69]

There are many reasons to doubt the appropriateness of a free-wheeling, highly contextual, strongly political approach to compliance in multilateral environmental agreements, particularly those in which states with a wide range of power, influence, and wealth are included, and most emphatically those in which penalties, including exclusion from privileges, are contemplated. As with reporting obligations and the Paris Agreement's stocktaking exercise, compliance procedures benefit greatly from the forms of depoliticization that Huggins argues may be brought about through careful attention to procedural rules and safeguards. The dynamism of the process may be significantly tempered as a result, as common procedures, available conclusions, and appropriate responses are brought to bear. However, if dynamism is understood not only to be reflected in changes to the content of rules but also in the putting into motion of components of the regime, the development of legal norms and approaches that shape and discipline the operation of metrics within regimes may be considered to be a crucial aspect of a regime's dynamic operation.

5. Conclusion

The narrative that has law in decline and metrics in the ascendant in international environmental governance is strongly supported by two milestones in 2015: the adoption of the SDGs and the Paris Agreement. The former does indeed strongly suggest a loss of patience with IEL and the identification of another avenue. The largely parallel operation of the SDGs and IEL is problematic, and, if points of intersection and interaction are not developed, is likely to create difficulties in both parallel tracks. This chapter has explained these dynamics and unpacked how the profoundly disappointing results of multilateral efforts opened the space for bureaucratic, technocratic, and expert-driven solutions, which catalysed the turn to metrics, and performance-oriented cognitive standards, and relocated the dynamism in IEL outside of the normative realm. I have also argued that there are some indications in the Paris Agreement of the renewed potential of legality to promote the requisite dynamism while at the same time interacting in potentially fruitful ways with cognitive approaches. The Paris Agreement, which is in many important respects built around NPM approaches and strategies, is in other, perhaps equally

69 ibid 71.

important respects, an indication of the greater potential for legal normativity to shape its implementation and development.

In a more speculative register, the interaction between the logics of metrics and norms which the architecture of the Paris Agreement fosters could promote the dynamism of the Agreement and the climate regime more generally. The procedural obligations with which the climate regime is already rife and to which the Paris Agreement adds significantly will impose strictures and constraints; indeed, they are designed to do precisely this. Yet the manner in which they do so may make possible a more dynamic and fruitful interaction between metrics and norms, science and law, by rendering these two sets of logics mutually supporting.

PART IV
FORCES OF CHANGE

8

Resurgent Authoritarianism, Rights, and Legal Change

*Wayne Sandholtz**

1. Introduction

International legal norms and institutions are under stress across a range of domains, from the use of force, to trade and investment, to human rights. The World Trade Organization (WTO) Appellate Body is in suspension. Three Latin American states[1] have withdrawn from the International Centre for Settlement of Investment Disputes (ICSID) Convention and others have threatened to follow. Foreign military interventions—in Libya, Ukraine, and Syria, and Yemen, among others—have strained the prohibition on the use of force. Burundi and the Philippines have withdrawn from the International Criminal Court, Venezuela denounced the American Convention on Human Rights, and Russia has been expelled from the European Court of Human Rights after its invasion of Ukraine. And, more broadly, rising authoritarianism is eroding basic rights defined in core international instruments. These developments and others suggest to many that the post-World War II international legal order may be on the brink of far-reaching change.

One of the key drivers of the current period of international legal change is resurgent authoritarianism. As Ginsburg has recently noted, autocratic governments use international law and legal institutions in fundamentally different ways than do democracies.[2] Not only that, but with the number of authoritarian regimes and their assertiveness on the rise, they may be in the process of constructing an 'authoritarian international law'.[3] Authoritarian regimes appear to favour a transactional approach to international relationships and emphasize traditional international law principles and norms of sovereignty, non-interference, self-determination, and territorial integrity. They tend to prefer bilateral 'deals' to multilateral institutions

* Professor and John A McCone Chair in International Relations, Department of Political Science and International Relations and Gould School of Law, University of Southern California, USA.

[1] Bolivia, Ecuador, and Venezuela.

[2] Tom Ginsburg, 'Authoritarian International Law?' (2020) 114 American Journal of International Law 221. In this study, I use the terms 'authoritarian' and 'autocratic' interchangeably. In some analytical contexts it might be useful to draw distinctions between the two, but not here.

[3] Ginsburg (n 2).

Wayne Sandholtz, *Resurgent Authoritarianism, Rights, and Legal Change* In: *The Many Paths of Change in International Law*. Edited by: Nico Krisch and Ezgi Yildiz, Oxford University Press. © Wayne Sandholtz 2023.
DOI: 10.1093/oso/9780198877844.003.0008

that involve external scrutiny and enforcement. Authoritarians are likely to avoid third-party dispute resolution (international courts and tribunals) in favour of one-on-one negotiations.[4]

The more destructive effects of resurgent authoritarianism will occur at the domestic level. Research has shown that international human rights law (IHRL) affects rights in practice when it empowers domestic actors to vindicate their rights through political mobilization and litigation.[5] That is, domestic social, political, and judicial arenas are where IHRL becomes effective. Authoritarian regimes curtail the domestic accountability mechanisms through which IHRL can enhance respect for rights. As the number of authoritarian regimes grows, and as those regimes tighten their grip on power, the international human rights legal regime loses effectiveness where it matters most: at the domestic level. This essay thus contributes two insights to the larger project: (1) international legal change is not always progressive but can also move in a non-liberal direction; and (2) for international human rights law—and probably for other domains of international law as well—crucial pathways of change go through domestic institutions and practices.

This study takes up the question of resurgent authoritarianism and its likely effects on international law. The focus will be on IHRL, for three reasons. First, international human rights law is one of the most distinctive defining features of the post-war liberal international order. For the first time, individual persons became subjects of international law, with legal rights and duties. Secondly, IHRL is the foundation of international rule of law in general. In this perspective, the international rule of law requires more than the 'mere existence of a legal order' that allows states to pursue their interests vis-à-vis each other.[6] As Nardin puts it, '[t]he international rule of law exists to the extent that states conduct their relations on the basis of laws that limit and not simply enable policy.'[7] In its most ambitious version, this perspective sees international human rights as the essence of a global constitutionalism in which individual rights and freedoms set boundaries to the powers of the state.[8]

[4] Ginsburg (n 2) 225, 257.

[5] Sally Engle Merry, *Human Rights and Gender Violence: Translating International Law into Local Justice* (University of Chicago Press 2006); Beth A Simmons, *Mobilizing for Human Rights: International Law in Domestic Politics* (CUP 2009); Karen J Alter, *The New Terrain of International Law: Courts, Politics, Rights* (Princeton University Press 2014).

[6] Gianluigi Palombella, 'The Rule of Law Beyond the State: Failures, Promises, and Theory' (2009) 7 International Journal of Constitutional Law 442, 454.

[7] Terry Nardin, 'Theorising the International Rule of Law' (2008) 34 Review of International Studies 385, 400.

[8] Stephen Gardbaum, 'Human Rights as International Constitutional Rights' (2008) 19 European Journal of International Law 749; Stephen Gardbaum, 'Human Rights and International Constitutionalism' in Jeffrey L Dunoff and Joel P Trachtman (eds), *Ruling the World? Constitutionalism, International Law, and Global Governance* (CUP 2009) 233; Mattias Kumm, 'The Cosmopolitan Turn in Constitutionalism: On the Relationship between Constitutionalism in and beyond the State' in Dunoff and Trachtman (eds), Ruling the World?, 258; Wayne Sandholtz, 'Resurgent Authoritarianism and the International Rule of Law' Berlin Potsdam Research Group 'The International Rule of Law—Rise

Thirdly, authoritarian regimes are not necessarily incompatible with basic international legal structures in security (the use of force), economic relations, or the environment. With respect to the use of force, liberal Western powers may be more likely than autocracies to test the limits of Article 2(4), as the examples of Kosovo (1999), Iraq (2003), Libya (2011), and Syria (2017) demonstrate. On trade, China—the world's leading authoritarian power—has invested heavily in developing international trade law capacity and has been adept at working within the WTO legal system.[9] And it is the US that is primarily responsible for blockading the WTO Appellate Body.[10] Trump withdrew the US from the Trans-Pacific Partnership (which essentially went ahead without the US), handing China a chance to assume trade leadership in the crucial Asia-Pacific region, which it did with the Regional Comprehensive Economic Partnership.[11] On the environment, when Donald Trump withdrew the US from the Paris Climate Accord, Xi Jinping announced that China would take the lead in international efforts to deal with climate change.[12] In other words, authoritarian regimes regularly work within international legal institutions that meet specific interests.[13]

In contrast, authoritarianism directly undermines international human rights norms. Whereas authoritarian regimes can effectively advance their interests within other international legal regimes (in economics, security, and the environment), their drive to remain in power inevitably leads them to curtail basic civil and political rights enshrined in regional and global treaties. Moreover, authoritarians target three essential categories of rights in order to suppress opposition and retain power: (1) access to justice in independent courts; (2) freedom of expression and the press; and (3) freedom of civil society to organize and participate in public life. These three sets of rights and freedoms are essential for holding governments

or Decline?' (2019) Working Paper Series No 38; Alec Stone Sweet and Jud Mathews, *Proportionality Balancing and Constitutional Governance: A Comparative and Global Approach* (OUP 2019).

[9] Gregory Shaffer and Henry Gao, 'China's Rise: How it Took on the U.S. at the WTO' [2018] University of Illinois Law Review 115

[10] Keith Johnson, 'How Trump May Finally Kill the WTO' *Foreign Policy* (9 December 2019) <https://foreignpolicy.com/2019/12/09/trump-may-kill-wto-finally-appellate-body-world-trade-organization/> accessed 4 June 2022.

[11] Amy Mackinnon, 'The World's Largest Trade Agreement Doesn't Include the United States' *Foreign Policy* (16 November 2020) <https://foreignpolicy.com/2020/11/16/largest-trade-agreement-rcep-asia-pacific-united-states-china/> accessed 4 June 2022; Mireya Solís, 'Trump Withdrawing from the Trans-Pacific Partnership' (*Brookings Institute*, 24 March 2017) <www.brookings.edu/blog/unpacked/2017/03/24/trump-withdrawing-from-the-trans-pacific-partnership/> accessed 4 June 2022; Mireya Solís and Jennifer Mason, 'As the TPP Lives On, the U.S. Abdicates Trade Leadership' (*Brookings Institute*, 9 March 2018) <www.brookings.edu/blog/order-from-chaos/2018/03/09/as-the-tpp-lives-on-the-u-s-abdicates-trade-leadership/> accessed 4 June 2022.

[12] Colum Lynch and Robbie Gramer, 'China Rises in U.N. Climate Talks, While U.S. Goes AWOL' *Foreign Policy* (7 May 2019) <https://foreignpolicy.com/2019/05/07/china-rises-united-nations-climate-change-talks-u-s-trump-goes-awol-environment-diplomacy-global-warming/> accessed 4 June 2022.

[13] Ginsburg recognizes that authoritarians demonstrate 'more innovation in and commitment to international economic law' than other areas of international law; see Ginsburg (n 2) 225.

accountable; even the holding of elections becomes a hollow ritual if citizens are unable to organize politically, participate in campaigning and lobbying, publicly express demands and points of view, and have recourse to justice when those (and other) rights are abridged. Once citizens have no means of holding state authorities accountable, violations of virtually every other kind of right can follow. The three core rights examined here, then, are the primary bulwark of the international human rights legal order. The analysis thus focuses on IHRL as the domain where resurgent authoritarianism is most likely to bring about change in international law.

The first section of this study introduces and defines authoritarian resurgence and situates it in the context of the international human rights legal order. Section 2 examines how authoritarianism diminishes the effectiveness of human rights institutions at the international level and assesses the likely consequences for the international legal order. The third section focuses on the front line in applying IHRL in practice: the domestic level. Authoritarian strategies curtail or destroy the primary mechanisms through which domestic actors can hold governments accountable for rights violations and press them to uphold their obligations under IHRL. Section 4 examines sources of resilience in international human rights law and offers some evidence suggesting that authoritarians may not have an easy path and that this third wave[14] of authoritarianism may also ebb. The conclusion offers final reflections.

2. Resurgent Authoritarianism and the 'Zone of Liberalism'

Authoritarianism is resurgent, across world regions and across regime types. Entrenched authoritarians have intensified their repression (Azerbaijan, Burundi, Cambodia, Egypt, Iran). Countries that had appeared to be consolidating democracies (Brazil, Hungary, Philippines, Poland, Turkey) are now seen as 'backsliders'. Most troubling, as Lührmann and Lindberg note, whereas the previous wave of autocratization affected 'electoral autocracies' almost exclusively, 'almost all contemporary autocratization episodes affect democracies'.[15] Democratic decline has occurred even in established democracies like India, Israel, and the US.

Authoritarians in the twenty-first century differ from their predecessors in that they are far more likely to come to power democratically as opposed to through *coups*.[16] In the current period, authoritarian leaders or parties often gain power through democratic elections, then gradually and incrementally erode essential democratic institutions.[17] Or, as Frantz and Kendall-Taylor put it:

[14] Anna Lührmann and Staffan I Lindberg, 'A Third Wave of Autocratization is Here: What is New about it?' (2019) 26 Democratization 1095, 1105.

[15] ibid 1103.

[16] Erica Frantz and Andrea Kendall-Taylor, 'The Evolution of Autocracy: Why Authoritarianism Is Becoming More Formidable' (2017) 59 Survival 57, 60–61.

[17] ibid 94–98.

> Contemporary autocrats are coming to power through a process of 'authoritarianisation', or the gradual erosion of democratic norms and practices. Democratic leaders, elected at the ballot box through reasonably free and fair elections, are slowly undermining institutional constraints on their power ... in ways that make it difficult to pinpoint the moment at which the break with democratic politics occurs.[18]

The twenty-first century version of authoritarianism also tends to differ from earlier ones in its primary tools and strategies for staying in power. One difference is that today's authoritarians generally (though not always) rely less on brutal physical repression. Autocrats in the 1960s and 1970s routinely resorted to arbitrary detention, torture, disappearances, and extrajudicial killing to suppress dissent and eliminate opponents.[19] Today's authoritarians often exploit formally legal processes to subvert democratic institutions. These 'autocratic legalists' tend to

> hijack constitutions ... to benefit from the superficial appearance of both democracy and legality within their states. They use their democratic mandates to launch legal reforms that remove the checks on executive power, limit the challenges to their rule, and undermine the crucial accountability institutions of a democratic state.[20]

The resurgence of authoritarian practices in recent decades has been so dramatic that it is apparent in a variety of indicators. For several years, Freedom House has been calling attention to the erosion of democracy and the rise of authoritarianism. Its 2018 annual report, titled *Democracy in Crisis*, declared that democratic values were 'under assault and in retreat globally' and that '[p]olitical rights and civil liberties around the world deteriorated to their lowest point in more than a decade in 2017'.[21] The 2020 document reported that '2019 was the 14th consecutive year of decline in global freedom' and that 'the negative pattern affected all regime types'.[22] In fact, twenty-five of forty-one 'established democracies' (those with at least twenty consecutive years of democracy prior to 2006) experienced declines over the past fourteen years.[23] The Varieties of Democracy (V-Dem) 2020 report

[18] ibid 60.

[19] Of course, many of today's authoritarians employ the same kinds of physical violence: extrajudicial killings in the Philippines, large-scale detentions of journalists in Turkey, mass arrests of Uighurs in China and their transfer to concentration camps, and more. The point here is that many of today's autocrats do not rely on violent repression but instead hollow out democratic institutions using ostensibly legal means.

[20] Kim Lane Scheppele, 'Autocratic Legalism' (2018) 85 University of Chicago Law Review 545, 547.

[21] Freedom House, *Freedom in the World 2018: Democracy in Crisis* (2018) <https://freedomhouse.org/report/freedom-world/2018/democracy-crisis#anchor-one> accessed 4 June 2022.

[22] Freedom House, *Freedom in the World 2020: A Leaderless Struggle for Democracy* (2020) <https://freedomhouse.org/report/freedom-world/2020/leaderless-struggle-democracy> accessed 4 June 2022.

[23] ibid 10.

concurs, finding that '[f]or the first time since 2001, democracies are no longer in the majority'.[24] And the declines have occurred not just in countries that were already autocracies, but in democracies: '[O]ver the last decade, the rise in electoral autocracies is mainly the result of democracies gradually breaking down. Seven of these became electoral autocracies over the last year from 2018 to 2019.'[25]

A surge in the number of autocracies and the concomitant decline in the proportion of democracies in the world amount to a shrinking of the 'zone of liberalism'.[26] The 'zone of liberalism' refers to the set of liberal states (ie those instantiating electoral democracy, basic civil and political rights, the rule of law, and market economies) and relations among them.[27] International human rights law achieves its most ample fulfilment in a zone of liberalism because its constituent states (1) place effective limits on public authorities that ensure fundamental individual rights, and (2) sustain a rule-based system of peaceful relations among themselves.[28] As Slaughter argued, international relations among liberal states differ qualitatively from international relations outside of them.[29] In this perspective, what is worrisome is that even well-established democracies have slipped into authoritarian practices and some have dropped into the autocratic category.

Of course, international human rights law has never been truly international, much less universal. It has always been weakly implemented or routinely violated in large swathes of the world. This is not meant as a criticism; IHRL has always been and must always be in part aspirational. It affirms values and norms, establishes standards, motivates policy entrepreneurs and social movements, and can empower victims and their advocates. But as the liberal community shrinks, the consequences for the international human rights legal regime could be significant. A contracting zone of liberalism would: (1) make it more difficult for liberal states to pressure or encourage non-compliant states to improve their human rights performance; (2) make it easier for authoritarian states to resist external pressure, both because there will be fewer liberal states to pressure them and more fellow autocrats to support and shield them; and (3) debilitate international human rights

[24] Seraphine F Maerz and others, 'Autocratization Surges—Resistance Grows: Democracy Report 2020' (2020) 27 Democratization 909.

[25] ibid 13.

[26] For my purposes, 'liberalism' is a set of ideas and institutions centred on electoral democracy, basic civil and political rights, the rule of law, and market economies (in all their varieties; see Peter A Hall and David W Soskice, *Varieties of Capitalism: The Institutional Foundations of Comparative Advantage* (OUP 2001)). Liberal states are those that largely embody these institutions in practice; see Alec Stone Sweet, 'A Cosmopolitan Legal Order: Constitutional Pluralism and Rights Adjudication in Europe' (2012) 1 Global Constitutionalism 53, 56.

[27] Alec Stone, 'What Is a Supranational Constitution? An Essay in International Relations Theory' (1994) 56 Review of Politics 441; see Stone Sweet (n 26).

[28] Stone Sweet (n 26); Alec Stone Sweet and Clare Ryan, *A Cosmopolitan Legal Order: Kant, Constitutional Justice, and the European Convention on Human Rights* (OUP 2018)

[29] Anne-Marie Slaughter, 'International Law in a World of Liberal States' (1995) 6 European Journal of International Law 503.

institutions (treaty bodies, courts, and similar organs) as authoritarian states make up a larger share of their membership (more on this below).

The analytical framework for assessing change in IHRL must be one in which national, regional, and international levels are interconnected. This is not a question of 'monism' versus 'dualism'. Rather, it is a recognition that IHRL constitutes a 'transnational legal order' (TLO).[30] A TLO consists of legal norms and practices that develop and settle through processes that involve multiple kinds of actors (social, political, legal) across multiple levels, from the local to the global. The process is recursive, as developments at the international level affect those at the domestic level, and vice versa.[31] The international human rights legal order integrates domestic, regional, and international levels, each with its own sources of human rights law tied together by (1) an underlying theory of constitutionalism; (2) common substantive norms, and (3) interlinked rights institutions.

The international human rights legal order is grounded in rights-based limits on government authority—the essence of modern constitutionalism. That order includes broadly overlapping rights charters at global, regional, and domestic levels. Rights charters, in turn, are associated with judicial and quasi-judicial institutions at all three levels that assess state acts for their congruence with rights norms. In the following section I assess the likely effects of resurgent authoritarianism on IHRL at the international level.

3. Authoritarianism and the International Human Rights Regime

Rising authoritarianism is likely to weaken international human rights law, not by dissolving or modifying the body of international human rights treaties but by weakening, evading, and resisting the mechanisms that give it effect. Put differently, the next decade or two may not see significant change in formal international human rights law. Rather, if authoritarian modes of politics and governance continue to spread and become entrenched, the practices of IHRL—and therefore its effectiveness—will be diminished. Equally important, the dynamic 'ratcheting up' of rights protections over time may pause or be muted. The argument here takes as given that international law is more than a set of legal rules. My approach has affinities with Brunnée and Toope's interactional theory of international legality. In

[30] Terence C Halliday and Gregory Shaffer, 'Transnational Legal Orders' in Terence C Halliday and Gregory Shaffer (eds), *Transnational Legal Orders* (CUP 2015). See also Sally Engle Merry, 'Firming Up Soft Law' in Halliday and Shaffer (eds), Transnational Legal Orders, 374; Paulette Lloyd and Beth A Simmons, 'Framing for a New Transnational Legal Order' in Halliday and Shaffer (eds), Transnational Legal Orders, 400; Leigh A Payne, 'The Justice Paradox?' in Halliday and Shaffer (eds), Transnational Legal Orders, 439.

[31] Halliday and Schaffer, 'Transnational Legal Orders' (n 30).

their account, the legitimacy of international law—and thus the sense of obligation held by actors—is based on factors that interact to create legitimacy and engender in legal subjects the 'fidelity' that leads to compliance.[32] International human rights law will therefore be weakened, even if the formal law remains unchanged, to the extent that authoritarian regimes undermine 'practices of legality'.

The international human rights legal order consists of the network of human rights treaties, both global and regional, plus their associated institutions. Those institutions include the human rights treaty bodies, the Human Rights Council and its Universal Periodic Review (UPR) process, and the regional human rights courts. Rising authoritarianism is unlikely to lead to the abandonment of existing human rights treaties. Treaty withdrawal—the open rejection of human rights principles and norms—would offer little in the way of payoffs and could generate some costs. No leader, regardless of how abusive of rights domestically, wants to be seen as opposing or rejecting human rights outright. Thus the 'wholesale rejection of rights is rare'.[33] Authoritarians deploy the rhetoric of democracy and human rights, even as their actions erode rights in practice. And, instead of explicitly spurning human rights, autocratic governments routinely justify rights violations by invoking other basic norms, 'like counterterrorism, sovereignty and non-interference' or 'traditional values'[34] as a means of shielding themselves from international accountability.

Rather than seeking to dismantle formal international law, authoritarians can gradually hollow out the institutions designed to monitor state human rights practices and promote compliance with human rights treaties. These include the UN Human Rights Council, ten human rights treaty bodies,[35] three regional human rights courts,[36] and sub-regional courts with human rights jurisdiction.[37] Authoritarian states resist intrusive international human rights mechanisms and continually emphasize norms of sovereignty and non-interference in domestic affairs. After all, their rights-repressive measures are a key autocratic tool for holding onto power. As the zone of authoritarianism expands, it will become easier for authoritarians to weaken international human rights institutions from within.

[32] Jutta Brunnée and Stephen J Toope, *Legitimacy and Legality in International Law: An Interactional Account* (CUP 2010) 55, 101, 119

[33] Stephen Hopgood, Jack Snyder, and Leslie Vinjamuri (eds), 'Conclusion: Human Rights Futures' in *Human Rights Futures* (CUP 2017) 316.

[34] ibid.

[35] For general information about the human rights treaties bodies, see Office of the High Commissioner for Human Rights, *Monitoring the Core International Human Rights Treaties* (2020) Office of the High Commissioner for Human Rights <www.ohchr.org/EN/HRBodies/Pages/Overview.aspx> accessed 4 June 2022.

[36] The European Court of Human Rights (ECtHR), the Inter-American Court of Human Rights (IACtHR), and the African Court on Human and Peoples' Rights (ACtHPR).

[37] These include the Economic Community of West African States (ECOWAS) Court and the East African Community (EAC) Court.

Authoritarian governments tend to participate in human rights bodies in ways that meet formal requirements (eg filing reports) but in non-substantive, pro forma ways. They can also take more active steps. China and Russia, for example, have regularly 'used [their] veto in the Security Council to shield other authoritarian countries from international demands to protect human rights and to block interventions that would force governments to end abuses'.[38] Autocracies also inhibit human rights initiatives in the General Assembly. Boockmann and Dreher report a clear difference in the voting behaviour of democracies and autocracies with respect to human rights resolutions in the General Assembly. Across different measures of democracy, the more autocratic a country is, the more likely it is to vote against a human rights resolution.[39]

The Human Rights Council offers another example. For the 2020 Council session, nearly half of the membership (twenty-one out of forty-seven) consisted of autocracies (see Table 8.1), despite the formal requirement that members of the Council have a strong record of respecting human rights.[40] China, the largest and most influential autocracy, took an assertive approach after its election to the Human Rights Council in 2013. China proposed its first resolutions in the Council in 2017 and 2018. 'Both resolutions emphasized national sovereignty, called for quiet dialogue and cooperation rather than investigations and international calls to action, and pushed the Chinese model of state-led development as the path to improving their vision of collective human rights and social stability'.[41] The strong presence of autocracies in the Council undermines its credibility as a mechanism for encouraging states to improve their rights performance.

The Human Rights Council also administers the UPR. Every state is reviewed on a five-year cycle. The review considers a report submitted by the state under review, plus additional documents provided by human rights organizations, other UN treaty bodies and agencies, and domestic stakeholders. Each country review produces a report that contains questions, comments, and recommendations.[42] Not surprisingly, the nature and quality of state participation varies widely. In a 2009 report, the non-governmental organization UN Watch rated the quality of countries' participation in the UPR process.[43] Among the sixteen states whose role was rated as 'destructive', all but two were autocracies under the V-Dem

[38] Jessica Chen Weiss, 'A World Safe for Autocracy? China's Rise and the Future of Global Politics' (2019) 98 Foreign Affairs 92, 95

[39] Bernhard Boockmann and Axel Dreher, 'Do Human Rights Offenders Oppose Human Rights Resolutions in the United Nations?' (2011) 146 Public Choice 443, 455–58.

[40] Ted Piccone, *China's Long Game on Human Rights at the United Nations* (Brookings Institution 2018) <www.brookings.edu/wp-content/uploads/2018/09/FP_20181009_china_human_rights.pdf> accessed 4 June 2022.

[41] Piccone (n 40) 4.

[42] OHCHR (n 35).

[43] Negative points were given to interventions that praised or covered up for the country being reviewed, while positive scores were awarded for challenges to rights-violating countries.

Table 8.1 Autocracies in the Human Rights Council, 2020

Country	V-Dem regime type	Term expires
Afghanistan	Electoral autocracy	2020
Angola	Electoral autocracy	2020
Armenia	Electoral autocracy	2022
Bahrain	Closed autocracy	2021
Bangladesh	Electoral autocracy	2021
Burkina Faso	Electoral autocracy	2021
Cameroon	Electoral autocracy	2021
Democratic Republic of the Congo	Electoral autocracy	2020
Eritrea	Closed autocracy	2021
Fiji	Electoral autocracy	2021
Libya	Closed autocracy	2022
Mauritania	Electoral autocracy	2022
Nigeria	Electoral autocracy	2020
Pakistan	Electoral autocracy	2020
Philippines	Electoral autocracy	2021
Qatar	Closed autocracy	2020
Somalia	Closed autocracy	2021
Sudan	Closed autocracy	2022
Togo	Electoral autocracy	2021
Ukraine	Electoral autocracy	2020
Venezuela (Bolivarian Republic of)	Electoral autocracy	2022

Note: Regime types from the Varieties of Democracy (V-Dem) project. Total Council membership = 47.

classification.[44] In addition, the nature of states' recommendations differs across regime types. Democracies tend to recommend changes to domestic law and governance. Authoritarian states target their recommendations to joining or ratifying international human rights treaties, rather than encouraging domestic change.[45]

[44] UN Watch, *Mutual Praise Society: Country Scorecard and Evaluation of the Universal Periodic Review System of the U.N. Human Rights Council* (2009) <https://unwatch.org/mutual-praise-society/> accessed 4 June 2022.

[45] Mi Hwa Hong, 'Legal Commitments to United Nations Human Rights Treaties and Higher Monitoring Standards in the Universal Periodic Review' (2018) 17 Journal of Human Rights 660, 661.

The strategy of participating in international human rights institutions in ways that weaken them manifests itself in other ways. Authoritarian states can go through the motions of submitting the periodic reports required in most human rights treaty bodies, but without accepting external criticisms or committing to substantive reforms. For example, Creamer and Simmons find that autocracies are as likely as democracies to file the reports required by the Committee against Torture. But '[d]emocracies generally submit reports that identify implementation and compliance shortcomings and that respond to concerns of the treaty-monitoring body—autocracies, much less so.'[46] A similar dynamic likely holds in the other human rights treaty bodies.

Autocracies are also increasing their 'pushback' against regional human rights courts. Of course, some degree of state resistance to international human rights courts and non-compliance with their judgments is 'normal' state behaviour.[47] But authoritarian states are more likely than democracies to reject, ignore, or refuse to implement adverse judgments. Autocracies might also go further. For instance, the Russian Constitutional Court (prior to Russia's expulsion from the Council of Europe) asserted the right to selectively implement (or reject) judgments of the European Court of Human Rights. States can also withdraw from regional human rights systems, as Venezuela did from the IACtHR in 2012.

Still, authoritarian states will not be able to curtail the authority of the regional human rights courts on their own. Authoritarian regimes routinely criticize human rights courts and fail to comply with their judgments, which amounts to resistance or 'pushback'. But pushback is 'normal' behavior in the context of international courts: states of all stripes complain about adverse judgments and about 'activist' courts. There is no evidence that the regional human rights courts respond to pushback from authoritarian regimes by exhibiting greater deference (eg declining to find rights violations). Indeed, diluting their rights jurisprudence in response to criticism from authoritarians would undermine the courts' legitimacy. In fact, some of the more aggressive challenges to human rights courts in the last decade or so have come from democracies. In both the European and Inter-American systems, democratic states have recently engaged in backlash, which goes beyond the usual forms of resistance by seeking to curtail the authorities or jurisdiction of a

[46] Cosette D Creamer and Beth A Simmons, 'Do Self-Reporting Regimes Matter? Evidence from the Convention Against Torture' (2019) 63 International Studies Quarterly 1051, 1053.

[47] See the recent work on 'backlash' against international courts, including Wayne Sandholtz, Yining Bei, and Kayla Caldwell, 'Backlash and International Human Rights Courts' in Alison Brysk and Michael Stohl (eds), *Contracting Human Rights: Crisis, Accountability, and Opportunity* (Edward Elgar 2018) 159; Daniel Abebe and Tom Ginsburg, 'The Dejudicialization of International Politics?' (2019) 63 International Studies Quarterly 521; Karen J Alter, James T Gathii, and Laurence R Helfer, 'Backlash against International Courts in West, East, and Southern Africa: Causes and Consequences' (2016) 27 European Journal of International Law 293; Mikael Rask Madsen, Pola Cebulak, and Micha Wiebusch, 'Backlash against International Courts: Explaining the Forms and Patterns of Resistance to International Courts' (2018) 14 International Journal of Law in Context 197.

court.[48] So far, the backlash attempts in Europe and the Americas have not been successful.

In Europe, the states parties convened from 2012 to 2018 a series of 'High Level Conferences' aimed at examining the performance of the Court and considering reforms. The UK, in particular, proposed an agenda that would have reined in the ECtHR's competences. But the declarations (Brighton Declaration and Copenhagen Declaration) that emerged from the conferences highlighted the shortcomings of the member states in applying the ECHR and emphasized the obligation of states to implement the Court's judgments. They affirmed the Court as the authoritative interpreter of the Convention and did nothing to roll back the Court's authority.[49] In the Americas, a set of states with left-leaning governments demanded reforms of the Inter-American Commission on Human Rights that would have trimmed its authority and brought it under greater state control. The challenge to the Commission played out in a series of meetings from 2011 to 2014. Governments and civil society organizations that were supportive of the Inter-American Human Rights System mobilized against the effort to rein in the Commission. In the end, the Commission emerged with its authority intact. The reforms approved by the member states were those that the Commission itself had proposed. In short, neither effort succeeded in reducing the authority of the courts or inducing them to reverse important precedents.[50]

Finally, Ginsburg has argued that authoritarian states will advance new international legal norms and create supportive institutions designed to solidify their hold on power. The primary example of this effort is the Shanghai Cooperation Organization (SCO), which Ginsburg describes as 'a critical step in the development of authoritarian international law'.[51] The SCO has concluded treaties that

[48] On the distinction between resistance and backlash, see Sandholtz and others, 'Backlash' (n 48).

[49] Protocol no 15 mentions subsidiarity but only in the non-binding preamble; it does not in fact do anything to bring the Court under increased state control. Though states have not curtailed the ECtHR's authority or jurisdiction, some analysts have argued that the Court has moderated its own behaviour in response to the pushback. For instance, Madsen et al note that the Court has entered fewer judgments against the UK finding violations (Madsen and others (n 48)), though a causal connection has not been established. Helfer and Voeten find that dissents claiming that the Grand Chamber of the ECtHR has tacitly reversed precedents in a rights-regressive direction have increased in the last ten years; see Laurence R Helfer and Erik Voeten, 'Walking Back Human Rights in Europe?' (2020) 31 European Journal of International Law 797; for a sceptical view of that claim see Alec Stone Sweet, Wayne Sandholtz, and Mads Andenas, 'Dissenting Opinions and Rights Protection in the European Court: A Reply to Laurence Helfer and Erik Voeten' (2021) 32 European Journal of International Law 897. Stiansen and Voeten present evidence that the Court has exercised 'restraint' toward consolidated democracies that have criticized it; Øyvind Stiansen and Erik Voeten, 'Backlash and Judicial Restraint: Evidence from the European Court of Human Rights' (2020) 64 International Studies Quarterly 770.

[50] Ezequiel Gonzalez Ocantos and Wayne Sandholtz, 'The Sources of Resilience of International Human Rights Courts: The Case of the Inter-American Court' (2022) 47 Law & Social Inquiry 95. The only successful challenge to an international court's authority is that directed at the South African Development Community Tribunal; see Alec Stone Sweet and Wayne Sandholtz, 'The Law and Politics of Transnational Rights Protection: Trusteeship, Effectiveness, Backlash' [2022] Governance 105.

[51] Ginsburg (n 2) 249.

enhance the ability of member governments to silence regime critics and opponents by mobilizing 'cross border cooperative repression'.[52] The treaties oblige states to criminalize and punish the 'three evils' of terrorism, separatism, and extremism, which are defined so broadly as to include not just material acts but also 'ideology and practice'.[53] States commit to cooperation in extraditing and prosecuting violators from the other states. Though these repressive dimensions of the SCO are indeed ominous, the SCO is a sub-regional organization with only eight members,[54] and the repressive tools it supports likely cover forms of autocratic cooperation that would take place anyway. Moreover, it is doubtful that similar norms and bodies could be constructed at the global or even the regional level.

In sum, authoritarians seek to hollow out international human rights bodies, giving the appearance of participation but doing so in ways that weaken the institutions and diminish their credibility.

4. Authoritarianism and Domestic Rights Accountability

Though the international human rights regime is a multi-level legal order, with fundamental norms and key institutions at the international and regional levels, the domestic arena plays an especially crucial role. As former judge Diego García-Sayán of the Inter-American Court of Human Rights put it: 'states are supposed to be the actors performing the leading role' in the human rights regime.[55] One of the contributions of this analysis is to show that, even if authoritarians do not alter formal human rights norms and institutions at the global level, the international human rights legal regime can undergo significant, rights-regressive change through backsliding at the domestic level.

International human rights law may be the substantive domain in which Koh's transnational legal process model—arguing that international law has effects on state behaviour to the extent that it is internalized domestically—works best.[56] One of the few broad and stable findings in scholarship on IHRL is that it has practical effects mainly at the domestic level, to the extent that it empowers people to mobilize political pressure and to litigate for rights.[57] International human rights law improves human rights practices when domestic actors—journalists,

52 ibid 248.

53 ibid 251.

54 The original members of the SCO were China, Kazakhstan, Kyrgyzstan, Russia, Tajikistan, and Uzbekistan; India and Pakistan joined in 2017.

55 Diego García-Sayán, 'The Inter-American Court and Constitutionalism in Latin America' (2011) 89 Texas Law Review 1835, 1836.

56 Harold Hongju Koh, 'Why Do Nations Obey International Law?' (1997) 106 Yale Law Journal 2599 and Harold Hongju Koh, 'The 1998 Frankel Lecture: Bringing International Law Home' (1998) 35 Houston Law Review 623.

57 Merry, *Human Rights and Gender Violence* (n 5); Simmons, *Mobilizing* (n 5).

activists, victims, advocates, civil society organizations, elected officials, and judges—leverage international human rights law to expose and condemn violations; pressure governments to hold perpetrators accountable; gain justice for victims; and change domestic laws and how they are enforced. Rising authoritarianism undermines IHRL by vitiating the primary mechanisms through which IHRL affects rights in practice, at the domestic level. The point is that authoritarian practices undermine the domestic mechanisms and institutions through which people can seek to vindicate the full panoply of rights.

It is more useful to define authoritarianism by what it *does* (its core practices) than by what it *is not* (ie it is not democratic). Defining authoritarianism by its core practices is especially important in the current period because it allows us to identify authoritarian shifts in countries that have been and are still fully or partially democratic. Authoritarian practices—in whatever type of regime they are found—aim to eliminate accountability.[58] Authoritarian practices weaken or curtail the mechanisms by which other actors can criticize, oppose, and punish a government. Research has converged on three key clusters of rights that authoritarians target in order to consolidate unaccountable power: the right to judicial recourse in independent courts, which entails the authority to review government acts for their consistency with basic rights; the right to freedom of expression, especially freedom of the press; and the right to assemble and organize.[59] These three sets of rights are crucial because once they are compromised or eliminated, authoritarians have a firmer grip on power and are less constrained from violating other rights.

Core authoritarian practices thus undermine essential means of holding governments accountable. The right to free expression is essential if rights violations are to be exposed, publicized, and condemned. Civil society is crucial for mobilizing pro-rights actors in both political and judicial realms. Civil society organizations (CSOs) pressure government officials, marshal support for candidates, organize direct political action, and engage in 'naming and shaming'. In the judicial realm, CSOs are crucial in locating victims, providing them with legal assistance, and representing them in judicial proceedings. Independent courts are essential for ensuring that the laws that protect rights are applied, even against state officials.

I evaluate the extent to which countries that have experienced an authoritarian shift from 2011 to 2020 show increased use of the three core authoritarian practices. I make use of two measures for each of the three core authoritarian

[58] Marlies Glasius, 'What Authoritarianism is … and is Not: A Practice Perspective' (2018) 94 International Affairs 515, 521.

[59] David Beetham, 'Authoritarianism and Democracy: Beyond Regime Types' (2015) 13 Comparative Democratization 2; Glasius (n 59) 515; Jan-Werner Müller, *The Rise and Rise of Populism?* (Penguin Random House Grupo Editorial 2017); Cas Mudde and Cristóbal Rovira Kaltwasser, *Populism: A Very Short Introduction* (OUP 2017); Aziz Z Huq and Tom Ginsburg, 'How to Lose a Constitutional Democracy' (2018) 65 UCLA Law Review 78; Scheppele (n 20); Robert R Kaufman and Stephan Haggard, 'Democratic Decline in the United States: What Can We Learn from Middle-Income Backsliding?' (2019) 17 Perspectives on Politics 417.

Table 8.2 Average number out of six indicators showing an authoritarian shift, 2011–2020

	Countries that:			
	Dropped to a more authoritarian level (N)	Did not drop to a more authoritarian level (N)	Difference	Significant?
Average number of six authoritarian strategy indicators	3.58 (90)	2.27 (63)	1.31	yes ($p = 0.0000$)

Note: The number of countries in each group is indicated in parentheses. Countries are included if they did not have a score of less than 0.300 on the *v2x_liberal* variable for both 2011 and 2020. Cuba and Equatorial Guinea, for example, were thus excluded because they had scores that classified them as non-democratic for both years. The results are similar if the cutoff on the *v2x_liberal* variable is 0.400. Data from the Varieties of Democracy (V-Dem) Project.

practices,[60] all of which are taken from the V-Dem project.[61] In what follows, I refer to these measures as the 'six authoritarian practices'. A country has undergone an authoritarian shift if its liberal democracy score declines over the previous decade (2011 to 2020).

The data show clearly that states moving toward greater authoritarianism deploy the core authoritarian practices to a striking degree. Table 8.2 reports the average number of the six authoritarian practices that increased among states that underwent an authoritarian shift, compared to states that did not. The difference between the two groups of states is substantial and significant. In addition, many of the countries that have moved in an authoritarian direction have seen an increase in all or nearly all of the six authoritarian strategy indicators. Among the 90 states with a decrease in the measure of democracy, eight show greater authoritarianism in all six indicators and 24 (including the United States) show it in five.

Authoritarian leaders who have implemented the three core practices are not hard to find. The consolidated autocratic regimes of Vladimir Putin in Russia and Xi Jinping in China have broadly achieved the three core authoritarian goals of establishing political control over the judiciary, eliminating independent news media, and repressing the ability of civil society to organize and engage in political activity. Both have clamped down effectively on human rights and pro-democracy

[60] The measures of authoritarian practices are: (1) undermine judicial independence: *Government attacks on the judiciary* and *Court packing*; (2) curtail freedom of expression: *Freedom of discussion* and *Harassment of journalists*; and (3) constrain civil society: *CSO entry and exit* and *CSO repression*.

[61] Michael Coppedge and others, *V-Dem Country-Year Dataset v10* (2020); Michael Coppedge and others, *V-Dem Codebook v10* (2020).

NGOs by restricting foreign funding or prohibiting it altogether.[62] Hungary's Viktor Orbán may be the most accomplished implementer of authoritarian practices within a hitherto liberal democratic state. The new constitution pushed through by Orbán in 2011 (with a supermajority for his Fidesz party in parliament) gave his government control of the judiciary and allowed Orbán to pack the Constitutional Court.[63] A new media law brought virtually all publicly supported radio and television under Orbán's control, with the result that 'the public networks are more tightly supervised today than they were in the final period of the communist regime'. Fidesz also gained control over the country's newspapers.[64] The Law and Justice Party (PiS) in Poland has followed a similar path, if not as openly and comprehensively as Orbán and Fidesz in Hungary. The PiS government first subordinated the Constitutional Tribunal, then the Supreme Court, the ordinary courts, and the National Council of the Judiciary.[65] It moved against press freedom and civil society as well; it 'enacted changes to media laws that promote government messaging; has sought to regulate NGOs; and, in March 2017, it passed legislation limiting rights to assembly'.[66]

President Recep Tayyip Erdoğan of Turkey has assiduously pursued the three core authoritarian practices. He has closed down more than 100 independent news organizations and led the world each year from 2016 through 2018 in arrests of journalists (only to take second place to Xi's China in 2019).[67] He packed the courts with loyalists. Erdoğan has taken advantage of the Covid-19 pandemic to further stifle dissent and press freedom.[68] Following the same pattern, Rodrigo Duterte implemented the authoritarian practices after winning election in 2016 in the Philippines. His government 'cracked down on the independent press, jailed a senator who investigated his death-squad past, and engineered the ouster of an independent minded chief justice of the Supreme Court'.[69] Tanzania under President

[62] Thomas Carothers, 'The Backlash Against Democracy Promotion' (2006) 85 Foreign Affairs 55; Tom Ginsburg and Aziz Z Huq, *How to Save a Constitutional Democracy* (University of Chicago Press 2018) 50.

[63] Paul Lendvai, 'The Transformer: Orban's Evolution and Hungary's Demise' (2019) 98 Foreign Affairs 44, 51.

[64] Lendvai (n 65).

[65] Christian Davies, 'Hostile Takeover: How Law and Justice Captured Poland's Courts' (Freedom House 2018) <https://freedomhouse.org/report/analytical-brief/2018/hostile-takeover-how-law-and-justice-captured-polands-courts> accessed 4 June 2022; Anna Sledzinska-Simon, 'The Polish Revolution: 2015–2017' (*International Journal of Constitutional Law Blog*, 2017) <www.iconnectblog.com/2017/07/the-polish-revolution-2015-2017/> accessed 4 June 2022.

[66] Frantz and Kendall-Taylor (n 16) 62.

[67] Elana Beiser, 'China, Turkey, Saudi Arabia, Egypt Are World's Worst Jailers of Journalists' (2019) Committee to Protect Journalists <https://cpj.org/reports/2019/12/journalists-jailed-china-turkey-saudi-arabia-egypt/>accessed 4 June 2022.

[68] Marc Pierini, 'Emerging From the Pandemic, Turkey Rolls Out a More Assertive Foreign Policy' (2020) Carnegie Endowment for International Peace <https://tinyurl.com/mwstm2ex> accessed 4 June 2022.

[69] Sheila S Coronel, 'The Vigilante President: How Duterte's Brutal Populism Conquered the Philippines' (2019) 98 Foreign Affairs 36, 42

John Magufuli took a similar course. Magufuli's government weakened the judiciary 'through executive appointments without independent parliamentary vetting'. It clamped down on the media through a law empowering it 'to suspend and close media outlets for reporting on allegations of corruption and human rights violations'. A similar law granted the government 'sweeping powers to police the internet'.[70] Amnesty International reported that a series of new laws since 2019 has restricted the operations of NGOs and established greater government control over NGO activities.[71] Egypt under Abdel Fattah al-Sisi and Nicolás Maduro's Venezuela have seen the same kinds of authoritarian policies. And, as the V-Dem data showed, such examples could be multiplied over dozens of countries.

Authoritarian resurgence has weakened the domestic accountability mechanisms that are essential for giving effect to international human rights legal norms. International human rights law can be a tool for actors who press their own governments to live up to their international human rights commitments. Advocates, activists, the news media, and the broader public itself can expose abuses, denounce violators, demand accountability, and bring political and legal pressure on governments to fulfil their human rights treaty commitments—but only if the channels for engaging in those activities remain open. Naturally, authoritarian governments consistently target the essential mechanisms of accountability: independent courts, freedom of expression and the press, and the ability of civil society to organize and participate in public life. These mechanisms are crucial to people's ability to deploy international human rights law in their local contexts.

5. The Resilience of Rights

As authoritarian regimes become more numerous and consolidate their power, the international human rights legal order faces erosion from above and below. At the international level, authoritarian regimes do not seem likely to mount an all-out assault on formal human rights law by denouncing treaties and dropping out of related institutions. Rather, they can weaken those institutions by participating in purely pro forma ways; engaging in human rights talk while reasserting sovereignty and non-interference; and shielding each other from international accountability. At the domestic level, the erosion of mechanisms of accountability seems to portend even greater damage to the international human rights legal order. It is through domestic action—political and judicial—that IHRL can improve human

[70] Tom Odula, 'Tanzania Intensifies Repression ahead of Polls, Says Report' (2020) Associated Press <https://apnews.com/article/virus-outbreak-john-magufuli-health-media-newspapers-1f502c763c52c11aade72154a0ecf28a> accessed 4 June 2022.

[71] Amnesty International, 'Tanzania: Laws Weaponized to Undermine Political and Civil Freedoms Ahead of Elections' (2020) <www.amnesty.org/en/latest/news/2020/10/tanzania-laws-weaponized-to-undermine-political-and-civil-freedoms-ahead-of-elections/> accessed 4 June 2022.

rights fulfillment. Authoritarians constrict or close off the avenues for rights-promoting domestic action.

At the international level, as the zone of liberalism shrinks, the burden of maintaining the complex of treaty bodies, human rights courts, and related institutions (like the Human Rights Council) will fall on the remaining liberal democracies. Much will depend on whether the democracies are willing to hold themselves to high rights standards and to continue to press the authoritarians to respect rights. Whether the democracies are willing to sustain a long and slow-moving struggle for rights will partly depend, in turn, on whether domestic publics value rights and support some degree of rights internationalism. On that score, the US and Europe are likely to play major roles. With a new administration in place as of January 2021, the US has already taken steps to show that it will be a more active promoter of democracy and human rights on the international stage. The European Union has laid out pro-democracy priorities in its foreign policy, though it must still find a way to confront and sanction the authoritarian canker in Hungary and Poland.

What sources of resilience does the international human rights regime possess? 'Resilience' refers to the capacity of institutions to resist efforts to curtail their authority and competences. The resilience of international and regional human rights orders is a function of the degree to which they become more fully embedded (or incorporated) in a greater variety of domestic contexts. Regional and global human rights, as I have argued, become effective at the domestic level as they are incorporated and deployed by different kinds of actors. We should expect greater resilience of international human rights legal orders to the extent they have become embedded more extensively in more countries. That embeddedness can occur in domestic law (including constitutions, legislation, and jurisprudence), in legal education and the practice of law, in government institutions, in civil society organizations, and in broader public awareness and acceptance.

Signs of the embeddedness of human rights are visible. The attempts at backlash against the ECtHR and the IACtHR—which aimed to trim the powers of the regional human rights systems—failed. Neither system saw its authorities meaningfully reduced. The resilience of the regional systems is due in large part to their embeddedness in domestic law, institutions, and society. The European Convention and the jurisprudence of the ECtHR are widely incorporated in domestic legal systems and applied by domestic judges. Similarly, the Inter-American Human Rights System has become embedded domestically in many countries of the region, in constitutions, legislation, and judicial interpretation; legal clinics; national rights institutions; and civil society organizations. Indeed, the mobilization of NGOs played a major role in defeating the effort to trim the Inter-American Commission's powers.[72]

[72] Gonzalez Ocantos and Sandholtz (n 51). The 'new constitutionalism' in Latin America has linked domestic constitutional orders and international human rights increasingly tightly; see Armin von

More broadly, part of the critique of the human rights sceptics has been that the global human rights movement has become insular, captivated by its own illusions, and detached from the everyday concerns of real people.[73] Underlying this critique is an unsupported presumption that ordinary people do not care about rights. In fact, there are good reasons to think that the opposite is true. As Dancy and Fariss point out, human rights are popular relative to other discourses available for making political claims. They note that '[t]he global volume of written and verbal references to human rights shows few signs of contraction, and the respect that local populations have for human rights organizations is higher than some would expect'.[74] People value human rights institutions because they 'remain a site through which individuals empower themselves, seek meaning together, and resist cruelty'.[75] If that is the case, then authoritarian repression also has its limits. Authoritarians often take power promising to serve the people and bring about deeper democracy. They deliver the opposite, undermining their own legitimacy.[76]

In fact, there is evidence that people living under authoritarian regimes continue to value democracy and rights and are willing to resist the autocrats. As Kenneth Roth, executive director of Human Rights Watch, has argued, '[W]hile the autocrats and rights abusers may capture the headlines, the defenders of human rights, democracy, and the rule of law are also gaining strength. The same populists who are spreading hatred and intolerance are spawning a resistance.'[77] Freedom House, in its most recent global report, makes a similar point: 'A striking number of new citizen protest movements have emerged over the past year, reflecting the inexhaustible and universal desire for fundamental rights.'[78] Evidence provides tentative support for what might otherwise be seen as the wishful thinking of professional human rights do-gooders.

An IPSOS poll in twenty-eight countries found that only three in ten respondents stated that human rights were *not* a problem in their country. In addition, '[e]ight in ten people surveyed stress the importance of having laws that protect human rights in their country and *more than half say they make their life better*.'[79]

Bogdandy and others (eds), *Transformative Constitutionalism in Latin America: The Emergence of a New Ius Commune* (OUP 2017).

[73] Stephen Hopgood, *The Endtimes of Human Rights* (Cornell University Press 2013); Samuel Moyn, *The Last Utopia: Human Rights in History* (Harvard University Press 2010); Eric A Posner, *The Twilight of Human Rights Law* (OUP 2014).

[74] Geoffrey Dancy and Christopher Fariss, 'The Heavens Are Always Fallen: A Neo-constitutive Approach to Human Rights in Global Society' (2018) 81 Law and Contemporary Problems 86.

[75] ibid 100.

[76] Yascha Mounk, 'The Dictators' Last Stand: Why the New Autocrats Are Weaker Than They Look' (2019) 98 Foreign Affairs 138.

[77] Kenneth Roth, 'World's Autocrats Face Rising Resistance' (2019) Human Rights Watch <www.hrw.org/world-report/2019/keynote/autocrats-face-rising-resistance> accessed 4 June 2022.

[78] Freedom House, *Freedom in the World 2020* (n 22).

[79] Nicolas Boyon, Yves Bardon, and Chloe Morin, 'Human Rights in 2018' (2018) IPSOS <www.ipsos.com/en-us/news-polls/global-advisor-human-rights-2018#> accessed 4 June 2022 (emphasis added).

A number organizations active in human rights were 'widely seen as doing a good job', including the United Nations, the International Committee of the Red Cross, Amnesty International, International Federation for Human Rights, Lawyers Without Borders, and Human Rights Watch.[80] The Global Protest Tracker, produced by the Carnegie Endowment for International Peace, documents 'antigovernment protests worldwide since 2017' involving more than 1,000 people. The data list twenty-nine such protests in countries rated by Freedom House as 'not free' and forty-nine protests occurring in countries classified as 'partially free'.[81] And new V-Dem data on 'pro-democracy mass mobilization'[82] found 'all-time highs in 2019'. A number of findings stand out:

- 'Citizens are taking to the streets in order *to defend civil liberties and the rule of law*, and to fight for clean elections and *political freedom*.'
- 'During 2019, citizens in 29 democracies mobilized against autocratization, such as in Bolivia, Poland, and Malawi.'
- 'Citizens staged mass protests in 34 autocracies, among them Algeria, Hong Kong, and Sudan.'
- 'In 22 countries, pro-democracy mass protests have been followed by substantial democratization during the last ten years.'[83]

As Carothers puts it:

> all this attention on the decline of democracy has obscured a story that is just as important: many authoritarians, dictators, and other nondemocratic leaders are also in trouble. Just like their peers in free countries, many citizens in nondemocracies are deeply frustrated with their political systems and have in the last several years been acting on that unhappiness by challenging those in power.[84]

Even some of the most aggressive authoritarians have faced large-scale mass protests, including Erdoğan in Turkey[85] and Orbán in Hungary.[86]

[80] ibid.

[81] Carnegie Endowment for International Peace, 'Global Protest Tracker' (2020) <https://carnegieendowment.org/publications/interactive/protest-tracker> accessed 4 June 2022.

[82] I treat 'pro-democracy' mobilization as essentially coterminous with pro-rights mobilization, since democracy (at least in its 'liberal' model, which is the focus in this chapter) depends on and is in part defined by the presence of civil and political rights.

[83] Maerz and others (n 24) (emphasis added).

[84] Thomas Carothers, 'Dictators in Trouble: Democracy Isn't the Only System under Stress' *Foreign Affairs* (6 February 2020) <https://tinyurl.com/bdfw8hxn> accessed 4 June 2022.

[85] Mark Lowen, 'Turkey's Erdogan Defends Istanbul Election Re-run Amid Protests' (*BBC News*, 7 May 2019) <www.bbc.com/news/world-europe-48184149> accessed 4 June 2022; Mark Lowen, 'Erdogan's Party Suffers Blow after Istanbul Re-run Poll Defeat' (*BBC News*, 24 June 2019) <www.bbc.com/news/world-europe-48739256> accessed 4 June 2022.

[86] Helene Bienvenu and Marc Santora, 'Thousands of Hungarians Protest Against Newly Elected Leader' *New York Times* (2018) <www.nytimes.com/2018/04/14/world/europe/hungary-protest-orban.

Anti-authoritarian popular movements have sometimes managed to dislodge autocrats. Anti-government protests in Ethiopia began in 2015 and continued until the prime minister, Hailemariam Desalegn, resigned in February 2018.[87] In Sudan, mass protests against the autocratic Omar al-Bashir started in December 2018, and the military removed al-Bashir from power in April 2019.[88] When the autocratic president of Algeria, Abdelaziz Bouteflika, announced his candidacy for a fifth term in February 2019, he triggered massive peaceful demonstrations. Bouteflika stepped down in April 2019.[89] The successful popular protest movements did not immediately produce democracy. But the point is that repression can reach its limits and that publics are often willing to defy the autocrats—a sign of the resilience of rights.

In short, international human rights norms may be more embedded in civil society around the globe than many have presumed. The more human rights norms and institutions are embedded domestically, the greater the sources of resilience of regional and international human rights regimes.

6. Conclusion

This exploration of authoritarian resurgence and change in the international human rights legal order contributes to our understanding of the paths of change in international law. My analysis offers two relevant insights: (1) international legal change is not always progressive but can also move in a non-liberal direction; and (2) for international human rights law—and probably for other domains of international law as well—crucial pathways of change go through domestic institutions and practices. This study also proposes more questions.

First, the analysis emphasized the crucial role of domestic politico-legal mechanisms and processes in driving change in the international legal order. Because domestic arenas are the front line in applying and giving effect to international human rights legal norms, much of the action in terms of systemic legal change necessarily happens there. A question going forward is: to what extent are domestic

html> accessed 4 June 2022; Nick Thorpe, 'Budapest Election: Hungary's Orban in Shock Defeat' (*BBC News*, 14 October 2019) <www.bbc.com/news/world-europe-50039847> accessed 4 June 2022.

[87] The Guardian, 'Ethiopian Prime Minister Resigns after Mass Protests' *The Guardian* (15 February 2018) <www.theguardian.com/world/2018/feb/15/ethiopia-prime-minister-hailemariam-desalegn-resigns-after-mass-protests> accessed 4 June 2022.

[88] BBC News, 'Sudan Coup: Why Omar al-Bashir Was Overthrown' (*BBC News*, 15 April 2019) <www.bbc.com/news/world-africa-47852496> accessed 4 June 2022.

[89] Adam Nossiter, 'Hopes Fade for New Political Course in Algeria a Year After Popular Uprising' *New York Times* (2020) <www.nytimes.com/2020/10/04/world/africa/algeria-protests-politics.html> accessed 4 June 2022; Adam Nossiter, 'Military's Preferred Candidate Named Winner in Algeria Election' *New York Times* (2019) <www.nytimes.com/2019/12/13/world/africa/algeria-election-protest.html?action=click&module=RelatedLinks&pgtype=Article> accessed 4 June 2022.

developments an important motor of international legal change in other domains? An initial proposition would be that in areas where the conduct to be regulated by international law is primarily domestic and even local, the domestic level will be a crucial site of international norm change. That condition is most likely met by international environmental law, where the point of rule-making is to affect the choices that millions of actors make every day. Individual choices at the domestic level are probably less relevant to international law on security and the use of force. International economic law (trade and investment) probably falls somewhere in between, with private transnational economic actors playing a central role.

Secondly, I have argued that the formal content of international human rights could well remain unchanged. Authoritarians would seem to have little to gain from the effort that would be required to scrap global human rights treaties or enact new ones embodying more autocracy-friendly norms. Instead, they can do what they have often done already, namely, engage in cheap talk, giving lip service to human rights while denying that they are doing anything wrong or that outsiders have any right to question their domestic practices. They can assert limits to human rights norms based on traditional international law principles (sovereignty and non-interference) or on new counter-norms (like combating terrorism, extremism, and separatism).[90] Authoritarians can hollow out international human rights institutions by going through the motions of reporting and responding, but without accepting negative findings regarding themselves or their fellow autocrats. What this suggests is that we need to recognize and understand modes of norm change that do not alter the substantive content of norms. That is, 'change in the substantive content of rules is only one form of change; norms can also shift along other dimensions, including strength, formality, specificity, and authoritativeness.'[91]

Authoritarian resurgence appears to be changing IHRL on the dimensions of strength and authoritativeness. And yet signs of resilience are visible. The regional human rights courts have come through episodes of backlash—when states sought to trim their powers—with their authority intact. More broadly, domestic backlash against the authoritarians, motivated at least in part by human rights norms, has emerged in diverse settings around the world. Clearly, the paths of change in IHRL do not have a fixed endpoint.

[90] Alexander Cooley, 'Authoritarianism Goes Global: Countering Democratic Norms' (2015) 26 Journal of Democracy 49; Ginsburg (n 2).

[91] Wayne Sandholtz, *Prohibiting Plunder: How Norms Change* (OUP 2007) 23.

9

The Future of the Oceans

The Role of Human Rights Law and International Environmental Law in Shaping the Law of the Sea

*Seline Trevisanut**

1. Introduction

The law which regulates the use of the oceans is one of the oldest branches of international law. It is consequently deeply rooted in traditional understandings of foundational principles, such as sovereignty and territory. Notwithstanding this, the law of the sea has developed and was codified in the second half of the twentieth century, keeping in mind the necessary interaction of the legal regime with changing circumstances, in particular with technological developments and the emergence of international environmental law. The multiplication of activities and of users at sea, however, emphasizes the importance of the legal framework which is required to not only interact with environmental law, but increasingly to interact with refugee and human rights law.

The interaction with refugee and human rights law is, however, more difficult than with environmental law because, for instance, the law of sea is particularly state-centric and marginally deals with the 'human' element of maritime activities.[1] On the one hand, the 1982 Law of the Sea Convention (LOSC)[2] contains no mentions of 'human rights' and only a few of its provisions concern the treatment of individuals submitted to states' authority (eg the duty to render assistance in Article 98 LOSC). On the other hand, the LOSC contains treaty-based mechanisms of interaction with international environmental law (eg the so-called 'rules of reference' in Part XII of the LOSC).

The present contribution will compare the LOSC/international environmental law interaction with the LOSC/human rights law interaction in order to identify the factors and pathways that facilitate or hinder the impact of environmental law and human rights law on the LOSC. This analysis aims to offer tools to better

* Professor of International Law and Sustainability, School of Law, Utrecht University, Utrecht, The Netherlands. The research for this contribution was conducted, thanks to the financial support of the European Research Council under the European Union's Horizon 2020 research and innovation programme (Grant Agreement No 639070 – SUSTAINABLEOCEAN).

[1] For general discussion about the place of humans in the law of the sea, see *inter alia* Irini Papanicolopulu, *International Law and the Protection of People at Sea* (OUP 2018).

[2] United Nations Convention on the Law of the Sea (opened for signature 10 December 1982, entered into force 16 November 1994) 1833 UNTS 397 (hereafter LOSC).

Seline Trevisanut, *The Future of the Oceans* In: *The Many Paths of Change in International Law.* Edited by: Nico Krisch and Ezgi Yildiz, Oxford University Press. © Seline Trevisanut 2023. DOI: 10.1093/oso/9780198877844.003.0009

understand how international environmental law and refugee law have impacted the law of the sea and are shaping the future of the oceans. In particular, the chapter will show how the field has been transformed through the activities of alternative paths, at a time when the traditional lawmaking processes stalled. In this regard, the chapter showcases the importance of the multilateral pathway (through the resolutions and decisions of international organizations and treaty bodies), the bureaucratic pathway (by means of explanatory instruments adopted by the international organizations and diplomatic conferences), and the private authority pathway (by virtue of activities of professional associations and organizations).[3]

I will then focus on two case studies: the legal framework of search and rescue (SAR) operations which is anchored in a specialized treaty system (namely, the 1979 SAR Convention[4]) but has developed and changed through the action of United Nations High Commissioner for Refugees (UNHCR);[5] and the legal framework applicable to offshore energy projects, which is characterized by the participation of multiple and diverse actors, by sectoral and geographical fragmentation, and by unconventional lawmaking.[6]

2. Protecting Humans in Search and Rescue Operations

2.1 The International Legal Framework of Search and Rescue Services

The duty to render assistance at sea is set out in Article 98 LOSC as follows:

1. Every State shall require the master of a ship flying its flag, in so far as he can do so without serious danger to the ship, the crew or the passengers:

[3] Nico Krisch and Ezgi Yildiz, 'The Many Paths of Change in International Law: A Frame' in Nico Krisch and Ezgi Yildiz (eds), *The Many Paths of Change in International Law* (Oxford University Press 2023).

[4] International Convention on Maritime Search and Rescue (opened for signature 27 April 1979, entered into force 22 June 1985) 1405 UNTS 119 (hereafter SAR Convention).

[5] Some of the arguments presented in the second part of this chapter are an updated and revised version of parts of the chapter Seline Trevisanut, 'The Contribution of the UNHCR to Ocean Governance' in David Joseph Attard (ed), *The IMLI Treatise on Global Ocean Governance*, vol 2: *UN Specialized Agencies and Global Ocean Governance* (OUP 2018) 243–57.

[6] Unconventional lawmaking in the law of the sea encompasses a broad spectrum of lawmaking processes and actors; it includes not only lawmaking processes beyond states but also beyond international cooperation. Unconventional lawmaking encompasses different ways actors (state and non-state, public and private) which operate at the international level are developing standards of behaviour to regulate varied maritime activities, beyond traditional top-down lawmaking, beyond the structures of the Law of the Sea Convention. For a detailed analysis of those processes, see Natalie Klein (ed), *Unconventional Lawmaking in the Law of the Sea* (OUP 2022). Some of the arguments presented in the second part of this chapter are an updated and revised version of parts of the chapter Seline Trevisanut, 'Unconventional Lawmaking in the Offshore Energy Sector: Flexibilities and Weaknesses of the International Legal Framework' in ibid 163–83.

(a) to render assistance to *any person found at sea* in danger of being lost;
(b) to *proceed with all possible speed to the rescue of persons in distress*, if informed of their need of assistance, in so far as such action may reasonably be expected of him; [. . .] (emphasis added)

Before the adoption of the LOSC, two other international treaties had codified the content of the duty to render assistance: the 1974 Convention on the Safety of Life at Sea (SOLAS Convention) and the 1979 Search and Rescue Convention (SAR Convention). The latter was brought about in the wake of instances of non-rescue at sea during the Indochinese crisis and aimed at clarifying the need to identify the recipient of the obligation actually to perform the rescue operations and the consequences of their performance. As a result of its repetition in treaties and domestic legislation, and in the light of state practice, even if not always uniform,[7] today the duty to render assistance is recognized as a principle of customary law.[8]

The SAR Convention aims to create an international system for coordinating rescue operations that guarantees their effectiveness and safety. States parties are thus invited to conclude SAR agreements with neighbouring states to regulate and coordinate SAR operations and services in an agreed maritime zone. Such agreements are designed technically and operationally to implement the obligation set out in Article 98(2) LOSC, which provides that, where needed, neighbouring states should cooperate through regional agreements to promote and maintain adequate and effective SAR services.[9] Such agreements also diminish the risk of non-rescue incidents. Moreover, they represent an economic advantage for the contracting

[7] The content of the obligation is still debated. In particular, the disagreement focuses on the obligations of the coastal state in whose SAR zone the rescue operation takes place, and on the place where the rescued persons can disembark. See the debate between Mediterranean states (namely, Italy, Malta, and Spain) within the IMO; IMO, 'Measures to protect the safety of persons rescued at sea, Compulsory guideline for the treatment of persons rescued at sea', submitted by Spain and Italy (13 February 2009) FSI 17/15/1; IMO, 'Measures to protect the safety of persons rescued at sea, Comments on document FSI 17/15/1', submitted by Malta (27 February 2009) FSI 17/15/2. For a comment on this issue, see Patricia Mallia, 'The MV Salamis and the State of Disembarkation at International Law: The Undefinable Goal' (May 2014) 18 *ASIL Insights* <www.asil.org/insights/volume/18/issue/11/mv-salamis-and-state-disembarkation-international-law-undefinable-goal> accessed 17 June 2022; Seline Trevisanut, 'Search and Rescue Operations in the Mediterranean: Factor of Cooperation or Conflict?' (2010) 25 International Journal of Marine and Coastal Law 523.

[8] UN Commission on International Law, 'Commentary on Draft Article 12 of the United Nations Convention on the High Seas' (1956) UN Doc A/3179. Many have then supported the customary nature of the obligation; see, inter alia, Richard Barnes, 'Refugee Law at Sea' (2004) 53 International and Comparative Law Quarterly 49; Efthymios Papastravidis, *The Interception of Vessels on the High Seas: Contemporary Challenges to the Legal Order of the Oceans* (Hart Publishing 2013) 294; Trevisanut, 'Search and Rescue Operations' (n 6) 527.

[9] Art 98(2) LOSC states: 'Every coastal State shall promote the establishment, operation and maintenance of an adequate and effective search and rescue service regarding safety on and over the sea and, where circumstances so require, by way of mutual regional arrangements cooperate with neighbouring States for this purpose.'

parties to the extent that they can share the costs arising from organizing and carrying out SAR operations.

Carrying out rescue operations at sea, however, does not exhaust the duty to render assistance, which extends to the disembarkation of the rescued persons in a place of safety. Sea-borne migration and related humanitarian crises have strikingly highlighted this point. The Maritime Safety Committee (MSC) of the IMO adopted two resolutions that amended both the SOLAS[10] and SAR Conventions,[11] and which entered into force on 1 July 2006. Consequently, pursuant to Article 4.1-1 of Chapter V/33 of the SOLAS Convention and Chapter 3.1.9 of the Annex of the SAR Convention, the coastal state responsible for the search and rescue region in which the SAR operation took place shall exercise 'primary responsibility' to ensure that the 'survivors assisted are *disembarked* from the assisting ship and delivered to *a place of safety*' (emphases added). According to the MSC Guidelines,[12] a 'place of safety' means a location where the rescue operations can be considered as completed. In accordance with Principles 6.13 and 6.14 of the Guidelines, the rescue unit can be the place of safety, but only provisionally. In fact, the text insists on the role that the flag state and the coastal state should play in substituting for the master of the rescuing vessel.

Moreover, pursuant to the same guidelines, the state in whose SAR zone the operation took place has the duty to provide or, at least, to secure a place of safety for the rescued persons (Principle 2.5). This Principle does not include a right of entry into the territory of this state by the rescued persons or a right of access to the ports of the coastal state by the rescuing unit. It simply requires that the coastal state carries out the SAR operations and brings them effectively to an end, ie by not leaving the rescued persons (whatever their status)[13] at sea or in any other unsafe situation. Keeping in mind that the MSC Guidelines are not binding, Principle 2.5 suggests that the coastal state has a 'residual obligation' of allowing disembarkation on its own territory when it has not been possible to do so safely anywhere else.[14] This has been clarified by the IMO Facilitation Committee (FAL), which adopted

[10] MSC.153 (78) 20 May 2004.

[11] MSC.155 (78) 20 May 2004.

[12] MSC.167 (78) 20 May 2004.

[13] The issue concerning the denial of disembarkation by coastal states was mainly raised in instances where irregular migrants and asylum-seekers were among the rescued persons. On the issue see, inter alia, Andreas Fischer-Lescano, Tillmann Löhr, and Timo Tohidipur, 'Border Controls at Sea: Requirements under International Human Rights and Refugee Law' (2009) 21 International Journal of Refugee Law 256; Guy S Goodwin-Gill, 'The Right to Seek Asylum: Interception at Sea and the Principle of Non-Refoulement' (2011) 23 International Journal of Refugee Law 443; Efthymios Papastravidis, 'The EU and the Obligation of Non-Refoulement at Sea' in Francesca Ippolito and Seline Trevisanut (eds), *Migration in the Mediterranean: Mechanisms of International Cooperation* (CUP 2015) 236; Seline Trevisanut, 'The Principle of *Non-Refoulement* at Sea and the Effectiveness of Asylum Protection' (2008) 12 Max Planck Yearbook of United Nations Law 205–46.

[14] For a contrary opinion, see Papastravidis, *The Interception of Vessels* (n 7) 299.

the 'Principles relating to administrative procedures for disembarking persons rescued at sea'[15] in January 2009. Principle 3 establishes that: '[i]f disembarkation from the rescuing ship *cannot be arranged swiftly elsewhere*, the Government responsible for the SAR area *should accept the disembarkation of the persons rescued* in accordance with immigration laws and regulations of each Member State into a place of safety under its control in which the persons rescued can have timely access to post rescue support' (emphasis added).

The fact that the FAL had to intervene clearly indicates that the 2004 amendments to the SAR and SOLAS Conventions have been insufficient to enhance the safety of persons rescued at sea and to clarify the content of the applicable legal obligations. The MSC Guidelines and the FAL Principles set out how these amendments should be implemented, but these suggestions have not yet been taken up in practice.

2.2 The UNHCR and the Development of the Search and Rescue Legal Framework

The UNHCR has had a fundamental influence in the recognition of the customary nature of the obligation to render assistance at sea. The Indochinese crisis gave the decisive impetus for the adoption of an international legal framework in the field of rescue at sea, with the adoption of the Search and Rescue (SAR) Convention and the Safety of Life at Sea (SOLAS) Convention. In particular, the adoption of the SAR Convention in 1979 is closely linked to the adoption of the resettlement programmes discussed above and the beginning of the cooperation between the IMO and the UNHCR.

2.2.1 The Indochinese crisis

The UNHCR's action consisted of promoting initiatives and giving support to the existing multilateral cooperation programmes that dealt with the rescue and resettlement of refugees found at sea. This mode of action took shape in particular with the management of the 'boat people' crisis stemming from the Vietnam War.[16] The United Nations were involved in the reconstruction process following the Peace Treaty of Paris of 1973, but the fate of the boat people took an international significance only in the second half of the 1970s.[17]

Considering thatthe UNHCR can only operate on the territory of states that have authorized it and does not have its own means to intervene at sea, the agency could

[15] FAL.3/Circ.194, 22 January 2009.

[16] Lakshamana Chetty, 'Resolution of the Problem of Boat People: The Case of a Global Initiative' [2001] ISIL Yearbook of International Humanitarian and Refugee Law 144ff.

[17] ibid 145ff.

then only intervene once the migrants had reached the country of destination or of transit. However, at that time, the main recipient countries, namely Thailand, Malaysia, and Singapore, were not parties to the 1951 Geneva Convention or the 1967 Protocol. The UNHCR interventions were therefore aimed at getting the attention of states parties to the Refugee Convention, which were likely to provide support and aid for the construction and management of camps.

In connection with, and in addition to, the humanitarian emergency, other problems emerged: to determine who should intervene on the high seas to rescue migrants, and what were the areas of competence and responsibility of the interested states. The then High Commissioner, Hartling, emphasized: 'we must not ask a drowning man how he came to be in those straits. Still less is there time to question if he has relatives abroad, is bilingual, skilled or physically or mentally handicapped. Asylum, at least temporarily, must be given immediately and durable solutions [. . .] must be devised in response to humanitarian needs, needs that are surely self-evident.'[18]

The mixed composition of the migratory flows and their increasing number generated strong hostility among the public in recipient countries. Instances of non-rescue and denials of disembarkation multiplied. The intergovernmental conference held in Geneva in July 1979 made it clear that the crisis could not be solved within the UNHCR because the agency did not have, and still does not have, competence in the field of navigation, specifically for rescue operations. In Geneva, the UNCHR then called the parties to cooperate, in a spirit of solidarity, and presented a programme to that effect.

The focal point of the 1979 conference was temporary asylum, which implied a subsequent multilateral cooperation programme on resettlement of refugees.[19] In 1979, the DISERO (Disembarkation Resettlement Offers) programme was created and provided a first solution to the refusal of disembarkation by destination states.[20] Participating states undertook to accept a predetermined quota of refugees/displaced persons in order to encourage vessels to perform their rescue obligations by guaranteeing them entry and disembarkation. Unfortunately, the practice of ignoring vessels in distress continued. The main issue for rescuing vessels was the economic cost of rescue operations. A rescue operation often implied a variation of the navigational route, with consequent loss of time and, thus, consequent economic loss.

[18] Opening Statement by the United Nations High Commissioner for Refugees, in Consultative Meeting with Interested Governments on Refugees and Displaced Persons in South East Asia (Geneva 11–12 December 1978) <www.unhcr.org/en-us/admin/hcspeeches/3ae68fce4c/opening-statement-mr-poul-hartling-united-nations-high-commissioner-refugees.html> accessed 17 June 2022.

[19] Sten A Bronée, 'The History of the Comprehensive Plan of Action'(1993) 5 International Journal of Refugee Law 534.

[20] 'Problems Related to the Rescue of Asylum-Seekers at Sea', EC/SCP/42 <www.unhcr.org/excom/scip/3ae68cbc20/problems-related-rescue-asylum-seekers-sea.html> accessed 17 June 2022.

In 1982, the Working Group of Government Representatives on the Question of Rescue and Asylum Seekers at Sea issued an appeal to the flag states to encourage vessels flying their flag to carry out rescue operations on the high seas and to adhere to the DISERO programme.[21] The problem of so-called 'flags of convenience' or 'open-registry countries' then emerged.[22] On the same occasion, the Working Group suggested that the master of the ship, in the fulfilment of his or her obligations, 'should not be in any way held liable for undertaking rescue'. This disclaimer did not, however, solve the problem of the economic cost of rescue operations. The following year, the UNHCR proposed the *Guidelines for the Disembarkation of Refugees*,[23] in which the agency took an active role both at the operational and financial levels:

> On request, UNHCR will reimburse shipowners for costs, which are specially related to the care of refugees rescued at sea, not exceeding US$ 5 per refugee. Furthermore, UNHCR can reimburse shipowners for expenditures incurred in connection with disembarkation of refugees […], reimbursement of such incidental expenditures should not exceed US$ 5,000 per ship. […] Expenses incurred by shipowners, as a direct consequence of rescue […] cannot be covered by this programme.

The same document contained a Proposal for a Scheme for the Rescue at Sea Resettlement Offers that sought to respond to another concern of flag and port states, namely the resettlement of rescued refugees. Within the RASRO (Rescue at Sea Resettlement Offers) programme the flag state could ask for an anticipated funding of the costs linked to the arrival of refugees/displaced persons and to their subsequent integration. At the same time, the coastal states would receive resettlement guarantees in exchange for authorizing disembarkations. The RASRO programme became operational on 1 May 1985,[24] and fifteen states participated therein.[25]

The UNHCR also continued its dialogue with shipowners and masters expanding the project to the reimbursement of their costs associated with rescuing

[21] 'Report on the Meeting of the Working Group of Government Representatives on the Question of Rescue of Asylum Seekers at Sea held in Geneva 5–7 July 1982 (24 August 1982).

[22] On the issue of flag of convenience and open-registry state see, inter alia, Dr Ademuni-Odeke, 'An Examination of Bareboat Charter Registries and Flag of Convenience Registries in International Law' (2005) 36 Ocean Development and International Law 339; Doris König and others, 'Flags of Convenience' [2009] Max Planck Encyclopedias of International Law.

[23] UNHCR, 'Problems Related to the Rescue of Asylum-Seekers in Distress at Sea' (1 September 1983) Annex 1 <www.unhcr.org/excom/scip/3ae68ccf8/problems-related-rescue-asylum-seekers-distress-sea.html> accessed 17 June 2022.

[24] 'Report of the United Nations High Commissioner for Refugees' (1 August 1986) UN Doc A/41/12, para 92.

[25] Australia, Canada, Denmark, Finland, France, Greece, Japan, New Zealand, Norway, the Netherlands, the United Kingdom, Spain, the US, Sweden, and Switzerland.

boat people (the *Rescue at Sea Reimbursement Project*).[26] It also intensified its cooperation with the International Maritime Organization (IMO), which, after reaching an agreement with the UNHCR in December 1984, put at the disposal of the latter an expert to assist in matters relating to rescue at sea.[27] Despite the significant contribution of the DISERO and RASRO programmes in managing and reducing the number of arrivals, the countries of first asylum continued to express their concerns and voiced the need to find definitive solutions to the problem. The central point of the debate remained the issue of resettlement. In June 1989, the International Conference on Indochinese Refugees was held in Geneva. It marked a worldwide breakthrough in the management of one of the most important migratory crises, thanks in particular to the adoption of the Comprehensive Plan of Action (CPA).[28] The CPA outlined the role which the UNHCR can play in facilitating and organizing international cooperation for the management of irregular migration by sea. During the Indochinese crisis, the UNHCR deeply influenced the way in which cooperation took place and the content and fulfilment of any agreements concluded between the countries involved, including the cooperation in the field of search and rescue at sea.

2.2.2 Interinstitutional dialogue and normative developments

The IMO is one of the first institutions with which the UNHCR signed a memorandum of understanding. Cooperation between the two agencies dates back to 1970.[29] These fifty years have allowed the development of the conventions mentioned above and subsequent amendments of principles and standards aimed at facilitating rescue operations at sea in compliance with refugee law and, more generally, human rights law. Following this policy goal, and according to the comprehensive approach to the migratory phenomenon inaugurated with the CPA, the UNHCR has organized in close collaboration with the IMO a series of meetings specifically devoted to the rescue at sea of migrants between 2002 and 2014.

One of the major results of the cooperation between the UNHCR and the IMO was the publication in 2006 of a leaflet entitled *Rescue at Sea: A Guide to Principles and Practice as Applied to Migrants and Refugees*.[30] This document incorporates in particular the 2004 amendments to the SAR and SOLAS Conventions. It emphasized the specific measures and precautions that the rescuing vessel shall adopt

[26] UNHCR, 'Problems Related to Rescue of Asylum Seekers at Sea' (8 July 1985) para 8 <www.unhcr.org/excom/scip/3ae68cbc20/problems-related-rescue-asylum-seekers-sea.html> accessed 17 June 2022.

[27] UN Doc A/41/12 (n 23) para 139.

[28] As mentioned, the CPA mainly dealt with settlement issues and will thus not be analysed in depth here. For further information on the CPA, see, inter alia, Bronée (n 18); Chetty (n 15).

[29] Executive Committee, 'Follow-up to ECOSOC Resolution 1995/56, Information Note on the Development of Operative Memoranda of Understanding' (4 January 1996) EC/46/SC/CRP.8, 2.

[30] IMO/UNHCR, 'Rescue at Sea: A Guide to Principles and Practice as Applied to Migrants and Refugees' <www.unhcr.org/publications/brochures/450037d34/rescue-sea-guide-principles-practice-applied-migrants-refugees.html> accessed 17 June 2022; the leaflet was updated in 2015.

when there are refugees or asylum-seekers among the rescued migrants. It then recalled the duty of the captain of the rescuing unit to protect asylum-seekers, to inquire about their presence on board, eventually to communicate it to the UNHCR, and to disembark them only when all guarantees of protection for the personal safety of the asylum-seekers, including the principle of *non-refoulement*,[31] have been confirmed. The document clearly incorporates the Guidelines developed by the IMO MSC concerning the interpretation of the 2004 amendments to the SAR and SOLAS Conventions. Principle 6.17 of the MSC Guidelines provides: 'The need to avoid disembarkation in territories where the lives and freedoms of those alleging a well-founded fear of persecution would be threatened is a consideration in the case of asylum-seekers and refugees recovered at sea.'[32]

A meeting on 'Refugees and Asylum-Seekers in Distress at Sea—How Best to Respond?' was held in Djibouti in 2011. The meeting aimed to discuss with governments and other stakeholders, such as the UNHCR, possible cooperation mechanisms in order to share burdens and responsibilities related to distress at sea situations involving refugees and asylum-seekers.[33] The discussion was based on a background paper prepared by the UNHCR[34] in which the agency presented possible tools for organizing and enhancing cooperation. The discussions focused on two tools in particular: a model framework for cooperation and mobile protection response teams. The model framework builds upon the experience of the UNHCR during the Indochinese crisis and tries to repeat the success of the CPA.[35] It also mirrors the efforts within the IMO concerning a Regional Agreement on Concerted Procedures Relating to the Disembarkation of Persons Rescued at Sea for the Mediterranean region.[36]

The mobile protection response teams are supposed to be temporary teams which would include experts, with different backgrounds, from several governments, the UNHCR, other international organizations, and non-governmental organizations. These teams could be established on a stand-by basis and deployed, on request, to support and develop host government capacity in the reception and processing of rescued persons upon arrival.[37] Both tools thus target the treatment of refugees and asylum-seekers from the moment of the disembarkation.

The UNHCR also suggested the development of standard operating procedures (SOPs) for shipmasters in the event of a distress at sea situation involving refugees

[31] ibid.

[32] See above (n 11).

[33] The Summary Conclusions and other related documents from the Djibouti meeting are available at <www.refworld.org/pdfid/4ede0d392.pdf> accessed 17 June 2022.

[34] UNHCR, 'Background Paper: Refugees and Asylum-Seekers in Distress at Sea—How Best to Respond? Expert Meeting in Djibouti, 8–10 November 2011' (October 2011) <www.refworld.org/docid/4ec211762.html> accessed 17 June 2022.

[35] Anja Klug, 'Strengthening the Protection of Migrants and Refugees in Distress at Sea through International Cooperation and Burden-Sharing' (2014) 26 International Journal of Refugee Law 1.

[36] IMO Facilitation Committee, 37th session, FAL 37/6/1, 1 July 2011.

[37] ibid 59.

and migrants.[38] Those procedures are meant to supplement the 2006 leaflet elaborated by the UNHCR in cooperation with the IMO. The background paper interestingly attempts to provide a definition of a distress situation that would trigger SAR obligations:

> SAR activities should be initiated wherever there are indications that a vessel or the conditions of the people on board do not allow for safe travel, creating a risk that people may perish at sea. Relevant factors include overcrowding, poor conditions of the vessel, or lack of necessary equipment and expertise.[39]

This definition is an important attempt by the UNHCR to contribute to the existing legal framework by offering a harmonized interpretation of the material scope of application of the SAR system. Moreover, the SOPs would ideally be incorporated in 'industry best practices' in conjunction with the International Chamber of Shipping (ICS).[40] In 2015, the ICS published the second edition of *Large Scale Rescue Operations at Sea, Guidance on Ensuring the Safety and Security of Seafarers and Rescued Persons*,[41] which is intended to be complementary to the IMO/UNHCR *Rescue at Sea* leaflet.[42] However, the 2015 ICS Guidance does not specify any rule of conduct for the members of the crew in case refugees or asylum seekers are rescued. To the contrary, it affirms that 'the Master has no authority, obligation or responsibility for listening to, acting upon or communicating information concerning the legal status of rescued persons or applications for asylum'.[43]

Last but not least came the High Commissioner's 2014 Dialogue on Protection at Sea.[44] This meeting addressed many of the challenges that the never-ending migratory and humanitarian crisis in the Mediterranean poses. It consisted of a key element of the UNHCR's two-year *Global Initiative on Protection at Sea*.[45] The main goal of the Global Initiative is to support states in order to:

> reduce loss of life at sea, as well as exploitation, abuse and violence experienced by people travelling irregularly by sea, and [. . .] establish protection-sensitive responses to irregular mixed migration by sea.[46]

[38] UNHCR, 'Background Paper: Refugees and Asylum-Seekers in Distress at Sea' (n 33).
[39] ibid.
[40] Djibouti meeting, Summary Conclusions, para 17.
[41] ICS, *Large Scale Rescue Operations at Sea* (2nd edn, 2015) 3 <https://www.ics-shipping.org/wp-content/uploads/2015/01/large-scale-rescue-at-sea-min.pdf> accessed 17 June 2022.
[42] IMO/UNHCR (n 29).
[43] ICS (n 40).
[44] Seventh High Commissioner's Dialogue on Protection Challenges (Geneva 10–11 December 2014) <www.unhcr.org/high-commissioners-dialogue-on-protection-challenges-2014.html> accessed 17 June 2022.
[45] UNHCR, High Commissioner's Dialogue on Protection Challenges: Protection at Sea, Global Initiative on Protection at Sea (Geneva 1 May 2014) <www.unhcr.org/5375db0d9.html> accessed 17 June 2022.
[46] ibid 1.

The UNHCR has once again affirmed the importance of the SAR regime, encouraged compliance with it, and repeated the need for further cooperation, in particular at the regional level.[47] At the 2014 meeting, the UNHCR together with the IMO, the International Organization for Migration (IOM), the Office of the United Nations High Commissioner for Human Rights, and the UN Office on Drugs and Crime (UNODC) issued a *Joint Statement on Protection at Sea in the Twenty-First Century*. In this document, the UN bodies once more draw attention to how the many lives lost at sea are challenging the 'time-honored tradition of rescue at sea enshrined in international law', which applies 'regardless of the migration status of the persons in distress at sea'.[48] Once again, the UNHCR affirmed the customary nature of the duty to render assistance and the need to interpret this obligation within its normative context,[49] which includes refugee law and human rights law when dealing with migrants at sea.

3. Protecting the Environment in Offshore Energy Operations

The implementation and the development of the law of the sea are tightly interlinked with technological development. The legal framework needs to be both highly specialized and at the same time flexible. The specialization[50] is guaranteed by the sectoral fragmentation at the global level and the geographical fragmentation at the regional level. The flexibility is pursued through unconventional law-making by international organization and treaty bodies at both global and regional levels.

3.1 Sectoral and Geographical Fragmentation

The offshore energy sector has considerably expanded in the last thirty years. Commentators talk about an 'offshorization'[51] of energy production. The expansion

[47] ibid 2. See also UNHCR, High Commissioner's Dialogue on Protection Challenges: Protection at Sea, Background Paper (Geneva 11 November 2014) <www.unhcr.org/5464c3dc9.html> accessed 17 June 2022.

[48] Joint Statement on Protection at Sea in the Twenty-First Century (Geneva 10 December 2014) <www.unhcr.org/news/press/2014/12/548825d59/unhcr-iom-imo-unodc-ohchr-joint-statement-protection-sea-twenty-first-century.html> accessed 17 June 2022.

[49] Art 31(3)(c) of the Vienna Convention on the Law of Treaties ((opened for signature 23 May 1969, entered into force 27 January 1980) 1155 UNTS 331) provides that, when interpreting a treaty: 'There shall be taken into account, together with the context: ... (c) Any relevant rules of international law applicable in the relations between the parties.'

[50] '[S]pecialisation accommodates various needs and concerns if the states engage in international law-making, and states perceive that their individual positions are better respected in these special regimes that in a global one'; Gerhard Hafner, 'Pros and Cons Ensuing from Fragmentation of International Law' (2004) 25 Michigan Journal of International Law 858–59.

[51] Tarik Dahou, 'La politique des espaces maritimes en Afrique. Louvoyer entre local et global' (2009) 116 Politique africaine 10.

of the sector multiplied the risks associated with this activity, in particular when we consider the increased exploitation of deep-water resources. The Deepwater Horizon disaster in April 2010[52] is of course a clear example of the risks associated with deep water oil and gas exploitation. No framework convention regulates the offshore energy sector. The legal framework developed in a fragmented manner following a problem-based approach at the global level and a geographical approach at the regional level.

3.1.1 The sectoral fragmentation at the global level

The LOSC contains a series of obligations, which set out the jurisdictional framework for conducting offshore energy activities and for the protection of the marine environment. Pursuant to Articles 60 and 80, coastal states have exclusive rights to authorize the construction and exclusive jurisdiction over installations in respectively their exclusive economic zone (EEZ) and continental shelf. The Convention also contains a series of obligations for the protection of the marine environment in Part XII.[53]

Article 208 LOSC specifically regulates the prevention, reduction, and control of the pollution from seabed activities subject to national jurisdiction, for instance the pollution generated by the offshore oil and gas industry located in the EEZ or continental shelf. Coastal states are required to adopt laws, regulations and measures that 'shall be no less effective than *international rules, standards and recommended practices and procedures*' (Article 208.3, emphasis added).[54] Moreover, states, 'acting especially through *competent international organizations or diplomatic conference*, shall establish global and regional rules, standards and recommended practices and procedures to prevent, reduce and control pollution of the marine environment referred to in paragraph 1' (Article 208.5, emphasis added). This provision builds an important 'bridge' between the LOSC and other relevant normative sources, which are not necessarily generated from treaties but derive

[52] The Deepwater Horizon was a mobile offshore drilling unit that was operated at a depth of more than 1,500m in the Gulf of Mexico. Following an explosion in April 2010, killing eleven crew members, the rig sank, and an oil spill affected more than 1,000km of coastline Ruwantissa Abeyratne, 'The Deepwater Horizon Disaster—Some Liability Issues' (2010) 35 Tulane Maritime Law Journal 125.

[53] See the general obligations in arts 192–94 LOSC; for a recent interpretation of those articles in relation to the construction of installations and artificial islands, see Permanent Court of Arbitration, *The South China Sea Arbitration* (*The Republic of Philippines v The People's Republic of China*) (Award) [2016] PCA Case 2013-19, 175, paras 983ff.

[54] The LOSC does not define concepts such as 'international rules', 'standards', and 'recommended practices and procedures', which also remain vague in practice. See, inter alia, Bernard Oxman, 'The Duty to Respect Generally Accepted International Standards' (1991–92) 24 New York University Journal of International Law and Politics 109ff; Seline Trevisanut, 'La Convention des Nations Unies sur le droit de la mer et le droit de l'environnement: développement intrasystémique et renvoi intersystémique' in Hélène Ruiz Fabri and Lorenzo Gradoni (eds), *La circulation des concepts juridiques: le droit international de l'environnement entre mondialisation et fragmentation* (Société de législation comparée 2009) 416.

from the work of relevant actors, such as international organizations, diplomatic conferences, and professional associations.[55]

The integration within the LOSC of future developments in the field of environmental protection is also guaranteed by Article 237 LOSC which consists of a specific compatibility clause between the Convention and obligations deriving from other agreements on the protection and preservation of the marine environment. This provision facilitates the application of the LOSC in the relevant normative context and of environmental law instruments in the context of marine environment protection.[56] Many international instruments are relevant here: those tackling a particular source of pollution and its consequences,[57] and those regulating wider questions relevant for the protection of the environment. For instance, the United Nations Framework Convention on Climate Change (UNFCCC) and the 1992 Convention on Biological Diversity (CBD) apply in areas under the jurisdiction of the coastal state, ie its territorial waters, continental shelf and EEZ, and integrate principles such as precaution and sustainable development in the context here analysed.

The duty to perform an environmental impact assessment (EIA) is one of the restrictions to the way in which states treat their natural resources.[58] EIA can be defined as:

> a governmentally controlled procedure by which scientific assessment is made—together with public participation—of the proposed activity the impacts of which may be harmful. Its goals include improving the quality of the information to enable decision-makers to make better decisions from the viewpoint of the environment and raise in general the level of public participation in environmental decision-making.[59]

To perform an EIA in relation to any activity that might have consequences for the environment is now considered an obligation of customary nature.[60] The LOSC

[55] Catherine Redgwell, 'Mind the Gap in the GAIRS: The Role of Other Instruments in LOSC Regime Implementation in the Offshore Energy Sector' in Nigel Bankes and Seline Trevisanut, *Energy from the Sea: An International Law Perspective on Ocean Energy* (Brill Nijhoff 2015) 40.

[56] Trevisanut, 'La Convention des Nations Unies' (n 53) 414ff.

[57] See eg the Convention on the Prevention of Marine Pollution by Dumping of Waste and Other Matter (opened to signature 29 December 1972, entered into force 30 August 1975) 1046 UNTS 138 (hereafter London Dumping Convention) and the Protocol to the Convention on the Prevention of Marine Pollution by Dumping of Wastes and Other Matter (opened to signature 7 November 1996, entered into force 24 March 2006) 36 ILM 1 (hereafter 1996 London Protocol).

[58] Richard Barnes, *Property Rights and Natural Resources* (Hart 2009) 234–40.

[59] Timo Koivurova, 'Could the Espoo Convention Become a Global Regime for Environmental Impact Assessment and Strategic Environmental Assessment?' in Robin Warner and Simon Marsden (eds), *Transboundary Environmental Governance. Inland, Coastland and Marine Perspective* (Ashgate 2012) 326.

[60] *Pulp Mills on the River Uruguay (Argentina v Uruguay)* (Judgment) [2010] ICJ Rep 14 [205]ff; ITLOS, *Responsibilities and obligations of States sponsoring persons and entities with respect to activities in the Area* (Advisory Opinion) [2011], ITLOS Reports 2011, p 10, para 145.

provides for the direct obligation[61] to conduct an EIA and of monitoring in Articles 204, 205, and 206. The latter in particular provides that, when states have 'reasonable grounds for believing that planned activities under their jurisdiction or control may cause substantial pollution of or significant and harmful changes to the marine environment, they shall, as far as practicable, assess the potential effects of such activities on the marine environment'. States are also supposed to monitor the risks and effects of pollution resulting from activities under their jurisdiction (LOSC Article 204) and to communicate the results of such assessment and monitoring (LOSC Article 205).

Under the 1991 Convention on Environmental Impact Assessment in a Transboundary Context (Espoo Convention), parties have a duty to require an EIA in order to 'prevent, reduce and control significant adverse transboundary environmental impact from proposed activities'[62] and must establish procedures which permit public participation. Pursuant to the Espoo Convention Guidance, a non-binding instrument adopted by the meeting of the parties in 2004,[63] the domestic EIA procedure should include the necessary provisions so that:

> (a) the public is informed on any proposals relating to an activity with potential adverse environmental impacts in cases subject to an EIA procedure in order to obtain a permit for a given activity; (b) the public in the areas likely to be affected is entitled to express comments and opinions on the proposed activity when all options are open before the final decision on this activity is made; [...] (d) in making the final decision on the proposed activity, due account is taken of the results of the public participation in the EIA procedure.[64]

The 2003 Protocol on Strategic Environmental Assessment (SEA)[65] to the Espoo Convention allows the public to be involved in the decision-making process earlier than in general EIA procedure. An SEA involves:

> the evaluation of the likely environmental, including health, effects, which comprises the determination of the scope of an environmental report and its

[61] 'It should be stressed that the obligation to conduct an environmental impact assessment is a direct obligation under the Convention and a general obligation under customary international law'; ITLOS, *Responsibilities and obligations of States* (n 59) para 145.

[62] Art 2(1) of the Convention on Environmental Impact Assessment in a Transboundary Context (opened for signature 25 February 1991, entered into force 10 September 1997) 1989 UNTS 309 (hereafter Espoo Convention).

[63] Meeting of the Parties to the Convention on Environmental Impact Assessment in a Transboundary Context, Guidance on Public Participation in Environmental Impact Assessment in a Transboundary Context, Decision III/8, Report of the Third Meeting (13 September 2004) ECE/MP.EIA/6, Annex VIII.

[64] ibid para 14.

[65] Protocol on Strategic Environmental Assessment to the Convention on Environmental Impact Assessment in a Transboundary Context (opened for signature 21 May 2003, entered in force 10 July 2010) 2685 UNTS 140 (hereafter SEA Protocol).

preparation, the carrying out of public participation and consultations, and the taking into account of the environmental report and the results of the public participation and consultations in a plan or programme.[66]

The Espoo Convention and its SEA Protocol enhance the transparency in the performance of the assessment and monitoring obligations by opening those procedures to non-state actors. They thus enhance the safety of oil and gas operations by guaranteeing better control over the planned and performed activities, thanks to the participation of unconventional actors. Their reach is however limited to transboundary situations. The existing regional instruments take diverse approaches to the conduct of EIAs.

3.1.2 The geographical fragmentation at the regional level

Four regional sea conventions have a protocol or annex specifically dedicated to offshore activities. First, Annex III on the Prevention and Elimination of Pollution from Offshore Sources to the Convention for the Protection of the Marine Environment of the North-East Atlantic (OSPAR Convention) contains an obligation to use 'best available techniques' and 'best environmental practices' (Article 2) and a specific provision on the management of disused installations and pipelines (Article 5). The latter article was modified by the OSPAR Decision 98/3 on the Disposal of Disused Offshore Installations,[67] which requires the full removal of any disused equipment.

Secondly, Annex VI on the Prevention of Pollution from Offshore Activities to the Helsinki Convention on the Protection Marine Environment of the Baltic Sea Area[68] also invites contracting parties to make use of best available techniques and practices. Annex VI contains then a very detailed provision on environmental impact assessment and monitoring (Regulation 8). Moreover, '[i]n order to monitor the consequent effects of the exploitation phase of the offshore activity studies [. . .] shall be carried out *before* the operation, at *annual intervals* during the operation, and *after* the operation has been concluded.'[69] Regulation 8 is, at the moment, the most detailed international provision regulating EIAs in the offshore oil and gas sector.

[66] Art 2(6) SEA Protocol (n 64).

[67] Commission of the Convention for the Protection of the Marine Environment of the North-East Atlantic (22–23 July 1998) OSPAR 98/14/1-E, Annex 33.

[68] The Helsinki Convention had been amended many times since 1992. Any reference made in the present text refers to the last version as in force in 2008, and as available on the website on the Baltic Marine Environment Protection Commission—Helsinki Commission (HELCOM) at <www.helcom.fi> accessed 17 June 2022. Annex VI of the Helsinki Convention concerns the prevention of pollution from offshore activities and its text is available at <www.helcom.fi/about-us/convention/annexes/annex-vi> accessed 17 June 2022.

[69] Emphasis added.

Thirdly, the Offshore Protocol to the Barcelona Convention for the Protection of the Mediterranean Sea Against Pollution[70] consists of a quite detailed instrument which aims at covering the complete life cycle of offshore operations. In setting a number of mandatory requirements for the authorization procedure (Articles 4–7), the protocol focuses on the role of both authorizing states and the industry, ie the operator, in assessing the environmental impact of a planned activity, in monitoring it, and in reacting to possible emergencies.[71] The central role of the industry is also evident in Section IV of the Protocol on safeguards, namely on safety measures, contingency plans, and emergency response (Articles 15–21). The Mediterranean Action Plan,[72] adopted within the framework of the Offshore Protocol, aims in particular at encouraging the adoption of further safety measures at the regional level, in the time frame of 2016–24.[73] In relation to the development of regional standards and guidelines, the document emphasizes the need of common rules for EIAs,[74] highlighting in this way the shortcomings of the global legal framework and the crucial importance of such a procedure.

Fourthly, the Offshore Protocol to the Kuwait Regional Convention for Co-operation on the Protection of the Marine Environment from Pollution, unfortunately, does not contain a clear and general obligation of environmental impact assessment as it allows contracting parties not to require such an assessment before a new activity starts. When a contracting state decides not to request an EIA, it 'shall consider' performing a survey of the marine environment (Article IV.2). Contracting parties then have a wide margin of discretion under this instrument, which is, however, limited by the global legal framework analysed above.

3.2 Unconventional Lawmaking by the IMO and Global Treaty Bodies

Many international institutions participate in the development of the legal framework at the global and regional levels, and they often do so by adopting soft law instruments and by dialoguing with the stakeholders of the relevant economic sector. Soft law instruments[75] have mainly been adopted in order to set common

[70] UNEP(OCA)/MED IG.4/4 <https://wedocs.unep.org/rest/bitstreams/2336/retrieve> accessed 17 June 2022.

[71] Seline Trevisanut, 'The Role of Private Actors in the Offshore Energy Industry' (2014) 29 International Journal of Marine Coastal Law 645.

[72] Mediterranean Offshore Action Plan in the framework of the Protocol for the Protection of the Mediterranean Sea against Pollution resulting from Exploration and Exploitation of the Continental Shelf and the Seabed and its Subsoil, UNEP(DEPI)/MED IG.22/28 <https://wedocs.unep.org/rest/bitstreams/8381/retrieve> accessed 17 June 2022.

[73] ibid 214.

[74] ibid 220.

[75] See in particular the instruments elaborated by the IMO, which has taken the lead in recent years concerning the elaboration of standards and best practice related to the offshore industry, eg IMO,

standards in the field of safety and pollution control. At the global level, the IMO has in particular taken the lead concerning both the treatment of disused installations and pollution by dumping. It has elaborated some guidelines for the removal of installations[76] and is the depositary of the London Dumping Convention.[77] However, its role in the development of the regulatory framework in relation to the offshore oil and gas industry has raised some criticism.[78]

The IMO mandate, as amended, includes 'the general adoption of the highest practicable standards in matters concerning *maritime safety* […] and prevention and control of *marine pollution from ships*'.[79] Notwithstanding this, the IMO Legal Committee has pointed out: 'while pollution directly arising from exploration/exploitation is however not of direct concern of IMO, the Organization may contribute to the establishment of international regulations.'[80] The IMO Legal Committee, in particular, supports the development of guidance for states in their effort to conclude arrangements at the bilateral and regional level on liability and compensation issues connected to transboundary pollution damage, resulting from offshore oil exploration and exploitation.[81] Not all IMO contracting parties, however, support what they perceive as an unjustified extension of the IMO mandate.[82] This undermines the 'generally accepted' character of the rules and standards which the organization elaborates.

General acceptance needs then to be assessed on the basis of the subsequent practice of states. Within the London Dumping system, Lyons for instance suggests that, unlike the 1972 London Convention, its 1996 Protocol does not yet qualify as a global rule under the LOSC because it has gained general acceptance only in some regions of the world.[83] This also suggests that the 1996 Protocol may be regarded as generally accepted international rules and standards (GAIRS) in

Guidelines for safety zones and the safety of navigation around offshore installations and structures, SN.1/Circ.295, 7 December 2010.

[76] IMO, Res A.672 (16) of 19 October 1989.

[77] London Dumping Convention (n 56).

[78] Some states and some commentators have raised several points of criticism about the role of the IMO in the development of rules and standards concerning offshore installations. The details of such debate are beyond the scope of the present chapter. For a critical voice, refer to J Ashley Roach, 'International Standards for Offshore Drilling' in Myron H Nordquist and others (eds), *The Regulation of Continental Shelf Development, Rethinking International Standards* (Martinus Nijhoff 2013) 107.

[79] Convention on the International Maritime Organization (opened for signature 6 March 1948, entered into force 17 March 1958) 289 UNTS 3 (emphasis added).

[80] See 'Implications of the United Nations Convention on the Law of the Sea for the International Maritime Organization' (19 January 2012) IMO Doc LEG/Misc.7 Annex, 18.

[81] See IMO Doc LEG 99/14, 24 April 2012, para 13.16.

[82] Roach (n 77) 105. See also Aldo Chircop, 'The International Maritime Organisation' in Donald R Rothwell and others (eds), *The Oxford Handbook of The Law of the Sea* (OUP 2015) 429.

[83] Youna Lyons, 'The New Offshore Oil and Gas Installation Abandonment Wave and the International Rules on Removal and Dumping' (2014) 29 International Journal of Marine and Coastal Law 506, 510. For an opposing view, see Alexander Proelss, *United Convention on the Law of the Sea, A Commentary* (OUP 2017) 464.

some areas of the world where the majority of relevant states have ratified it; so as regional GAIRS and not global rules. The 1996 Protocol could also fall within the definition of best environmental practices, as required by some regional instruments analysed above, namely the OSPAR and Helsinki Conventions.

Aside from the IMO, the treaty bodies of the CBD[84] have played an important role in the regulation of the offshore energy sector, specifically concerning the EIA procedures. As already mentioned, EIA obligations are a cornerstone of the legal regime. If the Espoo Convention is regarded as a potential global standard, it remains a regionally born instrument which applies to transboundary contexts. The CBD Convention and further developments concerning its Article 14 are thus important pieces of the regulatory mosaic.

Article 14 of the CBD provides for an international obligation to submit to EIA procedure any activity which might significantly impact biodiversity, internally or transboundary.[85] In order to support the integration of biodiversity considerations in EIA procedures, the Conference of the Parties (COP) of the CBD adopted in 2006 the Voluntary Guidelines on Biodiversity-inclusive Impact Assessment.[86] The lawmaking powers of COPs within multilateral environmental agreements are highly debated and beyond the scope of the present chapter.[87] What is important here is the assessment of the normative value of the non-binding instrument which is the outcome of the decision-making process. Although not formally binding, the 2006 Voluntary Guidelines are considered to have 'high normative value because they have been negotiated under the auspices of the CBD and adopted by the [COP]'.[88] Of less normative value are, for instance and according to Craik, the Draft Guidance on biodiversity-inclusive strategic environmental assessment.[89] The SEA Draft Guidance 'was not "adopted" by the parties, but rather the document produced by the Secretariat was "endorsed", indicating agreement with the content but an unwillingness to give the document greater normative status'.[90] The instruments adopted by the parties through the COP and, thus, whose content was 'subscribed' by the parties could even amount to 'subsequent agreements by

[84] Convention on Biological Diversity (opened for signature 5 June 1992, entered into force on 29 December 1993) 1760 UNTS 79 (hereafter CBD).

[85] For a detailed analysis of art 14 CBD, see, inter alia, Neil Craik, 'Biodiversity-Inclusive Impact Assessment' in Michael Faure (ed), *Elgar Encyclopedia of Environmental Law*, vol III (Edward Elgar 2017) 431–44.

[86] COP 8 Decision VIII/28, <www.cbd.int/decision/cop/?id=11042> accessed 17 June 2022.

[87] COPs do not possess international legal personality and are not considered international organizations. Whether their lawmaking powers can be justified on the basis of the theory of 'implied powers' is thus contested. For a treatise of the issue, see, inter alia, Jutta Brunnée, 'COPing with Consent: Law-Making Under Multilateral Environmental Agreements' [2002] Leiden Journal of Internatioal Law 1; Francesca Romanin Jacur, *The Dynamics of Multilateral Environmental Agreements, Institutional Architectures and Law-Making Processes* (Editorial Scientifica 2013) 161ff.

[88] Craik (n 84) 436.

[89] CBD Executive Secretary (2006), Voluntary guidelines on biodiversity-inclusive impact assessment, Annex II, UN Doc UNEP/CBD/COP/8/27/Add.2.

[90] Craik (n 84) 437–38.

which the underlying treaty is interpreted in the sense of Art. 31.1(a)' of the Vienna Convention on the Law of Treaties.[91] Moreover, the 2006 Voluntary Guidance benefits from the external support of other guideline documents with a similar content, such as the resolutions of the Ramsar Convention COP 2008[92] and the Convention on Migratory Species COP 2002.[93] They 'operate collectively to reinforce the principles associated with biodiversity-inclusive impact assessment'[94] and, consequently, increase each other's normative value.

Unconventional lawmaking also allows linking biodiversity-inclusive EIA with human rights law. Consider the International Finance Corporation Performance Standards and related guidance notes,[95] the UN Guiding Principles on Business and Human Rights,[96] or the Organisation for Economic Co-operation and Development Guidelines for Multinational Enterprises.[97] These instruments are also relevant for the offshore energy industry, when considering the impact of the sector on indigenous and local communities. Unconventional lawmaking here allows the circumvention of the lack of will about SEA outside the regional context of the Espoo Convention.

3.3 Unconventional Lawmaking by Regional Seas Treaties Bodies

The regional seas treaties play an important role in regulating the offshore energy sector in the absence of a specialized global instrument. The institutional framework is however very diverse, in line with the very different levels of integration in the respective regions and does impact the lawmaking processes.

The OSPAR Commission and the Helsinki Commission (HELCOM) are strong treaty bodies which can also adopt binding decisions. but which also make extensive use of non-binding instruments to regulate in particular the protection of the marine environment. A clear example is the OSPAR Guidance on Environmental

91 Georg Nolte, 'Subsequent Agreements and Subsequent Practice of States Outside of Judicial or Quasi-judicial Proceedings', Third Report for the ILC Study Group on Treaties over Time (2012).

92 Ramsar Convention Conference of the Parties, 'Environmental Impact Assessment and Strategic Environmental Assessment: updated scientific and technical guidance' (28 October–4 November 2008) Res X.17, Annex.

93 Convention on Migratory Species Conference of the Parties, 'Impact Assessment and Migratory Species' (18–24 September 2002) Res 7.2.

94 Craik (n 84) 436.

95 See in particular Performance Standard 6 on Biodiversity Conservation and Sustainable Management of Living Natural Resources <www.ifc.org/wps/wcm/connect/topics_ext_content/ifc_external_corporate_site/sustainability-at-ifc/policies-standards/performance-standards/ps6> accessed 17 June 2022.

96 Available at <www.ohchr.org/documents/publications/guidingprinciplesbusinesshr_en.pdf> accessed 17 June 2022.

97 Available at <http://mneguidelines.oecd.org/guidelines/> accessed 17 June 2022.

Considerations for Offshore Windfarm Development.[98] The OSPAR Guidance complements the relevant obligations of the Espoo Convention,[99] offering valuable guidelines on the minimum content of EIAs for all stages of the life of offshore wind farms, from location to decommissioning. Also, the HELCOM Recommendation 18/2 on Offshore Activities[100] reiterated that, in case of offshore oil and gas exploitation activities, it is necessary for states to assess the environmental status of the area in which the project is proposed to be located before any activity takes place. While the requirements set out under Annex VI should apply as a minimum standard, the Recommendation highlights that when the nature of the area so requires, states must apply more stringent requirements.

Little has so far come out of the Barcelona and Kuwait Conventions' treaty bodies, which do not have the same institutional features as the OSPAR Commission and the HELCOM. The Kuwait Convention and its Protocols are implemented by the Regional Organization for the Protection of the Marine Environment (ROPME).[101] The ROPME is in charge of developing guidelines for assisting contracting states; however, no guideline is available on the ROPME official website. It seems that the ROPME has not so far exercised its drafting functions.

In the Mediterranean context, the institutional framework of the Barcelona Convention consists of several bodies,[102] including a Meeting of the Parties (MOP) and the Barcelona Convention Offshore Oil and Gas Group (BARCO OFOG), the latter created in 2014. The BARCO OFOG is a technical body for the exchange of best practices, knowledge, and experiences between its members to assist the parties in promulgating international rules, standards, and recommended practices and procedures pursuant to Article 23 of the Barcelona Offshore Protocol.[103] The periodic examination and review of the Offshore Action Plan, adopted by the MOP in 2016, has also been assigned to it.[104] The Offshore Action Plan aims at operationalizing the harmonization of regional practices in the implementation of the Mediterranean Offshore Protocol, considering 'relevant existing standards

[98] OSPAR Guidance on Environmental Considerations for Offshore Wind Farm Development, ref no 2008-3.

[99] Similarly, wind farms are also included in the amended Annex of the Espoo Convention (n 61).

[100] HELCOM Recommendation 18/2, adopted 12 March 1997, Attachment a.

[101] The ROPME was created in 1979 pursuant to art XVI of the Kuwait Convention. According to the information available on its official website <http://ropme.org/1_WhoWeAre_EN.clx#> accessed 17 June 2022, '[t]he main objective of ROPME is to coordinate efforts of the eight Member States towards protection the marine and coastal environment and ecosystems in the ROPME Sea Area against marine pollution and stressors that might be induced from developmental activities or/and other drivers of change'.

[102] For a complete overview of the Barcelona Convention bodies, see <www.unenvironment.org/unepmap/who-we-are/governing-and-subsidiary-bodies> accessed 17 June 2022.

[103] Decision IG.21/8 (2014), Follow up Actions regarding the Offshore Action Plan, UNEP/MED. IG.21/9, Annex.

[104] Decision IG/22/3 (2016), Mediterranean Offshore Action Plan in the framework of the Protocol for the Protection of the Mediterranean Sea against Pollution resulting from Exploration and Exploitation of the Continental Shelf and the Seabed and its Subsoil, DOC UNEP/MED IG.22.

and guidelines in this field'.[105] One of the outputs of the Action Plan is the adoption by the MOP of the 2019 Mediterranean Offshore Guidelines and Standards on the Disposal of Oil and Oily Mixtures.[106] The normative value of the Guidelines relies on two arguments, invoked by the document itself. First, the Barcelona MOP adopted the Guidelines pursuant to specific objectives of the Action Plan, and thus pursuant to a mandate agreed upon by the contracting parties.[107] Secondly:

> [t]his guidance has been derived from international best practices as outlined by organisations and institutions such as the Secretariat of the Convention for the Protection of the Marine Environment of the North-east Atlantic (OSPAR), International Finance Corporation (IFC)/World Bank and the International Association of Oil and Gas Producers (IOGP), as well as from countries with mature oil and gas industry with well-developed regulatory frameworks, such the UK, Norway, the Netherlands and the US.[108]

As mentioned above concerning the guidelines adopted by some global treaty bodies, the cross-referencing reinforces the principles enshrined in the guidelines, each increasing the other's normative value.

3.4 Unconventional Lawmaking by Unconventional Actors

The expansion of the offshore sector has buttressed the role of private actors at the international level. They are increasingly involved in the implementation and enforcement of international rules, but also in lawmaking processes. On the one hand, civil society—in particular local communities—can actively impact the decision-making process thanks to their participation rights, guaranteed, inter alia, by the Aarhus Convention[109] and the Espoo Convention.[110] On the other hand, private actors financially involved in the activities—for example investors and insurance companies—bear (indirect) obligations under specific international

105 ibid s II.2.2, specific objectives 7 and 8, 220ff.

106 Decision IG.24/9 (2019), Mediterranean Offshore Guidelines and Standards: (a) Common Standards and Guidance on the Disposal of Oil and Oily Mixtures and the Use and Disposal of Drilling Fluids and Cuttings; (b) Common Standards and Guidelines for Special Restrictions or Conditions for Specially Protected Areas (SPA) within the Framework of the Mediterranean Offshore Action Plan, UNEP/MED IG.24/22, 471ff.

107 Decision IG.24/9 (2019) 471–72.

108 ibid 476.

109 Aarhus Convention on Access to Information, Public Participation in Decision-Making and Access to Justice in Environmental matters of the United Nations Economic Commission for Europe (opened for signature 25 June 1998, entered into force 30 October 2001) 2161 UNTS 447.

110 Espoo Convention (n 61).

instruments, such as the above-mentioned Barcelona Offshore Protocol[111] and the IMO Removal Guidelines.[112]

The latter element is particularly problematic because international law does not have 'teeth' to directly act against private actors, and private actors might disguise reality through self-regulation.[113] For instance, before the Deepwater Horizon incident, BP had a very good reputation concerning the environmental standards of the company; it was considered a safe company. After the incident, the BP National Commission continued to encourage 'self-regulation and co-regulation following the example of other economic sectors, such as fisheries, chemical industry, nuclear power industry'.[114] It justified this approach by affirming that governments cannot compete with private-sector salaries for the most talented experts.[115] '[S]elf-regulation is an instrument whose very rationale is versatility; it can be portrayed as nonlaw, as soft law, and even as law. Thus, the character of regulation becomes decisive, not the content of the rules.'[116] However, self-regulation should not become 'a substitute of government but serves as an important supplement to government oversight'.[117]

'[F]irms are no longer simply accountable under local law, but to international norms and standards, such as those promulgated by International Labour Organization (ILO), the Universal Declaration of Human Rights (UDHR), and corporate best practices.'[118] In the offshore energy sector, this is not as straightforward. Companies have developed a 'green sensibility' and invested in 'greening' their image by declaring their respect for international law obligations. Several oil and gas companies have adopted, in particular since the Deepwater Horizon disaster, codes of conduct where they affirm their recognition of international norms for the protection of the marine environment.[119] The internal codes of conduct are

[111] Protocol for the Protection of the Mediterranean Sea against Pollution Resulting from Exploration and Exploitation of the Continental Shelf and the Seabed and its Subsoil to the Convention for the Protection of the Mediterranean Sea Against (opened for signature 14 October 1994, entered into force 24 March 2011) 2742 UNTS 77 (hereafter Barcelona Offshore Protocol).

[112] IMO, Guidelines and Standards for the Removal of Offshore Installations and Structures (n 76).

[113] '[E]ntity self-generated standards empower them to manage the data-driven construction of their reality'; Larry Catá Backer, 'Transparency and Business in International Law: Governance between Norm and Technique' in Andrea Bianchi and Anne Peters (eds), *Transparency in International Law* (CUP 2013) 499.

[114] BP National Commission, 'Industry's Role in Supporting Health, Safety and Environmental Standards: Options and Models for the Offshore Oil and Gas Sector', Staff Working Paper No 9 2.

[115] ibid.

[116] Katja Creutz, 'Law versus Codes of Conduct: Between Convergence and Conflict' in Jan Klabbers and Touko Piiparinen (eds), *Normative Pluralism and International Law, Exploring Global Governance* (CUP 2013) 167.

[117] BP National Commission, Final Report, ch 8 'Safety and Industry' (2011) 234.

[118] World Bank Group, 'Corporate Social Responsibility Practice. Strengthening Implementation of Corporate Social Responsibility in Global Supply Chains' (October 2003) 1.

[119] See, inter alia, BP, 'Our Code, Our Responsibility' <https://www.bp.com/content/dam/bp/business-sites/en/global/corporate/pdfs/who-we-are/our-code-our-responsibility.pdf> accessed 17 June 2022; Total, 'Code of Conduct, Our Values in Practice' <https://totalenergies.com/sites/g/files/nytnzq121/files/atoms/files/total_code_of_conduct_va_0.pdf> accessed 17 June 2022; Shell, 'General Business Principles' <www.shell.com/about-us/our-values/_jcr_content/par/relatedtopics.stream/1643027598

certainly not binding but they can produce normative effect. In fact, they consist of a sort of declaration that the company is aware of the existing legal framework and could be considered as relevant practice when assessing the content of the applicable due diligence obligations. Moreover, the codes of conduct, as relevant practice, can consist of 'best available practice', thus feeding the international legal framework and clarifying the meaning of certain obligations.

The codes of conduct are also relevant for 'corporate ocean responsibility' (COR), namely an ocean-focused corporate social responsibility (CSR) initiative. There is no agreed definition of COR or CSR. According to the World Bank, CSR is '[t]he commitment of business to contribute to sustainable economic development working with employees, their families, the local community, and society at large to improve their quality of life, in ways that are both good for business and good for development'.[120] Accordingly, COR could be defined as the commitment of business to contribute to the sustainable use of the oceans working with employees, their families, local communities, and society at large to improve the quality of the oceans, in ways that are good for business, for development, and for the environment. The COR legal framework is composed of different categories of standards and 'embodies non-binding general principles of responsible conduct and technical guidelines […] directly addressing business operators, and those formally addressing States with recommendations to be complied with by private operators'.[121] Similarly to CSR, COR aims to fill in the details of international legal principles, either conventional or customary, that provide for the protection of common concerns, such as the environment, and focusing the private companies' attention on the needs of the society in which they operate. It can thus play an important role in preventing pollution and environmental disasters by pushing companies to put in place the necessary prevention mechanisms. It can also be a tool for mitigating damage and compensating losses once a disaster has occurred.[122]

Private actors in the offshore energy sector are not only individual companies, but also professional associations. In the US, for instance, the American Petroleum Institute (API) has played a dominant role in developing safety standards. But it has also regularly resisted 'agency rulemakings that government regulators believe would make those operations safer', and has favoured 'rulemaking that promotes industry autonomy from government oversight'.[123] At the EU level, the pressure exercised by some representatives of the industry, such as Oil and Gas

209/6b4a23c6d8b47b0fd3e8e3b9fe955e59431f9c83/shell-general-business-principles-2014.pdf> accessed 17 June 2022.

[120] World Bank Group (n 117).

[121] Angelica Bonfanti and Francesca Romanin Jacur, 'Energy from the Sea and the Protection of the Marine Environment: Treaty-Based Regimes and Ocean Corporate Social Responsibility' in Bankes and Trevisanut (eds) (n 54) 73–74.

[122] ibid 78ff.

[123] BP National Commission (n 116) 225.

UK,[124] contributed to changing the proposed instrument from a regulation to a directive.[125]

Professional associations play different roles in the international legal framework. They can guarantee a certain level of safety. The Offshore Pollution Liability Association (OPOL),[126] for instance, is a private agreement between certain European states[127] and the major participants in their offshore industries. Most participating states now require applicants for offshore exploration, exploitation, and pipe-laying licences to be a party to OPOL. Industry is also important in order to collect high-quality and comprehensive data to ensure science-based standard-setting.[128] The International Regulators' Forum (IRF) is a group of offshore health and safety regulators for the oil and gas industry, created in order to promote information sharing and collaboration through joint programmes. The participants in the IRF Global Offshore Safety are: Australia (National Offshore Petroleum Safety Authority); Brazil (National Agency of Oil, Gas and Biofuels); Canada (Canada Newfoundland and Labrador Offshore Petroleum Board & Canada-Nova Scotia Offshore Petroleum Board); Netherlands (State Supervision of Mines); New Zealand (Department of Labour); Norway (The Petroleum Safety Authority); United Kingdom (Health and Safety Executive); and United States (Bureau of Ocean Energy Management Regulation and Enforcement). The Forum is a very important network for the exchange of information and the collection of data. However, it consists of very different administrations, with different mandates and priorities, at different regulatory levels, and with different expertise. Consequently, the type and the quality of data might diverge. There is no guarantee of coherence at the domestic level concerning the standard-setting activity that such a network generates.[129]

[124] 'We [Oil and Gas UK] believe the EC would best achieve its goal through a properly worded Directive, instead of Regulation. [...] A properly worded Directive would encourage member states which do not currently achieve the recognised high standards present in the North Sea, to do so in a way which blends with their established legislation. This would protect the existing strong safety regime in the UK, minimise disruption to operators and regulators and eliminate the additional risk that the Regulation presents'; Oil and Gas UK, Proposed Regulation on Offshore Safety <www.oilandgasuk.co.uk/ProposedEURegulation.cfm> accessed 17 June 2022.

[125] For a comment, see Lorenzo Schiano di Pepe, 'Offshore Oil and Gas Operations in the Mediterranean Sea: Regulatory Gaps, Recent Developments and Future Perspective' in Juste Juste Ruiz and Valntin Bou Franch (eds), *Derecho del mar y sostenibilidad ambiental en el Mediterráneo* (Tirant Lo Blanch 2014) 379.

[126] Under the Offshore Pollution Liability Agreement (concluded on 4 September 1974), operating companies agree to accept strict liability for pollution damage and the cost of remedial measures with only certain exceptions, up to a maximum of US $250,000,000 per incident. Within this limit there may also be included the cost of remedial measures undertaken by the party to OPOL involved in the incident. For more information, see <www.opol.org.uk> accessed 17 June 2022.

[127] The European states in which OPOL applies are: United Kingdom and Northern Ireland (including Isle of Man), Denmark (including Faroe Islands and Greenland), Germany, France, Ireland, the Netherlands, and Norway.

[128] BP National Commission, 'Collecting High Quality, Objective, Comprehensive Data' Staff Working Paper No 18, 2011.

[129] Trevisanut, 'The Role of Private Actors' (n 70).

Another interesting and recent example is the International Renewable Energy Agency (IRENA). According to Article 2 of IRENA's Statute, its objective is to promote the adoption and sustainable use of all forms of renewable energy, including marine renewable energy. It does not have the competence to issue legally binding standards on the operation of marine renewables but can be a starting point for providing advice and monitoring in relation to policy, capacity building, and collaboration, and it can function as a clearing house for research and best practices used in different regions.[130] In that sense, the IRENA, in collaboration with renewable energy professional associations, such as the International Electrotechnical Commission (IEC), has collected renewable energy standards and relevant patents.[131] Furthermore, it has published renewable energy technology briefs relating to ocean thermal energy conversion, salinity gradient energy, and tidal and wave energy.[132] While these briefs outline the environmental impact of marine renewable energy activities, they are not aimed at providing for environmental standards to inform the due diligence standard of states in regulating and monitoring those activities. Consequently, none of these documents provides any international standards within the meaning of Article 208 LOSC.

The IRENA collaborates with specialized professional associations in the development of standards of operation specifically tailored for offshore renewable energy devices.[133] In general, these standards are not legally binding on either states or the industry. However, their embeddedness in the international legal framework can upgrade their normative impact on state or industry conduct. Depending on their institutional source and the form and procedure by which they are adopted, these legally non-binding pronouncements may become relevant as interpretative guidance or standard of proof that a state has (or has not) shown due diligence.

4. Conclusion

The 'LOSC was never intended to be a "one stop shop" for the regulation of all offshore activities.'[134] As a framework convention, it accommodates necessary

[130] Glen Wright, 'The International Renewable Energy Agency: A Global Voice for the Renewable Energy Era?' [2011] Renewable Energy Law and Policy Review 267.

[131] 'Irena Platform Supports Renewable Energy Innovation, Quality and Collaboration', see IRENA website: <www.irena.org/newsroom/pressreleases/2015/Jul/New-IRENA-Platform-Supports-Renewable-Energy-Innovation-Quality-and-Collaboration> accessed 17 June 2022.

[132] IRENA Ocean Energy Technology Briefs <www.irena.org/publications/2014/Jun/IRENA-Ocean-Energy-Technology-Briefs> accessed 17 June 2022.

[133] IRENA (2013) 'International Standardization in the Field of Renewable Energy' <www.irena.org/-/media/Files/IRENA/Agency/Publication/2013/Inventory_renewable_energy_standards.pdf?la=en&hash=9E18027869BB956421143C768963EE945FAE7926> accessed 17 June 2022.

[134] Catherine Redgwell, 'The Never Ending Story: The Role of GAIRS in UNCLOS Implementation in the Offshore Energy Sector' in Jill Barrett and Richard Barnes (eds), *Law of the Sea: UNCLOS as a Living Treaty* (BIICL 2016) 184.

changes and developments, either by explicitly referring to external sources of law (ie the GAIRS) or by using generic terms. In the latter case, the ICJ affirmed that, 'where the parties have used generic terms in a treaty, the parties necessarily having been aware that the meaning of the terms was likely to evolve over time, and where the treaty has been entered into for a very long period or is "of continuing duration", the parties must be presumed, as a general rule, to have intended those terms to have an evolving meaning'.[135] The Convention was negotiated more than forty years ago and has been in force for twenty-eight years at the time of writing. Many of the other treaties mentioned have also come to a certain maturity phase in their lives and have changed over time through a combination of pathways.

Three pathways of change[136] are mainly relevant here. First, the multilateral pathway highlights the role of international organizations and treaty bodies in adopting resolutions and decisions, which have complemented and, sometimes, changed the meaning of certain obligations. Some prime examples are the resolutions of the UNHCR ExCom in relation to the content of the duty to render assistance.

Secondly, the importance of the bureaucratic pathway assuredly emerges from the analysis of the explanatory instruments adopted by the competent international organizations and diplomatic conferences. Change is buttressed here through guidelines and handbooks, which encourage best practices and can crystallize in GAIRS to ultimately become binding through the transformative mechanism of the LOSC rules of reference. This can clearly be observed in the guidelines of the COPs of the CBD and of the Espoo Convention in relation to the duty to conduct an EIA and the content of the relevant procedures.

Thirdly, and lastly, the private authority pathway plays a key role in the offshore energy sector, in the absence of one competent international organization and because of the scattered legal framework. This pathway is well known and established in the traditional sector of oil and gas extraction, through the self-regulation of the industry and the key role played by professional associations and organizations (eg ICS, OPOL, IRF). The growing sector of renewable energy production seems to follow in the footsteps of the oil and gas industry, but in a more centralized, and maybe coherent way, through the IRENA.

If the LOSC was never to be a '"one stop shop" for the regulation of all offshore activities',[137] much of its evolution is now removed from the traditional lawmaking processes and states are no longer uniquely in charge of its further development. Those pathways are shaping the future of the oceans.

[135] *Dispute regarding Navigational and Related Rights* (*Costa Rica v Nicaragua*) (Judgment) [2009] ICJ Rep 213 [66].

[136] Krisch and Yildiz (n 2).

[137] Redgwell, 'The Never Ending Story' (n 133) 184.

10

World Trade Law and the Rise of China

Struggles over Subsidy Rules

*Nina Teresa Kiderlin**

1. Introduction

It seems intuitive to think that if the distribution of political power shifts, law eventually follows, as new powers want political changes to ultimately be reflected in the law. However, established actors typically want the law to remain stable and therefore resist legal change. When and how are shifts in global power structure then brought into international law?

One of the greater shifts in geopolitics in recent history has been the rise of China, and it has put the international order under significant strain.[1] The question this chapter will explore is to what extent this shift has resulted in change in international law, and especially in world trade law. The WTO has been a key arena of conflict between the US and China in recent years, well before the Trump years.[2] What happens when a new, potentially powerful, (state) actor enters the scene of an already existing and established legal regime such as international trade law? How did China, whose international trade law profession was underdeveloped (or virtually non-existent) prior to its accession to the WTO, manage to use the WTO dispute settlement system to push for change.

International trade law is a particularly suitable field for an inquiry into the effects of geopolitical shifts on international law, because—especially in the form it found in the WTO Agreements—it is widely seen as a reflection of a particular economic vision associated with the dominant powers of the 1990s. The WTO Agreements tend towards neoliberal market liberalization, mainly due to pressure from the US and, to an extent, the European Union during the Uruguay Round. Developing countries challenged this dominance in the Doha Round and

* PhD Researcher in Anthropology and Sociology, Graduate Institute of International and Development Studies, Geneva, Switzerland.

[1] Gregory Shaffer, *Emerging Powers and the World Trading System* (CUP 2021) 11.

[2] Aseema Sinha 'Understanding the "Crisis of the Institution" in the Liberal Trade Order at the WTO' (2021) 97 International Affairs 1521; John Mearsheimer 'The Inevitable Rivalry' (2021) 100 Foreign Affairs 48; Marco Bronckers 'Trade Conflicts: Whither the WTO' [2020] Legal Issues of Economic Integration 221.

Nina Teresa Kiderlin, *World Trade Law and the Rise of China* In: *The Many Paths of Change in International Law*. Edited by: Nico Krisch and Ezgi Yildiz, Oxford University Press. © Nina Teresa Kiderlin 2023.
DOI: 10.1093/oso/9780198877844.003.0010

prevented the further extension of this approach through treaty-making, but they did not achieve a rebalancing on this route either as negotiations largely ended in gridlock. Meanwhile, societal contestation—particularly in the area of environmental regulation—has created legitimacy issues for the WTO, adding to the pressures the organization finds itself under, but has not led to formal changes in existing agreements either.[3]

Yet, change in trade law does not necessarily have to come through state-led processes. In fact, this field of international law is particular not only because of its ideational orientation, but also because of the centrality of the 'judicial' path of change, embodied in the WTO dispute settlement system and the jurisprudence of the panels and the Appellate Body (AB).[4] In light of the clogged nature of state or multilateral paths, the focus for change agents in this field soon shifted towards the judicial path, and it is here that we have seen most movement, especially under the influence of the AB from the mid-1990s until 2019, when the AB itself became blocked as the US prevented the appointment of new members. Change processes in world trade law over the past decades have then also largely come about through shifts in the interpretation by WTO dispute settlers.[5]

China, too, has been among the change agents using the judicial path at the WTO, and it has been quite successful in using it for its own interests and to advance its global economic and political position.[6] This was aided by the fact that, as we will see in more detail later in the chapter, China invested significant resources into building its own trade law capacity to further global influence.[7] This contributed to the country being perceived as a credible rival to Europe and the US in shaping, changing, and developing international trade law. The change in turn has resulted in political shifts, impacting the political (im-)balance between China and the Western world.

This chapter traces China's rise and its consequences at the WTO, especially with a view to understanding how the country utilizes home-grown capacity for international trade law, and how these developments can embody a global political shift in power. In the WTO context the AB could achieve (lasting) impactful change and might have therefore been an obvious choice of forum to push for change. In other areas of international law, where one does not have a similar focal point or decisive

[3] Robert Howse, 'The World Trade Organization 20 Years On: Global Governance by Judiciary' (2016) 27 European Journal of International Law 9.

[4] Richard Steinberg, 'Judicial Lawmaking at the WTO: Discursive, Constitutional, and Political Constraints' (2004) 98 American Journal of International Law 247; Gregory Shaffer, Manfred Elsig, and Sergio Puig, 'The Extensive (but Fragile) Authority of the WTO Appellate Body' (2016) 79 Law & Contemporary Problems 237.

[5] Howse (n 3); Gregory Messenger, *The Development of World Trade Organization Law: Examining Change in International Law* (OUP 2016).

[6] Shaffer (n 1).

[7] Gregory Shaffer and Henry Gao, 'China's Rise: How it Took on the US at the WTO' (2018) 1 University of Illinois Law Review 115; Shaffer (n 1) 18.

body, it might be less likely that change can be pursued (successfully) through judicial bodies.

Pressures of geopolitics are especially encapsulated in the case of subsidy regulation at the WTO—the focus of our inquiry here. Subsidy regulation, a seemingly niche topic, provides a magnifying glass through which we can observe how disagreements between economic and political systems play out in a specific issue-area. The WTO's subsidy rules were not ideally suited to dealing with economies with a blurred boundary between public and private actors, and China soon pushed back against the wide application of these rules on its state-owned entities. This led to a (limited) interpretive shift among WTO dispute settlement bodies, but also to contestation on the part of, in particular, the US, which saw this issue as increasingly significant in the context of the developing trade conflict with China in the early 2010s. As we will see below, the issue seemed relatively settled for several years before the AB took a step back towards the US position later in the decade, when the crisis over AB appointments was already well advanced. Subsidy disciplines have become an element in discussions about general WTO reform,[8] and one could even go as far as to argue that the future of the WTO hinges on them as they represent the ultimate test for whether the institution can accommodate a strong non-market based economy—and whether it can strike a balance between the demands of different types of economies within it.[9]

2. China's Challenge to International (Trade) Law

The impact of China's rise on the international order has been much debated in recent years, and observers diverge on whether China will grow within existing rules and institutions or whether, and to what extent, it is bound to challenge them.[10] For international law, too, expectations differ, though many commentators highlight the renewed emphasis on state sovereignty and challenges to human rights-related norms as well as pushes towards a broader accommodation of authoritarian forms of governance.[11] As for WTO law, however, expectations have been largely about a relative degree of continuity—avoiding major ruptures and instead working within the system to generate a greater alignment with its interests—yet potentially

[8] Shaffer (n 1).

[9] Dukgeun Ahn, 'Why Reform is Needed: WTO "Public Body" Jurisprudence' (2021) 12 Global Policy 61.

[10] John Ikenberry (2008) 'The Rise of China and the Future of the West: Can the Liberal System Survive?' (2008) 87 Foreign Affairs 23.

[11] Tom Ginsburg, 'Authoritarian International Law' (2020) 114 American Journal of International Law 221.

coupled with moves towards creating more favourable structures in a regional context.[12]

China has struggled with multiple aspects of international trade law and policy since its accession to the WTO, which took fifteen years to negotiate, and which contained agreements widely seen as imposing heavy burdens of adjustment on the country—heavier burdens yet than on other accession states.[13] Much of this struggle is related to China's political economy and its particular state-centred set-up even after the end of the Cold War, when many formerly Communist states adapted to a more market-based, neoliberal, privatized economic model. Generally, the central issue between China and the WTO, no matter how many disputes are adjudicated, returns to the seemingly incompatible nature between China's legal system and the legal and economic structure and concepts underlying the WTO.

The most obvious path towards change in WTO rules would have been the multilateral one—the different 'rounds' of multilateral trade negotiations in the WTO context. As China's accession to the WTO coincided with the launch of the Doha Round, many observers assumed that China would play an active role in those negotiations and ultimately have a (significant) impact.[14] However, their prediction did not materialize. This could be due to the negotiation approaches adopted by China, which were different from those of other, more central actors at the WTO. At the beginning, China seemed to be a more quiet presence at the negotiations and only towards the end of the Doha Round did it attempt to become part of the core decision-making group.[15] Despite the fact that it was a member of the G-20 and had submitted its first negotiating proposal only six months after accession, it operated not as a lead actor but instead often rather as an observer.[16] A variety of explanations have been advanced for this behaviour. One possibility could be that the Chinese government, which had been under the spotlight and scrutiny of the WTO community for so many years during accession negotiations, needed some time to implement the newly assumed commitments which were, as mentioned, more stringent than those of other WTO members upon accession.[17] Due to that, China attempted to argue that they should be considered on a par with

[12] Henry Gao, 'How China Took on the United States and Europe at the WTO' in Gregory Shaffer (ed), *Emerging Powers and the World Trade System* (CUP 2021) 174; Henry Gao, 'A New Chinese Economic Law' in Shaffer (ed), Emerging Powers and the World Trade System, 222.

[13] Julia Qin, 'WTO-Plus Obligations and their Implications for the World Trade Organization Legal System—An Appraisal of the China Accession Protocol' (2003) 37 Journal of World Trade 483. So far, only Russia has had a longer negotiation process to accession—it took eighteen years.

[14] Henry Gao, 'China's Participation in WTO Negotiations' (2012) 1 China Perspectives <https://journals.openedition.org/chinaperspectives/5823> accessed 17 June 2022.

[15] ibid.

[16] ibid.

[17] Aaditya Mattoo, 'China's Accession to the WTO: The Services Dimension' (2003) 6 Journal of International Economic Law 299; Nicholas Lardy, *Integrating China into the Global Economy* (Brookings 2002).

other recently added members and not make the same level of concessions during the Doha Round as other leading economies, which meant they attempted to not make aggressive demands and to keep a lower profile so as to not attract attention from other states.[18] In this light, it is possible to interpret China's 'lack of success' during the Doha Round as a strategic choice, albeit an ultimately unsuccessful one as the flexibility awarded to recently added members was not extended to China. In a similar vein, some scholars have argued that China had a lack of expertise in terms of procedural and substantive rules.[19] Furthermore, developing countries and established large trading countries alike regarded China as a threat instead of an ally, complicating the access to informal information.[20]

The Doha Round soon ran into difficulties, in particular due to deadlocked North-South relations, and actors paid more attention to other paths of change, especially the judicial one, given the particularly strong institutionalization of dispute settlement in the WTO context. This held for China, too, and it did not only concern the subsidy issues this chapter focuses on. Originally a hesitant participant, let alone initiator, in WTO litigation, China had changed its approach by the mid-2000s. Their cases pertained to a variety of issues, amongst others import tariffs and the non-market economy status of China at the WTO.[21] The increased focus on dispute settlement was accompanied by attempts to change procedural rules, for example by requesting special and differential treatment in DSU negotiations with a view to requiring developed countries to exercise due restraint in their cases against China.[22] China also proposed to boost the rights of third parties to allow them to attend all substantive meetings of the panel instead of only the first meetings.[23] This shift towards litigation, however, would not have been possible without serious investments in capacity, which have recently been highlighted, especially by Greg Shaffer and his co-authors.[24] It is to these efforts that we will now turn.

3. Generating Trade Law and Litigation Capacity

As mentioned above, in the years directly following accession China was more a silent observer than a rule maker or challenger. However, as of the mid-2000s

[18] WTO, Ministerial Conference, 5th session, Cancun, Statement by HE Mr Lu Fuyuan, Minister of Commerce of China (2003) WT/MIN(03)/ST/12.

[19] Gao 'China's Participation in WTO Negotiations' (n 14).

[20] ibid.

[21] Mark Wu, 'The 'China, Inc.' Challenge to Global Trade Governance' (2016) 57 Harvard International Law Journal 261.

[22] Specific Amendments to the Dispute Settlement Understanding—Drafting Inputs from China (2003) TN/DS/W/51/Rev.1.

[23] ibid.

[24] Shaffer (n 1).

it changed its behaviour and began contesting rules of international trade law through litigation. This shift to the judicial path was crucial to China's more recent successes and position of influence at the WTO, as I will discuss below. China (as well as other countries) spent their early years at the WTO sometimes trying to engage in proceedings through statements and operated largely through the multilateral pathway.[25] However, as Nicolas Lamp demonstrates, many countries chose not to pursue multilateral options further and ultimately shifted to the judicial path in order to gain more influence at the WTO and to push the organization (and with it the field of international trade law) to adapt to their regional or domestic priorities.[26]

In the case of China, this shift is particularly remarkable as international trade law is one of very few areas in which the country agreed to conflict resolution by means of an international court or quasi-court.[27] Yet the expertise necessary for countries to succeed through litigation does not materialize overnight but requires a significant effort. Therefore, it is important to take a closer look at what is underlying this shift on a domestic level.

China's accession to the WTO has not just been a catalyst for restructuring their state-owned enterprises (SOEs) but has also spurred the development and formation of the international trade law profession in the country.[28] From the start, the Ministry of Justice was acutely aware of their internal shortcomings in terms of lack of English language fluency and trade law capacity.[29] They set out a ten-year strategy to rectify these deficits as early as 2001. This strategy plan outlined that training abroad for currently practising lawyers and law students would be crucial to build a legal profession, which could compete with those of other countries at the WTO. The Ministry placed particular emphasis on incentivizing foreign-trained Chinese lawyers to return and practise trade law domestically in order to fulfil the demands of the country's 'market economic construction and development'[30] between 2001 and 2010. Building this capacity was a top priority of the Department of Trade and Commerce and the Department of Treaty and Law within the Ministry

[25] See Nico Krisch and Ezgi Yildiz, 'The Many Paths of Change in International Law: A Frame' in Nico Krisch and Ezgi Yildiz (eds), *The Many Paths of Change in International Law* (Oxford University Press 2023).

[26] See Nicolas Lamp, 'Arrested Norm Development: The Failure of Legislative-Judicial Dialogue in the WTO' Working Paper, Queen's University, 2021.

[27] Henry Gao, 'China's Ascent in Global Trade Governance: From Rule Taker to Rule Shaker, and Maybe Rule Maker?' in Carolyn Deere-Birkbeck (ed), *Making Global Trade Governance Work for Development* (CUP 2011) 153

[28] On the following, see especially Henry Gao, 'How China Took on the United States and Europe at the WTO' in Shaffer (ed), Emerging Powers and the World Trade System (n 12) 174.

[29] Ministry of Justice, China, 'Notice No. 030, Opinions of the Ministry of Justice on Accelerating the Reform and Development of the Legal Profession after China's Accession to the WTO' (2001) <www.lawinfochina.com/display.aspx?lib=law&id=2970&CGid> accessed 17 June 2022. LawinfoChina is a legal database run by Beijing University.

[30] ibid.

of Foreign Affairs in the early 2000s.[31] Subsequently, the Department of Treaty and Law organized study trips to Washington DC for delegations of selected scholars, practising lawyers, and ministry employees where they were taught at Georgetown University by Professor John Jackson.[32] Simultaneously, the government put in place programmes for Chinese law professors to assist the Ministry of Commerce in developing, enhancing, and implementing their WTO strategy.[33]

In the early years, post-accession China relied heavily on non-Chinese law firms to litigate disputes at the WTO, as there was no domestic law firm with experience in the area.[34] Yet the government insisted on additionally hiring domestic firms to support international (often French) firms and learn from their legal practices and knowledge.[35] In the early 2000s around ten domestic law firms worked on WTO cases, narrowing to five over the years, one of which is part of the original group of ten, while the others are more recent additions. The remaining five involved in WTO cases are amongst the largest 'full-service' firms in the country, as opposed to the original ten which were mainly boutique firms.[36] The lawyers practising in the currently hired law firms are younger overall and have significant experience in firms abroad (in Europe and the US) whilst those in the early days were older, distinguished domestic lawyers, without experience practising abroad but with strong domestic government ties.[37] This is exemplary for the development of the Chinese international trade law capacity domestically. Domestic law firms were further incentivized to be involved with WTO cases as these gave the firms direct access to government officials, particularly in the Ministry of Commerce, and increased influence over other areas of regulation that is drafted by the Ministry, such as the regulation of competition laws and foreign investment. There is a clear distinction between cases that are argued before a WTO panel—in these instances the government hires foreign (American or European) and domestic law firms to collaborate.[38] If cases do not reach the stage of litigation before a panel, or in cases in which China acts as a third party in panel proceedings, the Chinese government primarily hires domestic law firms.[39]

[31] Sida Liu and Hongqi Wu, 'The Ecology of Organizational Growth: Chinese Law Firms in the Age of Globalization' (2016) 122 American Journal of Sociology 798.

[32] Shaffer and Gao (n 7).

[33] ibid.

[34] Han Liyu and Henry Gao, 'China's Experience in Utilizing the WTO Dispute Settlement Mechanism' in Gregory Shaffer and Ricardo Meléndez-Ortiz (eds), *Dispute Settlement at the WTO: The Developing Country Experience* (CUP 2011) 137.

[35] Randall Peerenboom, 'Economic Development and the Development of the Legal Profession in China' in Margaret Woo and Mary Gallagher (eds), *Chinese Justice: Civil Dispute Resolution in Contemporary China* (CUP 2013) 114.

[36] ibid.

[37] Peerenboom (n 35); Liu and Wu (n 31).

[38] Shaffer and Gao (n 7).

[39] ibid 151.

Simultaneously, China attempted to expand their capacity at the WTO secretariat which is often a strong force behind the drafting of panel and AB reports.[40] In 2010, there were only five Chinese staff members in the WTO Legal Affairs Division and the AB secretariat out of 629 in total and compared with 181 French and 72 British staff members.[41] This could be partly attributed to the WTO language requirements of French or Spanish, which led China, India, Brazil, and other developing countries to submit a proposal for diversifying the WTO secretariat.[42] By 2021, the numbers of Chinese staff members had increased to sixteen[43]—still a modest number in absolute terms, but a threefold increase over the situation a decade earlier.

This indicates that, from the early days of Chinese accession to the WTO, the government was acutely aware of how to best use the tools at their disposal and that they had a strategic plan for how to push their own interests, using the same avenues available to everyone else. Their efforts at building own capacity play a crucial part in China's attempts to change international trade law in order to align its interpretation with China's own economic and political vision and to avoid having to submit to the neoliberal, US-centric status quo prevalent in the 1990s.[44] A case in which these attempts—and some of their success—is observable are the changes around subsidy regulation at the WTO. To appreciate the impact of those changes it is important to first consider the historical context from which they emerged.

4. Subsidies and State-Owned Enterprises in China

China's large state-owned sector differed from (Eastern European) non-market economies in that China did not embrace mass privatization whilst other countries often implemented large-scale privatizations early in their economic reform process.[45] China instead opted to develop a 'socialist market economy', in which the market sets prices whilst public ownership remains dominant and coexists with a smaller private sector. In the late 1990s, China did reduce state ownership,

[40] See Joost Pauwelyn and Kristof Pelc, 'Who Guards the Guardians of the System? The Role of the Secretariat in WTO Dispute Settlement' (2022) 116 American Journal of International Law 534.

[41] Pasha Hsieh, 'China's Development of International Economic Law and WTO Legal Capacity Building' (2010) 13 Journal of International Economic Law 997.

[42] WTO, Committee on Budget, Finance and Administration—Joint Proposals on the Improvement of Diversification of the WTO Secretariat (4 November 2009) WT/BFA/W/191, by Brazil, China, Cuba, Ecuador, India, Pakistan, and South Africa.

[43] WTO, 'Overview of the WTO Secretariat' <www.wto.org/english/thewto_e/secre_e/intro_e.htm> accessed 17 June 2022.

[44] James Gaathii and Sergio Puig, 'The West and the Unraveling of the Economic World Order: Thoughts from a Global South Perspective' in David Sloss (ed), *Is the International Legal Order Unraveling?* (OUP 2023).

[45] Julia Qin, 'WTO Regulation of Subsidies to State-Owned Enterprises (SOEs)—A Critical Appraisal of the China Accession Protocol' (2004) 7 Journal of International Economic Law 863.

promoting foreign investment and private enterprises, as well as allowing SOEs to be sold or go bankrupt.[46] By 1999, SOEs made up a 28 per cent share of the gross national industrial output, compared to 76 per cent in 1980.[47]

The remaining sectors dominated by SOEs were oil, energy, metal, chemicals, machinery, finance, insurance, rail and air transportation, telecommunications, and medical services. Many of them were economically inefficient due to their historical SOE structure,[48] which resulted in substantial, non-performing loans being extended from state-owned banks to a large number of SOEs.[49] The Chinese government anticipated increased market competition following their entry into WTO, evident in their attempts to reform the SOE sector in the late 1990s, selling off SOEs at increased pace, restructuring and listing them on domestic or foreign stock exchanges.[50] In that sense, the WTO accession can be understood as another step in Chinese SOE reform. Nevertheless, China continued providing subsidies to SOEs, which can be grouped under three columns: subsidies to sustain and revive loss-making SOEs, subsidies to privatize and restructure SOEs, and subsidies provided to foster key SOEs.[51] Some of these might have actually been motivated by the drive to reform the SOE sector.[52] However, they might still negatively affect the trade interests of other WTO members, clearly presenting a challenge to the system. Balancing the interest in SOE reform requiring subsidization and at the same time protecting the interests of other members was bound to be difficult for the WTO.

China became a member of the WTO in 2001. In the years leading up to accession, the overwhelming expectation from policymakers and academics was that China would reform their SEOs, privatize and liberalize them, and adapt to the predominant neoliberal WTO system. Some were acutely aware that the systems of, on the one hand, private enterprises operating in the existing world trade and investment structure and a large, protected, privileged, state-owned sector on the other hand were incompatible and could not easily coexist.[53] Shortly after the accession it became clear that one of the areas of strong contention in the years to come would be possible subsidy reform.[54] Early expectations that China would

[46] ibid.

[47] Xiaolu Wang 'State-owned Enterprise Reform: Has it Been Effective?' in Ross Garnaut and Ligang Song (eds), *China 2002: WTO Entry and World Recession* (Asia Pacific Press 2002) 29.

[48] ibid.

[49] US-China Economic and Security Review Commission '2004 Report to Congress' (2004) 77.

[50] Julia Qin, 'WTO Regulation of Subsidies to State-Owned Enterprises (SOEs)—A Critical Appraisal of the China Accession Protocol' (2004) 7 Journal of International Economic Law 863.

[51] Qin, 'WTO Regulation' (n 45).

[52] ibid.

[53] Gary Hufbauer, 'China as an Economic Actor on the World Stage: An Overview' in Frederick Abbott (ed), *China in the World Trading System: Defining the Principles of Engagement* (Kluwer Law International 1998).

[54] John Jackson, 'The Impact of China's Accession on the WTO' in Deborah Cass, Brett Williams, and George Barker (eds), *China and the World Trading System* (CUP 2003) 19.

adapt to the WTO system were not fulfilled, and instead China began lobbying efforts to mould wider WTO frameworks to adapt them to their own economic understanding.[55]

The Accession Protocol set out a number of provisions directly and indirectly targeting the management of subsidies in an economy with a large number of state-owned enterprises.[56] The most prominently featured ones are provisions around an SOE-based specificity test and authorization for the importing country to permanently use alternative benchmarks to identify and calculate Chinese subsidies. The Accession Protocol also excludes China from invoking the privatization exception that is available to other developing country members under the Agreement on Subsidies and Countervailing Measures (SCM Agreement).[57] The Chinese Accession Protocol refers here to the 'right to trade' related to the import and export of goods.[58] It was interpreted narrowly, meaning that in practice the extension of obligations to non-discriminatory and non-discretionary treatment extends the obligation from mere border measures and applies to all enterprises (whether private, state-owned, or joint ventures).[59] This limits China's ability to utilize the exception provisions the General Agreement on Tariffs and Trade (GATT) had originally allowed for developing and transitioning members.[60] China agreed not to invoke any of the exceptions normally in place for developing countries, which grant special treatment with regard to domestic subsidies.[61]

Under the Accession Protocol China is not obliged to privatize their SOEs. Instead, the Protocol requires China to ensure that its SOEs will operate in line with market economy principles.[62] Furthermore, China agreed to eliminate all export subsidies upon accession, which is a deviation from past practices in which developing and transition economy members had seven to eight years to eliminate subsidies.[63] The Protocol also requires China to notify the WTO of any subsidy (within the meaning of Article 1 of the SCM Agreement), but the notification does not strictly include the obligation to identify subsidies provided by state-owned banks.[64]

55 Messenger (n 5).

56 Protocol on the Accession of the People's Republic of China, WT/L/432 (2001) WTO.

57 Certain subsidies related to developing country members' privatization programmes are not actionable multilaterally (SCM Agreement, art 29). Developing country members (whilst respecting countervailing measures) are entitled to more favourable treatment regarding termination of investigations if the level of subsidization or volume of imports is small.

58 Accession Protocol (n 56) art 5.1.

59 ibid art 5.2.

60 *China—Measures Related to the Exportation of Various Raw Materials* (30 January 2012) Report of the Appellate Body, WT/DS394-5-8/AB/R, 293, excluding the possibility of China's recourse to art XX GATT for its obligation to eliminate export duties under art 11.3 of the Accession Protocol, as (unlike art 5.1) there was no *specific* reference to 'China's right to regulate in a manner consistent with the WTO Agreement'.

61 Report of the Working Party on the Accession of China (WTO 2001) WT/MIN(01)/3, para 171.

62 ibid para 46.

63 Accession Protocol (n 56) s 10.3, SCM Agreement, arts 27.2, 27.3, 27.4, 29.

64 Accession Protocol (n 56) s 10.1.

China has privatized a large number of former state-owned enterprises before and after WTO accession, but the government has retained ownership of some strategically important companies.[65] Many of these enterprises have been performing well economically, largely due to their close relation to the government and its support as well as the possibility of accessing financing through state-owned commercial banks.[66] In particular, this access to financing streams has given rise to the argument that these enterprises have an unfair advantage in the marketplace. The US has therefore argued that many of the state-owned enterprises and state-owned commercial banks are 'public bodies' under Article 1.1(a)(1) SCM Agreement, that they are therefore subject to WTO subsidies disciplines, and that countervailing duties (CVDs) can be used in response to subsidies provided by them. As a result, the US has introduced CVDs on many goods from China.[67]

For China then, the question of what constitutes a 'public body' became of pressing concern with a view to their SOEs. This raised broader questions about the regulation of subsidies in the WTO context and especially its interpretation in a context—that of a non-market economy—for which it was not initially conceived.

5. Subsidy Regulation at the WTO

Historically, subsidy regulation within international trade law broadly, and at the WTO specifically, has been used by different global actors as the basis to push for and advance specific assumptions and state structures concerning the relationship between state and market. However, many legal issues in the field remained unclear for many decades.[68] The 1947 GATT did not actually define the term subsidy. A subsidy code was originally developed by the Tokyo Round 1973–79 (although it did not contain a precise definition of a subsidy either) and the Uruguay Round elaborated on the original Subsidies Code and incorporated it into the WTO. The SCM Agreement, part of the package of WTO Agreements, was more specific than any of the previous documents in that it attempted to define the term 'subsidy', though it leaves underspecified a number of elements, among them the term 'public body'.[69]

'Subsidy' is defined by Article 1.1 of the SCM Agreement as a financial contribution that is made by a government or any public body within the territory of a member through a (potential) direct transfer of funds or liabilities, government

[65] Peter Nolan, 'Globalisation and Industrial Policy: the Case of China' (2014) 37 The World Economy 747

[66] ibid.

[67] 'Countervailing Duty Investigation of Coated Free Sheet Paper from the People's Republic of China—Whether the Analytical Elements of the Georgetown Steel Opinion Are Applicable to China's Present-Day Economy' (US Department of Commerce 2007) C-570–907.

[68] Messenger (n 5).

[69] ibid.

revenue, or a government providing goods and services beyond general infrastructure, or a government making payments to a funding mechanism directly or through a private body, or the conferring of a benefit.[70] The three key elements are the 'financial contribution' by 'government or public body', which confers a 'benefit'. Government support for business is a common occurrence in all types of economies, but if it is labelled as subsidization, it entails legal consequences and in particular makes it possible for other countries to enact CVDs to offset the benefit derived from the subsidy. Yet, the line between government support and subsidization is difficult to draw and has given rise to significant contestation. The US understood the SCM Agreement as an opportunity to form a body of rules cementing the transatlantic agreement under US hegemony and to influence the manner in which other states engaged in privatizations.[71] Over time, it emerged that the US and Europe acted as partners in trade regulation vis-à-vis developing countries.[72] Traditionally, the US negotiators sought to include in WTO disciplines as many forms of governmental subsidies as possible, except those which are part of technology and environmental programmes.[73]

The SCM Agreement reflects this in part, but the openness of some of its terms allows for ongoing contestation. Especially the meaning of 'public body' has continued to be a battleground where transatlantic concepts and approaches of subsidy regulation have been challenged by others, in particular China and to some extent India. Problems with it arise especially for economies in which state-owned enterprises occupy an important role, as the SCM Agreement seems to give preference to states that do not involve governmental bodies in the market and relies on a model of a liberal state in which public and private are separated. This issue has been of particular importance to China due to the large number of state-owned enterprises, as government subsidies had historically caused much concern with their trading partners.[74] Signalling this, the China Accession Protocol is the only WTO discipline containing rules on subsidization of SOEs, setting out criteria under which subsidies to SOEs are to be treated as 'specific' and therefore 'actionable' under the SCM Agreement.[75] In terms of general rules, GATT Article XVII (State Trading Enterprises) is the only WTO provision referring explicitly to SOEs intending to ensure that members do not make use of state trading enterprises to circumvent or avoid GATT obligations.[76] Whilst the SCM Agreement

[70] Agreement on Subsidies and Countervailing Measures (15 April 1994) art 1.1, Marrakesh Agreement (hereafter SCM Agreement).
[71] Sarooshi (n 50).
[72] Messenger (n 5).
[73] ibid.
[74] Qin, 'WTO Regulation' (n 45).
[75] ibid; Accession Protocol (n 56) art 10(2).
[76] WTO, *Canada—Measures Related to Exports of Wheat and Treatment of Imported Grain* (6 April 2004) WT/DS276/R, paras 6.39, 6.89, 85; *Canada—Measures Relating to Exports of Wheat and Treatment of Imported Grain* (30 August 2004) WT/DS276/AB/R, para 85 (stating that art XVII 1(a) is an 'anti-circumvention' provision).

does not per se differentiate between SOE and private entity subsidization it does contain exceptions related to SOE subsidies. First, it provides an exception for subsidies granted by a developing country regarding a privatization programme and secondly, it contains an exception for subsides utilized by a transition economy member facilitating transformation from centrally planned to market economy.

It is challenging to identify any 'hidden subsidies' in non-market economies as the benchmark of the market is missing. Approaches developed with a view to this challenge in the GATT prior to the creation of the WTO tend to start from a pure version of a country 'which has a complete or substantially complete monopoly of its trade and where all domestic prices are fixed by the State', but they eschew less clearcut cases.[77] After the end of the Cold War, most former non-market economies transformed from centrally planned economies to market economies and the issue became less pressing. One member country that remained a non-market economy was Cuba, which normally informs the WTO that it does not maintain or grant subsidies falling within the meaning of Article 1(1) and Article 2 of the SCM Agreement.[78] With very little practice at an institutional level concerning subsidies from non-market economies, issues of Cuban export subsidization were largely dealt with through individual countries' national laws on countervailing duties.[79]

6. Shifts in the WTO Case Law

While the definition of subsidies—and especially that of 'public bodies' as the authors of subsidies—was not entirely settled by the SCM Agreement, several decisions of WTO panels developed a clearer stance focused on government control, thus opening the door relatively wide to include a host of SOEs among public bodies. The 2005 *Korea-Commercial Vessels* case was in many ways exemplary of this trend. The case centred on the Korean export-import bank, which offered financing and loan guarantees to support domestic businesses, and which—according to the South Korean argument—could not be regarded as a 'public body' as it pursued commercial interests.[80] The panel, however, did not focus on whether a commercial or governmental purpose was pursued, or whether the bank acted on the basis of governmental authority. Instead, it found that the SCM Agreement envisioned a straightforward approach to the distinction between public and private bodies. For the panel, the decisive criterion here was whether an entity is

[77] Agreement on Interpretation and Application of Articles VI, XVI and XXIII of the General Agreement on Tariffs and Trade (10 November1980) BISD 26S/26-28.

[78] WTO, *Notification of Subsidies by Cuba* (1 July 2003) G/SCM/N/95/CUB.

[79] John Jackson, *The World Trading System: Law and Policy of International Economic Relations* (MIT Press 1997); Robert Lantz, 'The Search for Consistency: Treatment of Nonmarket Economies in Transition under United States Antidumping and Countervailing Duty Laws' (1995) 10 American University International Law Review 993

[80] *Korea—Measures Affecting Trade in Commercial Vessels* (7 March 2005) WT/DS273/R.

controlled by the government, in which case any action by that entity falls under Article 1.1(a)(i) of the SCM Agreement.[81] The same test was pursued in *EC—Large Civil Aircraft*,[82] and it came to be regarded as the settled state of the law.[83]

Up until that point, it had been US policy not to apply CVDs to countries considered as non-market economies (NMEs), such as China. Yet, starting in 2006, the US changed course, distinguished the Chinese economy from the (Soviet) model that had led to the earlier policy, and began to impose CVDs on a host of products from China (as well as other contemporary NMEs), with significant economic ramifications.[84]

As part of a challenge to this new practice, the earlier settlement around the notion of a public body in subsidy regulation came undone. In *US—AD/CVDs (China)*, China sought to obtain a different interpretation of the meaning of the term 'public body' with respect to state-owned enterprises and banks declared as such by US authorities.[85] The US contended that, as a public body in the past had been determined by governmental control, SOEs were automatically to be considered as 'public bodies'. China, in contrast, argued that previous panel decisions should not be followed and presented its own interpretation. The panel sided with the US, even as it noted that there was no general definition for 'public body'.[86] It pointed out that it would be challenging to come up with an abstract definition as different jurisdictions defined 'public bodies' differently in their own law, and 'some of these go well beyond government agencies or similar organs of government, and include, inter alia, government-owned or -controlled corporations providing goods and/or services'.[87] The panel reviewed the provisions in French and Spanish and came to the conclusion that the main question that had to be answered was whether state-owned enterprises and state-owned commercial banks are public or private bodies specifically under the SCM Agreement.[88] The panel focused on the relationship between public and private, not on the one between 'public body' and 'government', thus distinguishing the issue from that before the AB in *Canada—Dairy*,[89] which had taken governmental and non-governmental functions into account. As a result, the panel reaffirmed the previous jurisprudence and focused

[81] ibid paras 7.49–50.

[82] *European Communities and Certain Member States—Measures Affecting Trade in Large Civil Aircraft* (30 June 2010) WT/DS316/R.

[83] Daniel Bethlehem and others, *The Oxford Handbook of International Trade Law* (OUP 2009).

[84] Matthew Kennedy, 'China's Role in WTO Dispute Settlement' (2012) 11 World Trade Review 555.

[85] *United States—Definitive Anti-Dumping and Countervailing Duties on Certain Products from China* (22 October 2010) WT/DS379/R. See also Dukgeun Ahn, 'United States—Definitive Anti-dumping and Countervailing Duties on Certain Products from China' (2011) 105 American Journal of International Law 761.

[86] ibid.

[87] *US—Definitive Anti-Dumping and Countervailing Duties on Certain Products from China* (n 85).

[88] ibid.

[89] *Canada—Measures Affecting the Importation of Milk and the Exportation of Dairy Products* (13 October 1999) WT/DS103/AB/R W/DS113/AB/R.

on control as the distinctive criterion, with the public sector under state control and private enterprises privately controlled:[90] '[w]e consider that interpreting "any public body" to mean any entity that is controlled by the government best serves the object and purpose of the SCM Agreement.'[91] Majority government ownership was taken to be 'clear and highly indicative evidence of government control, and thus of whether an entity is a public body for purposes of the SCM Agreement'.[92]

This was the not the outcome China had pushed for, and it accordingly brought the case before the AB. China argued that ownership in and of itself was not determinative and that the key criterion should not be whether an entity is controlled by the government, but instead whether the entity exercises governmental *authority*.[93] The AB largely followed this argument.[94] It found that the US had to demonstrate that an SOE exercised 'government functions', creating constraints on US CVD practices against Chinese imports.[95] The AB stated that governmental control or delegation may, but need not, be indicators of the public nature of a body: 'the precise contours and characteristics of a public body are bound to differ from entity to entity, State to State, and case to case.'[96]

Even though this move generated considerable legal uncertainty,[97] many saw it as a momentous move: it 'effectively transformed the "public body" test into a "government action" test'.[98] It was also a move taken over the explicit opposition of important WTO members, including not just the US, but also the EU, Canada, Mexico and Turkey, among others,[99] As was to be expected, the AB decision was strongly contested by the US Trade Representative as it destabilized the control test set forth in previous decisions and challenged existing US CVD practice.[100] If implemented, it would have largely removed benefits provided by SOEs from the remit of CVDs as the burden of evidence to demonstrate actual exercise of governmental authority was too high,[101] especially because SOEs in China are mostly

[90] *US—Definitive Anti-Dumping and Countervailing Duties on Certain Products from China* (n 85) para 8.69.

[91] ibid para. 8.79.

[92] ibid para. 8.135.

[93] Messenger (n 5).

[94] *US—Definitive Anti-Dumping and Countervailing Duties on Certain Products from China* (n 85) 611.

[95] ibid 318, 543.

[96] ibid.

[97] Joost Pauwelyn, 'Treaty Interpretation or Activism? Comment on the AB Report on *United States—Ads and CVDs on Certain Products from China*' (2013) 12 World Trade Review 235.

[98] See the statement by Turkey, in WTO, Dispute Settlement Body, Minutes of Meeting (9 June 2011) WT/DSB/M/294, para 107. See also Ahn, 'Why Reform is Needed' (n 9).

[99] See hereafter *US—Definitive Anti-Dumping and Countervailing Duties on Certain Products from China*, WT/DS379/R (n 85) paras 8.42–8.52.

[100] Melissa Lipman, 'WTO Rejects US Duty Double-Counting in China Fight' (*LAW360*, 11 March 2011) <www.law360.com/articles/231712/wto-rejects-us-duty-double-counting-in-china-fight> accessed 17 June 2022.

[101] Weihuan Zhou, Henry Gao, and Xue Bai, 'Building a Market Economy through WTO-Inspired Reform of State-Owned Enterprises in China' (2019) 68 International and Comparative Law Quarterly 977.

non-transparent as regards their governance structure, which will often make it impossible for an investigating authority to provide the evidence required.[102]

The US did not shift its approach either and continued to rely on 'meaningful control' as the core criterion. Yet, even despite this lack of implementation, the AB decision represented a victory for China in terms of pushing forward its own views and agenda. Several important countries—among them Brazil, India, and Saudi Arabia—had supported the Chinese position in the proceedings. And even governments that disagreed on substance recognized that the AB finding would 'serve as a reference for the conduct of any investigating authority', and that no grounds existed to call into question the legitimacy of the decision.[103]

The AB approach was consolidated in the following years, especially in response to a broader challenge by China to US CVD determinations. In 2014, a WTO panel found that these determinations, based as they were on the previous criteria (government control and ownership), were not in compliance with the standard set out by the AB in 2011.[104] Most third-party interveners had suggested that the panel follow the AB, and the US did not even appeal this point. In a parallel case, however—brought by India and concerning SOEs with a similar role to China's—the panel initially decided not to follow the AB's approach, applied the traditional, 'meaningful control' standard, and sided with the US.[105] It was, however, soon reversed on appeal. The AB's decision in late 2014 largely insisted on the prior AB jurisprudence and, while indicating some flexibility, continued to focus on 'governmental authority' as the core yardstick.[106]

By the mid-2010s, therefore, the legal standard applied in such cases had clearly changed compared to what it was a decade earlier. The shift in the understanding of 'public body' under the SCM Agreement may not have become fully consolidated, as contestation and instances of non-compliance continued, especially on the part of the US. It nevertheless resulted in a new balance of argument and provided a new reference point for the legal debate, reflected, for example, in the way in which the law came to be presented in trade law textbooks.[107] Even though the typical threshold for 'subsequent practice'—with a concurring practice or agreement of the parties to a treaty—had not been met, the law had, for all practical purposes,

[102] Chad Bown and Jennifer Hillmann, 'WTO'ing a Resolution to the China Subsidy Problem' (2019) 22 Journal of International Economic Law 557.

[103] See eg the statement by Mexico and the European Union, in WTO, Dispute Settlement Body, Minutes of Meeting (n 98) paras 103 and 112.

[104] *United States—Countervailing Measures on Certain Hot-Rolled Carbon Steel Flat Products from India* (14 July 2014) WT/DS436/R.

[105] ibid.

[106] *United States—Countervailing Measures on Certain Hot-Rolled Carbon Steel Flat Products from India* (8 December 2014) WT/DS436/AB/R.

[107] See eg Joost Pauwelyn, Andrew Guzman, and Jennifer Hillman, *International Trade Law* (Wolters Kluwer 2016) 507; Peter van den Bossche and Werner Zdouc, *The Law and Policy of the World Trade Organization: Text, Cases and Materials* (CUP 2017) 783.

changed, and it would have been unprofessional to restate the law on the basis of the previous control test.

A few years later, this relative consolidation was again called into question. Several reports by panels and the AB after 2018 were somewhat more deferential to US views and further added to the uncertainty about the applicable standards.[108] Still, they kept generating friction, including through a separate opinion of one AB member, and the US appealed even a favourable panel ruling out of opposition to the starting point chosen, which continued to focus on 'governmental functions'.[109]

These decisions were already adopted in the midst of the crisis surrounding, and eventually incapacitating, the AB. The 'public body' jurisprudence also features prominently among the points of concern of the US regarding the AB,[110] and it is likely to have contributed to the US challenge to the AB and its decision to block the appointment of new members (a development also discussed by Mark Pollack in his chapter in this volume[111]). The EU, too, has raised concerns about the 'narrow interpretation' of the notion of 'public body' and identified subsidies through SOEs as one of the areas in which a 'rebalancing of the rules' of the WTO is necessary.[112] Without a functioning dispute settlement system, understandings of the current state of the law are in any event bound to diverge more over time.

7. Conclusion

Power shifts do not translate automatically into changing international legal rules. Instead, rising powers need to find pathways to align the law more closely with their visions and preferences, and they will often find the typical, state-driven processes of multilateral negotiations blocked because of a reluctance of other countries to accommodate their rise. This has been on display most vividly in the trade context, in which WTO negotiations since the onset of the Doha Round have been fraught with controversy and have hardly led to meaningful results, partly because of claims for a stronger role by a coalition of developing countries, in particular the BRICs. Other state-led paths for change at the WTO—especially through decisions of intergovernmental bodies—were also not used, or not usable, by governments.[113]

[108] See Ahn, 'Why Reform is Needed' (n 9) 64.

[109] ibid.

[110] US Trade Representative, Report on the Appellate Body of the World Trade Organization (February 2020), 82–89. <https://ustr.gov/sites/default/files/Report_on_the_Appellate_Body_of_the_World_Trade_Organization.pdf> accessed 17 June 2022.

[111] Pollack, this volume.

[112] EU, 'Concept Paper: WTO Modernisation' <https://www.wita.org/atp-research/eu-concept-paper-on-wto-reform/> accessed 17 June 2022.

[113] See Lamp (n 26).

China, a rising power and with misgivings about the outcome of the accession negotiations, understood early during its membership that it had to shift away from, or at least complement, a negotiation-driven multilateral path if it wanted to inform policy and change norms in its own interest. International trade law lent itself to such a shift—especially a shift to a judicial path—as it is (or was then) organized around a central dispute settlement body holding much power when it comes to attempts to change legal norms in the field. The clogged paths of multilateralism then resulted in the judicial pathway being more or less the only path open to change attempts.

As we have seen in this chapter—and as is developed much further by Shaffer in his recent book—the Chinese government invested significantly in its capacity to use this path to its advantage, in particular by creating domestic legal expertise in WTO law and urging Chinese law firms to generate capacity in the field. It also pushed for greater representation in the WTO secretariat in order to enable its views to be better reflected in the preparation of decisions, including those of panels and the AB in dispute settlement. As a result of its greater confidence in this field, by 2006 China not only defended its trade policies as a respondent in WTO cases, but it also began bringing its own cases against the US and the EU.[114] As a result, China began to shape WTO jurisprudence and in effect international trade law with a view to constraining US and EU attempts to impose measures against Chinese imports.

It is difficult to causally link Chinese investments to particular outcomes, but it is clear that the Chinese push towards litigation has borne fruit in various respects.[115] In this chapter, I have traced its attempt to change the subsidies regime in order to constrain the use by other countries, in particular the US, of CVDs against benefits deriving from state-owned entities, including banks. As we have seen, this attempt was relatively successful as the AB in the 2010s moved away from the common understanding of a crucial term—'public body'—that had prevailed until then.

Subsidy reform is an example of China playing the Western game, and rather successfully at that. It is imperative not to re-read this story in terms of China making its own rules, but instead as one of China using strategies which were also at the disposal of, and often used by, Western countries. The rules of international trade law were defined largely by Western countries, and the WTO dispute settlement mechanism was a way of giving them teeth. China has been challenging them not by actively pushing back against the rules themselves, but rather by occupying the spaces made available by existing rules. As a result of this, through the work of its lawyers China has taken on a leading role in developing transnational legal processes in international trade law, sometimes with ripple effects and wide-reaching

[114] Cui Huang and Wenhua Ji, 'Understanding China's Recent Active Moves on WTO Litigation: Rising Legalism and/or Reluctant Response?' (2012) 46 Journal of World Trade 1281.

[115] Wu (n 21); Shaffer and Gao (n 7).

consequences for other members and their respective economic and political systems. The AB itself moved to the centre of a power contest between states and their fundamentally different understandings and visions for a global economy.

International legal change in this instance—and in other areas of WTO areas as well—has travelled on the judicial pathway, with a limited ability of (even important) states to block shifts in meaning brought about by the AB. Even as the US vigorously contested the reinterpretation of 'public body', most actors in the field soon acknowledged that the law had changed. The contestation prevented full consolidation, though, and it had more tangible effects later on, once the US had moved towards the '' option of incapacitating the AB by blocking new appointments. It was at that point that panels and the AB returned to a greater measure of openness to US policies, butit was too late to rescue the AB.

This points to a series of potentially important insights about change in international law. It seems to confirm the framing paper's conjecture that change can indeed take place despite major divergences among states if alternative paths are available, as in this case the judicial pathway. It also suggests that it is then the institutional dynamics on the relevant pathway that condition outcomes and determine to what extent the positions of states have an influence. In this case, both the Chinese and the US positions are likely to have had an impact on the WTO panels and the AB—in line with the finding by Sergio Puig and Jeff Kucik in their contribution to this volume that strong signals about challenges (especially non-compliance) provoke responses by the AB[116]—yet their positions were not determinative of the outcome. However, we also see that the relative autonomy of the judicial pathway had serious limits once the US shifted to all-out opposition and, thanks to the institutional rules in place at the WTO, managed to unilaterally disempower the AB. Institutional rules vary across institutions, of course, and discontent with the European Court of Human Rights may have had a more limited impact in part because of that difference.[117] But backlash can take different forms, and states may find ways of derailing change if institutions overstretch their *marge de manoeuvre*. The paths of change in international law are hardly ever straight.

[116] Jeffrey Kuick and Sergio Puig, this volume.

[117] See also Mikael Madsen, Pola Cebulak, and Micha Wiebuch, 'Backlash against International Courts: Explaining the Forms and Patterns of Resistance to International Courts' (2018) 14 International Journal of Law in Context 197.

PART V
SITUATING CHANGE

11

The Appellate Body's Judicial Pathway

Precedent, Resistance, and Adaptation

Jeff Kucik and Sergio Puig***

1. Introduction

What are the limits of change of international law in highly judicialized environments? The World Trade Organization's (WTO) Appellate Body (AB) provides a good case study of the limits of the judicial pathway of international law.[1] The AB is unique: an international, multilateral, and appellate court with general jurisdiction over an entire area of WTO members' policy, routinely interpreting a discrete number of treaties. Initially regarded as a significant step forward in international trade law enforcement, the AB's difficulties arose quickly, in part due to the role of their decisions. Today, the future of the body is uncertain.[2]

There are different ways to tell the story of the rise and downfall of the AB. We choose one that highlights the limits of the judicial pathway of change.[3] Despite a formal rule against the application of precedent, the AB has become rather consistent in the use of prior decisions as it gains authority.[4] Yet, in following a de facto precedent norm, the AB has often given an expansive treatment to its own decisions, including in sensitive areas such as the regulation of anti-dumping duties.[5]

The extension of precedent did not go unnoticed by the most active (and powerful) members of the organization, including the US. The parties to these

* Associate Professor of Political Science and Law (by courtesy) at the University of Arizona.
** Evo DeConcini Professor of Law and Director, International Trade and Business Law Program at the University of Arizona.

[1] Jeffrey L Dunoff and Mark A Pollack, 'The Judicial Trilemma' (2017) 111 American Journal of International Law 225.

[2] Cosette D Creamer, 'From the WTO's Crown Jewel To Its Crown Of Thorns' (2019) 113 American Journal of International Law Unbound 51; see also Gregory C Shaffer, 'A Tragedy in the Making?: The Decline of Law and the Return of Power in International Trade Relations' (2019) 43 Yale Journal of International Law 37.

[3] Nico Krisch and Ezgi Yildiz, 'The Many Paths of Change in International Law: A Frame' in Nico Krisch and Ezgi Yildiz (eds), *The Many Paths of Change in International Law* (Oxford University Press 2023).

[4] Other articles have discussed the role of precedent in the demise of the AB. See James Bacchu and Simon Lester, 'The Rule of Precedent and the Role of the Appellate Body' (2020) 54 Journal of World Trade 183; Mariana Clara de Andrade, 'Precedent in the WTO: Retrospective Reflections for a Prospective Dispute Settlement Mechanism' (2020) 11(2) Journal of International Dispute Settlement 262 <doi.org/10.1093/jnlids/idaa006> accessed 14 October 2022.

[5] Jeffrey Kucik and Sergio Puig, 'Extending Trade Law Precedent' (2021) 54 Vanderbilt Journal of Transnational Law 539.

Jeff Kucik and Sergio Puig, *The Appellate Body's Judicial Pathway* In: *The Many Paths of Change in International Law.* Edited by: Nico Krisch and Ezgi Yildiz, Oxford University Press.
DOI: 10.1093/oso/9780198877844.003.0011

disputes, often the states on the losing side of the case, reacted by complaining, delaying, and, eventually, by failing to comply with the decisions of the WTO's 'judicial' body. Non-compliance represented a challenge to the legal authority of an international dispute body. The decline in compliance rates became a strong signal of dissatisfaction of states—a backlash against the WTO's authority.[6] This resistance raises the question: how did the AB adapt to such strong signalling by states?

We believe, based on our evidence, that the AB has adapted precedent more often by narrowing and distinguishing its own decisions when members failed to comply with rulings.[7] This suggests that while the judicial path is not generally adept for radical transformations, legal bodies can be sensitive to—and can adjust to—political backlash. Yet, that adaptation also has limits. Changes that upend complex balances of power, including expansive readings of the law, might generate additional backlash.

Why do we focus on how the AB applies prior rulings in the face of non-compliance? From one point of view, reliance on precedent is unsurprising given international legal bodies' incentives to generate predictability. However, as the WTO illustrates, leaning too heavily on precedent can cause political problems. A trade dispute decision can alter treaty commitments and applying it as binding may expose the body to resistance from dissatisfied governments that do not agree with that interpretation. One way to show resistance to judicial overreach—perhaps the most radical way—is by failing to abide to the decisions of the body.[8]

Dispute settlement bodies are not unaware of this tension. These bodies often face a choice: in the face of non-compliance, adjudicators can stick with past precedent, a strategy we have termed elsewhere the 'legal coherence' approach. This approach prioritizes coherence across decisions but risks upsetting (even more) the member states. This behaviour is what some WTO members argue about the AB—ie, that the AB adheres to overly stringent readings of the law, and, therefore, strong members like the US have decided not to cooperate. Alternatively, adjudicators can adapt decisions over time in response to the dissatisfaction governments

[6] Jeffrey Kucik, Lauren Peritz, and Sergio Puig, 'Legalization and Compliance: How Judicial Activity Undercuts the Global Trade Regime' (2022) British Journal of Political Science 1, arguing that 'extending previous decisions can reduce the flexibility that states include deliberately in their agreements [and finding] strong evidence that extending precedent reduces on-time compliance. It also leads to longer delays before members comply.'

[7] Jeffrey Kucik and Sergio Puig, 'Do International Dispute Bodies Over-reach?' (2022) 66 International Studies Quarterly 1

[8] Kal Raustiala and Anne-Marie Slaughter, 'International Law, International Relations and Compliance' in Walter Carlnaes, Thomas Risse, and Beth A Simmons (eds), *The Handbook of International Relations* (Sage 2002) 538. See also Karen J Alter, Emilie Marie Hafner-Burton, and Laurence R Helfer, 'Theorizing the Judicialization of International Relations' (2019) 63 International Studies Quarterly 449 (explaining how compliance in the context of delegation is difficult because governments often do not control the timing, nature, or extent to which political and policy decisions are adjudicated).

express in different ways—and by doing so prevent a possible backlash. We have termed this the 'adaptation' approach.[9]

We have investigated this choice and its implications for the WTO and the judicial pathway. Here, we describe our approach in the context of this book relating to change in international law. As we explain, our findings speak not only to the validity of current criticisms of the WTO, which paint the AB as politically naïve, but also to the role of signalling and authority in the judicial path—the behaviour of states to legal interpretations as the main agents of change. By implication, the results speak to how international adjudicators apply precedent strategically and are, potentially, less beholden to legal coherence than is commonly argued. Paradoxically, change is a common feature of the judicial path, but it is constrained by the limited 'autonomy' of judicial bodies from states that can use compliance as a 'control tool' of change.[10]

The chapter is organized as follows. Section 2 discusses the competing incentives of ICs that inform our hypotheses with respect to the judicial path of change. Section 3 discusses our recent empirical work on this point. Section 4 uses the framework of this volume and our empirical results to propose ways in which the AB of the WTO case helps to improve our understanding of change in international law in highly legalized environments.

2. Precedent and the Competing Incentives of International Courts

After having been initially regarded as a significant step forward in trade law enforcement, the AB's difficulties arose quickly. Dissatisfaction with the AB decisions has contributed to a decline in compliance rates in recent years. Total compliance rates, measured as bringing policy into conformity with WTO rulings, fell across the membership by more than 10 per cent in the last decade. Some believe that the change in behaviour is, in part, connected with the decision in *US—Continued Zeroing* as well as *US—Stainless Steel (Mexico)*, which introduced the concept that, 'absent cogent reasons' to deviate from precedent, WTO adjudicators should

[9] Kucik and Puig, 'Do International Dispute Bodies Over-reach?' (n 7) (noting that the results reveal that the AB is more likely to adapt precedent in the wake of past non-compliance, implying that the AB is arguably more responsive than common criticisms suggest. The evidence shows a strong, positive correlation between past non-compliance and adaptation whereas the correlation is negative between past non-compliance and following precedent.)

[10] See Jacob Katz Cogan, 'Competition and Control in International Adjudication' (2008) 48 Vanderbilt Journal of International Law 411, 420. (providing a taxonomy for controlling international courts (internal and external) and five categories of external controls over courts: (1) mandates; (2) rules it can apply; (3) staffing; (4) budget; and (5) ability to make and apply decisions).

follow it. Some states saw this decision as overreach as the AB indicated its intention to follow a strong norm of precedent.[11] Hence, declining compliance rates.

Given that non-compliance sends a clear signal of dissatisfaction, we hypothesize that adjudicators face a choice. How do they handle decisions that failed to induce compliance when those issues arise again in future disputes? The AB can attempt to reinforce the strength of past rulings by directly applying—that is, following—previous decisions. Alternatively, the AB can adapt precedent in the hope that new rulings are more palatable to governments. Here we explain how we tested these competing hypotheses after discussing precedent as a judicial technique, a technique that ensures some consistency, but also enables changes in law through 'judicial' means.

2.1 The Use of Precedent and the Judicial Path

Precedent as a judicial technique typically means following prior readings. In this sense a rigid application of precedent is the antithesis of change—it is stability at its best. However, while precedent typically means following prior readings, a more nuanced understanding of how courts actually apply precedent allows legal scholars to move away from an unhelpful binary. Judges can utilize (and often do use) the plasticity encountered in legal discourse to distinguish prior readings, or to change their prior decisions without necessarily overriding precedent.[12]

This behaviour of changing or refining a prior reading can have added value for the judicial body. For example, distinguishing precedent can bolster the importance of previous readings or generate greater coherence in legal interpretations over time. Scholars also recognize other ways to adapt precedent—most notably, narrowing.[13] Narrowing takes place in instances where the best prior reading applies, but where the court decides to shrink the scope of that reading to have a more limited bearing on the decision at hand. By doing so, at least in international law, overly broad readings of states' commitments can be avoided. Narrowing precedent can be done slowly over time, or by abruptly interpreting a precedent less broadly than it might have been construed otherwise. It is generally done slowly, often noticed only by communities of practice deeply immersed in the legal doctrines and practice of that subject. Yet, narrowing precedent means that the court, without directly disregarding its own precedent, is able to trim back its reach.

[11] Roger P Alford, 'Reflections on US—Zeroing: A Study in Judicial Overreaching by the WTO Appellate Body' (2006) 45 Columbia Journal of Transnational Law 196, 197.

[12] Harlan G Cohen, 'Theorizing Precedent in International Law' Interpretation in International Law 268 (Andrea Bianchi et al eds. 2015) <digitalcommons.law.uga.edu/cgi/viewcontent.cgi?article=2286&context=fac_artchop> accessed 14 October 2022.

[13] Richard M Re, 'Narrowing Precedent in the Supreme Court' (2014) 114 Columbia Law Review 1861, 1869.

Courts may also use precedent where it does not apply clearly to the case at hand. In order to do so, judges may read and apply a precedent more broadly, effectively extending precedent so that it applies to the current case. Extending precedent involves the widening of a prior reading's *ratio decidendi*—this is the opposite of narrowing. This can occur when the court adopts a justificatory approach to a precedent that extends the application to domains not previously covered by the prior decision. As such, extending precedent goes a step beyond a simple following of prior readings. It adheres to that reading but applies it to a different set of facts or issues.

Thus, at a high level of generality, and with many caveats, the use of precedent is not a binary choice and can refer to, at least, four possible outcomes. When a prior reading clearly applies, a court may follow that precedent through a simple, direct, and mechanical application of a previous decision or it may extend precedent by applying that past reading to a new circumstance, effectively expanding the scope of previous rulings. Conversely, it may narrow precedent through a refinement of those past readings. When a precedent may not necessarily apply, the court can distinguish the current reading from the previous one by explaining why invoking a prior decision is inappropriate. We consider both behaviors – narrowing and distinguishing – examples of adaptation.[14]

In the next section, we discuss how we employed our data set that included more than 5,500 applications of precedent at the WTO to test if the AB was more likely to adapt in the face of non-compliance with its prior decisions. This, in turn, can serve to think more broadly about the judicial path of change in complex judicial settings.

2.2 Exploring the Judicial Path through Non-compliance

The use of precedent in ICs could be understood as two competing choices for a court when it comes to affirming its prior choice in the face of pushback. On the one hand the 'legal coherence' approach predicts that because courts place a premium on consistency across cases, judges will follow prior decisions. A rich vein of legal studies literature shows that coherence can bolster a court's authority, and this applies doubly to international legal systems, which have extra incentives to rule predictably given their contested legitimacy.[15] Moreover, in a world where states guard their trade policy sovereignty fiercely, consistent decisions can reduce the court's exposure to accusations of bias or arbitrariness. Thus, legal coherence—bolstered

[14] See David L Shapiro, 'In Defense of Judicial Candor' (1987) 100 Harvard Law Review 731, 739–40.

[15] See generally Karen J Alter, Laurence R Helfer, and Mikael Rask Madsen, 'How Context Shapes the Authority of International Courts' (2016) 79 Law and Contemporary Problems 1, 11–12; see also Thomas M Franck, 'Legitimacy in the International System' (1998) 82 American Journal of International Law 705.

by a strict adherence to precedent—lends greater credibility to the court. It reduces the chance that rulings appear arbitrary, capricious, or politically motivated.[16]

In addition to the court's incentives, there are institutional and sociological factors at play. The secretariats and operational staff of many ICs, including the WTO, are legal professionals, not political appointees. Lawyers who litigate and hear disputes are trained to value candour to the law. That does not mean they are blind to political context. However, the likelihood is that these actors see consistent interpretations of the law as a positive feature of the system.[17]

In light of these incentives, the 'legal coherence' approach implies that adjudicators respond to non-compliance with prior decisions by following precedent. Following precedent involves the direct application of a previous decision to a current dispute. For example, the AB considered ten previous rulings in its decision on *US—1916 Act (EC)*, one of the WTO's many disputes over anti-dumping duties. The AB followed the cited precedent in each instance. This included several references to the highly influential *EC—Hormones* decision. In *EC—Hormones*, the AB made important rulings relating to the burden of proof that complainants must meet when relying on scientific evidence to allege trade discrimination. The AB also ruled in *EC—Hormones* that panels have discretion over whether to grant third parties 'enhanced' rights. The AB upheld both of these findings in its subsequent ruling on *US—1916 Act (EC)*. That is to say, it followed precedent.

The AB has been asked to consider a previous ruling in almost every decision, a practice that has naturally increased over time as WTO case law expands. By 2015, references to previous rulings were so frequent that the average number of individual precedents interpreted in a given AB ruling was 58 [SD: 50.6]. The AB follows precedent over 75 per cent of the time, a significant majority, which is what we would expect from any legal body concerned with coherence (Table 11.1). However, that 75 per cent may seem low if coherence was the only goal. That is why it is also important to notice that the AB adapts precedent in nearly 15 per cent of its applications of prior readings. These are split relatively evenly between decisions that distinguish (7 per cent) and those that narrow (8 per cent) prior readings. Adapting precedent 15 per cent of the time might sound rare, but it cuts against the incentives to remain consistent. It shows that the AB is willing, on a regular basis, to drift from its previous decisions, which it has done at a relatively consistent rate over the course of the WTO's existence. The question is: when and where is the AB more likely to adapt? It turns out that the majority of adaptations

[16] For a similar discussion, see Laurence R Helfer and Erik Voeten, 'Walking Back Human Rights in Europe?' (2020) 31 European Journal of International Law 797.

[17] See Gregory Shaffer, Manfred Elsig, and Sergio Puig, 'The Extensive (but Fragile) Authority of the WTO Appellate Body' (2016) 79 Law and Contemporary Problems 237, 271; Joost Pauwelyn, 'Minority Rules: Precedent and Participation Before the WTO Appellate Body' in Joanna Jemielniak, Laura Nielsen, and Henrik Palmer Olsen (eds), *Judicial Authority in International Economic Law* (CUP 2016).

Table 11.1 Precedent use by the WTO's Appellate Body[a]

Precedent Type	Total Number	Previous Compliance	Prev. Non-Compliance
Follows	3,744	1455 (39%)	2289 (61%)
Adapts	636	180 (28%)	456 (72%)
Narrows	351	110 (31%)	241 (69%)
Distinguishes	285	70 (25%)	215 (75%)
Other	540	192 (36%)	348 (64%)

[a]Kucik and Puig, 'Do International Dispute Bodies Over-reach?' (n 7).
Note: 'Other' includes mentions of previous rulings without a definitive application in the current dispute. The share of applications adapted is higher after non-compliance (14.74 per cent) than after compliance (9.85 per cent).

(72 per cent) occur after the *cited* dispute ended in non-compliance. Put another way, when a previous ruling failed to induce compliance, the AB adapts in future considerations of similar issues. This is because the AB faces competing incentives.

As we have explained in our study of precedent, there is another approach by a dispute settlement body in the face of non-compliance.[18] While the coherence approach, wherein adjudicators adhere faithfully to past legal decisions, may sound politically naïve in the face of pushback from governments, the 'legal adaptation' approach sees change as an effort to manage political backlash. In this sense, rather than hammering the same legal nail repeatedly, an alternative approach is that legal bodies modify precedent in the face of situations that threaten the court's authority.

2.3 Change and Adaptation of Precedent

In practice, adaptation may occur merely because some facts of the current dispute differ from previous cases and therefore the body may focus on the differences between cases. But in making a choice, adjudicators might be interested in two, related goals: promoting compliance with the law and limiting the occurrence of future disagreements.[19] In other words, the premise behind many ICs, including the AB, is that promoting compliance is in the shared interest of the WTO as well as the WTO's member governments.

[18] ibid.
[19] In the context of the WTO, art 22.1 of the Dispute Settlement Understanding states that 'prompt compliance with [DSB rulings] is essential in order to ensure effective resolution of disputes to the benefit of all Members'.

Adapting precedent—ie, shrinking or differentiating legal interpretations of treaty text over time—provides one way to demonstrate responsiveness to government dissatisfaction. As mentioned earlier, adaptation can take two forms.

First, adjudicators can distinguish the current dispute from the cited precedent. For example, the AB may decide that a past ruling does not apply to the case at hand or that there is not a compelling legal argument to lean on a prior decision. That is what happened in *Chile—Price Band System*, where the AB rejected Argentina's reference to the previous rulings in *Canada—Periodicals.* In that previous case, the AB considered obligations under the General Agreement on Tariffs and Trade (GATT) (1994) Article II:1(b), which states that certain products are exempt both from 'ordinary customs duties' and from 'other duties or charges'. These two obligations were interpreted to be 'part of a logical continuum'. In *Chile—Price Band System*, the AB distinguished precedent, stating that the two components of Article II:1(b) were distinct obligations and should be interpreted separately when evaluating the disputed measures. Distinguishing precedent offers a way to determine that the precedent does not apply to the case at hand, and it may open the door for a new or different legal analysis.[20]

The second form of adaptation is narrowing. Narrowing occurs when the AB restricts the scope of previous decisions. For example, the AB may decide that a previous ruling was too vague (or too far-reaching) in its application. In response, the AB can refine its jurisprudence by narrowing precedent. That is what happened in *US—Foreign Sales Corporations (FSC)*, a case under the WTO's Subsidies and Countervailing Measures Agreement, where the European Communities challenged US tax policies relating to 'foreign sales corporations'. In the *US—FSC* ruling, the AB narrowed the scope of *Canada—Dairy*. That previous decision included an expansive definition of export subsidies under the Agreement on Agriculture of the WTO. The AB previously stated that direct payments by, and 'revenue foregone' to, a government authority both constituted export subsidies in general. However, in *US—FSC*, the AB effectively narrowed by refining the definition of subsidies only to foregone revenues that are 'otherwise due'. This important distinction limits the precedent. The prior interpretation of 'payments' in Article 9.1(c) of the Agreement on Agriculture, which extended to the definition of 'subsidy' under the Agriculture and Subsidies and Countervailing Measures (SCM) Agreements, was narrowed. In essence, *US—FSC* whittled down *Canada—Dairy* because incentives other than payments such as grants or payouts would no longer qualify as prohibited subsidies.[21]

[20] World Trade Organization, 'Chile—Price Band System and Safeguard Measures Relating to Certain Agricultural Products: Report of the Appellate Body' (WT/DS207/AB/R).

[21] World Trade Organization, 'United States—Tax Treatment for 'Foreign Sales Corporations: Report of the Appellate Body' (WT/DS108/AB/R). Notice that the initial interpretation of the word 'payments' in *Canada—Dairy*, in the specific context of art 9.1(c) was an expansive one, imputing into its meaning, 'payment in kind' which may be read to include foregone revenue. In *US—FSC*, the AB effectively shrinks the meaning of subsidy for the entire agreement to mean only foregone revenue in a move that

In the above examples, both cited disputes, *Canada—Periodicals* and *Canada—Dairy*, failed to result in on-time compliance by a generally compliant member. The respondent in both cases, a member with a strong voice at the WTO, resisted the ruling, sending a signal of dissatisfaction with the decision. In the subsequent rulings, made in view of that prior non-compliance, AB adapted its position, saying that those precedents did not apply universally. As such, distinguishing and narrowing precedent both provide the AB with alternatives to strict adherence to prior rulings. These techniques also provide an alternative to directly overruling a precedent entirely. Wholly overturning a previous ruling would come at a high cost for the body since it could be perceived as an admission that the prior decision was wrong. In this way, breaking entirely from precedent, as distinct from adaptation, could worsen backlash against the AB. It is telling that, in twenty-five years, the AB has never entirely overruled a previous interpretation.[22] Only specific panel decisions are reversed on occasion.[23]

Hence, the 'legal adaptation' approach predicts that the AB is more likely to adapt precedent when there was non-compliance with past rulings. The idea is that the court, seeing the limits of its previous decisions, adapts the law in response to political resistance. Such behaviour is consistent with the idea that adjudicators are strategic and care more about being perceived as effective than as correct. There is also some evidence that adaptation has downstream benefits. Compliance is actually (slightly) more likely after AB decisions that adhere less strictly to following precedent. As a result, the AB may reasonably anticipate that, despite an interest in legal coherence, adaptation offers a way to promote the Dispute Settlement Body's (DSB) ultimate goals.[24]

We acknowledge an alternative explanation for why adjudicators adapt precedent. Namely, the AB sometimes hears arguments that do not apply directly to the case at hand. Litigants may cite extraneous precedents when making their legal arguments. Litigants themselves behave strategically, introducing certain legal arguments specifically to establish useful precedents for the future. Given widespread use of judicial economy and the fact that AB is an appeals court, the mere existence of an AB decision is prima facie evidence that the AB considered the legal issue fundamental to the dispute. In other words, for our analysis, the AB will have

all but destroys the young and fragile precedent set in *Canada—Dairy*, and creates expansive implications for the entire Agreement on Agriculture, with that limited interpretation.

22 The closest the AB has come to overruling precedent is with regard to pre-WTO panel reports. For example, the rejection of the processes and production methods analysis in the first *Tuna—Dolphin* case—although even then the AB did it carefully and not explicitly citing the precedent.

23 Out of the 420 legal claims ruled on the AB in DS1-450, the AB differed from the panel report on only 113 occasions—ie 27 per cent of the time.

24 The AB adapts precedent about 15 per cent of the time per dispute. In dispute rulings that adapt above the mean, downstream compliance rates are 47.6 per cent. In rulings below the mean—ie, that follow precedent more closely—compliance rates are 36.1 per cent. We do not test those downstream implications directly in this chapter. Rather, we focus on the AB's decision.

the tendency to 'filter out' references to disputes where the precedent simply does not apply.

3. Testing Change by Looking at Adaptation

3.1 Design

To examine AB behaviour, we collected data on precedent applications in the first one hundred AB decisions (spanning 1995–2015). An individual 'precedent application' is each instance in which the AB interprets references to prior findings. These may be brought to the AB's attention in arguments by the complainant, respondent, or a third party. Given the DSB's heavy reliance on judicial economy, whereby panels and the AB typically rule on only a small set of claims made in each dispute, we do not code for the manner in which each precedent is introduced. The data contain 5,518 unique applications.

We were interested mainly in whether the AB follows or 'adapts' rulings in the wake of past non-compliance. As mentioned, adaptation can take two forms. The AB can distinguish the current issue from a previous one by ruling that a prior decision does not apply to the dispute at hand. The AB can also narrow a previous ruling, refining the scope of the cited precedent. Both application types represent alternatives to strict adherence to prior findings. We coded each application of a prior ruling for whether it follows or adapts—that is, whether the AB sticks to the cited decision or whether it modifies that decision in some meaningful way.

Like many legal systems, the AB typically follows its past rulings, doing so 75 per cent of the time. By contrast, the AB adapts precedent 15 per cent of the time. Adaptations are meaningful. They cut against courts' traditional emphasis on legal coherence, and they can potentially amend past doctrines by distinguishing prior cases or by narrowing formal grounds. That is how we believe judicial change happens: by slow evolution and reassessment of the law or its context of application. Each adaptation, in that sense, can represent an incremental change in how the law is read and applied.

Using this precedent data, we conducted a large-n analysis, which correlates AB behaviour with past (non-)compliance. Our main explanatory variable is noncompliance with the previous (cited) ruling. Non-compliance is coded using data from Peritz.[25] Peritz codes compliance in terms of tangible policy changes. Under WTO law, respondents do not necessarily need to dismantle their policies if they lose a dispute. They can 'comply' with WTO rulings merely by absorbing retaliation. However, policy change is, in our view, the more meaningful test. The Peritz

[25] Lauren Peritz, *Delivering on Promises: The Domestic Politics of Compliance in International Courts* (University of Chicago Press 2022).

data measure whether a respondent made concrete efforts to dismantle WTO-illegal measures.

Our sample of precedent applications is reasonably balanced between citations of disputes that ended in compliance (44 per cent) and those that ended in non-compliance (56 per cent). However, adaptations are far more likely given past non-compliance. Approximately 70 per cent of all adaptation occurs when the cited dispute previously resulted in non-compliance.

3.2 Results

Our results show a strong, positive correlation between non-compliance with a past dispute and adaptation of precedent in the dispute at hand. Conversely, there is a negative, though less significant, correlation between prior non-compliance and following precedent. We infer that the AB is more likely to adapt precedent in the wake of past non-compliance, implying that the AB is arguably more responsive than common criticisms suggest.

The substantive effects of our analysis are presented in Figure 11.1.

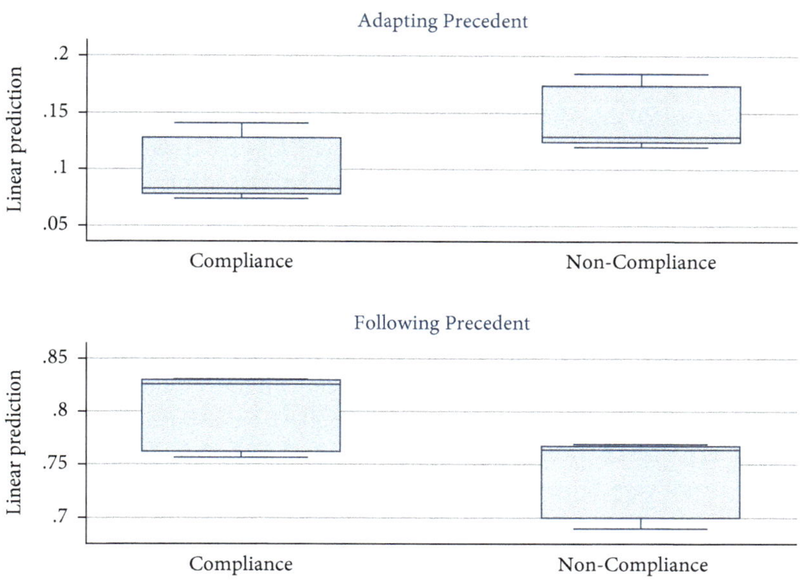

Figure 11.1 Adapting precedent is more likely after non-compliance[a]

Note: The top pane graphs the point predictions for adapting precedent given compliance (0.10 [0.07, 0.14]) or non-compliance (0.14 [0.12, 0.18]). The bottom pane graphs the point predictions for following precedent given compliance (0.79 [0.75, 0.83]) or non-compliance (0.74 [0.69, 0.77]).

[a] ibid.

The AB is 45 per cent more likely to adapt precedent when the cited ruling failed to induce compliance in the past. The point prediction is 0.10 [0.07, 0.14][26] after compliance. The point prediction is 0.14 [0.12, 0.18] after non-compliance. The absolute difference (0.04) may appear small. However, it is substantively meaningful given the fact that the AB, like so many legal bodies, typically follows precedent.

Figure 11.1 also shows the point predictions for our estimates of whether the AB follows precedent. Given past compliance, the AB is more likely to follow the previous reading (0.79 [0.75, 0.83]). However, following is less likely in wake of non-compliance. Contingent on non-compliance, the predicted rate of following is 6 points lower (0.73 [0.69, 0.77]).

The estimates were robust to a wide variety of estimation techniques and model specifications. We started with bivariate estimations, which were consistent across ordinary least squares regression, fixed effects for the citing dispute, and maximum likelihood estimation. We also included a wide variety of controls, including indicators for disputed issue-area, traits of the AB members, and the use of judicial economy. Disputed issue-area is especially important since some GATT/WTO Agreements are disputed more frequently. Notably, these include subsidies and anti-dumping. It is possible that the AB may be more or less likely to adapt precedent in highly sensitive areas of the law.

The controls do not alter our core results. They are generally insignificant. However, we do find a significant correlation between adaptation and whether the US was the respondent in the cited dispute. Given that the US is a vocal critic of the AB and given that it has the political influence and market power to resist rulings, it makes sense that the AB may adapt precedent in an effort to address the US's concerns. If so, this finding is important. It suggests that the AB is more responsive—at least, more than commonly argued—to political backlash from one of the WTO's largest members. Even here, following previous rulings remains the most common form of precedent. But there is more adaptation after non-compliance than we otherwise witness.

Finally, our analysis recognizes that past non-compliance is non-random. For example, in sensitive areas like anti-dumping, the high number of disputes may itself be evidence of persistent non-compliance. Once a respondent (eg the US) fails to comply with some ruling A, it leads to follow-on disputes B, C, and D. The interconnectedness between disputes is a concern for any large-n analysis of legal systems. In our case, it means that the AB's decision today is affected by a series of decisions in disputes that may date back many years. Drawing from the large-n literature, we model non-random selection into non-compliance.[27] The core finding

[26] Brackets include 95 per cent confidence interval.

[27] Strong correlates of past non-compliance, such as the number of third-party participants in the cited dispute, are poor predictors of precedent use. The relevant diagnostic tests for two-stage estimation give us confidence that the system of equations is suitably identified.

holds when attempting to correct for this bias. While controlling for the predictors of past behaviour by respondents, there remains a strong correlation between non-compliance and adaptation.

The extended design and empirical analysis can be consulted in the related papers.[28]

4. The Judicial Path and Precedent

Based on our empirical results we believe that states may exercise different pressures on the 'receptors' of change. One way that pressure can be especially significant is by delaying compliance or by non-complying with decisions of judicial-like bodies. In our case study of the AB of the WTO, we find that the judicial change was limited and perhaps insufficient to reverse the backlash against the body. However, we think that the judicial pathway of change is available, but rocky in part because states tend to be zealous in protecting the nature and extent of the legal obligations they commit to. In this final section, we develop our argument with reference to the framework of this book.

4.1 The Paths Framework and Judicial Change

In the introduction to this volume, Krisch and Yildiz propose a framework of five ideal-typical pathways that explain change in international law. The authors recognize that change is contingent to actors that are 'recognized as authorit[ies]', including judicial authorities like the AB. Yet, each path differs in meaningful ways and rely on different types of authority.[29] The different paths have their own mechanisms through which change occurs or upon which actors rely to propose change attempts. The paths serve different purposes, and their effectiveness is contingent on different conditions.

In this chapter we are concerned with what Krisch and Yildiz call the judicial pathway. In particular, in this path:

> Change ... is recognized as the result of decisions and findings of courts and quasi-judicial bodies. It relies on judicial expert authority and often also on the delegation from states, and typically comes about through mechanisms of (broader or narrower) interpretation or channeling of views expressed in other legal instruments (both soft and hard)—without open claims to effecting change.

[28] For a discussion of our results, see Kucik and Puig, 'Do International Dispute Bodies Overreach?' (n 7).

[29] Krisch and Yildiz, this volume.

> International courts are the typical anchor of this path, but institutions such as the UN human rights treaty bodies or the OECD National Contact Points feature here as well, just as much as national courts when they interpret international (rather than national) law.[30]

In addition, Krisch and Yildiz argue that to usefully conceptualize these pathways, we need to think in three stages that affect change. The first is the selection stage, where change agents choose and activate a pathway to realize their vision of change. In the judicial pathway this could be located in the decision to bring or participate in litigation before the organization instead of ignoring a violation or settling a dispute. The second stage is that of construction. Here the actors and authorities associated with the pathway process the change attempt and generate statements about the status of the norm in question—confirming or refuting the change attempt or finding some middle ground—or avoid a positioning. In the context of judicial change, this stage involves the adjudicatory body deciding on the interpretation of a rule and the possible consequences of that interpretation. The third stage is the reception stage, 'where the outcome of [the] construction stage is appraised by a broader range of actors'.[31] In this stage that state and other 'constituencies of compliance' react by accepting or pushing against the plausible change resulting from legal interpretations.

International judicial actors are most relevant in the last two stages. ICs may attempt change by issuing a judicial interpretation, which is then either fully accepted, partially accepted, or rejected by state authorities and other relevant constituencies. According to Krisch and Yildiz, '[a]ctors in the reception stage will assess a proposed change on substance but also on pedigree. If the actors and institution at the construction stage are recognized as authorities, members of the community of practice will often defer to them even if they disagree with the result.'[32]

A key point made by Krisch and Yildiz is the observation that different pathways operate in different conditions. For one, change constructed by judicial actors will be limited by factors that affect the authority of ICs, including *ex-ante* and *ex-post* mechanisms of state control over a court. One of those tools—perhaps the most powerful tool of control—is the state resistance to compliance. One hypothesis resulting from this observation is that the judicial change may operate with 'less support by, or even in the face of objections from, states'.[33] This is a relevant point, and we believe that the conditions of the judicial pathway might indeed enable change even in the face of resistance to comply. However, there is a limit to that as states—or, at the very least powerful states that can dictate terms of agreement—have

[30] ibid.
[31] ibid.
[32] ibid.
[33] ibid.

mechanisms to push back against unwelcome or undesirable changes. Chief among these mechanisms, as we observed from our analysis, is non-compliance with unpalatable precedents, which might cement into the jurisprudence and become settled law. Therefore, compliance and resistance operate as signalling for adjudicators to create incentives for the IC to reverse course. As we now explain, this observation can help to refine the theory of judicial change proposed by Krisch and Yildiz in two ways.

4.2 The AB and Judicial Change

We have found that the AB, despite having incentives to uphold prior rulings, modifies precedent regularly—especially in the face of resistance to comply with rulings. Our results also show that the AB is less intransigent than its critics argue; it is more likely to adapt if members failed to comply with previous decisions.

These findings have implications for understanding change in international law and to refine the story of change at the WTO, including the role of the Trump administration in the current crisis.[34] Conceptually, our chapter highlights the tension between the judicial path and cooperation between states. The judicial pathway has clear limits imposed by states, and often exercised by *ex-post* control tools. The tension between independence and control is not unfamiliar to states that delegate to ICs the ability to decide disputes resulting from the application of international agreements. In fact, controlling the effects of the decision of ICs, by establishing limits on the effects of precedent, may be an important way to avoid undesirable evolutions or changes of the rules. The more 'binding' a precedent is, the more likely it is that precedent can lead to permanent changes over time.

As the AB case demonstrates, as ICs try to increase their authority, often by prioritizing precision and legal coherence, they effectively may strip away some of the term's flexibility, deterring policy experimentation as well as political bargaining over the legality of controversial policies. At that point states are left with limited tools to control the work of ICs and repair the effects of their decisions. One important way is by signalling the distaste for resistance, either delays or non-compliance. In this sense, the judicial pathway is limited by methods of *ex-post* control of courts, including non-compliance. Such tools operate as determinants of real, permanent change.

Judicial authorities in charge of enforcing international law are not blind to potential backlash. In fact, our results show that these authorities can be rather subtle

[34] See Pollack, this volume (highlighting that '[t]he administration of United States (US) President Donald Trump is the most significant "change agent" in the international legal order in recent decades' including at the WTO).

in addressing and in responding to pressures.[35] One of the ways in which adjudicators navigate this tension and the political realities of international law enforcement is by adapting, that is, narrowing or distinguishing precedent. At the WTO adjudicators seemed rather aware of—and attempted to adapt to—backlash from the organization's membership, in particular the US.[36]

More generally, the case of the adjudicatory system of the WTO shows the relationship between the 'construction' and the 'reception' stages of change. The construction of legal change is of course dependent on the judicial authorities that might enable change selected by strategic litigation or otherwise. Yet, the reception of that change in systems with sophisticated dispute settlement processes operates in the long-term horizons—the eventual acceptance by states needs to happen for change to effectively succeed. Hence, systems of constant adjudication may invite complex dynamics that make them less, rather than more, nimble to change. This is because, from the standpoint of domestic political officials, international agreements need to result in net political gains relative to political costs. And, from the perspective of adjudicators, their decisions should remain effective and result in compliance. This calculation, of course, depends on how judges assess the general likelihood that states (and other actors) will comply. The AB had, we believe, become relatively confident about its authority and only noticed the depth of dissatisfaction late in the game. Hence, the story of adaptation is perhaps one of 'too little too late'.[37]

Our results also illustrate a mechanism by which ICs learn and evolve in light of change. Rather than adhering to a strict interpretation of the law, rulings shift and adapt over time, as in other areas of law. That is not to deny that areas of contention remain unchanged. However, it appears that international law, as law in general, is always in motion. As such, our findings are also relevant for studies of international agreement life cycles. To understand change across time, one has to account for the behaviour of different actors, including international judicial bodies, but also the officials that will need to comply with the rules. While the judicial change depends heavily on the strategic behaviour of litigants, authorities, in particular judicial authorities, should possess a certain level of political knowledge to manage or control

[35] On this point, see Mark A Pollack, 'Trump as a Change Agent in International Law: Ends, Means, and Legacies' (2022) <ssrn.com/abstract = 4137754> accessed 14 October 2022. See also Wolfgang Streeck and Kathleen Thelen, *Beyond Continuity: Institutional Change in Advanced Political Economies* (OUP 2005) 1–39.

[36] See Nicolas Lamp, 'Arrested Norm Development: The Failure of Legislative-Judicial Dialogue in the WTO', manuscript on file with the authors, noting, in particular:

> [I]f the WTO Membership had clarified the interpretation of the Anti-Dumping Agreement after the first 'zeroing' case, decades of litigation could have been avoided. And if the WTO Membership had instructed the Appellate Body how it should deal with situations in which it could not meet its 90-day deadline, it could have spared itself many acrimonious debates in the Dispute Settlement Body and prevented the frustration with the Appellate Body from mounting.

[37] We thank Krisch and Yildiz for this point.

political dissatisfaction that could hamper legal change. As put by Pollack in this volume, law can also produce negative feedbacks and '[s]elf-undermining institutions, by contrast, "can cultivate the seeds of their own demise," by producing negative feedbacks and increasing demands for change over time.'[38]

Future work should look more closely at whether adaptation helps resolve lingering resistance to change. It also remains to be seen whether adaptation promotes downstream compliance, a hypothesis that we did not test, but which could be fertile ground for expanding our research. It will take several more years before the recent crisis in Geneva is resolved—and before we observe compliance decisions with ongoing trade disputes. In the interim, this chapter shows that looking at the content of trade rulings, not just the outcomes, reveals a more nuanced, strategic approach to change. The crisis of the WTO is not simply the result of the 'activism' of the AB, but certainly it is a significant part of it.[39]

5. Conclusion

What is the pathway of change of international law in highly judicialized environments? In many systems with such environments, governments have expressed concern that courts use legal decisions and subsequent precedent to change the law. In particular, the resistance to the WTO AB's behaviour caused gridlock in the system when the US starting to veto the reappointment of AB members. Was the AB indifferent to the backlash caused by the perceived change through the judicial path?

By looking at twenty years of practice of the 'World Trade Court', this chapter contributes to this conversation about the limits of change in international law. It clarifies the role of the judicial pathway and how resistance to complying with rulings may serve as a mechanism to limit change. As we explained, the application of precedent through a strong *stare decisis* norm at the AB led to dissatisfaction beyond the point at which governments were willing to cooperate. But our results also show that the WTO is adaptive when it needs to be. Despite a strong norm to

38 Pollack (n 35); referencing Avner Greif and David D Laitin, 'A Theory of Endogenous Institutional Change' (2004) 98(4) American Political Science Review 633–52, 634; see also Laurence R Helfer, 'Overlegalizing Human Rights: International Relations Theory and the Commonwealth Caribbean Backlash against Human Rights Regimes' (2002) 102 Columbia Law Review 1832, 1832–911.

39 See also Lamp (n 38), noting that 'the crisis in WTO dispute settlement is not simply the result of the "activism" of the WTO Appellate Body or the United States' turn away from the "rules-based international order", but rather reflects deeper flaws in the institutional design of the World Trade Organization. A good starting point to illuminate these flaws is the distinction with which I began this article, namely, the distinction drawn by the European Economic Community in the 1980s between the "two activities involved in dispute settlement": "resolution of the conflict on the one hand and authoritative interpretations of GATT provisions on the other". The two activities are in tension because they require different actors to exercise control over the process of dispute settlement.'

follow prior rulings, the AB has modified precedent regularly—especially in the face of past non-compliance.

This important finding has at least two implications for the framework proposed by Krisch and Yildiz. On the one hand, we note that judicial change is limited by the receptors of legal change. These receptors might express dissatisfaction by failing to comply, rendering ICs decisions ineffective. On the other hand, we observed that authorities, in particular adjudicators, must also be strategic with respect to the change enabled with their decisions. In the end, the judicial pathway will be conditioned by the ability of their decisions to result in compliance. An IC that prioritizes change over authority might see backlash that renders them ineffective.

12

Whose International Law is Changing?

The Practice of Fragmented Communities Constructing Legal Change

*Dorothea Endres**

1. Introduction: A Trajectory of Change?

In Hindu mythology, Mahabali is a demon-king. At least when the higher castes tell the story. Narrating the same story, the Dalits display Mahabali as a heroic icon of justice.[1] The same practice, storytelling, produces opposing images of the same character in the story. Yet, Brahmans and Dalits have little cause to contest the other group's account of the story. The two characters of Mahabali exist in parallel. Similarly, international law is composed of communities of practice (CoPs) that at times coexist in parallel. Consequently, their evaluation of the same attempt at change can result in solidification of the norm in one CoP, yet in the sidelining of the same norm in another. These divergences do not necessarily lead to contestation. In particular when the change in question is incremental, CoPs may coexist while holding divergent views of what the law is.

Incremental change happens in a recursive dynamic,[2] structured in recurring phases of selection, construction, and reception.[3] As has been elaborated by Nico Krisch and Ezgi Yildiz in this volume, actors take up legal norms in the selection stage, construct legal change in the construction phase, and receive legal change in the reception phase.[4] International legal change is recursive in that it 'involves numerous iterations of law-making and implementation' between a wide range of actors.[5] Susan Block-Lieb and Terence Halliday distinguish between vertical and horizontal levels of recursivity: vertically, local, national, and global levels are

* PhD Researcher in International Law, Graduate Institute of International and Development Studies, Geneva, Switzerland; Research Assistant, Faculty of Law, University of Geneva.

[1] This was elaborated by the Indian scholar Jotirao Phule in 1873 in his book Gulamgiri. Cited in Gail Omvedt, *Seeking Begumpura—The Social Vision of Anticaste Intellectuals* (Navayana 2008) 166–67.

[2] Susan Block-Lieb and Terence C Halliday, *Global Lawmakers: International Organizations in the Crafting of World Markets* (CUP 2017) 26–27.

[3] Nico Krisch and Ezgi Yildiz, 'The Many Paths of Change in International Law: A Frame' in Nico Krisch and Ezgi Yildiz (eds), *The Many Paths of Change in International Law* (Oxford University Press 2023) 15–17.

[4] ibid.

[5] Block-Lieb and Halliday (n 2) 26.

Dorothea Endres, *Whose International Law is Changing? The Practice of Fragmented Communities Constructing Legal Change* In: *The Many Paths of Change in International Law*. Edited by: Nico Krisch and Ezgi Yildiz, Oxford University Press.
 DOI: 10.1093/oso/9780198877844.003.0012

linked; horizontally, international actors are involved in 'multiple rounds of interactional engagements in their various claims to law-making authority'.[6] The idea of 'multiple rounds' refers to recurring phases of legal change: actors select certain norms in order to construct a legal change that then has to solidify in order to be successful.[7] For incremental legal change, in particular legal change that is not primarily secured by treaty-making or jurisprudence, this solidification is however a very murky process. Regularly, the degree of solidification of a legal change is unclear. In particular, different communities will have diverging opinions on the degree of solidification of a change. Hence, in order to pin down the extent to which a legal change has been 'successful', it is crucial to look at the practices registering or sidelining legal change. Those practices differ depending on issue-areas or type of actor, but also, and most importantly, within the same issue-area and amongst the same type of actors. In other words, we may find within one issue-area several communities composed of a variety of actors that are linked through common practices. Consequently, actors of the same issue-area may be members of different CoPs, and members of those different CoPs within the same issue-area will account differently for 'successful' legal change. For instance, investment tribunals' statements on 'what investment is' diverge without chronological logic, but by reference to assumptions about the legal basis on which investment arbitration operates.[8]

The identification of legal change in the reception stage of incremental legal change then becomes a heuristic exercise depending on the composition of the issue-area.[9] If one of the parallel communities is more closely linked to the issue-area, a change only being recognized in a specific, possibly very small community may become portrayed as successful for the whole issue-area—and vice versa. Thus, I argue that divergent CoPs may produce divergent accounts of change. And that the reception of legal change within the issue-area may identify legal change in accordance with one community's finding, neglecting the existence of parallel communities' views. If the composition of the community has been considered as 'critical because it makes and shapes the law',[10] I argue it is also critical for the evaluation of the success of legal change—for asking 'whose law is changing'.

Inquiring into the question of 'whose law it is', scholarship has produced insightful analyses on contestation and acceptance. The question is often framed in a manner that presumes that the answer will reflect conflict. For example, Frank Harvey and John Mitton ask whose norm it is when talking about norm

[6] ibid.
[7] Krisch and Yildiz (n 3) 11–12.
[8] See section 3.3.
[9] Krisch and Yildiz (n 3) 12.
[10] Sandesh Sivakumaran, 'Making and Shaping the Law of Armed Conflict' (2018) 71 Current Legal Problems 119, 131.

antipreneurs,[11] and Block-Lieb and Halliday ask, 'whose law?' in order to highlight the role of competition and conflict in the process of making international law.[12] In contrast, this chapter looks at instances when different, divergent norms are produced in parallel yet without necessarily being perceived as conflicting. This is in particular due to the fact that divergent understandings of norms are not engaged with.

Different CoPs value and devalue legal change based on different shared premises. Consequently, in order to establish whose law is changing, two points are crucial: the actor and the practice. First, the actors' position in the frame in which the practice has meaning determines to some extent the value the practice has for the CoP in question. As we will see later in the chapter, the International Committee of the Red Cross (ICRC) enjoys a different position within the field of international humanitarian law (IHL) than the Appellate Body (AB) of the World Trade Organization (WTO) in the field of trade law. Secondly, different practices have different effects on the solidification of legal change. Furthermore, the same practice can vary in its effects depending on the broader structure in which it is embedded. Academics and judges may both engage in the practice of interpretation, but their interpretations have different effects on the solidification of legal change.

And yet, some judges and some academics join together in opposing other judges and other academics—all of them engaging in the same practice of interpretation. For instance, different CoPs can start emerging from such coalitions of opposition. As long as those coalitions engage in open conflict, the general solidification of change can be—at least to some extent—determined by evaluating the success of one coalition. However, if the starting point is less explicitly one of disagreement, members of one community may drift apart incrementally, and eventually resolve into two parallel communities coexisting without explicitly contesting the other group—albeit devaluing their propositions.

This argument will be elaborated in two steps. In the first step, I will present the theoretical concept of CoPs and how this concept can be useful for conceptualizing change in international law, and present the theoretical entry point for the second part, elaborating how one can make sense of divergent stages of solidification of legal change within the same issue-area or within the same group of actors. In the second step, I will introduce three examples to demonstrate the relevance of CoPs in international law for the analysis of legal change.

The first two examples look at state practice and its impact on international legal change. An example from the WTO demonstrates how the same legal norm used by different groups of states receives very different reactions. The second example

[11] Frank Harvey and John Mitton, 'Whose Norm Is It Anyways? Mediating Contest Norm-Histories in Iraq (2003) and Syria (2013)' in Alan Bloomfield and Shirley V Scott (eds), *Norm Antipreneurs and the Politics of Resistance to Global Normative Change* (Routledge 2017).

[12] Block-Lieb and Halliday (n 2) 265–321.

looks at how the practice of armed conflict affects the recognition of legal change in IHL. The final example explores the limits of the widely advanced argument that legal change is furthered by practices of interpretation in international litigation. Looking at international investment arbitration, I show that, while change-by-precedent is true for one CoP, a parallel community privileges bilateral investment treaties as the primary source of reference and consequently produces different accounts of legal change.

Ultimately, I demonstrate how CoPs in international law may develop parallel yet diverging understandings on what the law is, and how and when it changes. I will show how those communities might clash in contestations but need not do so. Indeed, they may coexist in 'peaceful' non-recognition of the validity of parallel communities' practices. Furthermore, as I will show, it is also possible that CoPs coexist in parallel without dynamics of conflict or convergence. I conclude this chapter with a critical assessment of the perspective and positionality of researchers investigating legal change.

2. CoPs Changing International Law

2.1 Definition

I understand CoPs as groups of actors that are held together through performative, patterned acts that rely on shared knowledge. Practices are 'competent performances' in the sense that they are 'socially meaningful patterns of action, which, in being performed more or less competently, simultaneously embody, act out and possibly reify background knowledge and discourse in and on the material world'.[13]

Two elements of this definition are particularly relevant for this chapter. First, the use of 'competent' points to 'the fact that groups of individuals tend to interpret [the performance of practices] along similar standards'.[14] Thus, social recognition is crucial.[15] The second element is the role of background knowledge, which necessarily relies on collectivity for its production and implementation.[16] In fact, practices serve as 'structural, discursive and epistemic focal points'.[17] Those practices 'make possible common knowledge and enable actors to play the international game according to [...] mutually recognizable rules'.[18]

[13] Emanuel Adler and Vincent Pouliot, 'International Practices' (2011) 3 International Theory 1, 4.
[14] ibid 6.
[15] ibid.
[16] ibid 8, 17–18 and 29; see also Etienne Wenger, *Communities of Practice: Learning, Meaning, and Identity* (CUP 1998) 51–71.
[17] Adler and Pouliot. 'International Practices' (n 13) 21.
[18] Karin Tusting, 'Language and Power in Communities of Practice' in David Barton and Karin Tusting (eds), *Beyond Communities of Practice: Language Power and Social Context* (CUP 2005) 44–45.

This means that they also isolate actors from one another, and this isolation regularly happens more on the level of background knowledge than on the level of cognizant strategic action.[19] As section 3 elaborates, those distinctions do not necessarily correlate with the boundaries of specific fields of international law.

While Emanuel Adler and Vincent Pouliot's analysis of practices focuses on the strategic use of practices,[20] by emphasizing the dynamics of collectivity and background knowledge, this chapter highlights how the recognition of legal change depends on practices incorporating change. This incorporation can be strategic, but it can also be a by-product of other mechanisms.[21] What qualifies articulations or actions as practices is their institutionalization into a framework for meaningful interaction.[22] In that process, background knowledge enables the deciphering of the interactions' meaning and consequently becomes crucial.

In further distinction to Adler and Pouliot, who focus on politics rather than law, my focus is on change of law and not politics, though I understand law and politics to be profoundly intertwined.[23] Closer to my perspective, Silviya Lechner and Mervyn Frost highlight the relevance of rule-following as a fundamental element of practice theory, which provides for an important starting point for recognizing normative dimensions of practices.[24] Practices as relations between persons provide for normative 'stickiness' and durability of a socially meaningful framework—CoPs.[25]

However, such frameworks can be more or less stable, and more or less closed. Lechner and Frost identify the existence of norms through the detection of adverse reactions to norm violation.[26] From that perspective, norms constituting the framework of a CoP may provide for diverging adverse reactions within the same community—to an extent that the boundaries of the community become blurry.[27]

While different communities are constituted through different practices, those differences are secondary for the argument presented here. Whether the practice is at the core of communities' practices affects the particular shape of the communities, but does not determine the stability of the communities per se. It is that difference in stability of CoPs that I want to highlight. Of fundamental importance for

[19] See Pierre Bourdieu, *Esquisse d'une théorie de la pratique* (Librairie Droz 1972) 261 and 265.

[20] Adler and Pouliot, 'International Practices' (n 13) 9–13 and 20.

[21] See eg Davide Nicolini, *Practice Theory, Work, and Organization: An Introduction* (OUP 2013) 195–98.

[22] Silviya Lechner and Mervyn Frost, *Practice Theory and International Relations* (CUP 2018)3 and 18.

[23] See Tanja Aalberts and Thomas Gammeltoft-Hansen, *The Changing Practices of International Law* (CUP 2018) 37.

[24] Lechner and Frost (n 22) 11.

[25] ibid 16.

[26] ibid 15.

[27] In contrast, Bourdieu sees chronologically ordered structures: Pierre Bourdieu, *Esquisse d'une théorie de la pratique: précédé de trois études d'ethnologie Kabyle* (Seuil 2000) 284. This is possible for him because he sidelines the question of normative dimensions, highlighted in Lechner and Frost's perspective (relying on Wittgenstein in contrast to Bourdieu): Lechner and Frost (n 22) ch 3.

the stability of a CoP is the shared background knowledge, an assumption of 'what the law is'.

2.2 CoPs in International Law

2.2.1 Constituting CoPs

Relying on Tanja Aalberts' account of political and legal elements in international practice, I argue that actors interact based on what they consider to be law and, through that interaction, create diverse CoPs.[28] Those communities are based upon a common understanding regarding the signification of those practices. For instance, the recognized practice for settling disputes in the WTO is to conform to the AB's ruling.[29] However, a diversity of actors engaging in practices brings about dynamics of legal change that may lead not only to constitution but also to the opposite: dissolution or fragmentation of CoPs.[30] For instance, actors assessing what law is applicable for the regulation of an armed conflict often rely on the term '*lex specialis*'—and depending on their humanitarian or military background, they understand the term differently.[31]

Most scholarship recognizing a diversity of actors in international law sorts those actors according to issue-areas and/or generalizable characteristics such as private, state, and international institutions.[32] In the process of incremental legal change, these categories are useful for identifying the different capacities of participants.[33] However, these categorizations fall short of being able to theorize the registration of incremental legal change. They do not account for the same types of actors in the same issue-area potentially belonging to groups that recognize law and its change differently; their group identity is constructed through different practices.

To some extent, Anthea Roberts touches on this point when she identifies different ways of practising international law in different geographical settings.[34] However, while her account starts from geographical boundaries, my account

[28] Tanja E Aalberts, *Constructing Sovereignty between Politics and Law* (Routledge 2012) 78, 81 and 87; Margareta Brummer, 'Abandonment, Construction and Denial - The Formation of a Zone' in Tanja E Aalberts and Thomas Gammeltoft-Hansen (eds), *The Changing Practices of International Law* (CUP 2018) 39.

[29] This will be elaborated in detail in section 3.1.

[30] Thus, this goes beyond Adler and Pouliot's assertion that '[n]ew practices emerge out of authoritative definitions of truth and morality as promoted by certain segments of society; but this is hard work of reification and power struggle'. Emanuel Adler and Vincent Pouliot, 'International Practices: Introduction and Framework' in *International Practices* (CUP 2011) 27.

[31] This is elaborated in detail in section 3.2.

[32] See eg Malcolm Nathan Shaw, *International Law* (8th edn, CUP 2018) 155–209, 234–54, 924–32, 991–94.

[33] See eg Sivakumaran (n 10), in particular 128–30.

[34] Anthea Roberts, *Is International Law International?* (OUP 2017).

starts from different practices constituting different communities. Those communities can be based in different geographical spaces or not. What is crucial is that their practice can and does determine what they conceive of as international law, and how and when it changes.

Ingo Venzke supports this point in relation to state representatives, when he holds that distinct actors of specific branches of government may 'align themselves according to sectoral interests in order to act on the international level [...] and thus to gain advantage in competition on the domestic level'.[35] Venzke is of course not distinguishing between different phases of legal change, and if one were to categorize his thinking according to those categories, one would find it rather focused on interpretation as 'selection' phase, while the current project aims at delineating the practices relevant for the reception phase.[36] This difference is even more evident when Venzke identifies the authority of international courts or tribunals as 'the ability to establish content-laden reference points that participants cannot escape'.[37] As will be elaborated below, different actors situate themselves differently in their practice of referencing judicial decisions—thereby attributing different degrees of authority to different change attempts.[38]

2.2.2 Identifying communities

Identifying CoPs can be challenging. Tanja Aalberts sees states responding to developing rules and case law of international law and establishing their identity through those practices.[39] However, states are only one of many participants in interactions establishing and changing international law. In this game, I argue, it is the common background knowledge which determines the focal point around which CoPs are established.

Around that focal point, one can identify practices which determine what is inside and what is outside a given community.[40] For instance, enforcingcriteria for membership or mechanisms to settle disputes provide for practices that normalize certain values and behaviour, which ultimately ground background knowledge or assumptions of 'what the law is' and how it changes.[41] Actors not amenable to

[35] Ingo Venzke, *How Interpretation Makes International Law: On Semantic Change and Normative Twists* (1st edn, OUP 2012) 67.

[36] Venzke however also points to 'recognition of authority' by tribunals as inherent in their practice of referencing: Ingo Venzke, 'Understanding the Authority of International Courts and Tribunals: On Delegation and Discursive Construction' (2013) 14 Theoretical Inquiries in Law 381, 403.

[37] ibid 398.

[38] Inger-Johanne Sand, 'Varieties of Authority in International Law' in Ingo Venzke and Patrick Capps (eds), *Legal Authority beyond the State* (CUP 2018). For the argument advanced here it is sufficient to highlight that different actors attribute authority differently.

[39] Aalberts and Gammeltoft-Hansen (n 23) 29–30.

[40] Ole Jacob Sending and Ivan B Neumann, 'Banking on Power: How Some Practices in an International Organization Anchor Others' in Adler and Pouliot (eds), International Practices (n 30) 232.

[41] Aalberts (n 28) 81–82.

those criteria will be considered as 'outsiders' on the other side of the communities' boundary.[42] Their knowledge and contribution to or assessment of legal change is sidelined or dismissed. However, the boundaries and the practices reiterating them are constantly fluctuating and at times blurry.[43]

Hence, in looking for CoPs, three requirements are fundamental: (1) common background knowledge that builds the centre of the communities' identity and in that sense leads the members to consider certain knowledge as 'given', as 'normal'; (2) practices directed internally that reinforce the normalization of the common knowledge and identity; and (3) practices directed externally that determine the distinction between members and non-members.

2.2.3 The role of law in CoPs

Most of the recent scholarship using practice theory in international law focuses on judicial lawmaking,[44] ignoring the plethora of roles that law plays in CoPs in the international legal landscape. As I note in the following section, the role of judicial lawmaking for driving and registering legal change depends on the specific entanglement with other practices and the specific community it is relating to. In particular, judicial lawmaking is entangled with practices of international bureaucracies, academics, and state representatives.[45] Depending on the setting in which we find this entanglement, the same jurisprudential activity can be registered as legal change or sidelined.[46] This will be illustrated using three examples in section 3.

From this perspective, the distinction between political and legal practice is hard to determine. To some extent, this chapter relies on the idea of interactional establishment of legality to determine to what extent law is part of the practice and change in question. Jutta Brunnée and Stephen Toope base their interactional theory on Lon Fuller's moral philosophy, and in particular on his idea of law having distinct 'criteria of legality'.[47] In Brunnée and Toope's view, the legal character of practices depends on a shared understanding for its effectiveness, obligatory character, and quality as 'law'.[48] This provides a solid starting point for thinking about

[42] ibid 152.
[43] ibid 73–74.
[44] See Jeffrey L Dunoff and Mark A Pollack, 'A Typology of International Judicial Practices' in Andreas Follesdal and Geir Ulfstein (eds), *The Judicialization of International Law: A Mixed Blessing?* (OUP 2018); Ingo Venzke, 'Semantic Authority, Legal Change and the Dynamics of International Law' in Henrik Palmer Olsen and Patrick Capps (eds), *Legal Authority beyond the State* (CUP 2018).
[45] Nina Reiners provides for a convincing account of such entanglement in the context of human rights: Nina Reiners, *Transnational Lawmaking Coalitions for Human Rights* (CUP 2021) 37–8.
[46] For instance, different investment arbitration tribunals register different developments as solidified legal change. This will be elaborated in detail in section 3.3.
[47] Stephen John Toope and Jutta Brunnée, *Legitimacy and Legality in International Law: An Interactional Account* (CUP 2010) 26.
[48] ibid 33; see also Nico Krisch, 'Review: Brunée and Toope—Legitimacy and Legality in International Law: An Interactional Account' (2012) 106 American Journal of International Law 203, 203.

the way in which legal could be distinguished from political. However, as we will see below, in the international settings where actors and issue-areas and processes are multifaceted, fragmented, and entangled, more nuance is required: the practices which set up and rely on shared understandings are a lot less uniform than Brunnée and Toope imply.[49] In particular, as I point out in section 3, background assumptions vary considerably.

What is crucial, however, is Brunnée and Toope's fundamental point that legal characteristics are established and reinforced in interaction. Consequently, the qualification of legal change as 'successful' is also interactional. Depending on who interacts, this qualification can vary. In fact, different qualifications of the same change attempt can coexist without explicitly contesting each other. Conflict and contestation are more likely to arise when the change attempt emerges in the vicinity of strong international institutions centralizing the relevant practices. Pulling practices together, such institutions are likely to force diverging positions into direct conflict, and those conflicts are then authoritatively settled by that institution. As will be demonstrated in section 3.1, this used to be the case at the WTO.

3. Three Kinds of Communities

The stability of CoPs varies and is particularly dependent on the institutional setting in which the practices play out. The dynamics of opposition and incremental (dis-)agreement outlined above can have converging, diverging, or isolating effects on the CoPs concerned. Indeed, CoPs do not exist in an isolated and static way. To the contrary, depending on the dynamics provoked through practices, we find three different kinds of CoPs: convergent, divergent, and parallel.[50]

3.1 Convergent Community

For convergent communities, different ideas of 'what is the law' clash through practice and, consequently, the community converges around that practice. This will be illustrated using the example of the interpretation of Article XX(b) of the General Agreement on Tariffs and Trade (GATT), which allows for discrimination between countries with the same circumstances if 'necessary to protect human, animal or plant life or health'. In this example, the core question is how framing facts can push

[49] Toope and Brunnée (n 47) 56–87, 80–81 and 84–86; See also Krisch, 'Review: Legitimacy and Legality in International Law' (n 48) 205–06.

[50] It is important to keep in mind that there is seldom a CoP that is only constituted through one specific practice. The specific practice on which the examples focus are important practices but seldom the only practice constitutive of a specific community. Their role is highlighted in this chapter in order to demonstrate the role of practices for incremental legal change.

members of one community into clashes and how dispute settlement procedures may produce dynamics of convergence out of this.[51]

Very broadly, for WTO-focused trade law, the basic background assumption is that reduction of barriers is desirable, and the main actor is the nation state.[52] Furthermore, the AB is the central authority for the settlement of disputes.[53] These unquestioned assumptions form the centre of the community's identity.

Internal practices that reinforce the normalization of this common knowledge and identity are plentiful, the most important one being trade between actors that are based in two different countries—in other words, export and import. With respect to the differentiation between export and import, recent decades have considerably reshuffled states' positions,[54] leading to significant questioning of existing legal practices. States who were formerly respondents now also feature as claimants and vice versa. The example of legal change analysed here results from this reshuffling and demonstrates how dispute settlement can function as a practice of normalization: diverging opinions clash before the AB, and subsequently the AB's opinion on 'what the law is' becomes the standard for the entire community.

What is crucial here is the way in which facts are framed in order to enter the legal discourse. This practice of framing facts only makes sense in a setting in which clear argumentative structures are pre-given. This is particularly the case in judicial proceedings. The procedural law is assumed to ensure, inter alia, the correct filtering between relevant and irrelevant facts.[55] Practices may vary depending on the situatedness of the actor—as claimant, respondent, or judge—but the procedure fixes their interaction onto one authoritative outcome: the judge's ruling.[56] If practices may make way for diverging communities, the procedure before

[51] 'Framing Facts' is the practice of how facts are presented before a judicial body. This is a crucial practice translating (shifting) political positions into legal reasoning. The interpretive practices of judges depend considerably on these framings: this practice provides much of the form and substance on which the judges will base their interpretation. See Ana Luísa Bernardino, 'The Discursive Construction of Facts in International Adjudication' (2020) 11 Journal of International Dispute Settlement 175, 179–81. The judicial setting situates actors in very succinct positions towards one another. The claimant frames the facts to her advantage, the respondent tries to shift that frame to her advantage, the judge is then supposed to make an impartial decision. In short, 'framing facts' is a crucial legal practice for legal change. Venzke, *How Interpretation Makes International Law* (n 35) 53–54.

[52] Peter Van den Bossche and Denise Prévost, *Essentials of WTO Law* (2nd edn, CUP 2021) 2.

[53] This centrality is however limited to the field of WTO law and only present in one sequence of the chronological development of trade law. Joost Pauwelyn, 'The Transformation of World Trade' (2005) 104 Michigan Law Review 1, 25–26. Arguably the recent sidelining of the WTO AB originates in participants' questioning of the common background assumptions to the extent that even a central judicial body lacks the sufficient degree of authority to hold the community together. Joost Pauwelyn, 'WTO Dispute Settlement Post 2019: What to Expect?' (2019) 22 Journal of International Economic Law 297.

[54] Gilbert R Winham, 'The Evolution of the World Trading System — the Economic and Policy Context' in Daniel Bethlehem and others (eds), *The Oxford Handbook of International Trade Law* (OUP 2009) 25–27.

[55] Markus Benzing, *Das Beweisrecht vor internationalen Gerichten und Schiedsgerichten in zwischenstaatlichen Streitigkeiten* (Springer 2010) 11–12 and 174–88.

[56] In that vein, the Dispute Settlement Understanding, art 11 calls for an 'objective assessment of the facts of the case'. See, for a problematization of that idea of objectivity, Bernardino (n 51) 181–82.

judicial bodies tends to the opposite, to foster reunifications: 'By authoritatively stating what the law is, [judicial decisions] partake in [the law's] creation.'[57] That is, there is convergence.

The strategic use of interpretative practices has gained much attention in theorizations about international legal practices. In particular, the function of precedent in lawmaking practices in international trade law has been explored in great detail.[58] What will be highlighted here is the way in which diverging practices are forced to clash and to be reconciled because of the central position of the judicial body in the WTO system, the AB.[59] So, this example highlights the limits of such strategic interpretive practices, particularly in fields with strong central institutions.

As stated above, Article XX (b) GATT allows exceptions to WTO member states' obligations when those measures are necessary for the protection of human life or health. In the legal argument that has to be made, it is crucial to demonstrate that a 'risk' to health or human life made protective measures necessary.[60] Demonstrating 'risk' is however not primarily concerned with doctrinal questions, but with the establishment of facts. Consequently, these cases are regularly fought on the level of 'facts' rather than 'legal doctrine'.[61] More precisely, the core question at issue between the parties is how to deploy facts into the legal framework. This interpretive practice establishing facts within legal reasoning is particularly interesting with respect to legal change.

In defending its measures in *EC—Asbestos*, the European Community opposed requests to quantify the risk in question with the argument that a risk may be evaluated either in quantitative or in qualitative terms.[62] This practice was then reversed when challenging measures in *Brazil—Retreaded Tyres*. While 'the European Communities contend[ed], the Panel erred by not quantifying the reduction of waste tyres resulting from the Import Ban',[63] Brazil countered that the assessment of the Panel was correct because 'the [AB] expressly recognized, in *EC - Asbestos*, that "a risk may be evaluated either in quantitative or qualitative terms"'.[64] Indeed,

[57] Venzke, *How Interpretation Makes International Law* (n 35) 26.

[58] See Ingo Venzke, 'Making General Exceptions: The Spell of Precedents in Developing Article XX GATT into Standards for Domestic Regulatory Policy' (2011) 12 German Law Journal 1111.

[59] See section 2. Legal characteristics are established and reinforced through interaction. Here, the dispute settlement mechanism enforces this interaction. Furthermore, states participating in dispute settlement in front of the AB 'share an understanding of "what they are doing and why"'. Toope and Brunnée (n 47) 26 and 80; Emanuel Adler, *Communitarian International Relations: The Epistemic Foundations of International Relations* (Routledge 2005) 22.

[60] Steve Charnovitz, 'The WTO's Environmental Progress' (2007) 10 Journal of International Economic Law 685, 697–99.

[61] Gabrielle Marceau and Julian Wyatt, 'Trade and the Environment: The WTO's Effort to Balance Economic and Sustainable Development' in *Liber Amicorum Anne Petitpierre-Sauvain—de la responsabilité sociale et sociétale* (Schulthess 2009) 232.

[62] *EC—Asbestos* (2001) WT/DS135/AB/R, para 167.

[63] *Brazil—Retreaded Tyres* (2007) WT/DS332/AB/R, para 137.

[64] ibid para 138.

in *EC—Asbestos*, the European Union argued the exact opposite of what it advanced in *Brazil—Retreaded Tyres*.[65]

This is hardly surprising for anyone with basic knowledge of legal practices. The interests of the EC when it was defending its measure in *EC—Asbestos* were different from the interests of the EC when it was challenging Brazil's measure as an exporter of retreaded tyres to Brazil. This is simply good lawyering—to argue that a legal norm should be interpreted to the advantage of her clients.[66]

What makes this example striking is the evidence it provides for divergence of CoPs: health protection elements were introduced by the states of the Global North in *EC—Asbestos*. Then, these ideas were taken up by emerging economies for their own purposes in *Brazil—Retreaded Tyres*. This triggered opposition by the original 'inventors', the states of the Global North. Different positions in the structure of interpretive practice made the actors advance different arguments about what the law is. In effect, strands of the WTO community started to diverge into two separate communities.

However, the institutional structure of the field prevented this divergence. The AB provided a centripetal dynamic that pulled the diverging strands back together.[67] At the time, within the WTO system, the AB was the central point at which disputes almost necessarily ended up.[68] Authority for interpretation of WTO law was also quite centralized in the AB.[69] Consequently, interpretations clashed, and were authoritatively settled and reunified by the AB.[70] In that sense, this example is strikingly different from the much more ambiguous legal situation in the following example from the field of IHL or the Laws of Armed Conflict (LoAC).

3.2 Diverging Communities

In divergent communities, different ideas of 'what the law is' are not forced into a clash. But divergent background knowledge and conviction as to 'what the law is' makes actors devalue certain premises. Actors who have those devalued premises at the centre of their constituent practices may engage in reciprocal devaluation. Around those divergent premises, divergent communities may emerge. Divergent communities' identities develop and lead the members to consider different knowledge as 'given', as 'normal'. Legal developments may be discarded as unsuccessful change attempts in one group and at the same time considered as crucial changes

[65] Marceau and Wyatt (n 61) 232–33.
[66] See eg Jeffrey Lipshaw, *Beyond Legal Reasoning: A Critique of Pure Lawyering* (Routledge 2017) 8.
[67] Pauwelyn, 'The Transformation of World Trade' (n 53) 25–26.
[68] Winham (n 54) 28.
[69] Dominique Carreau and Patrick Juillard, *Droit international économique* (3rd edn, Dalloz 2007) para 48.
[70] *Brazil—Retreaded Tyres* (n 63) paras 140 and 146. See section 2.

in the other group. Since there is no central authoritative institution settling the conflict, these diverging accounts on legal change can coexist.

In the area regulating military behaviour in times of armed conflict, this is already evident in the way that body of law is denominated.[71] On the one side, lawyers using the terminology of IHL emphasize human dignity and human rights.[72] On the other side, lawyers using the terminology of Laws of War or LoAC tend to prioritize the principle of military necessity.[73] Despite being rooted in the same regulatory practices, here diverging values lead to diverging CoPs.

However, the two groups of lawyers do not exist in isolation.[74] Even if their evaluation of the success of a change attempt varies, they will still engage in overlapping knowledge and practice. Let me highlight this dynamic in the practice of conferencing.

Conferencing is a practice of assembling a community with similar interests and background in a specifically coordinated social setting.[75] Conferences provide focal points around which CoPs can evolve. Different conferences providing different focal points can, however, split up communities. In fact, within the same field of law, practitioners and academics often have diverging focal points for conferences. Similarly, diverging focal points of different conferences may reinforce diverging background assumptions. Different conference communities may develop diverging ideas about 'what the law is' in coexistence with other conference communities, devaluing divergent communities' standpoints.[76]

While it is recognized that international summits or conferences are a fundamental practice for the international order, providing centres of unity and furthering coherence, there is less consideration of how this same practice splits up the international order. In terms of legal change, the ICRC used to position itself as the principal forum convening states and driving convention-making.[77] Shifting

[71] David Luban, 'Military Necessity and the Cultures of Military Law' (2013) 26 Leiden Journal of International Law 315, 315.

[72] ibid 328–36.

[73] ibid 322–28. I will use the term 'LoAC/IHL' when addressing the field of law from a perspective that covers both the humanity and the military necessity focused communities. At the same time, as Luban points out, the separation in the use of the terminology is not absolute. Indeed, as it is a divergence and not a separation of communities, we see overlapping use of terminologies, ibid 318.

[74] Sivakumaran (n 10) 132.

[75] Lianne JM Boer and Sofia Stolk (eds), 'Backstage Practices of Transnational Law' in *Backstage Practices of Transnational Law* (Routledge 2019) 1–6.

[76] In this context, the present account of practice theory links to theorizations about epistemic communities or interpretive communities in international law. Those conceptualizations rely, however, on slightly different membership criteria, in particular with regards to the role of background knowledge and the relevant activities. See eg Andrea Bianchi, 'Epistemic Communities' in Jean d'Aspremont, Sahib Singh, and Andrea Bianchi (eds), *Concepts for International Law—Contributions to Disciplinary Thought* (Edward Elgar 2019); for a compelling account of interpretive debates in IHL, see Abhimanyu George Jain, 'The Implication of Sovereignty in Contemporary Interpretive Debates in IHL' (2018) 4 and 24–25 in particular.

[77] Emily Camins, 'The Past as Prologue: The Development of the "Direct Participation" Exception to Civilian Immunity' (2008) 90 International Review of the Red Cross 853, 872–79.

from state-focused to expert-driven paths of change, the setting has diversified considerably in recent decades. Conferences on the regulation of military conduct may attract more legal experts prioritizing military necessity. Conferences on humanitarian and human rights issues in times of armed conflict may assemble lawyers more interested in the protection of humanitarian values in times of war, and more ready to engage in considerations of human rights.[78]

With this in mind it is unsurprising that, when Seán MacBride sought to introduce human rights considerations into IHL at the 1968 International Conference on Human Rights in Tehran, a conference primarily assembling human rights lawyers, he met with no resistance.[79] Being the Secretary-General of the International Commission of Jurists, a member of the Irish Republican Army, and co-founder of Amnesty International gave him the authority to trigger the 'multilateral path' of the neighbouring field of IHL.[80] This was also possible because human rights conferences did not (and do not) tend to assemble people opposed to the use of human rights. In fact, the topic had not been on the agenda of the conference,[81] and yet discussions resulted in UN General Assembly resolution XXIII on human rights in armed conflicts, which was passed without opposition and only two abstentions.[82] At the same time, the fact that this proposition originated in a human rights conference may have made it all the easier for lawyers most distant from those considerations to discard even established principles of IHL as being overly informed by human rights.

This is illustrated in the use of the International Court of Justice's (ICJ) jurisprudence on the relationship between IHL and international human rights law (IHRL) in the Expert Process convened by the ICRC to define the notion of 'direct participation in hostilities' (DPH). One could argue that the ICJ issued a well-aligned series of judgments pronouncing general rules on the relationship between IHRL and IHL/LoAC. In the 1996 *Nuclear Weapons* case, the ICJ first qualified the relationship between IHRL and IHL/LoAC as governed by the principle of *lex specialis*.[83] The formulation '*lex specialis*' however only appears in the dissenting opinion of Judge Weeramantry:

> In principle, the right not arbitrarily to be deprived of one's life applies also in hostilities. The test of what is an arbitrary deprivation of life, however, falls to be

[78] Sivakumaran (n 10) 130–32.

[79] See, for a detailed account of MacBride's role, Amanda Alexander, 'A History of International Humanitarian Law' (2015) 26 European Journal of International Law 109, 118–19.

[80] Krisch and Yildiz (n 3) 10.

[81] Keith Suter, *An International Law of Guerrilla Warfare* (St Martin's Press 1984) 34; Alexander (n 79) 119.

[82] UNGA, 'Respect for Human Rights in Armed Conflicts (19 December 1968) A/RES/2444.

[83] *Legality of the Threat or Use of Nuclear Weapons* (Advisory Opinion) [1996] ICJ Rep 226.

> determined by the applicable lex specialis, namely, the law applicable in armed conflict which is designed to regulate the conduct of hostilities'.[84]

This formulation encouraged the interpretation that human rights continue to be applicable during war but will be displaced by the specific norms of IHL/LoAC. In 2004, the ICJ issued its *Wall* Advisory Opinion.[85] While the *lex specialis* principle remained part of the argument, the emphasis shifted to the complementarity of IHL/LoAC and IHRL norms.[86] In its 2005 decision in the *Armed Activities* case, the ICJ subscribed to complementarity: citing the *Nuclear Weapons* and *Wall* Opinions—however, and most importantly, without reference to '*lex specialis*'—the Court concluded that 'both branches of international law, namely international human rights law and international humanitarian law, would have to be taken into consideration'.[87] So the ICJ provided for a clear-cut judicial pathway of change.[88] Arguably, a court authoritatively settled the issue.

And yet, in the following years, proponents of the military necessity principle in the Expert Process aimed at defining the notion of 'DPH' (2003–08) vehemently contested the 'introduction' of human rights law into the Guidance, using as the *Nuclear Weapons* case as their principal reference, without addressing the subsequent cases.[89] Rather unusually, the newer ICJ jurisprudence was also barely addressed by the opposing group, the proponents of humanitarian considerations, though it would have supported their position.[90] One hypothetical explanation for this is the discursive contingency in this Expert Process. Opposing values of

[84] *Legality of the Threat or Use of Nuclear Weapons* (Advisory Opinion: Dissenting Opinion of Judge Weeramantry) [1996] ICJ Rep 429, 443.

[85] *Legal Consequences of the Construction of a Wall in the Occupied Palestinian Territory* (Advisory Opinion) [2004] ICJ Rep 136.

[86] ibid 106:

> [T]he Court considers that the protection offered by human rights conventions does not cease in case of armed conflict, save through the effect of provisions for derogation of the kind to be found in Article 4 of the International Covenant on Civil and Political Rights. As regards the relationship between international humanitarian law and human rights law, there are thus three possible situations: some rights may be exclusively matters of international humanitarian law; others may be exclusively matters of human rights law; yet others may be matters of both these branches of international law. In order to answer the question put to it, the Court will have to take into consideration both these branches of international law, namely human rights law and, as lex specialis international humanitarian law.

[87] *Armed Activities on the Territory of the Congo (Democratic Republic of the Congo v Uganda)* [2005] ICJ Rep 168, 216.

[88] See, for more detailed elaboration, Dorothea Endres, 'Case Study 8: Direct Participation in Hostilities' in Pedro Martínez Esponda et al (eds), *The Paths of International Law: Case Studies* (2023) 248 <https://papers.ssrn.com/sol3/papers.cfm?abstract_id=4430270>.

[89] See eg Nils Melzer, 'Third Expert Meeting on the Notion of Direct Participation in Hostilities Co-Organized by the ICRC and the TMC Asser Institute—Summary Report' (2005) 51–52; W Hays Parks, 'Part IX of the ICRC "Direct Participation in Hostilities Study": No Mandate, No Expertise, and Legally Incorrect' (2010) 42 International Law and Politics 769, 798–801.

[90] See Nils Melzer, 'Keeping the Balance between Military Necessity and Humanity: A Response to Four Critiques of the ICRC's Interpretive Guidance on the Notion of Direct Participation in Hostilities' (2010) 42 NYU Journal of International Law and Politics 831, 898–99.

military necessity and humanitarianism were set to clash, and this clash then happened to revolve around a random quote of a former Vice-President of the ICRC, Jean Pictet, sidelining the question of *lex specialis*.[91] Considered a hero to the humanitarian law community, Pictet's quote was unwelcome to those identifying with the military law community.[92]

From the available documents it seems that all people engaged in the discussion did assume '*lex specialis*' to be a term of art not needing elaboration, let alone proper referencing. And yet, they quite obviously understood different things when referring to '*lex specialis*'.[93] For some, '*lex specialis*' had been applied wrongly because the laws of war were not given clear priority over human rights considerations, and for others, '*lex specialis*' had been applied wrongly because human rights considerations had not been sufficiently taken into account.[94] In sum, both communities interpreted the term relying on their—diverging—background knowledge.

Comparing textbooks and jurisprudence, this difference would never become so evident. Even Yoram Dinstein, who favours military necessity, engages with the *lex specialis* principle in his textbook.[95] However, the majority of lawyers in the military necessity camp are not writing textbooks but instead are engaged in military activities.[96] Some of their constituent practices are fundamentally different from the constituent practices of humanitarian lawyers, of whom a large number are more engaged in assessing military practice than in its exercise.[97] They regularly either work in academia or in humanitarian organizations.[98]

[91] 'If we can put a soldier out of action by capturing him, we should not wound him; if we can obtain the same result by wounding him, we must not kill him. If there are two means to achieve the same military advantage, we must choose the one which causes the lesser evil.' ICRC Interpretive Guidance, at 82 (citing Pictet, *Development and Principles of International Humanitarian Law* (Martinus Nijhoff 1985) 75). For the discussion's focus on that quote, see eg Parks (n 90) 794; Ryan Goodman, 'The Power to Kill or Capture Enemy Combatants' (2013) 24 European Journal of International Law 819, 820. This transpired down to the level of national implementation: US Department of Defense, Law of War Manual (2023) 9, states the principle of *lex specialis* without acknowledging different interpretations thereof but engages in a critique of the Jean Pictet quote at 57.

[92] This points to another practice, the stylization of heroes for a given community.

[93] Melzer makes this point in 'Keeping the Balance between Military Necessity and Humanity' (n 90) 898–99.

[94] Jean-François Quéguiner, 'First Expert Meeting on the Notion of Direct Participation in Hostilities Co-Organized by the ICRC and the TMC Asser Institute—Summary Report' (2003) 8; Nils Melzer, 'Second Expert Meeting on the Notion of Direct Participation in Hostilities Co-Organized by the ICRC and the TMC Asser Institute—Summary Report' (2004) 18; Nils Melzer, 'Third Expert Meeting—Summary Report' (n 89) 51; Nils Melzer, 'Fourth Expert Meeting on the Notion of Direct Participation in Hostilities Co-Organized by the ICRC and the TMC Asser Institute—Summary Report' (2006) 9 and 78–79; Nils Melzer, 'Fifth Expert Meeting on the Notion of Direct Participation in Hostilities—Summary Report' (2008) 22.

[95] Yoram Dinstein, *The Conduct of Hostilities Under the Law of International Armed Conflict* (3rd edn, CUP 2016) 32-5.

[96] Eyal Benvenisti, 'Human Dignity in Combat: The Duty to Spare Enemy Civilians' (2006) 39 Israel Law Review 81, 82–83.

[97] See along those lines Luban (n 71) 318–22, 320 in particular.

[98] See Benvenisti (n 96) 82–83.

Thus, in contrast to the WTO, in this development of divergent CoPs, the ICRC's interest is not to escalate confrontations—it lacks capacity comparable to the WTO's AB to settle the conflict.[99] Instead, it attempts to push for legal change by stating authoritatively what the law is—or should be in their view[100] However, though the ICRC may construct an excellent study on customary IHL/LoAC or on DPH, the study's relevance is determined by the reception in CoPs.[101] While the customary IHL study is widely relied upon (even where the norm in the study is quite divergent from prior discourse),[102] the DPH study is only cited in order to mark the point where the divergent CoPs position themselves in relation to the study: at one end, military lawyers will only mark its existence and impracticability,[103] while at the other end, human-rights-favouring lawyers will push the construction much further, criticizing the guidance as insufficient.[104]

In sum, the different institutional structure of this field allows two CoPs to coexist without much explicit confrontation.[105] The ICRC, as a powerful institution of that international field, being necessarily closer to the CoP favouring humanitarian values,[106] is necessarily quite subjective in a conflict between this CoP and the CoP favouring military necessity.[107] At the same time, members of the humanitarian community are more engaged in the assessment than in the practice of military activity. Hence, the military lawyers, focusing on their own practice can also

[99] See along similar lines Nico Krisch, *Beyond Constitutionalism: The Pluralist Structure of Postnational Law* (OUP 2010) 291.

[100] The ICRC itself, of course, argues that no such attempt to push for change has been made. ICRC and Nils Melzer, *Interpretive Guidance on The Notion of Direct Participation in Hostilities under International Humanitarian Law* (ICRC 2009) 6. See Linus Mührel, 'The Authority of the ICRC' (Dissertation, Freie Universität Berlin 2022).

[101] Sivakumaran (n 10) 152; See also Emily Crawford, *Identifying the Enemy* (OUP 2015) 87. Crawford points out how the ICRC's guidance should be considered as a policy statement of the institution, not as a restatement of the law. Thus, the ICRC's authority to induce legal change appears rather limited.

[102] Sivakumaran (n 10) 141. However, even the reception of the ICRC Customary Law Study was not without contestation. See eg the US Department of Defense Law of War Manual (20123 at 181, refuting the ICRC Customary Law Study as well as the DPH Guidance. Even more explicit is the report of David Luban on the British government being 'pushed to issue the UK Military Manual (which had been stalled in the bureaucracy) because the ICRC was about to issue its own study of customary international humanitarian law and "we need to get in our retaliation in advance"', Luban (n 71) 315–49, fn 9.

[103] See eg the US Department of Defense Law of War Manual (2023) 235. Yoram Dinstein, 'Direct Participation in Hostilities' (2013) 18 Tilburg Law Review 3, 7–8.

[104] Ryan Goodman, 'The Power to Kill or Capture Enemy Combatants: A Rejoinder to Michael N. Schmitt' (2013) 24 European Journal of International Law 863, 864.

[105] Scholarship explains this as being enabled through legal indeterminacy. See Luban (n 71) 318–19 and 336–38 in particular; Adil Ahmad Haque, 'Indeterminacy in the Law of Armed Conflict' (2019) 95 International Law Studies 118.

[106] See, for a detailed account thereof, Els Debuf, 'Tools to Do the Job: The ICRC's Legal Status, Privileges and Immunities' (2015) 97 International Review of the Red Cross 319, 320–21 in particular.

[107] Luban notes that this increasing opposition between military and humanitarian lawyers may not always have been that explicit: Luban (n 71) 316–17.

easily discard the humanitarian lawyers' arguments as detached from 'realities of warfare'.[108] Hence, the divergent practices make relative coexistence possible.

This expert-based discourse on the law is entangled with relevant state practice.[109] Thus, 'whose practice is relevant' becomes crucial. We find here a divergent CoP based on states who engage with legal justifications of their military actions and states who do not reference these norms when engaging in violent conflict. In that sense, the common background knowledge diverges on the practice of applying law in times of war.[110] To illustrate, while North Atlantic Treaty Organization states and Israel are most explicit in justifying their military action according to IHL/LoAC standards, the majority of states engaged in armed conflicts tend to be significantly more reluctant to invoke these rules.[111] Consequently, experts, in discussions on 'what the law is', tend to rely on the examples from those states to a greater extent, neglecting the silence of the large majority of states.[112]

Let me demonstrate this problem by zooming in on the change attempt made by the ICRC to detail and thereby change the definition of DPH. The increasing number of multifaceted armed conflicts sidelines the general background assumption of interstate war as the stereotypical case for regulation.[113] In an interstate war, a dichotomy between civilian and soldier seems quite clear, and consequently the legal rule that soldiers can be the direct target of an attack, but not civilians, seems very clear as well.[114] The reluctance of states to qualify members of non-state armed groups as 'combatants' made the situation a little more complicated in conflicts involving non-state armed groups.[115] Since the dichotomy between soldier and civilian remains the core logic, combatants are equated with civilians. Civilians cannot be directly targeted, as long as they do not participate directly in hostilities.[116] Hence, the question of how to determine when and how a civilian can be

[108] See eg Melzer, 'Third Expert Meeting—Summary Report' (n 89) 52; Kenneth Watkin, 'Opportunity Lost: Organized Armed Groups and the ICRC Direct Participation in Hostilities Interpretive Guidance' (2010) NYU Journal of International Law and Politics 641, 662 and 680.

[109] Arguably, this is a case of an expert process intended to fill the gap left by states' reluctance to engage in conventional lawmaking. For Sivakumaran, it is representative of 'the age of the manual', Sivakumaran (n 10) 143. However, as we will see below, this expert-based path of change may actually also increase gaps.

[110] Adler and Pouliot, 'International Practices' (n 13) 17.

[111] This is not to say that Global South states are not participating in the lawmaking at all. See eg Alejandro Rodiles, 'International Humanitarian Law-Making in Latin America: Between the International Community, Humanity, and Extreme Violence' in Heike Krieger and Jonas Pueschmann (eds), *Law-making and Legitimacy in International Humanitarian Law* (Edward Elgar 2021); Balingene Kahombo, 'Sovereign Equality and Law-Making: How Do States from the Global South Shape International Humanitarian Law? An African Perspective' in ibid. Michael Bothe, 'Sovereign Equality and Law-Making: How Do States from the Global South Shape International Humanitarian Law? A Comment to Alejandro Rodiles and Balingene Kahombo' in ibid.

[112] Sivakumaran (n 10) 137.

[113] See eg Quéguiner (n 94) 4.

[114] Marco Sassòli, *International Humanitarian Law—Rules, Controversies, and Solutionas to Problems Arising in Warfare* (Edward Elgar 2019) paras 3.14–3.18. On the discussions during the drafting process regarding the definition of the civilians, see Geoffrey Best, *War and Law Since 1945* (OUP 1994) 115–23.

[115] Crawford (n 101) 18–20.

[116] Common art 3 of the Geneva Conventions.

considered to be participating directly in hostilities is at the core of the contemporary military practice of some states. Domestic legal and political interventions in the USA, UK, Germany, and Israel have pushed the evaluation of the legality of targeting practices to the forefront of debates on the military interventions of their countries.[117]

And yet, this leaves the majority of participants in contemporary armed conflicts outside the lawmaking picture. In effect, regarding the debate as to the relevance of other states' practices for the construction of LoAC/IHL, there seems little debate as long as the Global North has no interest in intervening. The ICRC-led Expert Process on the 'definition of DPH' was very narrowly focused on the state practice of USA, UK, Germany, and Israel.[118] Conversely, for instance, the practice of Cameroun, Nigeria, and Chad in their conflict with Boko Haram do not appear to ever have been on the table. In fact, sometimes it seemed as if the Taliban was the only non-state actor relevant for the definition of DPH, arguably because of the ongoing large-scale intervention of the Global North in the region where Taliban activity takes place.[119] Given the anonymization of documents on the Expert Process, there is no evidence to what extent representatives of other parts of the world were involved.[120] Thus, two alternative or complementary explications remain possible: that 'experts' were mainly from the Global North and/or expert knowledge focused on US military hegemony.

Interestingly, states whose practice is regularly ignored do not engage in open contestation. Even powerful states like India or China will not openly oppose change attempts in IHL/LoAC. They regularly resolve not to apply this body of law at all.[121] Qualifying internal conflicts as not amounting to the level of violence necessary for the applicability of IHL/LoAC to kick in, they aim at keeping their military practice outside the realm of IHL/LoAC. Given that 'IHL/LoAC experts' focus on the practice of the Global North, this practice can peacefully coexist with

[117] See, for the US, Naz K Modirazeh, 'Folk International Law: 9/11 Lawyering and the Transformation of the Law of Armed Conflict to Human Rights Policy and Human Rights Law to War Governance' (2014) 5 Harvard National Security Journal 225.

[118] See eg Melzer, 'Fifth Expert Meeting' (n 94) 14, 15, 24, 27; This is in contrast to the very exhaustive nature of the ICRC Customary Law Study: Sivakumaran (n 10) 135.

[119] In fact, there was a gradual shift from a focus at the beginning on private military companies, cyberwarfare, and the war on terror to an almost exclusive zooming into combatants in asymmetrical warfare. Michael N Schmitt, 'The Interpretive Guidance on the Notion of Direct Participation in Hostilities: A Critical Analysis' (2010) 1 Harvard National Security Journal 5, 10.

[120] Arguably, that anonymization is itself evidence of a tension between military and humanitarian lawyers in the Expert Process. Given that a considerable number of experts are said to have withdrawn their name from the final draft because it was giving too little weight to the principle of military necessity, the guidance now only represents the ICRC's view, and the Expert Process was anonymized. See ibid 6.

[121] See eg the conflict of the Indian government with the Communist (Maoist) party, classified as armed conflict by the Geneva Academy's database: <www.rulac.org/browse/conflicts/non-international-armed-conflict-in-india> accessed 9 November 2022. However, the Indian government treats this conflict as entirely outside the realm of IHL/LoAC: <www.mha.gov.in/sites/default/files/2023-04/FAQs_LWE_27042023.pdf> accessed 9 November 2022.

IHL/LoAC. The few states actively engaged in the application of IHL determine its change, and the states in armed conflict without reference to IHL/LoAC continue to follow their own set of rules. For the identification of 'successful change' in IHL/LoAC the consequence is striking: as long as the states of the Global North engaged in military conflict align, change in IHL/LoAC will seem extremely successful, and conversely, the contestation of one subgroup of the Global North obstructs change attempts in IHL/LoAC.

3.3 Parallel Communities

For parallel communities we see different ideas of 'what the law is' that ignore one another. If practices do not force those ideas to engage, parallel CoPs may co-exist. This will be illustrated using the example of defining 'investment' in arbitration that is based on the Convention of the International Centre for Settlement of Investment Disputes (ICSID). In this example, the core question is how the practice of framing law can lead to the existence of parallel communities. One of the most basic elements of interpretive practice in law is the substantiation of the argument with the correct legal basis.[122] In order to provide sound legal reasoning, the argument has to be based on authoritative sources of law. Opinions can, however, vary regarding the location of the authoritative source of law.[123] Consequently, framing law is a practice that can produce divergence—or even parallel coexistence—of communities.

Let us consider the example of the Salini test for defining investment in ICSID-based investment arbitration to identify CoPs.[124] This test defines the elements of 'investment'.[125] The practice is similar to the WTO example above in that it translates 'facts' into the realm of legal reasoning. However, the practice has developed in different directions. In fact, there are probably as many versions of the Salini test as there are arbitrators, perhaps even more. And yet, each award relying on the test

[122] Neil MacCormick, *Rhetoric and the Rule of Law: A Theory of Legal Reasoning* (OUP 2005) 33.

[123] Parameters for interaction may be clear so, in Toopes and Brunnée's conceptualization, conditions for a uniform CoP are given. However, the centre of authority is dispersed to an extent that opposing views are not forced into interaction. Thus, no uniform understanding of 'what the law is' emerges: Toope and Brunnée (n 47) 42 and 70–71.

[124] *Salini Costruttori SPA and Italstrade SPA v Kingdom of Morocco* (Decision on Jurisdiction) (16 July 2001) ICSID Case No ARB/00/4, para 52. Going beyond this paper's scope, let me nevertheless highlight the contingency of this change attempt's selection phase. The reason for the Salini test being the 'Salini test' and not the 'Gaillard test' is possibly the fact that the original argument, made by Gaillard, is basically only accessible in French university libraries.

[125] Dorothea Endres, 'Case Study 23: Legal Change of the Definition of "Investment" Within the Icsid Framework' in Pedro Martinez Esponda and others (eds), *The Paths of International Law. Case Studies* (SSRN 2023), 732–82.

references it as a somewhat 'stable' reference point. This stability is obtained by selective referencing of previous decisions and legal authorities.[126]

For this reference point, common background assumptions differ as to the understanding of 'what the law is' to the extent that parallel centres of the communities' identity emerge and in that sense lead the members to consider different knowledge as 'given' and 'normal'.[127] While it is barely debated that investment arbitration is based on a network of bilateral treaties, actors have different background assumptions as to how those bilateral treaties sit within the broader setting, for instance when they relate to ICSID.[128] Some actors consider bilateral treaties as establishing a multiverse of independent communities, while other actors consider ICSID as an additional element, and yet another group sees in ICSID the source of an overarching, constitution-like frame.[129]

The boundaries of these communities are fluid, but constantly recreated through the appointment of arbitrators and choice of legal representation before the tribunal.[130] Furthermore, the state being considered only as a defendant limits state agency considerably.[131] Those practices are common to all three identified communities. And yet, different background assumptions lead to different outcomes of these practices within the respective communities. In fact, the CoPs are different to the extent that they cite case law in line with their own argumentation without engagement with opposing views.[132]

When tracing the practice of framing of law, one can see confrontations between different opinions on 'what that law is' as engaged in semantic struggles 'with the decided interest of finding acceptance for their claims about the meaning of legal expressions and thus seek[ing] to influence what is considered (il)legal'.[133] However, those struggles often do not necessitate a confrontation with or changing of adversary opinions: framing what is perceived as an authoritative source of law and thereby sidelining other opinions can create coexisting CoPs within the same field of law. In this process, the practice of referencing becomes crucial. Regularly, in international law fields in which rules of precedent developed in a curious mishmash between legal cultures, the referencing of only judgments that support one's own position on 'what the law is' becomes established practice.[134]

[126] Thus, tribunals have the authority to establish reference points. However, those reference points are not sufficiently authoritative to make it impossible for participants to escape. See section 2.2.1.

[127] See also Endres (n 125) s 6.

[128] In that sense, practices setting up and relying on shared understandings are not uniform: different legalities emerge. See section 2.

[129] Jean Ho, 'The Meaning of "Investment" in ICSID Arbitrations' (2010) 26 Arbitration International 633, 644–46.

[130] See M Sornarajah, *Resistance and Change in the International Law on Foreign Investment* (CUP 2015) 409.

[131] Pierre-Marie Dupuy, *Droit International Public* (14th edn, Dalloz 2018) para 632.

[132] See, for a more detailed analysis, Endres (n 125) para 6 747–48.

[133] Venzke, *How Interpretation Makes International Law* (n 35) 40.

[134] Niccolò Ridi, 'The Shape and Structure of the "Usable Past": An Empirical Analysis of the Use of Precedent in International Adjudication' (2019) 10 Journal of International Dispute Settlement 200.

Without a centripetal judicial body, those practices can develop and coexist in parallel. Depending on what one cites, one joins a different community, and is recognized by and in that community.

The existence of parallel CoPs can be found in investment arbitration, with arbitrators relying on the idea of precedent, on the one hand, and arbitrators relying on the idea of case-specific application of convention and/or bilateral investment treaties (BITs), on the other hand. As in the previous example of LoAC versus IHL, the way in which the applicable law is identified divides the field into two groups that identify legal change in different ways.

This can be illustrated by the use of the Salini test. Indeed, the Salini test is simultaneously qualified as 'changed', 'outdated', or 'common' practice. Each of those qualifications relies to some extent on the practice of precedent, and yet confirms strikingly different 'legal change'.

In *Bayindir Insaat Turizm Ticaret Ve Sanayi AS v Islamic Republic of Pakistan*, relying on the preamble of the ICSID, the arbitrators see the definition as common practice.[135] And yet, in *Biwater Gauff (Tanzania) Ltd v United Republic of Tanzania*, relying on the parties' agreements, the arbitrators identify a change in the definition.[136] Conversely, in *RSM Production Corporation v Central African Republic*, relying on jurisprudence, the arbitrators set out a modification of the definition.[137]

What determines those different outcomes is a diverging background assumption about 'what the law is'. In fact, in the field of investment arbitration, we can group a community favouring the ICSID Convention as an authoritative focal point, a community giving preference to the individual bilateral investment treaties, and a community emphasizing some idea of precedent.

Those quite contradictory ideas of 'what the law is' can coexist in the same field of international law without taking much notice of one another. In investment arbitration this is particularly easy, because it is first and foremost composed of a network of bilateral treaties and case-specific tribunals.[138] An institution with centripetal powers comparable to the WTO AB is lacking, and hence contradictory views on legal change are not forced to clash and can coexist in parallel without any need for explicit and formal reconciliation. Furthermore, actor-positions in this field are significantly more cemented: states are always in the position of the defendant.[139] It is non-state actors, the investors, who will initiate the procedure and hence frame the claim. A situation in which the EC (or now the EU) could find itself in the reversed position akin to our first WTO example is a very unlikely scenario in the field of investment arbitration.

[135] ICSID Case No ARB/03/29 (Decision on Jurisdiction) (14 November 2005) para 137.
[136] ICSID Case No ARB/05/22 (Award) (24 July 2008) para 317.
[137] ICSID Case No ARB/07/2 (Decision on Jurisdiction and Liability) (7 December 2010) para 56.
[138] Ho (n 129) 644–46.
[139] Dupuy (n 131) para 632.

4. Conclusion: How to Determine Whose International Law is Changing?

A practice requires a certain level of repetition and reproduction in order to be recognized as a community's practice.[140] The elaborated examples have demonstrated how stability and change are intermingled in reproduced practices. Depending on the positionality of actors in that practice's framework, the legal change occurs and is accounted for differently.[141]

If we see coexisting CoPs registering legal change in divergent ways, understanding legal change as 'successful' when received in 'the issue-area' becomes challenging: where and how can we pin down the degree of success of legal change? If IHL is practised only by a handful of states, is the non-practice of all other states really irrelevant? If many arbitrators see the field of investment arbitration as a field interconnected through precedent, while others insist on the prevalence of states' agreement, where is the 'real' legal change?

The reception stage of legal change then becomes a somewhat heuristic exercise depending on the composition of the issue-area in which we are looking for the identification of legal change. As we have seen in the examples, if one of the parallel or diverging communities is more closely linked to the issue-area in question, change that is actually only recognized in a very small community may become portrayed as successful—and vice versa.[142] So, the challenge becomes how to identify the relevant community for the reception of legal change.

At this point the situatedness of the researcher becomes the crux.[143] Lechner and Frost highlight that the crucial question is not what practices exist, but 'what is the procedure that an observer must use for understanding them properly'.[144] Indeed, they argue that practices, as 'object[s] of intersubjective understandings of agents' are 'concrete social forms', which have to be described 'in concrete terms, by transcending categories that are abstract and invariant'.[145] Assumptions about the hegemonic power of some states or the belief in the authoritative power of courts and tribunals make researchers regularly follow one path over the other. The call for acknowledgement of those beliefs is hardly a new one, but the argument presented herein underlines the call's continuing importance.

This chapter has demonstrated the role of CoPs in international law and their impact on the construction and recognition of change in international law. First, the

[140] Christian Bueger and Frank Gadinger, 'The Play of International Practice' (2015) 59 International Studies Quarterly 449, 455–56.

[141] Along similar lines: Nico Krisch, 'Framing Entangled Legalities beyond the State' in Nico Krisch (ed), *Entangled Legalities Beyond the State* (CUP 2021) 15.

[142] See also section 3.1 and 3.3.

[143] Bourdieu, *Esquisse d'une théorie de la pratique* (n 27) 225–34; See also Lechner and Frost (n 22) 5–6 and 63.

[144] Lechner and Frost (n 22) 5.

[145] ibid 6.

chapter showed how an actor-centred approach highlights that the way in which incremental legal change happens depends fundamentally on the situatedness and background knowledge of the actors in question. Using the examples of practices playing out in the international order, I highlighted how different practices in different fields develop dynamics that can lead to diverging CoPs within the same issue-area. First, in the practice of interpretation, translating 'risk' into legal reasoning at the WTO, we could see how actors shift their practice according to their position. The centripetal power of the WTO solved emerging divergences by authoritatively settling the dispute. A second similar practice, the interpretative practice defining 'investment' in ICSID-based arbitrations, did not have a focal point akin to the WTO. This can allow for diverging communities to coexist without having to engage much with each other. This is further nuanced with respect to the community of states not engaging in the IHL/LoAC, which can coexist with the parallel community, sidelining IHL/LoAC as long as their actions do not clash. Lastly, the third practice of assembling members with the same interests in conferences or expert meetings can develop much dynamic for change—but the extent to which that change is recognized by parallel communities varies greatly.

The position of the interacting actors thereby constrains the degree of possible divergence. To the extent that practices develop dynamics that fragment communities, those fragmentations do not necessarily occur within or along issue-areas but may very well be entangled in between. One possible explanation for those divergences is recognition of change: expectations of consistency[146] are informed by different background assumptions and reinforced within different CoPs.

However, peaceful coexistence is a mere possibility only to the extent that the relevant communities' spheres do not clash. Recall the divergent depiction of Mahabali in Hindu mythology. In fact, Mahabali's depiction as a positive character faces considerable contestation by other castes. In Kerala in 2017, the Hindu Aikya Vedi (Hindu United Front) filed a lawsuit against the setting up of a Mahabali Memorial at a temple, forcing the two depictions into confrontation.[147]

[146] See Venzke, 'Understanding the Authority of International Courts and Tribunals' (n 36) 400–01.

[147] PK Yasser Arafat, 'Onam, Mahabali and the Narrow Imaginations of the Right' *The Wire* (4 September 2017) <https://thewire.in/politics/onam-mahabali-hindutva-right> accessed 9 November 2022.

13

A Quiet Revolution in the Making? The Changing State Authority in Treaty Interpretation

Fuad Zarbiyev[*]

1. Introduction

Very few topics in international law have attracted as much attention as treaty interpretation. The theme features prominently in the works of the founding figures of international law,[1] is a standard chapter in textbooks of international law[2] and has been the subject of many codification efforts by various institutions ranging from the Institut de Droit International and the International Law Commission (ILC) to the International Law Association.[3] Recent studies offering a systematic treatment of treaty interpretation or focusing on some specific aspects of the theme show that this remarkable interest is not about to fade.[4] But even a cursory glance at

[*] Associate Professor of International Law, Graduate Institute of International and Development Studies, Geneva, Switzerland.

[1] See eg Hugo Grotius, 'Book II Chapter 16: The Interpretation of Treaties' in Hugo Grotius (slightly abridged by AC Campbell), *On the Law of War and Peace* (Batoche 2001) 140; Emer Vattel, 'Chapter XVII: Of the Interpretation of Treaties' in Bela Kapossy and Richard Whatmore (eds), *The Law of Nations* (Liberty Fund 2008) 408.

[2] James Crawford, *Brownlie's Principles of Public International Law* (9th edn, OUP 2019) 364; Patrick Daillier, Mathias Forteau, and Alain Pellet, *Droit International Public* (8th edn, LGDJ 2009) 276; Peter Malanczuk and Alexander Orakhelashvili, *Akehurst's Modern Introduction to International Law* (8th edn, Routledge 2018) 265; Malcolm Shaw, *International Law* (8th edn, CUP 2017) 706; Alfred Verdross and Bruno Simma, *Universelles Völkerrecht: Theorie und Praxis* (3rd edn, Duncker Humblot 2010) 490; Benedetto Conforti, *Diritto Internazionale* (11th edn, Editoriale Scientifica 2018) 114.

[3] *'L'inteprétation des traités, Institut de Droit International, Session de Grenade, 11–20 April 1956' Annuaire de l'Institut de Droit International,* vol 46 (1956) 358–59; International Law Commission (ILC), Draft Articles on the Law of Treaties with Commentaries (1966) II Yearbook of the International Law Commission, UN Doc A/6309/Rev.1, 187–274; 'Final Report of the International Law Association Study Group on the Content and Evolution of the Rules of Interpretation' (29 November–13 December 2020) Kyoto.

[4] See Alexander Orakhelashvili, *The Interpretation of Acts and Rules in Public International Law* (OUP 2008); Ulf Linderfalk, *On the Interpretation of Treaties: The Modern International Law as Expressed in the 1969 Vienna Convention on the Law of Treaties* (2nd edn, Springer 2010); Malgosia Fitzmaurice, Olufemi Elias, and Panos Merkouris, *Treaty Interpretation and the Vienna Convention on the Law of Treaties: 30 Years On* (Brill 2010); Erik Bjorge, *The Evolutionary Interpretation of Treaties* (OUP 2014); Richard Gardiner, *Treaty Interpretation* (2nd edn, OUP 2015); Christian Djeffal, *Static and Evolutive Treaty Interpretation: A Functional Reconstruction* (CUP 2016); Irina Buga, *Modification of Treaties by Subsequent Practice* (OUP 2018).

Fuad Zarbiyev, *A Quiet Revolution in the Making? The Changing State Authority in Treaty Interpretation* In: *The Many Paths of Change in International Law.* Edited by: Nico Krisch and Ezgi Yildiz, Oxford University Press.
DOI: 10.1093/oso/9780198877844.003.0013

such a monumental production is sufficient to realize that what has virtually exclusively interested international lawyers is how treaty interpretation should proceed and what rules it should be guided by rather than who the actors that engage in it are, what kind of authority they can plausibly claim, and on what basis their competing claims to authority are resolved.[5] The lesson contained in Bishop Hoadly's famous comment that 'whoever hath an absolute authority to interpret any written or spoken laws, it is he who is truly the Law Giver to all intents and purposes, and not the persons who first spoke and wrote them'[6] may have been in the back of the mind of many, but it must have been seen as reinforcing the need for disciplining rules rather than calling for a careful study of how interpretive authority is distributed in the international legal order.

The ambition of this chapter is not to fill this unfortunate gap as such, but rather to reflect on the changing interpretive authority of one category of actors, namely the states. The different contributions to this volume make a strong point that, contrary to what the mainstream legal doctrine and the 'official' legal discourse might lead one to believe, many change processes in international law occur without states acting as drivers. Remarkably, however, even in 'state-empowered' institutions[7] typically highly deferential to states, there have been significant moves away from the state-centred position. This chapter focuses on one example of this, namely the position of the ILC on the interpretive authority of the parties to a treaty. Traditionally, the joint interpretation of a treaty by its parties was seen as the most authoritative interpretation of it. As Lassa Oppenheim stated, '[i]f [the contracting parties] choose a certain interpretation, no other has any basis. It is only when they disagree, that an interpretation based on scientific grounds can ask a hearing.'[8] This proposition was rarely challenged, linked as it was to common sense and 'reason'. But this state of affairs came under serious challenge in the recent work of the ILC on subsequent agreements and subsequent practice in relation to the interpretation of treaties, the Commission reaching the conclusion that joint interpretive agreements 'are not necessarily legally binding'.[9] Given the authority of the ILC, this conclusion is likely to be influential.

What this chapter attempts to do is to account for this 'quiet revolution' in the authority of treaty interpretation by the parties themselves. To do so, it moves beyond an actor-focused conception of authority and assesses state authority in treaty interpretation in light of the theory of authority offered by Kim Scheppele and Karol

[5] I am grateful to Phattharaphong Saengkrai for this point.

[6] Cited in John Gray, *The Nature and Sources of Law* (2nd edn, Macmillan 1921) 125.

[7] Sandesh Sivakumaran, 'Beyond States and Non-State Actors: The Role of State-Empowered Entities in the Making and Shaping of International Law' (2016) 55 Colombia Journal of Transnational Law 343.

[8] Lassa Oppenheim, *International Law: A Treatise* (Longmans, Green 1905) 559.

[9] See Commentary to Draft conclusion 3, in 'Draft conclusions on subsequent agreements and subsequent practice in relation to the interpretation of treaties with commentaries' (2018) II Yearbook of the International Law Commission, pt two, UN Doc A/73/10, 24 (hereafter 'Draft conclusions with commentaries').

Sołtan, which describes the latter as a function of attractiveness in a choice situation. My argument is that while the interpretive authority of the parties to a treaty has long appeared 'attractive' because it was obvious and persuasive, the landscape of the international legal order has progressively changed to give rise to a new social ecology in which treaty interpretation by the parties themselves is no longer seen as 'naturally' dispositive. I then focus on the ILC's work in that new environment and describe the mechanics of the 'quiet revolution' that the Commission initiated by opening the black box of state authority in treaty interpretation. In particular, I show that, for a variety of reasons ranging from lack of capacity for some to opportunistic considerations for others, states largely failed to engage with the Commission's conclusion, acting as collective 'bystanders' to what is likely to become a serious change in the authority regime of treaty interpretation.[10]

2. Assessing the Interpretive Authority of States

Most concepts of authority remain vulnerable to Michel Foucault's famous charge that political philosophy still needs 'to cut off the king's head' in its conceptualization of power relationships.[11] Foucault's point was that political theory had a tendency to analyse power as a matter of prescriptions and prohibitions, accounting for it in terms of some ultimate source, be it the person of the king or other similar alternatives. Despite serious attempts in the recent scholarship dedicated to authority in international affairs to broaden our understanding of authority relations beyond the prescriptions and prohibitions model, most analysts still remain focused on 'authority figures' in the form of persons, offices, and institutions.

Building on the theory of authority offered by Scheppele and Sołtan,[12] this chapter proposes to go beyond the actor-focused conception of authority.[13] According to Scheppele and Sołtan:

> Authority […] is not simply the right of actor A to get actor B to carry out A's will voluntarily. Instead, authority is found when actor B finds compelling particular properties of A, when A may be a person, a solution to a puzzle, or, more generally, any alternative in a choice situation. Authority is constituted not by person A willing a particular state of affairs which is then carried out, but rather by person B being attracted to the state of affairs offered by alternative A and voluntarily choosing that option over others.[14]

[10] See Nico Krisch and Ezgi Yildiz, 'From Drivers to Bystanders: The Varying Roles of States in International Legal Change'. <https://ssrn.com/abstract=4456773> accessed 25 August 2023.
[11] Michel Foucault, *Power: The Essential Works of Foucault 1954–1984* (The New Press 2001) 122.
[12] Kim Scheppele and Karol Sołtan, 'The Authority of Alternatives' (1987) 29 Nomos 169.
[13] ibid.
[14] ibid 170.

In this understanding, obviousness, 'the intuitive appeal of a particular solution for a particular problem',[15] is, for instance, likely to be a powerful basis for authority, considering that an alternative that can claim the advantage of obviousness reduces decision costs, is easier to agree on and more likely to secure an agreement.[16] Likewise, alternatives that can be persuasively justified are likely to look more attractive than others.[17]

Linking authority to attractiveness does not, however, mean that authority relations are a matter of subjective preference. Authority relations obtain precisely when attractiveness of an option is not a matter of personal choices, but have a social grounding in the form of 'a belief system' that supports it.[18] In other words, this understanding is fully in line with the 'triangular model of authority' which involves social practices, authority addressees, and authority in the sense that 'the recognition of authority [emanates] from social practices independent from an individual addressee's attitude'.[19]

As highlighted by Scheppele and Sołtan, the advantage of this approach is that authority is not to be regarded as the exclusive privilege of persons or offices, but can also be associated with 'texts, rituals, types of explanation, justifications, reasons or particular real or ideal social arrangements'.[20] Such an understanding of authority brings to light its fundamentally relative character, since the authority that an alternative can claim in a choice situation is not an on/off matter, but should be seen as 'a function of the strength of its resources'.[21] In other words, '[a]n alternative is not simply authoritative or not authoritative, but rather more or less authoritative depending on the resources which are possessed by that alternative.'[22] By focusing on authority-carrying properties, this conception of authority also makes it unnecessary to inquire whether a person or institution following an authoritative choice is carrying out an authority-holder's will or preferences.[23] Finally, unlike in conventional approaches, authority here is not a matter of unquestioning adherence and leaves ample room for resistance and contestation.[24]

Authority relations in the sense specified above typically intervene where power delineations through traditional formal entitlements or authoritative precedents are lacking. Treaty interpretation is precisely such an area. There is no formal legal instrument specifying the weight to which any interpretation is entitled in the

15 ibid 178.
16 ibid 187.
17 ibid 181.
18 Peter M Blau, 'Critical Remarks on Weber's Theory of Authority' (1963) 57 American Political Science Review 305, 307.
19 Nico Krisch, 'Liquid Authority in Global Governance' (2017) 9 International Theory 237, 244.
20 Scheppele and Sołtan (n 12) 170.
21 ibid 172–73.
22 ibid 173.
23 ibid 170.
24 For such an understanding of authority, see Michael Zürn, *A Theory of Global Governance: Authority, Legitimacy, and Contestation* (OUP 2018).

international legal order. As pointed out above, while there are formal rules clarifying how treaty interpretation should proceed and which means can be used in the process, the official regime of treaty interpretation is notoriously silent about the distribution of interpretive authority in international law. Efforts were made to formalize some authority entitlements in treaty interpretation, but they were typically resisted. The ILC's attempts to clarify the legal effects of pronouncements of expert bodies provide a good example. While the Special Rapporteur's early proposal suggested that those pronouncements 'may contribute to the interpretation of [the relevant] treaty',[25] a pushback from governments led the Commission to a less generous view in this regard.[26] The UN Human Rights Committee's early draft of General Comment 33 providing that the views adopted by the Committee in individual cases are legally binding and that they can be framed as subsequent practice of the states parties to the International Covenant on Civil and Political Rights is another example.[27] Several states rejected both views in their comments (with the US specifically describing them as an 'extraordinary assertion of authority'[28]), denying that the Committee had received such a mandate, and the Committee dropped both assertions in the final text of the General Comment.

In the absence of a formal allocation of the interpretive authority, the weight to which any actor's interpretation is entitled in the international legal order is informally grounded. The state authority in treaty interpretation is not an exception in this regard. Despite the large support that it has received in the literature, the proposition that an interpretive agreement by the parties to a treaty has conclusive effect is not set forth in any instrument. It is notably absent in the Vienna Convention on the Law of Treaties, the most authoritative instrument setting forth the rules of treaty interpretation which are consistently described as reflecting customary international law. During its work leading to the Vienna Convention, the ILC made several observations suggesting that the authority of such agreements could not be questioned. For instance, the Commission clarified that a subsequent interpretive agreement represented 'an authentic interpretation by the parties which must be read into the treaty for purposes of its interpretation'.[29] However, the Vienna

[25] 'Fourth Report on Subsequent Agreements and Subsequent Practice in relation to the Interpretation of Treaties' (2016) UN Doc A/CN.4/694, 36.

[26] The final conclusion specifies that '[t]he relevance of a pronouncement of an expert treaty body for the interpretation of a treaty is subject to the applicable rules of the treaty' and that the conclusion 'is without prejudice to the contribution that pronouncements of expert treaty bodies make to the interpretation of the treaties under their mandates'. Draft conclusion 13, 'Draft conclusions with commentaries' (n 9).

[27] HRC, 'Draft General Comment No 33 (Second revised version as of 18 August 2008)' (25 August 2008) UN Doc CCPR/C/GC/33CRP.3.

[28] Observations of the United States of America on the Human Rights Committee's General Comment 33 (22 December 2008) para 1 <https://2009-2017.state.gov/documents/organization/138852.pdf> accessed 15 February 2023.

[29] 'Reports of the International Law Commission on the second part of its seventeenth session and on its eighteenth session' (1966) II Yearbook of the International Law Commission, UN Doc A/6309/Rev.1, p 221.

Convention itself contains no such language. Also remarkable is the clarification that no hierarchy was implied among the interpretive means listed in the general rule of interpretation set forth in the Convention.[30]

There is also little authoritative support for the conclusive state authority in treaty interpretation in international case law. The advisory opinion of the Permanent Court of International Justice in *Question of Jaworzina* is commonly cited as the *locus classicus* on the matter. While the Court in that case did indeed point out that 'the right of giving an authoritative interpretation of a legal rule belongs solely to the person or body who has power to modify or suppress it',[31] the context of that statement was not treaty interpretation, but one involving the right of an intergovernmental conference to interpret its previous decision. The International Court of Justice has dealt with the argument of common understanding and interpretive agreements of the parties on several occasions but has never formulated a general statement to the effect that joint interpretive agreements are conclusive.[32]

But despite having no formal or precedential basis, the state authority in treaty interpretation has long enjoyed the advantage of obviousness and persuasiveness in the international legal order[33] for several reasons:

(a) International law has traditionally been state-centric, with the states being considered not just as one group of actors among others in international legal processes, but as 'pivotal' ones around which the entire international legal order allegedly revolved.[34] In this traditional picture, states have been portrayed not just as the addressees of international law, but also as the sole makers of it. In the case of custom, the state's central role is expressed either in the form of tacit or implicit state consent to customary rules or the exclusively state-focused definition of the practice required for the emergence of a customary rule. Even more forcefully, the law of treaties has been considered the bastion of consensualism in international law.[35] Among the

[30] ibid 220.

[31] *Question of Jaworzina (Polish-Czechoslovakian Frontier)* (Advisory Opinion) 6 December 1923, PCIJ Rep Series B No 8 (1923) 37.

[32] The Court pointed out in an advisory opinion that 'parties to treaties are in general free to agree on their interpretation', but the point was made in passing in response to an argument made by analogy with investment treaties in a case involving no issue having to do with the right of the parties to enter into interpretive agreements. *Judgment No 2867 of the Administrative Tribunal of the International Labour Organization upon a Complaint Filed against the International Fund for Agricultural Development* (Advisory Opinion) [2012] ICJ Rep 10 [43].

[33] So much so that, as Ingo Venzke points out, 'authoritative interpretations' and 'authentic interpretations' (joint treaty interpretations by the parties) have often been used interchangeably; see Ingo Venzke, 'Authoritative Interpretation' in *Max Planck Encyclopaedia of International Procedural Law*, para 2 <https://opil.ouplaw.com/view/10.1093/law-mpeipro/e3528.013.3528/law-mpeipro-e3528> accessed 15 February 2023.

[34] Philip Alston, 'The 'Not-a-cat' Syndrome: Can the International Human Rights Regime Accommodate Non-State Actors?' in Philip Alston (ed), *Non-State Actors and Human Rights* (1st edn, OUP 2005) 3. See also Krisch and Yildiz (n 10).

[35] Hubert Thierry, 'L'évolution du droit international: cours général de droit international public' in *Collected Courses of the Hague Academy of International Law*, vol 222 (Brill 1990) 36. See also ICSID,

> implications of the consensualist paradigm which permeates the whole body of the law of treaties is not only the basic threshold proposition that no state can be made a party to a treaty without its consent, but also the assumption that the very content of a treaty 'derives ... from the consent of the contracting States'.[36]

To put it in Foucault's words, such an understanding of international law offered 'an epistemological arrangement' that 'welcomed gladly' the view that states are masters of their treaties, making it appear like 'fish in water'.[37] Whether framed as 'patterns of culture',[38] 'the plausibility structure',[39] 'the structure of feeling',[40] or 'the spirit of the age',[41] an epistemological disposition that sees international law as a product of state consent is likely to have rendered state authority in treaty interpretation an obvious alternative.

(b) Another factor underpinning the compelling force of state authority in treaty interpretation has been the lack of plausible alternatives. For a long time, international law was a matter of intercourse among chancelleries, involving no third-party adjudicators, non-governmental organizations, or third-party beneficiaries. The very format of treaties—typically bilateral instruments setting forth specific rights and obligations for the parties—was inimical to the rise of plausible alternatives. Such circumstances are likely to have contributed to the authority of the joint interpretations of treaties by their parties.

(c) The international legal regime of treaty interpretation also reinforced state authority in treaty interpretation. During a considerable part of the history of the discipline, treaty interpretation was presented as a matter of a search for the common intention of the parties. The search for the common intention of the parties was of such paramount importance that it was thought that no technical rule of treaty interpretation should hinder it.[42]

Daimler Financial Services AG v Argentine Republic (Award) 22 August 2012, ICSID Case No ARB/05/1, para 168 ('Consent is ... the cornerstone of all international treaty commitments ... The primacy of the principle of consent runs through all types of treaty commitments entered into by states').

[36] *Request for Interpretation of the Judgment of 15 June 1962 in the Case concerning the Temple of Preah Vihear (Cambodia v Thailand)* (Judgment) 11 November 2013 [2013] ICJ Rep 281 [75].

[37] Michel Foucault, *Order of Things: An Archaeology of the Human Sciences* (Routledge 2002) 285.

[38] Ruth Benedict, *Patterns of Culture* (Harcourt 2005) 251.

[39] Peter L Berger and Thomas Luckmann, *The Social Construction of Reality. A Treaties in the Sociology of Knowledge* (Doubleday 1966) 154.

[40] Raymond Williams, *The Long Revolution* (Parthian 2011) 69.

[41] Vaughan Lowe, 'The Politics of Law-Making: Are the Method and Character of Norm Creation Changing?' in Michael Byers (ed), *The Role of Law in International Politics: Essays in International Relations and International Law* (OUP 2001) 220.

[42] Charles C Hyde, *International Law, Chiefly as Interpreted and Applied by the United States* (Little, Brown 1922) 69–70; John Westlake, *International Law, Part I: Peace* (CUP 1904) 282.

> Although he did not deny the practical utility of dedicated rules of treaty interpretation, Hersch Lauterpacht similarly recognized the central place of the intention of the parties in his report prepared for the Institut de Droit International, describing that intention as 'the law of the judge', 'a fundamental factor in the matter of treaty interpretation', or 'the primary object of interpretation'.[43]

When the common intention of the parties is seen as a guiding parameter in treaty interpretation, the parties to the treaty can plausibly claim significant authority, as actors best positioned to articulate that intention. What has been described as 'the paradox of knowing better'[44]—a third party pretending to know the common intention of the parties better than the parties themselves—can be plausibly addressed when the parties are in disagreement, but it becomes much harder to resolve when the parties have an interpretive agreement. Indeed, what the *ADF* tribunal observed with respect to interpretations issued by the Free Trade Commission of the North American Free Trade Agreement (NAFTA)—'[n]o more authentic and authoritative source of instruction on what the Parties intended to convey in a particular provision of NAFTA is possible'[45]—presumably describes a broader phenomenon of authorial authority, with authorship acting as a powerful mark of interpretive authority.[46]

This non-formal, substantive grounding of state authority in treaty interpretation comes at the cost of vulnerability to changes in relevant dynamics. Several developments in the international legal order have indeed undermined the 'naturalness' of the interpretive authority of states. The evolution of the official regime of treaty interpretation is arguably among such developments. While references to the common intention of the parties are still understandably present in the treaty interpretation discourse, the regime set forth in the Vienna Convention on the Law of Treaties is premised on the assumption that treaty interpretation is not 'an investigation *ab initio* into the intentions of the parties', but an exercise primarily based on the text, the latter being considered as the virtually exclusive medium used by the parties to express those intentions.[47] Arguably, this change in the object of interpretation has important consequences for the authority relations in treaty interpretation. The parties to a treaty may be said to be best positioned to clarify their common intention, but they can claim no such exclusivity when elucidating the

[43] See *Annuaire de l'Institut de Droit International*, vol 43 (1950) Tome I, 423 (author's own translation).

[44] Guy de Lacharrière, *La politique juridique extérieure* (Economica 1983) 172; Martti Koskenniemi, *From Apology to Utopia. The Structure of International Legal Argument* (CUP 2005) 347.

[45] ICSID, *ADF Group Inc v United States of America* (Award) 9 January 2003, ICSID Case No ARB (AF)/00/1, para 177.

[46] The privileged interpretive position of the authors of legal instruments is recognized in the adage *Ejus est interpretari legem cujus est condere*.

[47] 'Reports of the International Law Commission' (n 29) 220.

meaning of the text is considered to be 'the starting point and purpose of interpretation'.[48] In other words, state authority in treaty interpretation is likely to be less compelling in a regime in which the text is regarded as a primary object of treaty interpretation.

Another challenge to state authority in treaty interpretation has come from the rise of alternative interpreters.[49] A particularly prominent competing authority claimant in the international legal order has been third-party adjudicators that I broadly define as including any third party formally empowered to interpret treaties. Considered as transparent, impartial, and independent bodies subject to no force other than 'the force of the better argument',[50] such third parties can command significant authority in settings where those properties are highly valued, because they are largely lacking. This has been traditionally the case with the international legal order in which states have been seen as legally entitled to determine *uti singuli* what their legal rights and obligations are,[51] with impartial accounts of those rights and obligations remaining an exception. In such a system of 'boundless relativism',[52] interpretations offered by independent, neutral, and impartial sites such as international courts and structurally similar monitoring bodies can exert more attraction than 'interest-driven' interpretations advanced by the parties[53] for any actor interested in capitalizing on law's neutralizing and universalizing effects.[54]

In some areas of international law, non-governmental organizations have also arisen as credible alternative interpreters, with human rights and humanitarian law being prominent examples. Human rights non-governmental organizations (NGOs) use the channel of international adjudication to offer their interpretations of human rights treaties[55] and participate in human rights standard-setting.[56] The

48 'Third Report on the Law of Treaties, by Sir Humphrey Waldock, Special Rapporteur' (1964) II Yearbook of the International Law Commission, UN Doc A/CN.4/172, 56.

49 On the role of 'alternative authorities' to states, see also Krisch and Yildiz (n 10).

50 Jürgen Habermas, *The Theory of Communicative Action*, vol 1 (Beacon Press 1984) 25.

51 Leo Gross, 'States as Organs of International Law and the Problem of Autointerpretation' in George A Lipsky (ed), *Law and Politics in the World Community: Essays on Hans Kelsen's Pure Theory and Related Problems in International Law* (University of California Press 1953) 59; Hersch Lauterpacht, *The Development of International Law by the International Court* (CUP 1982); *Lake Lanoux Arbitration*, 24 ILR 101 (1961) 132; *Air Service Agreement*, 18 RIAA 443.

52 Paul Reuter, 'Principes de droit international public' (1961) 103 *Recueil des cours* 440.

53 Bruno Simma, 'Comment' in Rudiger Wolfrum and Volker Roeben (eds), *Developments of International Law in Treaty Making* (Springer 2005) 582.

54 Pierre Bourdieu, 'The Force of Law: Toward a Sociology of the Juridical Field' (1987) 38 Hastings Law Journal 805, 820.

55 See Heidi Haddad, *The Hidden Hands of Justice: NGOs, Human Rights, and International Courts* (CUP 2018).

56 NGOs played an active role in the development of the 'Siracusa Principles' on the derogation and limitation provisions of the International Covenant on Civil and Political Rights in 1984. See Theo van Boven, 'The Role of Non-Governmental Organizations in International Human Rights Standard-Setting: A Prerequisite of Democracy Trends in International Law' (1989) 20 California Western International Law Journal 207. Human Rights NGOs have also been active in submitting comments regarding draft general comments prepared by human rights treaty bodies. See eg 'Comments received

authority of the Pictet Commentaries to the Geneva Conventions authored by the staff members of the International Committee of the Red Cross is widely recognized both in practice and in academic circles.[57] The attractiveness of such alternative interpretations varies depending on the reputation, expertise, and perceived neutrality and impartiality of their authors, but the very fact of their existence undermines the notion that the parties-originated treaty interpretation is the only game in town.

The rise of treaties with third-party beneficiaries is arguably another factor weakening state authority in treaty interpretation. Human rights treaties and investment protection treaties are particularly worth mentioning in this context. Human rights treaties are typically described as being radically different from the interstate reciprocal bargaining model in the sense that obligations under those treaties are not intersubjective obligations among the parties, but 'objective obligations' with respect to all individuals subject to the jurisdiction of the parties.[58] This is sometimes seen as justifying a special regime for denunciation of or succession to such treaties.[59] It is also often relied on to grant lesser deference to indicators of state consent in treaty interpretation such as *travaux préparatoires* or the intention of the parties both in academic discourse and in practice.[60] The recent practice of human rights treaty bodies to open up their draft general comments for submissions from all interested parties is also presumably premised on the assumption that the normative content of human rights treaties is a matter of concern beyond the circle of the parties to those treaties.

State authority in treaty interpretation has been even more forcefully challenged in the context of investor-state arbitration. As is the case in human rights litigation initiated by individuals, only one of the parties in investor-state arbitration

with respect to the draft General Comment on the right of peaceful assembly' <www.ohchr.org/EN/HRBodies/CCPR/Pages/GCArticle21.aspx> accessed 15 February 2023.

57 Linus Mührel, 'Saying Authoritatively What International Humanitarian Law Is: On the Interpretations and Law-Ascertainments of the International Committee of the Red Cross' (PhD thesis on file at the Free University of Berlin 2019).

58 *Reservations to the Convention on Genocide* (Advisory Opinion) [1951] ICJ Rep 15, 23; *Ireland v United Kingdom*, App no 5310/71, 18 January 1978, para 239; *The Effect of Reservations on the Entry into Force of the American Convention on Human Rights (Arts 74 and 75)* (Advisory Opinion) OC-2/28, 24 September 1982, para 29.

59 UN Aide-Mémoire in connection with North Korea's denunciation of the Covenant, Ref C.N.467.1997.TREATIES-10, 12 November 1997 <https://treaties.un.org/doc/Publication/CN/1997/CN.467.1997-Eng.pdf> accessed 15 February 2023. See also, regarding automatic succession of human rights treaties, Menno Kamminga, 'State Succession in Respect of Human Rights Treaties' (1996) 7 European Journal of International Law 469.

60 Bernadette Rainey, Elizabeth Wicks, and Clare Ovey, *Jacobs, White, and Ovey: The European Convention on Human Rights* (OUP 2017) 66; David Harris and others, *Harris, O'Boyle, and Warbrick: Law of the European Convention on Human Rights* (OUP 2018) 22; George Letsas, 'Strasbourg's Interpretive Ethic: Lessons for the International Lawyer' (2010) 21 European Journal of International Law 509, 520; *Young, James and Webster v The United Kingdom*, App nos 7601/76 and 7806/77, 13 August 1981, para 52; *Sigurdur A. Sigurjónsson v Iceland*, App no 16130/90, 30 June 1993, para 35.

is also a party to the treaty and is in a position to put forward its views not only as a party to the dispute, but also as a party to the treaty. This asymmetrical situation is generally unproblematic, since a unilateral interpretation by one state of its treaty obligations is not treated as being entitled to special weight not only because it is emanating from one party,[61] but also because such an interpretation carries the risk of being self-serving.[62] But it becomes more challenging when the state as a party to the treaty secures an interpretive agreement with the other party to the treaty, especially so when the agreement intervenes during the pendency of the arbitration proceeding, because this possibility is not available to the investor. The issue came under the spotlight in the context of NAFTA when the NAFTA parties issued a document titled 'Notes of Interpretation of Certain Chapter 11 Provisions' in order 'to clarify and reaffirm the meaning of certain of [the] provisions' of Chapter 11 of NAFTA after 'having reviewed the operation of proceedings conducted' by Chapter 11 tribunals, [63] which included some ongoing proceedings in which the proper interpretation of those provisions was at issue. Granting such interpretive agreements a conclusive effect has been described as inconsistent with the due process of justice and the equality of arms by experts and practitioners in the field[64] and has led some tribunals to express a sense of unease.[65] Investors have also voiced concerns about the procedural unfairness entailed by the situation.[66]

3. Anatomy of a Revolution in the Making

The position of the ILC that joint interpretive agreements of the parties to a treaty are not necessarily binding is a very serious challenge to state authority in treaty interpretation given the considerable authority that the Commission enjoys

[61] As stated by the Appellate Body of the WTO: 'The purpose of treaty interpretation under article 31 of the Vienna Convention is to ascertain the *common* intentions of the parties. These *common* intentions cannot be ascertained on the basis of the subjective and unilaterally determined "expectations" of *one* of the parties to a treaty.' WTO, 'European Communities—Customs Classification of Certain Computer Equipment—Report of the Appellate Body' (5 June 1998) WT/DS62-67-68/AB/R, para 84 (emphasis original).

[62] See, by analogy, *Ahmadou Sadio Diallo (Republic of Guinea v Democratic Republic of the Congo)* (Merits, Judgment) [2010] ICJ Rep 639 [70] ('where a State puts forward a manifestly incorrect interpretation of its domestic law, particularly for the purpose of gaining an advantage in a pending case, it is for the Court to adopt what it finds to be the proper interpretation').

[63] NAFTA Free Trade Commission, 'Notes of Interpretation of Certain Chapter 11 Provisions' OXIO 553, 31 July 2001.

[64] Anthea Roberts, 'Power and Persuasion in Investment Treaty Interpretation: The Dual Role of States' (2010) 104 AJIL 179.

[65] See eg ICSID, *Magyar Farming Company v Hungary* (Award of 13 November 2019) ICSID Case no ARB/17/27, para 222 ('While the Contracting States remain the masters of their treaty, their control is limited by the general principles of legal certainty and *res inter alios acta, aliis nec nocet nec prodest*'); *HICEE BV v The Slovak Republic* (Partial Award) UNCITRAL, PCA Case no 2009-11, para 140.

[66] ICSID, *Mobil Investments Canada INC v Canada* (Award on Jurisdiction and Admissibility) 13 July 2018, ICSID Case no ARB/15/6, para 159.

regarding public international law matters. A close look at the reports prepared by the Special Rapporteur and the final conclusions and accompanying commentaries adopted by the Commission gives some clues as to the anatomy of the Commission's groundbreaking choice.

First of all, the Special Rapporteur engaged in a sustained work that can be characterized as discursive construction of unsettledness of the issue. What helped him considerably is the fact that, as described above, the authority of joint interpretive agreements of the parties is not settled in any formal rule of international law or any authoritative precedent. But the Special Rapporteur also tried to show that the matter was not settled by the Commission in the 1960s. For instance, he endeavoured to establish that, even though in the 1960s the Commission described the interpretations jointly offered in interpretive agreements by the parties as representing 'authentic interpretation[s] ... which must be read into the treaty for purposes of its interpretation', the Commission 'did not go quite as far as saying that such an interpretation is necessarily conclusive in the sense that it overrides all other means of interpretation'.[67] According to the Commentary, this conclusion finds support in the structure of Article 31 of the Vienna Convention on the Law of Treaties, which states that 'subsequent agreements and subsequent practice shall ... only "be taken into account" in the interpretation of a treaty' and establishes no hierarchy among the means of interpretation listed in that provision.[68] This exceedingly formalistic argument may not strike everyone as a plausible reading of the position of the Commission in the 1960s, but what is important for the purposes of this chapter is that the Commission needed to establish that no conclusive authority had been recognized to subsequent agreements by the Commission in the 1960s in order to be able to deny such authority.[69] In the same spirit, the Commentary contains no reference to the Advisory Opinion of the Permanent Court of International Justice in the *Jaworzina* case.

Another relevant consideration to bear in mind is that state authority in treaty interpretation is very much audience-sensitive and varies depending on 'the values, interests and expectations and cognitive frames' of the actors assessing it.[70] As Nico Krisch and Ezgi Yildiz observe, in many issue-areas, international lawyers do not display the level of cohesion and homogeneity characterizing a 'community'.[71] International legal scholars who have a state-centric conception of

[67] 'Draft conclusions with commentaries' (n 9) 25.
[68] ibid 24.
[69] Interestingly, according to the explanation provided with respect to the ISO environmental management standard 140001:2015, the difference between 'shall consider' and 'shall take into account' is as follows: 'When the standard uses the term consider, it means that it is necessary to think about the topic but it can be excluded. When the standard uses the phrase take into account, the topic must be thought about and cannot be excluded' <www.iso14001expert.com/2015/07/is-there-a-distinction-between-consider-and-take-into-account-in-iso-140012015/> accessed 15 February 2023.
[70] Julia Black, 'Says Who: Liquid Authority and Interpretive Control in Transnational Regulatory Regimes' (2017) 9 International Theory 286, 293.
[71] Krisch and Yildiz (n 10).

international law tend to see states as the owners of their treaties and treat their interpretive power accordingly.[72] We can expect a similar position from legal advisors to governments. Likewise, state authority in treaty interpretation is likely to be more readily recognized by interstate courts and tribunals than by other international courts. Interestingly, a variation can also be observed along the lines of national traditions of international law. For instance, in the French tradition of international law, the authority of the parties in treaty interpretation tends to be commonly taken for granted. These variations can also be observed in the composition of the Commission. For instance, Michael Wood, a former legal advisor to the Foreign Office, and Roman Kolodkin, a former legal advisor to the Russian government, were among the members of the Commission who objected to the Special Rapporteur's position regarding the authority of the joint interpretive agreements by the parties.[73] Coming from the French tradition of international law, Mathias Forteau and Maurice Kamto were among the most vocal opponents of the Special Rapporteur's position.[74] But these objections were relatively limited, which enabled the Special Rapporteur to stick to his position.

Equally relevant is the Commission's politics of the use of authorities. One of the rare monographs dedicated to the interpretation of the treaty by the parties is never mentioned in the Commentary, still less discussed in the Rapporteur's works.[75] The Commentary also dismissed the view contradicting the approach promoted by the Special Rapporteur as 'erroneous' and as merely 'the suggestions of some commentators',[76] with the relevant footnote containing no reference to highly reputed scholars (some of whom participated in the preparation of what became the Vienna Convention on the Law of Treaties within the Commission in the 1960s) and sources defending that view.[77] The Special Rapporteur's view is footnoted with citations to considerably lesser authorities supplemented in an exercise of circularity by a reference to his own Third Report for the Commission's Study Group

[72] See eg James Crawford, 'A Consensualist Interpretation of Article 31(3) of the Vienna Convention on the Law of Treaties' in Georg Nolte (ed), *Treaties and Subsequent Practice* (OUP 2013) 29, 31:

> [T]he parties to a treaty... own the treaty. It is their treaty. It is not anyone else's treaty... In the context of investment treaty arbitration there is a certain tendency to believe that investors own bilateral investment treaties, not the states parties to them ... That is not what international law says. International law says that the parties to a treaty own the treaty and can interpret it. One might say within reason, but one might not question their application of reason as they see fit.

[73] See, respectively, ILC, 'Summary Record of the 3160th meeting' (7 May 2013) UN Doc A/CN.4/3160, 4 and ILC, 'Summary Record of the 3261st meeting' (4 June 2015) UN Doc A/CN.4/SR.3261, 6.

[74] See, respectively, ILC, 'Summary Record of the 3205th meeting' (15 May 2014) UN Doc A/CN.4/SR.3205, 8 and ILC, 'Summary Record of the 3207th meeting' (20 May 2014) UN Doc A/CN.4/SR.3207, 5.

[75] See Ioan Voicu, *De l'interprétation authentique des traités internationaux* (Pedone 1968).

[76] 'Draft conclusions with commentaries' (n 9) 24.

[77] This list includes Manley Hudson, Arnold McNair, Robert Jennings, Arthur Watts, Paul Reuter, Mustafa Yasseen, and reference works such as Rudolf Bernhardt (ed), *Max Planck Encyclopaedia of Public International Law* (1984) or Jean Salmon (ed), *Dictionnaire de droit international public* (Elsevier Science Publishers 2001).

on Treaties over Time.[78] Also lacking is an explanation as to why the Commission itself took that allegedly 'erroneous' view just a few years back.[79]

The primacy of the text in the interpretive philosophy underpinning the Vienna Convention on the Law of Treaties was also mobilized by the Commission in order to relegate subsequent agreements and subsequent practice to a secondary position.[80] It is true that the Commentary insists that Article 31 of the Vienna Convention operates as 'a single integrated rule'.[81] But this did not prevent the Commission from reproducing the rule stated in Article 31, paragraph 1 of the Vienna Convention, according to which '[a] treaty shall be interpreted in good faith in accordance with the ordinary meaning to be given to its terms in their context and in the light of its object and purpose', in a separate paragraph before the paragraph referring to subsequent agreements and subsequent practice.[82] The Commentary clarified that:

> [t]he reiteration of article 31, paragraph 1, as a separate paragraph ... is intended to ensure the balance in the process of interpretation between an assessment of the terms of the treaty in their context and in the light of its object and purpose, on the one hand, and the considerations regarding subsequent agreements and subsequent practice in the present draft conclusions, on the other.[83]

Another notable aspect of the Commission's work on 'Draft conclusions on subsequent agreements and subsequent practice in relation to the interpretation of treaties' is that, while the Commission in the 1960s reserved the phrase 'authentic interpretation' for the interpretation of the treaty by the parties themselves, that expression is carefully avoided in Conclusion 3 dedicated to the general characterization of subsequent agreements and subsequent practice, the latter being described as 'authentic means of interpretation', another terminology used by the Commission in the 1960s.[84] This is a manifest attempt to diminish the importance that subsequent agreements and subsequent practice arguably had for the

[78] 'Draft conclusions with commentaries' (n 9) 25, fn 62.

[79] 'Guide to Practice on Reservations to Treaties with commentaries' (2011) UN Doc A/66/10/Add.1, 81 (stating that '[when the parties] agree on an interpretation, that interpretation prevails and itself takes on the nature of a treaty').

[80] Commentary to Draft conclusion 7, in 'Draft conclusions with commentaries' (n 9) 51–52:

> International courts and tribunals usually begin their reasoning in a given case by determining the 'ordinary meaning' of the terms of the treaty. Subsequent agreements and subsequent practice mostly enter into their reasoning at a later stage when courts ask whether such conduct confirms or modifies the result arrived at by the initial interpretation of the ordinary meaning (or by other means of interpretation.

[81] Commentary to Draft conclusion 2, in 'Draft conclusions with commentaries' (n 9) 20.

[82] ibid para 2.

[83] ibid.

[84] Commentary to Draft conclusion 3, in 'Draft conclusions with commentaries' (n 9) 10.

Commission in the 1960s,[85] with the Commission now highlighting that subsequent agreements and subsequent practice 'are ... not the only "authentic means of interpretation"' under Article 31 of the Vienna Convention.[86]

The Special Rapporteur's work also seems to have been heavily influenced by the rise of treaties with third-party beneficiaries and alternative interpreters. In his very first report, the Special Rapporteur referred to the assertion that 'the interpretation of treaties which establish rights for other States or actors is less susceptible to "authentic" interpretation by their parties'.[87] The examples taken from investment arbitration tend to suggest that the interpretive asymmetry between investors and the state party to the arbitration was a serious consideration in the Special Rapporteur's analysis.[88] The fact that the existence of alternative interpreters may also have been relevant is shown by the Commission's dedicated attention to pronouncements of expert treaty bodies.[89]

The foregoing considerations may explain what made the Commission's position about the legal effects of joint treaty interpretations by the parties possible. But one still needs to figure out how the ILC, whose main interlocutors are states and which normally cares about what is admissible to states,[90] could promote a position that seems to undermine state authority in treaty interpretation. One explanation that could be ventured is that the Commission knew from the beginning that its work on subsequent practice and subsequent agreement was not going to be submitted to an international conference with a view to the conclusion of a multilateral treaty.[91] The possibility for the work products of the Commission to never become a multilateral treaty is recognized in its Statute but has been more prominently used in the recent period. It is not a stretch to imagine that the Commission probably feels that it can take more freedom when its work is not subject to the test of acceptability at an intergovernmental conference.

[85] ibid 25. The Commentary is clear in this regard: 'The Commission has not employed the terms "authentic interpretation" or "authoritative interpretation" in draft conclusion 3 since these concepts are often understood to mean a necessarily conclusive, or binding, agreement between the parties regarding the interpretation of a treaty' (ibid).

[86] ibid 24.

[87] 'First Report on Subsequent Agreements and Subsequent Practice in Relation to the Interpretation of Treaties' (2013) UN Doc A/CN.4/660, 60, fn 75.

[88] ibid 70, paras 88–89; ILC, 'Second Report on Subsequent Agreements and Subsequent Practice in Relation to the Interpretation of Treaties' (2014) UN Doc A/CN.4/671, 62, paras 150–55.

[89] See Draft conclusion 12 and commentary thereto, in ILC, 'Draft conclusions with commentaries' (n 9). The Special Rapporteur also clarified that when judicial or quasi-judicial bodies existed, they could challenge interpretive agreements and their value. ILC, 'Summary Record of the 3446th meeting' (7 August 2018) UN Doc A/CN.4/SR.3446, 9.

[90] See Bruno Simma, 'The ILC's Work on State Responsibility: Personal Reflections' (*EJIL: Talk!*, 2 August 2021) <www.ejiltalk.org/the-ilcs-work-on-state-responsibility-personal-reflections/> accessed 15 February 2023 (describing the UN member states as the Commission's 'customers').

[91] 'Annex: Treaties over time in particular: subsequent agreement and practice' (2008) II Yearbook of International Law Commission, pt two, 156, para 22 ('The [...] goal of the consideration of the topic should be to derive some general conclusions or guidelines from the repertory of practice. Such conclusions or guidelines should not result in a Draft Convention').

It is true that the Commission works closely with the Sixth Committee of the UN General Assembly and submits its drafts to governments for comments and observations.[92] But it is a notorious fact that only a small minority of governments actually engages with the Commission's works. While states could be expected to be more pro-active when issues salient to their interestsare at stake ,[93] for a variety of reasons, a great majority of states do not react to the Commission's drafts even when they are invited and encouraged to do so. Some countries may be unaware of the details of the Commission's work due to the sheer amount of what they are expected to follow.[94] Others experience a severe lack of dedicated personnel or expertise.[95] There are also strategic reasons, having to do with states' unwillingness to tie their hands with public positions.[96] As Sandesh Sivakumaran points out, 'States tend not to want to formulate their position on an issue in the abstract; rather, they prefer to wait for situations in which they have to set out their position, for example, in pleadings before a court.'[97]

Despite the importance of the issue of state authority in treaty interpretation for all states, the Special Rapporteur's position about the legal effects of subsequent agreements and subsequent practice did not fare differently. Very few states engaged with the Special Rapporteur's position and only Greece[98] and Poland[99] objected to it, which enabled the Special Rapporteur to state that 'most States agreed' with the proposition that 'subsequent agreements and subsequent practice of the parties [do not] necessarily possess a conclusive, or legally binding effect'.[100] In other words, we are witnessing here a case of 'collective action incapacity'[101]

[92] For the interaction of the Commission with governments, see Danae Azaria, 'Codification by Interpretation: The International Law Commission as an Interpreter of International Law' (2020) 31 European Journal of International Law 188–89.

[93] Krisch and Yildiz (n 10).

[94] Sivakumaran (n 7) 382 (stating that '[i]nternational lawmaking and law-shaping bodies and processes have proliferated to such an extent that if State officials sought to respond to each and every output a state-empowered entity issued, they might have to spend all day, every day on this task').

[95] ibid 382–83; see also Yves Daudet, 'Rapport général' in *Société française pour le droit international, Colloque d'Aix-en-Provence* (Pedone 1999) 129, 164.

[96] Ramma Pradas Dhokalia, 'Reflections on International Law-Making and its Progressive Development in the Contemporary Era of Transition' in Raghunandan Pathak and Ramma Pradas Dhokalia (eds), *International Law in Transition—Essays in Memory of Judge Nagendra Singh* (Martinus Nijhoff 1992) 203, 226; Azaria (n 92) 191.

[97] Sivakumaran (n 7) 383. A seasoned governmental legal advisor once reported that a colleague from another country who was asked what his government's choice was between the principle of equidistance and equitable principles in the field of maritime delimitation replied that the response depended on which part of the country's costs was at issue. Lacharrière (n 44) 183.

[98] UNGA Sixth Committee, 'Summary Record of the 24th meeting' (31 October 2014) UN Doc A/C.6/69/SR.24, para 89.

[99] UNGA Sixth Committee, 'Summary Record of the 19th meeting' (30 October 2013) UN Doc A/C.6/68/SR.19, para 12.

[100] 'Fifth Report on Subsequent Agreements and Subsequent Practice in Relation to the Interpretation of Treaties by Georg Nolte, Special Rapporteur' (2018) UN Doc A/CN.4/715, para 30. The International Court of Justice interpreted the absence of reactions to the works of the International Law Commission as evidence of *opinio iuris*, see *Jurisdictional Immunities of the State (Germany v Italy; Greece intervening)* (Judgment) [2012] ICJ Rep 99 [77].

[101] Krisch and Yildiz (n 10).

empowering the Commission 'to fill the void left by the lack of response on the part of States'.[102]

What may have also helped with the Commission's position is that the statement that subsequent agreements and subsequent practice are not necessarily conclusive or legally binding only appeared in the Commentary and not in Conclusions as such. It is true that Conclusion 10 states that a subsequent interpretive 'agreement may, but need not, be legally binding for it to be taken into account'. But, as pointed out by a member of the Commission, this provision has to do with 'the legal nature or form of the agreement, rather than its consequence for legal interpretation'.[103] In other words, the provision makes clear that informal agreements or simple common understanding that may not take the form of a formally binding agreement can also be taken into account in treaty interpretation. However, the Special Rapporteur entertained the confusion between the form and effects of interpretive agreements. For instance, Poland's objection to the proposition that subsequent agreements are not necessarily binding was mentioned in the Fifth Report, but the Special Rapporteur pointed out that the objection would be dealt with in the context of the draft conclusion stating that a subsequent interpretive 'agreement may, but need not, be legally binding for it to be taken into account'.[104] In the same report, the Special Rapporteur even listed some states such as Austria and the UK as supporting his view about the legal weight of interpretive agreements while those states only supported the proposition about the legal nature or form of those agreements.[105]

4. Conclusion

Even though it has not received much attention so far, one of the most remarkable aspects of the recent work of the ILC on subsequent agreements and subsequent practice is its attempt to revisit state authority in treaty interpretation. While the proposition that join interpretive agreements are binding on treaty interpreters tended to be taken for granted, including by the Commission itself in its prior work, the recently adopted Conclusions on subsequent agreements and subsequent practice in relation to the interpretation of treaties deny that such agreements are necessarily binding.

This contribution attempted to account both for the traditional authority of joint interpretive agreements and the approach promoted by the Commission by building on a conceptualization of authority as a function of attractiveness. State

102 Sivakumaran (n 7) 385.
103 'Summary Record of the 3391st meeting' (1 May 2018) UN Doc A/CN.4/SR.3391, 9.
104 'Fifth Report on Subsequent Agreements and Subsequent Practice' (n 100) 10.
105 ibid 10, fn 56.

authority in treaty interpretation has long enjoyed the advantage of obviousness and persuasiveness in the international legal order, given the state-centric nature of international law, the dominance of the intention-focused treaty interpretation model, and the lack of plausible alternatives. But the Commission was able to capitalize on various factors challenging that 'obviousness' in order to open the black box of state authority in treaty interpretation.

In view of the institutional authority of the Commission, its position that the joint interpretation of a treaty offered by its parties is not necessarily binding is very likely to be influential in practice despite the 'soft' form of the Conclusions. As a matter of fact, the Special Rapporteur's explanation as to why interpretive agreements are not necessarily binding under the Vienna Convention has already been used in investment arbitration. [106] What is more remarkable here, however, is that the 'states as drivers of change processes of international law' model is called into question not just as a matter of practice—as reflected in the other contributions to this volume—but also in doctrinal construction in a rather traditional 'law-shaping'[107] institution such as the ILC.

[106] See *Bilcon of Delaware et al v Government of Canada*, PCA Case No 2009-04 (Award on Jurisdiction and Liability) 17 March 2015, para 430; ICSID, *Magyar Farming Company v Hungary* (n 65) para 218.

[107] Sivakumaran (n 7) 382.

14

The Path not Taken

On Legal Change and its Context

Ingo Venzke[*]

1. Introduction

Legal change must be understood in relation to its context. But how? It may happen that broader contexts fatefully determine legal change. As a general claim, however, such a view is hardly tenable. Curiously enough, it is unrealistic in its denial of law's relative autonomy, as I will argue. Legal change must be related to contexts without reducing the former to the latter. The question is not whether contexts matter, but rather, how and to what extent? And what counts as context?

An introductory example may illustrate the question and sharpen the discussion. I take it from the field of European human rights law but might have chosen other fields just as well. Change has been pervasive there, ranging from the now well-settled interpretation that the prohibition of torture includes the right of non-refoulement to the more recent interpretation that the right to life includes a right of protection from detrimental environmental effects.[1] Under the impact of jurisprudence from the European Court of Human Rights (ECtHR), the law has changed significantly, even though its primary text—the European Convention of Human Rights (ECHR)—has remained largely unchanged since it entered into force in 1953. Only the First Protocol to the Convention, which entered into force in 1954, is relevant for the more specific example.[2] Its Article 1 provides that '[e]very natural or legal person is entitled to the peaceful enjoyment of his possessions'.

* Professor of International Law and Social Justice, University of Amsterdam, Amsterdam, The Netherlands.

[1] On the changing interpretation of the prohibition of torture (Article 3, ECHR) see Seline Trevisanut, 'The Principle of Non-Refoulement at Sea and the Effectiveness of Asylum Protection' (2008) 12 Max Planck Yearbook of United Nations Law 205; Ezgi Yildiz, 'A Norm in Flux: The Development of the Norm Against Torture Under the European Convention from a Macro Perspective' (2016) iCourts Working Paper Series No 45. On the right to life (Article 2, ECHR) see Christina Binder and Haris Huremagić, 'Menschenrechtsverpflichtung zur Reduzierung von Treibhausgasemissionen' (2021) 1 Nachhaltigkeitsrecht 109; Dimitris Xenos, 'Asserting the Right to Life (Article 2, ECHR) in the Context of Industry' (2007) 8 German Law Journal 231, who focuses on *Öneryıldız v Turkey* App no 48939/99 (ECtHR, Grand Chamber, 30 November 2004), esp paras 89ff.

[2] For an overview of the protocols, see <www.echr.coe.int/Documents/Archives_evolution_Convention_ENG.pdf> accessed 3 November 2022.

Ingo Venzke, *The Path not Taken* In: *The Many Paths of Change in International Law.* Edited by: Nico Krisch and Ezgi Yildiz, Oxford University Press. © Ingo Venzke 2023. DOI: 10.1093/oso/9780198877844.003.0014

In a recent contribution, Silvia Steininger and Jochen von Bernstorff examine the gradual extension of human rights for corporations under the ECHR. Drawing on ideas from historical institutionalism, they focus on three critical junctures in that legal development.[3] First, they point to discussions about whether the right to property should also extend to *legal* or only *natural* persons, and whether it should be included in the Convention at all, which ultimately led to the right's relegation to the First Protocol. Secondly, Steininger and von Bernstorff turn to the ECtHR's judicial practice, which has, since the 1980s, extended the right to property to include far-reaching compensation, for example for reputation loss or decline in business clientele.[4] The Court has also allowed corporations to claim rights under the Convention generally, for instance under Article 6 on fair trial, thereby further assimilating legal to natural persons. Thirdly, the authors show how these developments have paved the way for extensive property protection in international investment law. These legal changes were contingent rather than necessary, they write. But the turns at each critical juncture did make good sense. Treaty-making in the 1950s was determined by the strictures of the Cold War and the relevant court judgments of the 1980s took off together with the rise of neoliberalism. If the legal developments were not necessary, how then to understand their contingency? How to turn claims about changes in the law's context into compelling understandings of legal change.

The example highlights what an understanding of legal change must achieve and where it can go wrong. First and foremost, the development of the law must indeed be understood in relation to broader contexts without reducing it to them. The present volume's editors aptly observe that the law 'will often reflect political constellations of its time … [but] it is not merely the mirror image of politics'.[5] When the judges of the ECtHR started granting far-reaching compensation to corporations, they acted in accordance with the tides of their time and arguably in their interest, but it would come at a loss of understanding if their actions were reduced to nothing but an expression of neoliberal conditions or institutional self-aggrandizement, just as it would be unconvincing to understand their actions as

[3] Silvia Steininger and Jochen von Bernstorff, 'Who Turned Multinational Corporations into Bearers of Human Rights? On the Creation of Corporate "Human" Rights in International Law' in Ingo Venzke and Kevin Jon Heller (eds), *Contingency in International Law: On the Possibility of Different Legal Histories* (OUP 2021) 280–95. On the notion of critical juncture, see Giovanni Capoccia and Daniel R Kelemen, 'The Study of Critical Junctures: Theory, Narrative, and Counterfactuals in Historical Institutionalism' (2007) 59 World Politics 341; Orfeo Fioretos, 'Historical Institutionalism in International Relations' (2011) 65 International Organization 367; Thomas Rixen, Lora Anne Viola, and Michael Zürn (eds), *Historical Institutionalism and International Relations: Explaining Institutional Development in World Politics* (OUP 2016).

[4] With reference to the ECtHR, *Tinnelly & Sons Ltd v United Kingdom* App no 62/1997/846/1052–53 (ECtHR, 10 July 1998); ECtHR, *Stratégies et Communications et Dumoulin v Belgium* App no 37370/97 (ECtHR, 15 July 2002).

[5] Krisch and Yildiz, this volume.

conclusively determined by the law, unaffected by ideological currents and, well, context.

But what is that context? For the editors, it is politics. But what then is politics? In the present contribution, I continue to probe difficulties that arise from putting international law in relation to broader contexts generally, be it political or otherwise. I take contexts to be composed of structures and actions that stand in a co-constitutive relationship. Structures are formed through the actions they stabilize or, the other way around, actors shape the structures that condition them.[6] Depending on particular theoretical traditions, other concepts for context could be system or field.[7] Those parallel traditions understand, as I also do, law as one such system or field. Just as politics is a context for law, law then is a context for politics. For law to be context, it needs to enjoy some relative autonomy from other contexts without being independent of them. A good way of understanding this relative autonomy is to see whether the law offers plausible reasons for its interpretation and development—a point that I will develop more fully.[8] These thoughts come together in thinking of international law as a practice, combining structural conditions with action and a sense for law's relative autonomy.[9]

To further think through how legal change relates to contexts, I build on work that explores contingency in international legal developments. *What was the path not taken?* This will be shown to be a productive question because it advocates for law's non-reductive contextualization. Contingency, I will continue to argue, marks the field of possibility, bordering on necessity on one side and chance on the other. What was possible within contexts and under circumstances as they stood? As the present volume's editors spell out further, international law certainly depends on politics.[10] While there are important variations in how to understand the political context, as the editors also detail, a traditionally important way is to turn to sovereign states and their will. Now, in a crucial passage of his legal philosophy, GWF Hegel writes that international law is 'tainted by contingency' because it 'always depends on particular sovereign wills'.[11] That may be so, but it only expresses

[6] See Anthony Giddens, *Central Problems in Social Theory. Action, Structure and Contradiction in Social Analysis* (Macmillan 1979); Pierre Bourdieu and Loïc JD Wacquant, *An Invitation to Reflexive Sociology* (University of Chicago Press 1992).

[7] See, respectively, Niklas Luhmann, *Law as a Social System* (OUP 2004); Pierre Bourdieu, 'The Force of Law: Toward a Sociology of the Juridical Field' (1987) 38 Hastings Law Journal 814.

[8] I will expand on this concept in section 3.1. For a circumspect discussion of how to conceive such relative autonomy, see Christopher Tomlins, 'How Autonomous Is Law?' (2007) 3 Annual Review of Law and Social Science 45. From the many specific accounts on this point, see in particular Gunther Teubner, *Recht als Autopoietisches System* (Suhrkamp 1989); Bourdieu (n 7); Yves Dezalay and Mikael Rask Madsen, 'The Force of Law and Lawyers: Pierre Bourdieu and the Reflexive Sociology of Law' (2012) 8 Annual Review of Law and Social Science 433.

[9] Tanja E Aalberts and Ingo Venzke, 'Moving Beyond Interdisciplinary Turf Wars: Towards an Understanding of International Law as Practice' in Jean d'Aspremont and others (eds), *International Law as a Profession* (OUP 2017) 287–310.

[10] Krisch and Yildiz, this volume.

[11] GWF Hegel, *Elements of the Philosophy of Right* (HB Nisbet tr, CUP 1991) 368, §333.

a relationship of dependence, not of possibility, unless the inquiry extends into the uncertainties of sovereign will. Could sovereign wills have been different? Why weren't they? In the German original, Hegel does not write of contingency (*Kontingenz*), but of *Zufälligkeit*, whose literal translation is 'coincidence', which is something quite different.[12] Exploring the contingency of international legal developments notably moves on from describing a relationship of dependence on other contexts, which it takes for granted, to ask about alternative possibilities under conditioning contexts. It is thus able to recognize law's relative autonomy, as opposed to just stipulating its rather obvious dependence.

I will continue by situating the question of contingency in the path of international law in response to idealist and realist accounts of legal change, and in reaction to difficulties that Third World Approaches to International Law (TWAIL) encountered when they turned to the possibilities of a different law (section 2). I will then focus on the drive to contextualize legal developments under the impact of political as well as legal realism and the challenges that arise in the practice of doing so (section 3). I then push back against that drive to contextualize legal developments, arguing that such developments not only tend to escape contexts, but that it is often far from clear what counts as context, and what to make of it (section 4). Each section thereby allows me to develop a key concept of my contribution. Whereas section 2 clarifies the notion of *contingency*, section 3 unfolds the idea of law's relative *autonomy*. That idea of autonomy connects, in short, to a distinct mode of justification and to the argument that the law seems to have its own causes that are equally significant as those that realist accounts see at work. Section 4 then expands on the understanding of legal *change* as a shift in argumentative burdens regarding claims about what is (il)legal, encompassing the change in legal reasons for future change. The section continues by asking what would make a difference. What would possibly be *path-breaking*? Is it not that political or economic structures ultimately catch up, and any moment of contingency in law's development flattens out in the long run? While occasionally compelling, I argue that such a view tends to overstate the determinacy of other contexts and underrate the law's side in its co-constitution of other contexts, including the political. But even then, a sense for legal paths not taken gets lost in *ex-post* rationalizations and narrative storytelling. The concluding section 5 returns to the question of what counts as law's context once more. The fundamental choice seems obvious—or is it? Why politics? Or what kind?

[12] GWF Hegel, *Grundlinien der Philosophie des Rechts*, Werke, vol 7 (Suhrkamp 1986) 500 §333: 'Die *Kantische* Vorstellung eines ewigen Friedens durch einen Staatenbund … setzt die *Einstimmigkeit* der Staaten voraus, welche auf moralischen, religiösen oder welchen Gründen und Rücksichten, überaupt immer auf besonderen souveränen Willen beruhe und dadurch mit Zufälligkeit behaftet bliebe.' Especially within the realm of English-language literature, contingency sometimes slides into the concept of chance. In other languages I read it is not possible to say, as is perfectly fine in English, that something is 'contingent on' something else, which only expresses a relationship of dependence but says nothing about possibilities.

2. Situating Contingency

Whereas the development of international law is viewed as a progressive unfolding in an *idealist* tradition, a *realist* tradition sees it as a mirror image of power politics. While the former is unconcerned with conditioning contexts, the latter has little patience for formal legal reasoning or claims about law's relative autonomy. Granted, this classic dichotomy has been under pressure. It still reverberates in contemporary debates, however. The contingency of international law has not been an issue for either side, neither for idealists who have embraced a strong teleology, nor for realists who reduced the law to its context of power politics. Taking their cues from political and legal realism, TWAIL scholars then turned to the history of international law not only to deride the law as an instrument of domination, but also to ask about possibilities for its change. They were thus pulled in opposite directions. The stronger their critique of international law as a handmaiden of the powerful, the weaker their claim that the law could change for the better, and vice versa. That is the uptake of situating contingency in international law's development: it demands law's utter contextualization while asking what else was possible within any broader context (C.).

2.1 Idealism

Many accounts of legal change have embraced a strong teleology rooted in religion, rationality, and in beliefs of progress.[13] When legal positivism emerged in the seventeenth century, it ran parallel, but never truly replaced, natural law theories. While, in short, the latter had come to understand the law as given to man, the former has held that law is man-made, subject to changing earthly conditions and political choices.[14] But natural law thinking notably lived on in cross-cutting background assumptions about the inherent rationality of the international legal order and its developments. Even if legal developments were related to historical conditions and concrete practices, it was in the form of an unfolding without relevant actors that would have come with particular interests. Following Samuel Moyn, many modern thinkers seem to 'have done little more than update Leibniz's old

[13] On the religious traces in the notion of progress and its derivative, (sustainable) development, see Thomas Skouteris, *The Notion of Progress in International Law Discourse* (Asser 2010); Jacobus A Du Pisani, 'Sustainable Development—Historical Roots of the Concept' (2006) 3 Environmental Sciences 83.

[14] The work of Hugo Grotius stands out as a bridge between the two approaches and shows that the contrast between them should not be overstated. See also Janne E Nijman, 'Grotius' Imago Dei Anthropology: Grounding Ius Naturae et Gentium' in Martti Koskenniemi, Mónica García-Salmones Rovira, and Paolo Amorosa (eds), *International Law and Religion: Historical and Contemporary Perspectives* (OUP 2017).

providentialist view that there is a hidden plan of nature, a cunning of reason, or a history working behind the backs of men, even if God did not author it'.[15]

The influential nineteenth-century Austrian public lawyer Georg Jellinek, for instance, rejected all bases for international law other than the free will of sovereign states. At the same time, however, he saw the law as an expression—objective, rational, and historically situated—of 'European civilized nations' (*Europäische Kulturvölker*).[16] For him, legal developments were those of a continuous, progressive realization of what European civilized nations required. Those nations did not appear, however, as actors with interests, but rather as mediaries of humanity. Such a strong teleology may well have been the common denominator for histories of international law into the twentieth century and beyond. It pictures international law, as Martti Koskenniemi put it, 'as the transformation of humankind's collective experience into a redemptive future'.[17] Even if they became less overt in their Eurocentric and colonialist outlook, later accounts have continued to depict legal change above all as a progressive realization of the will of the international community or the consciousness of humanity as a whole, writing the law's history as a long arch that ultimately bends towards justice.[18]

No plausible theory has survived concerning laws of history that would compel international law down a set path towards a singular future. And yet, several historical renderings continue to be marked by assumptions about a certain teleology, be it inherent in international law generally, or in specific legal doctrines. Since the work of Hugo Grotius, scholars have combined those assumptions with a commitment to positivism. The recent book on *Global Constitutionalism and the Path of International Law* is one case in point—committed to positivism, rejecting both utopianism (idealism) and scepticism (realism), it confidently posits that 'international law is continuously evolving from a modest arrangement to sophisticated institutionalism at its core', and it is quite certain in reading concrete legal developments as an embodiment of this process.[19] While such thinking is arguably most common among international lawyers, it is not alien to adjacent disciplines either. At least some accounts in international relations scholarship bear such an imprint,

[15] Samuel Moyn, 'From Situated Freedom to Plausible Worlds' in Venzke and Heller, *Contingency in International Law* (n 3) 515, 518.

[16] Georg Jellinek, *Allgemeine Staatslehre* (Häring 1914); see Jochen von Bernstorff, 'International Legal Scholarship as a Cooling Medium in International Law and Politics' (2014) 25 European Journal of International Law 977. Others are similar to Jellineck, such as Ernest Nys, *Les origines du droit international* (Castaignes Bruxelles 1894); see
Martti Koskenniemi, 'A History of International Law Histories' in Bardo Fassbender, Anne Peters, and Simone Peter (eds), *Oxford Handbook of the History of International Law* (OUP 2012) 943–70, 943.

[17] Koskenniemi, 'A History of International Law Histories' (n 16) 944.

[18] For a critical appraisal, see Thomas Skouteris, *The Notion of Progress in International Law Discourse* (Asser 2010); Sundhya Pahuja, *Decolonising International Law: Development, Economic Growth and the Politics of Universality* (CUP 2011) 117.

[19] Surendra R Bhandari, *Global Constitutionalism and the Path of International Law: Transformation of Law and State in the Globalized World* (Brill 2016), citation at 309.

especially under the impact of the buoyant 1990s. Those who have pictured the establishment of the International Criminal Court (ICC) as the pinnacle in the process of international constitutionalization may serve as a case in point.[20] Wayne Sandholtz has been more careful in his analysis of how norms change but has still linked that change to 'foundational metanorms of international society … that are at the core of *the* liberal Western tradition which is increasingly globalized'.[21] Contingency has been a non-issue. The possibility of alternative paths has not been denied, but if those paths existed, then only as aberrations.[22]

2.2 Realism

Legal and political realists have mounted convincing challenges to claims about the law's inherent rationality and the logics that drive the law's progression. At the turn of the twentieth century, Oliver Wendell Holmes' *The Path of Law* set out the programme of a social scientific study of the law, centred on what institutions with authority are likely to do. To Felix Cohen, abstract formal reasoning was *Transcendental Nonsense*.[23] Like others, they argued in the national setting of the US legal system.[24] Regarding international law, political rather than legal realists moved first. On the brink of the Second World War, EH Carr set out his masterful critique of utopian thinking to expose the 'real basis of the professedly abstract principles commonly invoked in international politics'.[25] He did not deny that actors also pursue normative principles but averred that those principles are typically reflections of self-interest.

After the War, émigré Hans Morgenthau set up the agenda of international relations scholarship in opposition to law and with a loud claim to social-scientific objectivity. In his well-known view, 'politics, like society in general, is governed by objective laws that have their roots in human nature'.[26] 'International Politics, like

[20] For a critical discussion see Theresa Reinold, 'Constitutionalization? Whose Constitutionalization? Africa's Ambivalent Engagement with the International Criminal Court' (2012) 10 International Journal of Constitutional Law 1076.

[21] Wayne Sandholtz, *Prohibiting Plunder: How Norms Change* (OUP 2007) 21 and 270.

[22] Geoff Gordon, 'The Time of Contingency in International Law' in Venzke and Heller, *Contingency in International Law* (n 3) 162–75.

[23] Oliver Wendell Holmes, 'The Path of Law' (1897) 10 Harvard Law Review 457. See also, in particular, Roscoe Pound, 'Philosophical Theory and International Law' (1923) 1 Bibliotheca Visseriana 71; Felix S Cohen, 'Transcendental Nonsense and the Functional Approach' (1935) 35 Columbia Law Review 809.

[24] They were, however, deeply influenced by the free-law movement (*Freirechtsschule*), see Rudolph von Jhering, *The Struggle for Law* (1915); Eugen Ehrlich, *Grundlegung der Soziologie des Rechts* (1913). On the fact of influence, see James E Herget and Stephen Wallace, 'The German Free Law Movement as the Source of American Realism' (1987) 73 Virginia Law Review 399.

[25] Edward Hallett Carr, *The Twenty Years' Crisis 1919–1939: An Introduction to the Study of International Relations* (HarperCollins 1946) 87

[26] Hans J Morgenthau, *Politics Among Nations* (6th edn, Peking University Press 2004) 4. In further detail, see Aalberts and Venzke (n 9). Morgenthau's anthropological foundation of realism was soon

all politics, is a struggle for power', he notably continued.[27] Invocations of international law could not bear on state actions, lest they were in sync with the prevailing balance of power. International law was deemed to depend on changing political conditions and bargains to be struck under them. It was reduced to that context with little, if any, autonomy of its own. In the following, I sidestep many of the further developments that political and legal realism has undergone since then, choosing instead to focus on drawing out three main implications for thinking about international legal change.

A first legacy of realist views has been to turn away from the law as a system of rules to instances of practice, to collecting diplomatic acts, treaties, and case law. That was the spirit of Arthur Nussbaum's influential *Concise History of the Law of Nations*, which notably warned against 'the deflecting influence of ideologies and hope'.[28] International law would change to the extent the repository of practice changed. That is as straightforward as it is dissatisfying. Whereas idealist accounts were marked by an overbearing teleology, chronicles of practice had no sense of direction.[29]

A second legacy has then been to write the history of international law as a succession of epochs marked by leading powers. Inspired by Carl Schmitt, who had embraced political realism in a historiographic apology of Nazi geopolitics in his *Nomos of the Earth*,[30] Wilhelm Grewes' *Epochs of International Law* offered an influential account in that vein, where the dominance of one power marks each passing legal epoch.[31] Just as idealists would not espouse a necessitarian view of the law, neither would realists. But they did not have a sense of international law's contingency either or in any event did not convey it. Saying that the law would have been different if states had acted differently under different power relations only proves the point. Such a claim only posits, like Hegel above, a relationship of dependence. But was there any possibility of a different law under the power relations as they prevailed?

The third implication of realism comes with a critical twist and leads to the necessity of providing precisely such an account of contingency. Third World

paralleled by structural reasons, see especially Kenneth N Waltz, *Man, the State, and War. A Theoretical Analysis* (Columbia University Press 1959).

27 Morgenthau, *Politics Among Nations* (n 26) 31.

28 See Koskenniemi, 'A History of International Law Histories' (n 16) 960. cf Nehal Bhuta, 'A Thousand Flowers Blooming, or the Desert of the Real? International Law and its Many Problems of History' (manuscript on file with the author, 2021).

29 cf Walter Benjamin, 'Über den Begriff der Geschichte (1940)' in *Gesammelte Schriften*, vols 1 and 2 (Suhrkamp 1974) 694 (Thesis III).

30 Carl Schmitt, *Der Nomos der Erde im Völkerrecht des Jus Publicum Europaeum* (Greven 1950); in English: Carl Schmitt, *The Nomos of the Earth* (Telos Press 2003).

31 Wilhelm G Grewe, *Epochen er Völkerrechtsgeschichte* (Nomos 1984); in English: Wilhelm G Grewe, *The Epochs of International Law* (Michael Byres tr, de Gruyter 2000); For a critical discussion, see also Nico Krisch, 'International Law in Times of Hegemony: Unequal Power and the Shaping of the International Legal Order' (2005) 16 European Journal of International Law 369.

Approaches to International Law have pioneered historical work in international law from a critically realist perspective.[32] They adopt a realist approach in rejecting assumptions about international law's gradual unfolding to serve the values of humanity—primarily because it seemed that the Third World was not included in that vision of humanity. They have been strong in exposing the many false universals in Eurocentric scholarship and practice.[33] By highlighting the practices of colonialism, TWAIL scholars have not only exposed the violence vested in international law, or in any event legitimized by it. They have also viewed colonialism as a transformative context, giving agency to both colonized and 'semi-peripheral' states.[34] Similarly, decolonization is depicted as a process of potentially universalizing international law, but primarily as a force that transforms it.[35] While realist in their outlook, however, few TWAIL scholars would give up on international law as an instrument of potential emancipation—not through the law as it stood, nor as it actually developed, but through law as they imagined that it could be.[36]

They thus had to think hard about the change they wanted to see simply because it would not come naturally. As much as they derided international law as a tool of subjugation and exploitation, they believed in its emancipatory potential because, to them, the law was also more than an expression of power-political contexts.[37] While they understood legal change against the background of other contexts, especially of economic structures and action, they recognized law's relative autonomy. They also held a concrete view on necessary agency. They argued that the change that they wanted to see should be brought about by the UN General Assembly, where decolonization had shifted majorities.[38] Perhaps TWAIL's first

[32] James Thuo Gathii, 'The Agenda of Third World Approaches to International Law (TWAIL)' in Jeffrey Dunoff and Mark Pollack (eds), *International Legal Theory: Foundations and Frontiers* (CUP 2022). cf Genevieve Painter, 'Contingency in International Legal History: Why Now?' in Venzke and Heller, *Contingency in International Law* (n 3) 44–59, 49.

[33] Gathii (n 32); BS Chimni, 'Third World Approaches to International Law: A Manifesto' (2006) 8 International Community Law Review 3–27. cf Martti Koskenniemi, 'Histories of International Law: Dealing with Eurocentrism' (2011) 19 Rechtsgeschichte 152–76, 175, TWAIL has pushed the realization that 'Europe, too, is just a continent with its particular interests and neurosis, wisdom and stupidity'.

[34] See Mohsen Al-Attar, 'Subverting Eurocentric Epistemology: The Value of Nonsense When Designing Counterfactuals' in Venzke and Heller, *Contingency in International Law* (n 3) 145–61.

[35] Anthony Anghie, 'Finding the Peripheries: Sovereignty and Colonialism in Nineteenth-Century International Law' (1999) 40 Harvard International Law Journal 1; Antony Anghie, *Imperialism, Sovereignty, and the Making of International Law* (CUP 2005); Arnulf Becker Lorca, *Mestizo International Law: A Global Intellectual History 1842–1933* (CUP 2014).

[36] See eg Makau W Mutua, 'What is TWAIL?' (2000) 94 American Society of International Law Proceedings 31–38; Mohammed Bedjaoui, *Towards a New International Economic Order* (UNESCO 1979). This may be a truism, however, since the statement relates to 'Third World Approaches to International Law'—where an outright rejection of international law may indeed be hard to find. There may be a wider bias because it is easier, surely for international lawyers, to identify those who have engaged with international law rather than argued against it entirely. Painter thus counsels caution: 'Let us not forget the places and the human and non-human lives that would rather be emancipated from international law than emancipated through it.' Painter (n 32) at 59.

[37] eg Bedjaoui (n 36).

[38] Bin Cheng, 'United Nations Resolutions on Outer Space: "Instant" International Customary Law?' (1965) 5 Indian Journal of International Law 23.

generation offered an account of international legal change that, in its take on the past and then open future, was overly optimistic. Its turn to history, in any case, has been eye-opening, as it reveals legal change as it should be seen: within the intricate dynamics of situated actors who utilize international law to advance their interests and convictions.

Later generations of TWAIL continued this trajectory but were less pronounced or less hopeful in their take on legal change. It was next to inevitable: the stronger their critique of international law as a tool of relentless domination, the less compelling would be their claims about possibly emancipatory change. If the law did change, then it was deemed superficial, only to update its categories and rules to better serve structural conditions of domination under evolving circumstances.[39] TWAIL scholarship has thus run into thinking hard about contingency in international law, as it has catered to the critical sensibilities both of wanting to show the possibilities of a different law as well as the determining forces that have driven the law down one path rather than another.[40] While both critical sensibilities may point in opposite directions, they are both crucial to keep inquiries about the possibilities of legal change on the terrain of contingency, situated precisely between necessity on one side and chance on the other, without collapsing into either.

2.3 Contingency

Thinking through contingencies in the path of international law probes what else could have happened within 'given' contexts.[41] It bears repeating that I understand contingency to mark the field of what is possible, bordering on necessity, on one side, and chance on the other. It is a modality that does not depend on what actually happens (*vel non*). Whatever happened, while possible, did not become necessary only because it happened.[42] What *is* could also *not be*. Likewise, something is not impossible only because it did not happen. It already merits emphasis, moreover, that contingency and necessity are modalities that are not inherent properties of any development. They are instead formed through experiences and expectations, as well as narrative emplotment, as I will continue to argue in section 4.[43]

In agreement with the present volume's framework, this setup of contingency ties the possibilities of legal change to different actions.[44] It is not unlike Marx who

[39] See the discussion in Al-Attar (n 34).

[40] Yemima Ben-Menahem, 'Historical Necessity and Contingency' in Aviezer Tucker (ed), *A Companion to the Philosophy of History and Historiography* (Blackwell 2009) 120.

[41] For the moment, I will set aside the assumption that contexts are never 'given', i.e. that the circumstances or conditions in which events take place are not fixed or predetermined, see section 4.

[42] Niklas Luhmann, *Kontingenz und Recht* (Suhrkamp 2013) 32–33.

[43] Luhmann (n 42) 44; Hayden White, *Metahistory: The Historical Imagination in Nineteenth Century Europe* (Johns Hopkins University Press 1973) 283.

[44] Introduction, in this volume at *9, stating that the pathways of change are actor-centric; see also the restatement in the conclusion, at *18.

spoke of co-constitutive structures and actors *avant la lettre* thus: '[m]en make their own history, but they do not make it just as they please; they do not make it under circumstances chosen by themselves, but under circumstances directly encountered, given and transmitted from the past.'[45] Thinking about contingency should be able to cover a lot of common ground.[46] And yet, it has occasionally been the victim of spats between those who want to defend spheres of freedom to act differently and others who challenged the overemphasis of seemingly free-floating actors in support of structural understandings for why things turned out the way they did.[47]

Understanding what else could have happened and what did happen, however, are two sides of the same coin.[48] Only with a keen sense of why things turned out the way they did is it possible to argue about how they could have turned out differently. Both sides of the coin in fact require each other across academic disciplines and theoretical traditions.[49] Nothing is per se novel or controversial about this claim. Still, thinking through the possibility of paths not taken is something that continues to linger in the background. Counterfactuals are often not made explicit or lack plausibility.[50]

While Steininger and von Bernstorff note that the legal changes they examined were contingent, the law's contextualization also revealed why the law developed the way it did. Their example illustrates a general point: the more one looks for contingency, the more it slips away, as Michele Tedescini put it.[51] Or as Genevieve Painter argues, contextualizing the law puts in motion a line of argument that is bound to find the law's fateful determination in that context.[52] Behind every possibility of a different law, a different trajectory of change, stand reasons that have compelled the law down one path rather than another. One question that stands out when putting the search for contingency into practice is thus when to stop looking for the next underlying reason—late enough, I submit, not to exaggerate possibilities that did not exist and early enough not to reduce all actions to

[45] Karl Marx, *The Eighteenth Brumaire of Louis Bonaparte* (Progress Publishers 1934) 10.

[46] Allan Megill, 'History's Unresolving Tensions: Reality and Implications' (2019) 23 Rethinking History 279.

[47] One of the most notorious targets for that latter critique is Niall Ferguson, *Virtual History: Alternatives and Counterfactuals* (Basic Books 1999). On the formative debate between EH Carr and Isaiah Berlin, see Susan Marks, 'False Contingency' (2009) 62 Current Legal Problems 1; Ingo Venzke, 'Situating Contingency in the Path of International Law' in Venzke and Heller, *Contingency in International Law* (n 3) 3–20.

[48] Aviezer Tucker, *Our Knowledge of the Past* (CUP 2004) 226.

[49] James D Fearon, 'Counterfactuals and Hypothesis Testing in Political Science' (1991) 43 World Politics 169; Philip E Tetlock and Richard Ned Lebow, 'Poking Counterfactual Holes in Covering Laws: Cognitive Styles and Historical Reasoning' (2001) 95 American Political Science Review 829; Tucker (n 48).

[50] Fearon (n 49).

[51] Michele Tedeschini, 'Historical Base and Legal Superstructure: Reading Contingency and Necessity in the *Tadic* Challenge' in Venzke and Heller, *Contingency in International Law* (n 3) 129–44.

[52] Painter (n 32).

a necessary expression of their context.[53] This is nothing other than the domain of history *tout court*: it does not stop asking why something happened until it is adequately explained, nor does it deny the possibilities of different action. For Reinhart Koselleck, inquiries into historical causation are in this way anthropologically centred:

> The historical facts of the past, as well as those of the future, are possibilities that either have been or can be realized and which preclude compelling necessity. Facts remain contingent, however much they can be grounded; they arise in the space of human freedom.[54]

Inquiring into the determining forces that ground all action does not lead towards necessitarian views of history, nor does probing alternative possibilities slide into chance. Historiography only makes sense on the presumption of contingency.[55] All that would otherwise be left to do would be to vindicate the laws of history (for which, once more, no plausible theory has survived), or to chronicle events while resigning oneself to the apparent incapacity to learn anything about them. This is what I see as the present volume's main aim: to provide a comprehensive explanation of the path of international law adequately, and as its main challenge, to do so without glossing over the possibility of paths not taken.

3. Law's Autonomy and Reasons for Change

The drive to contextualize legal developments, while per se uncontroversial, stumbles on difficulties when put into practice. How to contextualize legal change without reducing it to context, political or otherwise? And why not reduce it to its context? I have suggested that such a reduction would be, curiously enough, unrealistic as it would fail to account for the law's relative autonomy. Granted, law's relative autonomy is not a given. There are instances where the law may encounter its fateful determination within its context, essentially implying that, in that particular moment, the law lacks autonomy or normativity (A.).[56] But more often than

[53] cf Martti Koskenniemi, 'Histories of International Law: Significance and Problems for a Critical View' (2013) 27 Temple International and Comparative Law Journal 215–40.

[54] Reinhart Koselleck, *Futures Past: On the Semantics of Historical Time* (Columbia University Press 2004) 127. cf EH Carr *What Is History?* (Penguin 1982) 95, who makes the analogy between historical determination and causes of a crime: 'It would not, I feel sure, occur to any of those engaged in investigating the causes of crime to suppose that this committed them to a denial of the moral responsibility of the criminal.'

[55] See also Allan Megill, 'History's Unresolving Tensions: Reality and Implications' (2019) 23 Rethinking History 279.

[56] cf Koskenniemi, 'Histories of International Law' (n 53) 216, arguing that the law, as a normative phenomenon, cannot just be reduced to its context. See, more generally, Christoph Möllers, *Die Möglichkeit der Normen—Über eine Praxis jenseits von Moralität und Kausalität* (Suhrkamp 2016).

not, the law has a degree of relative autonomy, which means that legal reasons have to be treated as no less real than those arising from other, non-legal contexts (B.). Legal reasons can and often do matter as causes for legal decisions and developments (C.).

3.1 Legal Reasoning

Law's relative autonomy is more than a legal scholar's dogma. It is rooted in a variety of sociological traditions and related socio-legal theories.[57] Karl Marx, who is often portrayed as levelling the strongest critique of law's autonomy, supposedly relegating it to the ephemeral sphere of superstructure, in fact leaves space for it and even defends it.[58] At least parts of his oeuvre read as foreshadowing the now well-received proposition that law and society stand in a co-constitutive relationship.[59] In other words, the law is part of the societal conditions that shape it. The law bears on and is part of prevailing structures and conditions of action. Practically, this means that the law offers reasons that contribute to understanding legal decisions and legal change, especially those that pass through practices of interpretation.

A good way to understand law's relative autonomy relates to legal reasoning's distinct mode of justification and the social positions of particular actors in the field. There are some things that can and cannot be said in the operational legal discourse—boundaries that are loosely set by the rules of interpretation.[60] Moreover, interpreters enjoy different degrees of authority. The role of international courts and tribunals in shaping the legal discourse continues to stand out.[61] Their importance for law's relative autonomy also becomes clear when they are absent. But does this argument in support of law's relative autonomy not run into the critique of political and legal realists who revert to underlying power relations and discard formal legal reasoning as nothing but hollow words?

This question is crucial. It rightly locates questions about the context of legal change in concrete legal practice. Approaching the question requires a brief

[57] See eg Luhmann, *Law as a Social System* (n 7); Bourdieu (n 7).

[58] See Umut Özsu, 'The Necessity of Contingency: Method and Marxism in International Law' in Venzke and Heller, *Contingency in International Law* (n 3) 60–76; Marks (n 47); Grigory I Tunkin, 'Co-existence and International Law' (1958) 95 Collected Courses 1, 47: 'different elements of superstructure mutually influence each other and they also influence the development of the economic structure itself.'

[59] See, for a discussion of such readings, in particular EP Thompson, see Tomlins, 'How Autonomous Is Law?' (n 8) 50–52.

[60] In further detail, Ingo Venzke, *How Interpretation Makes International Law: On Semantic Change and Normative Twists* (OUP 2012) 46–57.

[61] On that judicial authority, see Armin von Bogdandy and Ingo Venzke, 'In Whose Name? An Investigation of International Courts' Public Authority and Its Democratic Justification' (2012) 23 European Journal of International Law 7.

diversion into issues of legal reasoning and interpretation,[62] only to then link them back to understandings of contingency in international legal developments more generally. Cutting through a variety of different approaches, I will focus on the challenges of legal realism. There are many debates in legal theory and practice about how to justify a claim about what is (il)legal. How to support claims about what the law is, what counts as a (right) source, and what counts as a (right) interpretation? At the same time, also those who have been invested in such debates recognize that, in practice, pragmatic considerations of how to win an argument prevail. This is not only the case for legal counsel but also for scholars and judges.[63] Already for Hersch Lauterpacht the mode of interpretation was not the determining cause of judicial decision, but the form in which the judge cloaks the results arrived at by other means.[64] Philip Jessup also wrote as much back in his canonic 1966 dissent, in which he critiqued the formalism of the International Court of Justice (ICJ) at great length while granting that interpretative arguments provide 'a cloak for a conclusion reached in other ways and not a guide to a correct conclusion'.[65]

Those who use and lay claims to the law are, as TWAIL scholars and others have carved out, invested in a struggle in which they seek to align the law with their interests or convictions—actors with interests or 'people with projects'.[66] Interpreters seek to pull the law onto their side. More often than not, justifications for one rather than another interpretation, and claims about how to justify interpretations, are subordinate to the goal of winning the argument. One might then wonder what is really going on below the surface of legal arguments.

[62] I understand *interpretation* as an argumentative practice in which reasons are offered to rationally motivate others. For present purposes, I can thus use interpretation interchangeably with *reasoning* or *arguing*. In the remainder of this section, I will still respond to the realist challenge that reasons are better discarded as rhetoric or violence. In further detail, see Ingo Venzke, 'The Practice of Interpretation in International Law: Strategies of Critique' in Dunoff and Pollack (eds) (n 32)). Also Iain Scobbie, 'Rhetoric, Persuasion, and Interpretation in International Law' in Andrea Bianchi and others (eds), *Interpretation in International Law* (OUP 2015) 61–77.

[63] Martti Koskenniemi, 'Between Commitment and Cynicism. Outline for a Theory of International Law as Practice' in *Collection of Essays by Legal Advisers of States, Legal Advisers of International Organizations and Practitioners in the Field of International Law* (United Nations 1999) 495.

[64] Hersch Lauterpacht, Restrictive Interpretation and the Principle of Effectiveness in the Interpretation of Treaties, 26 British Yearbook of International Law 48, 53 (1949).

[65] *South West Africa* (*Ethiopia v South Africa; Liberia v South Africa*) (Second Phase, Judgment) [1966] ICJ Rep 6 [355] (July 18) (dissenting opinion by Jessup).

[66] cf David Kennedy, *A World of Struggle: How Power, Law and Expertise Shape Global Political Economy* (Princeton University Press 2016); Susan Marks and Andrew Lang, 'People with Projects: Writing the Lives of International Lawyers' (2014) 27 Temple International and Comparative Law Journal 437.

3.2 Real Reasons

Even if actors were driven by the sincere conviction of making true, right, or just claims about the law, their claims are bound to remain partial.[67] This is one lasting lesson of much political and legal realism. While the categorical rejection of universal positions would be as unconvincing as their affirmation, no actor can escape their context, time, and space. In a debate about the laws of war, for example, it is clear that '[n]o one, after all, experiences the death of her husband or sister as humanitarian and proportional'.[68] Suggesting that the widow is biased and irrational for not agreeing with the claim that her husband's killing was legal would only add insult to injury. And even if, with shaky confidence, one were to abstract from the perspective of the widow, it is still hard to deny that interpretative claims stand under the spell of everyone's situatedness. That is also the case for judges, who are only human, including those on the bench of the ECtHR who expanded the rights of corporations in sync with the rising tides of neoliberalism. In a classically critical spirit, such a contextualization can possibly work towards greater awareness and reflexivity,[69] enabling inquiries into the socially constructed consciousness of actors.[70] What were they thinking?

Considerations of what is (il)legal expresses *social* beliefs. That is what the concepts of epistemic and interpretative communities want to capture. As such, the concepts have purchase. How else should the divide be understood between military and humanitarian lawyers when it comes to what they respectively call the laws of war or humanitarian law?[71] For understandings of legal change, locating interpretative practice within communities draws out constraints that bear on all action and, as the editors' framework has also highlighted, conditions for the reception of any interpretative claim.[72]

This take on the reality of legal practice and, by extension, factors that explain legal change or stasis are revealing and yet problematic. The reasons that actors offer in support of their claims about the law tend to fall off the radar.[73] That is most evident for understandings that resort to the concept of interpretative communities

[67] Outi Korhonen, 'New International Law: Silence, Defence of Deliverance?' (1996) 7 European Journal of International Law 1.

[68] Kennedy, *A World of Struggle* (n 66) 275.

[69] Isabel Feichtner, 'Critical Scholarship and Responsible Practice of International Law. How Can the Two be Reconciled?' (2016) 29 Leiden Journal of International Law 979; Sundhya Pahuja, 'Laws of Encounter: A Jurisdictional Account of International Law' (2013) 1 London Review of International Law 63.

[70] David Kennedy, 'The Turn to Interpretation' (1985) 58 Southern California Law Review 251, 255 .

[71] David Luban, 'Military Necessity and the Cultures of Military Law' (2013) 26 Leiden Journal of International Law 315; cf Stephan W Schill, 'Crafting the International Economic Order: The Public Function of Investment Treaty Arbitration and Its Significance for the Role of the Arbitrator' (2010) 23 Leiden Journal of International Law 401, 430.

[72] Krisch and Yildiz, this volume.

[73] cf Jan Klabbers, 'The Relative Autonomy of International Law, or the Forgotten Politics of Interdisciplinarity' (2005) 1 Journal of International Law and International Relations 35.

within which arguments are accepted if they resonate with the interpretive angles that a specific community shares.[74] That the community shares such an angle is a premise, not the result of arguments about the law. If the interpretative angle defines the community, what happens between communities other than brute competition? Between communities, it seems, international law is silent. International legal change would have to connect to changes in interpretative angles or to the balance of power not between nations but between interpretative communities.[75]

Realist schools of thought in international relations, via Morgenthau and onwards, have held that self-interest is the unshakable foundation for all action—including claims about the law. Some authors have suggested that arguments are merely cheap rhetoric, capable of offering new information at best, but unlikely to alter an actor's predisposition.[76] Competing constructivist schools of thought have always questioned the foundational role of self-interest. They have drawn attention to interests' social construction and have advanced the position that interests may indeed change through processes of arguing.[77] There really is no good reason for restricting the role of arguments to instrumentalist questions of how to get what we want and not to extend it to questions of what we want in the first place. What actors want is a given for realists at such a level of abstraction—power, wealth, maximizing interests (well, which?)—that it is often practically meaningless. For one, questions that seem instrumental—how to pursue given interests?—then quickly become questions of what actors really want. For another, explanations that turn to self-interest at least occasionally seem to turn in a loop of *ex-post* rationalization where interests are only inferred from the behaviour that they are supposed to explain.

Putting those difficulties aside, it follows from realist critiques that successful claims about what is (il)legal are best understood as an expression of power.[78] But any such claim may just as well meet with something like genuine agreement, or even induce a change in other actors' predispositions, either because they learn how they can better get what they want or what they really want. Realists, in short, claim to get closer to reality, but it is not so clear that they do.

[74] Stanley Fish, *Doing What Comes Naturally* (Duke University Press 1989) 141–42. Disagreement about how to interpret the law is, according to Fish, 'not ... a disagreement that could be settled by the text because what would be in dispute would be the interpretative "angle" from which the text was to be seen, and in being seen, made'.

[75] cf ibid 153, expressing his scepticism of general accounts of change, suggesting that it should be understood in the context of historical reconstruction instead.

[76] eg Jack L Goldsmith and Eric A Posner, *The Limits of International Law* (OUP 2005). The founding father of realism was much more nuanced and would defend the national interest as a point of reference but be less dismissive about the possibility of meaningful legal argument. See Oliver Jütersonke, *Morgenthau, Law and Realism* (CUP 2010).

[77] See, classically, Thomas Risse, 'Let's Argue!': Communicative Action in World Politics' (2000) 54 International Organization 1. See also Nicole Deitelhoff, *Überzeugung in der Politik* (Suhrkamp 2006).

[78] See, in agreement, Gregory Shaffer, 'The New Legal Realist Approach to International Law' (2015) 28 Leiden Journal of International Law 189, 206.

3.3 Which Reality? An Example of Reasons for Change

Why does a claimant who nowadays institutes proceedings at the ICJ need to argue that the respondent was 'aware, or could not have been unaware' of a dispute with the claimant?[79] The ICJ introduced such a jurisdictional requirement with its *Marshall Islands* judgment of 2016. The ICJ's majority of course asserted that there was nothing new about this requirement. The denial of novelty lies in the nature of the game, in the strictures of judicial legitimacy. But the decision did change the law in the sense that it redistributed argumentative burdens, which is clear to see in later legal practice. How to understand this change? What are the reasons for this decision to begin with, and for its reception?

It is not evidently wrong—unreal or surreal—to say that the ICJ, in its majority, declined the exercise of its jurisdiction in *Marshall Islands* due to the formal, legal reason that it found no dispute between the parties since the respondent was not aware (nor could have been) that a dispute existed. Such an understanding of the decision is, however, clearly incomplete. Dissenting judges have lamented how the majority's reasoning all too easily reveals that the real reasons lie elsewhere, certainly not in the existence *vel non* of a dispute. Commentators have for instance pointed out that all judges from nations who possessed nuclear weapons were in the majority that voted against the Court's jurisdiction (affirming the jurisdiction in that case would have put under scrutiny nuclear weapon states' duty to negotiate disarmament).[80] But realist understandings, which place reasons such as the distribution of nuclear weapons and judges' nationality centre stage, are equally partial as they no longer offer a view of legal reasons and of how the law operates.[81] No judge in the majority could justify the decision with a reference to the interest of their country of nationality (and the fact that they possessed nuclear weapons). Just as interpretations in law cut out what cannot be squeezed into the scope of legal reasons, realist approaches cut out an understanding of interpretations as a practice of normative argument.[82] That law is normative is in fact just another way of saying that it has some autonomy.[83]

For the law to function as law it must at least appear to have its own causes—such as the existence of a legal dispute between the parties as a condition for the ICJ's jurisdiction. And in order to succeed in law, actors need to argue with those causes to support their interpretations. That, and nothing more or less, is what law's

[79] *Obligations Concerning Negotiations Relating to Cessation of the Nuclear Arms Race and to Nuclear Disarmament* (*Marshall Islands v United Kingdom*) (Preliminary Objections) 5 October 2016, [41].

[80] See Nico Krisch, 'Capitulation in The Hague: The Marshall Islands Cases' (*EJIL Talk!*, 10 October 2016).

[81] Ino Augsberg, 'Some Realism about New Legal Realism: What's New, What's Legal, What's Real?' (2015) 28 Leiden Journal of International Law 457, 462 .

[82] Möllers (n 56) 69; Jürgen Habermas, *Faktizität und Geltung* (Suhrkamp 1992) 436.

[83] cf Natasha Wheatley, 'Law and the Time of Angels: International Law's Method Wars and the Affective Life of Disciplines' (2021) 60 History and Theory 311.

relative autonomy refers to. That this relative autonomy is real—not always, but at least often—has been recognized time and again, for instance by Max Weber when he suggested studying the states of mind of legal practitioners, above all judges, in order to get closer to the reality of the law.[84] Pierre Bourdieu likewise critiqued attempts at understanding a social practice such as legal interpretation through distanced external descriptions that explained those practices without regard for the reasons that the actors themselves have for their action. For him, 'far from being a simple ideological mask, such a rhetoric of autonomy, neutrality, and universality, ... is the expression of the whole operation of the juridical field'.[85] The legal field imposes constraints on the way of arguing that may well be the basis of law's relative autonomy, which, in turn, points to legal causes for change. That is also the case for thinking of legal change and relative autonomy in the tradition of understanding law as a social system.[86]

4. Context All the Way?

4.1 What Makes a Difference?

Even if legal change cannot be reduced to contexts, it is clear that, even within its relatively autonomous operation, the law eventually adapts to, accommodates, and absorbs changing contexts. There is only variation in degrees of autonomy and speeds of adjustment, over time, space, and legal regimes.[87] Several scholars have for example diagnosed shifts in international law in response to an overall rise in authoritarian populism.[88] Asking about paths not taken thus begs the question of what would have made a difference, also in the *longue durée*. Do prevailing political or economic structures not catch up eventually? Different judicial decisions or other instances of practice, even other choices in treaty-making, would often have made little more than a dent in international law's path, bending it into a detour, perhaps. But would they have been path-breaking?

[84] Alf Ross and Scandinavian legal realism made very similar suggestions. See Jakob VH Holtermann and Mikael Rask Madsen, 'European New Legal Realism and International Law: How to Make International Law Intelligible?' (2015) 28 Leiden Journal of International Law 211, 217–19.

[85] Bourdieu (n 7).

[86] Gunther Teubner, *Law as an Autopoietic System* (Blackwell 1993); Luhmann, *Law as a Social System* (n 7), especially ch 6. Also in this tradition, the relative autonomy of the law can of course be broken, so to speak, when it is taken over by political or economic systems; cf Marcelo Neves, 'Grenzen der Autonomie des Rechts in einer asymmetrischen Weltgesellschaft' (2007) 93 Archiv für Rechts- und Sozialphilosophie 363.

[87] Nico Krisch and Ezgi Yildiz, 'The Many Paths of Change in International Law: A Frame' in Nico Krisch and Ezgi Yildiz (eds), *The Many Paths of Change in International Law* (Oxford University Press 2023).

[88] Sandholtz, this volume. If the present is something like a critical juncture, then the outcome might however not be so settled, cf Michael Zürn, *A Theory of Global Governance: Authority, Legitimacy, and Contestation* (OUP 2018).

This has understandably been a hard question and a tall order for several recent contributions probing the contingency of international legal developments. In the examples of ECtHR jurisprudence and the ICJ decision in *Marshall Islands*, decisions might have been different but, as one might have expected, they did align to replicate with prevailing power structures. That is also the case in another example, one that Josef Ostransky offers on legal change in the regime of investment protection. The central arbitral decision to protect foreign investors' legitimate expectations as part of the guarantee of investors' fair and equitable treatment, he argues, was pulled out of thin air.[89] Stronger still, the leading precedent was also contradicted. There is, in short, nothing necessary about the legal developments that ended up corroborating the protection of investors' legitimate expectations. He argues further, however, that if investors' interests had not been accommodated in this way—as part of the guarantee of fair and equitable treatment—they would have been met through resort to other legal doctrines and concepts.[90] Even if the law had looked a bit different, it would essentially have been the same. It would not have made a difference.

What would it take for the law to be different? An obvious answer would be that changes are required in the context on which legal change depends. The pull of contextualization would even suggest that it is the only possible answer, at least in the long run. Prevailing structures—material, ideal, and everything in-between—would eventually catch up. Ostransky thus closes his account by convincingly arguing that real change would only be possible if the underlying political economy were to change.[91] Others have placed emphasis on changes in prevailing narratives, or on cutting across, and thereby irritating and breaking up, particular regime perspectives that otherwise hold the law captive.[92] The present volume's framework is likewise attuned to such 'discursive openings'.[93]

In the end, however, it seems once more that placing legal change in relation to its context sets in motion a line of argument that finds law's fateful determination in that context.[94] Such a conclusion, while often plausible, just as often has shortcomings. First, it underrates the degree of law's autonomy. Secondly, there is a risk

[89] Josef Ostřanský, 'From a Fortuitous Transplant to a Fundamental Principle of Law? The Doctrine of Legitimate Expectations and the Possibilities of a Different Law' in Venzke and Heller, *Contingency in International Law* (n 3) 424–40.

[90] ibid.

[91] ibid.

[92] Amanda Alexander, 'Narrative Contingency and International Humanitarian Law: Crimes against Humanity in Cixin Liu's Post-Humanist Universe' in Venzke and Heller, *Contingency in International Law* (n 3) 349–67; Kathryn Greenman, 'The Law of State Responsibility and the Persistence of Investment Protection' in Venzke and Heller, *Contingency in International Law* (n 3) 389–403, 403, concluding that 'resistance against investor-state arbitration also comes from developed countries and mainstream international investment lawyers but to the extent that such resistance stays within international law's structural biases and fails to work against fragmentation, it is unlikely to effect change'.

[93] Krisch and Yildiz, this volume.

[94] Painter (n 32); Tomlins, 'How Autonomous Is Law?' (n 8); Christopher Tomlins, 'After Critical Legal History: Scope, Scale, Structure' (2012) 8 Annual Review of Law and Social Science 31.

of overstating the degree to which any context is determinative. The indeterminacy of law has been rubbed in,[95] but other contexts may be rather similar in that regard. I have made the first point in section 3 above and now continue by focusing on the second, a reconsideration of the determinacy of law's context or, rather, its *in*determinacy.

4.2 The Indeterminacy of Context

What counts as context and what to make of it is often far from clear. As in the examples of legal change in human rights and investment law, neoliberalism is often a plausible point of reference, enabling compelling critiques of neoliberalism's trenchant operation. But the possibility of alternative legal arrangements tends to get lost.[96] Also under the spell of neoliberalism, the law continues to be ridden with tensions and remains to some degree pliable, not least because it is not so straightforward to ascertain what neoliberalism demands from the law. Struggles on the inside of the law, about what to do with those demands must be part of the story. No context speaks for itself, nor are its boundaries given—questions of what counts as context and how to read it are crucial sites of contingency.

It is for example common to read the 1977 First Additional Protocol (AP I) to the Geneva Conventions against the background context of anti-colonial struggle and the related constellation of power. With a more idealist bent it could be read, especially on account of the International Committee of the Red Cross (ICRC), as expanding the law's humanitarian objectives to new circumstances.[97] AP I notably ended up internationalizing 'armed conflicts in which people fight against colonial domination or alien occupation and against racist regimes in the exercise of their right of self-determination'.[98] As Emma Stone Mackinnon has recently shown, however, that outcome of AP I depended on the lawyers' battle over how to read the background. Neither power politics nor concerns for justice would dictate a specific outcome. Legal positions varied widely, also among those vested in anti-colonial struggles. Mackinnon thus concludes that '[l]aw is not simply determined by its context but is itself a site for argumentation over the meaning of that context'.[99]

[95] See the *loci classici* for international law, David Kennedy, 'Theses about International Law Discourse' (1980) 23 German Yearbook of International Law 353; Martti Koskenniemi, *From Apology to Utopia. The Structure of International Legal Argument* (CUP 2005).

[96] For an insightful account where, however, contingency gets lost, see Quinn Slobodian, *Globalists: The End of Empire and the Birth of Neoliberalism* (Harvard University Press 2018).

[97] Emma S Mackinnon, 'Contingencies of Context: Legacies of the Algerian Revolution in the 1977 Additional Protocols to the Geneva Conventions' in Venzke and Heller, *Contingency in International Law* (n 3) 317–34, at 318, with further references.

[98] Art 1(4) Additional Protocol I to the Geneva Conventions.

[99] Mackinnon (n 97) 320.

Law's relative autonomy, understood as a distinct mode of justification, keeps a distance from other contexts. Of course, determining factors for any decision are broader than overt legal reasons. But those legal reasons, I have already suggested, are in principle no less real.

4.3 *Ex-post* Rationalization and Historical Emplotment

There are three more challenges against which the drive of relating legal change to its context needs to struggle. First are tendencies of *ex-post* rationalization and, second, the difficulties of conveying contingency in an academic text without violating a specific discipline's standards or strictures. Third is the question that one might have expected first, but here it circles back to the beginning: which context—legal change in relation to what?

Social psychologist Baruch Fischhoff placed his pioneering work on the bias of hindsight squarely within discussions about historical methodology, subscribing to the view espoused by the historian Georges Florovsky that:

> [t]he tendency toward determinism is somehow implied in the method of retrospection itself. In retrospect, we seem to perceive the logic of the events which unfold themselves in a regular or linear fashion according to a recognizable pattern with an alleged inner necessity. So that we get the impression that it really could not have happened otherwise.[100]

In the specific domain of law, additional dynamics sustain the appearances of necessity.[101] Roberto Unger has famously blamed 'rationalizing legal analysis' as a mode of argument that creates 'false necessities'.[102] That mode of analysis continues to pervade many accounts of legal developments, especially those developments of the law that are carried along in the practice of adjudication. Similarly, many accounts are outright functionalist as though legal developments were a necessary response to societal challenges—as if economic globalization itself fatefully determined international trade or investment law, for instance. Some such explanations, as that of Ostransky discussed above, can claim considerable plausibility, but they also blend out alternative possibilities, including those alternatives that

[100] Georges Florovsky, 'The Study of the Past' in Ronald H Nash (ed), *Ideas of History*, vol 2 (EP Dutton 1969) 351, 369, quoted in Baruch Fischhoff, 'Hindsight ≠ Foresight: The Effect of Outcome Knowledge on Judgment Under Uncertainty' (1975) 1 Journal of Experimental Psychology: Human Perception and Performance 288, 288.

[101] See Ingo Venzke, 'What If? Counterfactual (Hi)Stories of International Law' (2018) 8 Asian Journal of International Law 403.

[102] Roberto Mangabeira Unger, *What Should Legal Analysis Become?* (Verso 1996) 36; Roberto Mangabeira Unger, *False Necessity: Anti-Necessitarian Social Theory in the Service of Radical Democracy* (Verso 2001); cf Duncan Kennedy, *A Critique of Adjudication* (Harvard University Press 1997) 18.

might have opened up through different understandings of the 'given' context and the challenges it creates. In legal practice, finally, the use of the past is unabashedly instrumental, used in support of claims in the present.[103] The operation of the law benefits significantly from hindsight, and even scholarly analyses conducted from a more distant perspective tend not to undermine this effect. At least part of the legitimacy of international law seems to rest on its past, which, given the specific burdens it carries, might not have been different. When compared to all these dynamics, asking about paths not taken sets off in the opposite direction, seeking out uncertainties about the law's path.

Even then, and in addition to all that has been said, how to express a sense of contingency in a text? I have suggested that inquiries into what happened and what else could have happened are indeed two sides of the same coin.[104] Following this analogy, however, it is just not possible to simultaneously see both sides of the coin without further ado. We can keep turning it around, but whenever we look at one side, it is difficult to also convey a sense of the other. And when we flip the coin, the side of contingency tends to land on its back, just as all the historical material, once it is put down into writing, expels a sense of contingency. Contingency tends to be banned narratively through disciplinary strictures and related emplotments.[105]

Another example helps to illustrate this point. Douglas Irwin recently offered a most informed account of the history of international trade law, including the fate of the International Trade Organization (ITO). The ITO's statute was backed by the US and was signed in 1948 by fifty-three of the then fifty-eight states. Will Clayton, chairman of the closing conference in Havana, had claimed, albeit with some exaggeration, that '[t]his may well prove to be the greatest step in history toward order and justice in economic relations among the members of the world community and toward a great expansion in the production, distribution and consumption of goods in the world'.[106] It did not happen. The ITO was never set up.

While this development contradicted the expectations of almost all actors at the time, it had become old news, also for Irwin. The US Congress did not ratify the statute, other countries turned away, and the ITO's statute ended in the dustbin of history.[107] The actions of the ITO's most ardent supporters are now rendered tragic as they approach the organization's preordained downfall. In contrast, as Irwin moves up to the 1990s, the establishment of the North Atlantic Free Trade Organization (NAFTA) comes as a surprise.[108] But contingency is lost again

[103] Anne Orford, 'On International Legal Method' (2013) 1 London Review of International Law 166; David Kennedy, 'Primitive Legal Scholarship' (1986) 27 Harvard International Law Journal 1.

[104] Tucker (n 48).

[105] Moyn (n 15).

[106] Statement by the Honourable William L Clayton at the final plenary session, on 23 March 1948, quoted in Richard Toye, 'The International Trade Organization' in Martin Daunton and others (eds), *The Oxford Handbook on the World Trade Organization* (OUP 2012) 85, 95.

[107] Douglas A Irwin, *Clashing Over Commerce: A History of US Trade Policy* (University of Chicago Press 2017) 502–05.

[108] ibid 636–42.

because early on Irwin foreshadows what is known—NAFTA was established. He thus conveys no sense that it was possible, perhaps even quite likely, that NAFTA would have failed. The certainty that is portrayed about NAFTA's establishment rather makes those who did not see it coming look a bit foolish and their anxieties overblown. If the first instance is rendered tragic, the second is comic.[109] Contingency is lost twice. The possibility of the ITO's success is repeatedly written out of existing histories that of course know what did and did not happen and are required to say so.

5. Conclusion

Why does the enigma of legal change persist? I have suggested that this has to do with difficulties when relating the law to contexts, political or otherwise. How to relate legal change to contexts without reducing the former to the latter? Thinking through law's contingency—the possibility of paths not taken—brings out those difficulties and helps to respond to them. It presses on the question of when to stop looking for the next underlying reason, one that promises to provide an explanation for why the law developed in the way it did. This inquiry, driven by the longing—disciplinary, professional, and human—to make sense of what happened, challenges us to determine when our exploration is truly comprehensive.[110] Giving in to this longing all too quickly risks producing myopic explanations of legal change that turn to the nearby reasons of ready-made stories—be it in an idealist, realist, or other grand narrative.

In the field of history, the turn to context in the 1960s arose out of a rejection of grand narratives.[111] In the field of international law, that is not equally true. Both idealist and realist accounts of international legal change have relied on context in their narratives. How else could they tell their stories and make their claims intelligible? They turned to different contexts: politics, for realists; justice, for idealists. They did so not to discard, but rather to support their grand narratives, either showcasing international law's evolution to better realize the values of humanity, or its trenchant operation as a handmaiden of domination.

EH Carr knew, writing on the brink of the Second World War and in the moment of his strongest critique of liberal idealism, that law, like politics, can be reduced neither to morality, nor to power. He saw it as a 'meeting place' for both.[112]

[109] For these modes of emplotment and their narrative effects, see White (n 43).

[110] On such a longing see, with further references, Venzke, 'What If?' (n 101).

[111] Quentin Skinner, 'Meaning and Understanding of the History of Ideas' (1969) 8 History and Theory 3.

[112] Carr, *The Twenty Years' Crisis 1919–1939* (n 25) 178. See also, more recently, Krisch, 'International Law in Times of Hegemony' (n 31), arguing that international law 'occupies an always precarious, but eventually secure position between the demands of the powerful and the ideals of justice held in international society'.

What then, finally, counts as context? In its turn to context, the field of history has always struggled to keep grand narratives from sneaking back in when it came to that question. How to choose the context and the histories that this choice creates? If anything, the recent high-flying debates about legal-historical methods in international law suggest that the answer does not lie there, in methods. As so often, those debates cloud disagreement about what to do in the present, about what the problem is perceived to be, and which practice or knowledge could possibly be emancipatory.[113] Accounts of legal change, including my own, will remain captive to that disagreement. The present volume sets out to fill gaps in understanding legal change in relation to politics. Those gaps are significant and much remains to be learned. After a long period of legal and political realism, the decision to consider politics as the context for law may seem obvious. But what kind of politics? Or, why politics?

[113] That, too, has been recognized and stressed repeatedly over time. Classically, White (n 43). See also Martti Koskenniemi, 'Vitoria and Us. Thoughts on Critical Histories of International Law' (2014) 22 Rechtsgeschichte—Legal History 119–38.

PART VI
EPILOGUE

15
Epilogue: Fragmentary Thoughts on Informal Change

BS Chimni[*]

1. Introduction

The problem of change in the international system, given the absence of a world state, is of central concern to students of international law. The changes may range from the gradual to the structural. Insofar as structural changes are concerned these are most often the result of exogenous factors captured by keywords such as capitalism, colonialism, imperialism, wars (both hot and cold), revolution, and decolonization. The resultant changes become part of the international legal order through formal sources such as treaties or customary international law. On the other hand, incremental or gradual changes are brought about through secondary pathways. While the formal doctrines and modes of change have received much attention in international legal scholarship, the subject of gradual change has been relatively neglected. The present volume is dedicated to gradual or informal change, defined as 'any modification of the burden of argument for a particular position on the content of the law'.

It is useful to distinguish the phenomenon of informal change from informal lawmaking. The latter leads to the creation of new rules while the former means changes in the interpretation and understanding of existing rules. The reasons for informal lawmaking today—as for instance in the case of internet law—are 'deep societal changes' that include 'the transition towards an increasingly diverse network society' and 'an increasingly complex knowledge society'.[1] In such cases formal modes of change, such as treaties, are not seen as suited for dealing with what are transitional, diverse, and complex developments, and norms of customary international law take time to emerge. Formal lawmaking may also not be ideal to deal with 'slender or thin' issues or where there is a sharp divergence of interests and perspectives among states. Finally, there may be the problem of 'treaty

* Distinguished Professor of International Law, Jindal Global Law School, Sonipat, India.

1 Joost Pauwelyn, Ramses A Wessel, and Jan Wouters, 'When Structures Become Shackles: Stagnation and Dynamics in International Lawmaking' (2014) 25 European Journal of International Law 733, 738–39.

BS Chimni, *Epilogue: Fragmentary Thoughts on Informal Change* In: *The Many Paths of Change in International Law*. Edited by: Nico Krisch and Ezgi Yildiz, Oxford University Press. © BS Chimni 2023. DOI: 10.1093/oso/9780198877844.003.0015

saturation'.[2] Thus, in contemporary times 'formal international law is stagnating in terms both of quantity *and* quality' and 'is increasingly superseded by "informal international law making" involving new actors, new processes, and new outputs'.[3] In the latter cases an option besides informal law-making is norm adjustment.

It is the case that every legal order has procedures, processes, and mechanisms that create space for 'norm adaptation'. As Brunnée and Toope point out, 'if the shared social understandings in which legal norms are grounded erode, or undergo a significant shift, law too will be under pressure to adjust'.[4] Informal change in the international legal order takes place through different pathways which include the bureaucratic, judicial, and private authority routes (and often involve more than one of them).[5] For instance, informal change is brought about by official bodies of experts by the mere act of codifying existing norms (as in the case of the International Law Commission (ILC)). Informal change can also be introduced by international organizations through issuing handbooks and guidelines in areas of domain expertise. An example of such informal change arguably is that produced by the UN High Commission for Refugees (UNHCR) *Handbook on Procedures and Criteria for Determining Refugee Status* under the 1951 Convention on the Status of Refugees.[6] It has influenced the interpretation and understanding of the term 'well-founded fear of being persecuted' by prescribing the application of both subjective and objective tests.[7] Likewise, in the post-Cold War era the World Bank influenced the development of international investment law through its Guidelines on Treatment of Foreign Direct Investment, of 1992.[8] Many of its prescriptions found their way into bilateral investment protection treaties or in multilateral texts such as the World Trade Organization (WTO) Agreement on Trade Related Investment Measures (TRIMS).

Informal change is also brought about by judicial or quasi-judicial bodies through advancing particular interpretations of existing norms and practices. Thus, for instance, Kiderlin shows how the interpretative mode has been used by the WTO Appellate Body to bring about gradual change in the law on subsidies.[9]

[2] ibid 738.
[3] ibid 734 (emphasis in original).
[4] Jutta Brunnée and Stephen J Toope, 'International Law and the Practice of Legality: Stability and Change' (2018) 49 Victoria University of Wellington Law Review 429, 445.
[5] Krisch had earlier proposed 'a framework for understanding the dynamics of international law beyond doctrinal categories …'; Nico Krisch, 'The Dynamics of International Law Redux' (2021) 74 Current Legal Problems 269, 271.
[6] The *Handbook on Procedures and Criteria for Determining Refugee Status* was first issued by UNHCR in 1979 and re-issued in 1992 and in 2019.
[7] For a view which challenges the understanding contained in the UNHCR Handbook, see James C Hathaway and WS Hicks, 'Is there a Subjective Element in the Refugee Convention's Requirement of "Well-Founded Fear"?' (2005) 26 Michigan Journal of International Law 505.
[8] Seymour J Rubin, 'World Bank: Report to the Development Committee and Guidelines on the Treatment of Foreign Direct Investment: Introductory Note' (1992) 31 International Legal Materials 1363.
[9] Kiderlin, this volume.

Judicial bodies can bring about more fundamental change by reconceptualizing a basic doctrine of international law. Thus, for instance, by insisting on the two-element test to identify a norm of customary international law—that of state practice and *opinio iuris*—the ICJ changed the understanding of a fundamental doctrine of international law.[10]

But beyond these secondary pathways there is also available, assuming a more inclusive definition of informal change, the power route to norm adjustment.[11] As Pollack shows, change can be initiated by a hostile response of leaders of powerful states to particular international law rules, practices, or institutions.[12] The reaction of President Trump (and subsequently President Biden) to WTO rules, in particular the dispute settlement provisions, is an example of a power-change dialectic that has led to changes in practice; albeit it has in the process diminished the international legal order, allowing other actors such as Russia to take the advantage of an international law-resistant ecology.

While the present volume discusses informal change in recent times it would be interesting to distinguish different historical periods with reference to pathways and the nature of informal change. What were the routes and mechanisms of norm adjustment in the colonial era? How was informal change achieved in the period after the October Revolution or after decolonization? A systematic historical study could shed much light on the significance of informal change over time, the nature of the international legal order, and the distinct pathways through which it is secured in different eras.

Broadly speaking, it can be said that over time it is powerful actors that have been more successful in bringing about informal change. Indeed, the history of international law can be told as a succession of phases in which dominant actors have in response to shifting contexts and interests brought about gradual change in the international legal order. However, change has also been ushered in by subaltern actors through collectively canvassing and pushing for change. In contrast to the power pathway this may be termed the resistance pathway, which can see norm adjustment at the initiative of weak states and civil society organizations.

Informal change does not happen suddenly. The stages through which informal change is brought about have been helpfully identified in this volume as 'selection', 'construction', and 'reception' stages. For this process to fructify in norm adjustment, the international legal order must have the internal resources and mechanisms to facilitate change and would need to be accompanied by an ideational environment in which such change is seen as justified.

[10] Werner, this volume. See also BS Chimni, 'Customary International Law: A TWAIL Perspective' (2018) 112 American Journal of International Law 1.

[11] A broader meaning of 'informal change' has to be used to include in its ambit the reconfiguring of formal institutional arrangements.

[12] Pollack, this volume.

2. Informal Change and the Relative Autonomy of International Law

The phenomenon of informal change therefore offers important theoretical insights into the nature and functioning of the contemporary international legal system. A significant insight is that the legal order possesses relative autonomy from the material substratum, that is, the logic of territory and the logic of capital that give it life. Put differently, the contemporary international legal order has an internal structure, logic, and dynamics that create space and processes for 'norm adjustment'. These elements bring into focus and play intramural drivers and modes of change in the international legal order. In fact, such is the complex nature of the internal composition and fluidity of the international legal order that it has invited an internal critique of international law by scholars like David Kennedy, Martti Koskenneimi, and more recently Jean d'Aspremont.[13]

While the international legal order is for the sake of simplicity and substantive characterization (such as for example colonial international law) viewed as a single block, in reality it consists of an amalgam of doctrines, principles, norms, institutions, and practices with distinct genealogies, thickness, and functional strengths. The decentralized nature of the international system means that these building blocks of the legal order are not always internally aligned. The internal critique points precisely to the tensions and conflicts in and between doctrines, principles, practices, etc to explain how situations of misalignment, norm conflict, or indeterminacy create space for informal change. In other words, state and non-state actors use existing lags and gaps in the legal order to advance interpretations and understandings of individual elements rooted in a particular vision or interest. On the theoretical plane, the rejection of the possibility of *non liquet* is a response to the lack of systematic development of international law.[14]

The space for gradual or informal change is also enhanced by the fact that distinct branches of international law are at different stages of development. This may call for transfer of ideas and practices from one sphere to another sphere of law—for example, from international human rights law to international climate law. The point is not simply about misalignment between different fields of international law and the resulting lags or gaps in the law but also about the distinctiveness of a decentralized legal order in which no orderly and methodical lawmaking takes place. There are always 'empty' legal spaces that can be filled through informal change. It is at least one reason why the writings or work of eminent experts and publicists

[13] For an analysis of the internal critique in the work of Kennedy and Koskenniemi, see BS Chimni, *International Law and World Order: A Critique of Contemporary Approaches* (2nd edn, CUP 2017) ch IV. See also Jean d'Aspremont, *International Law as a Belief System* (CUP 2017).

[14] See generally Hersch Lauterpacht, 'Some Observations on the Prohibition of '*Non Liquet*' and the Completeness of the Law' in FM van Asbeck (ed), *Symbolae Verzijl: Présentées au Prof J.H.W. Verzijl, à l'occasion de son LXXième anniversaire* (Nijhoff 1958) 196.

and decisions of international tribunals are considered subsidiary sources of international law.

The question of relative autonomy and informal change is also tied to the crucial question of reform in the international legal order. There are of course different views on the extent of autonomy of the international legal order—from deep structures such as the sovereign state system, capitalism, or patriarchy—and the possibilities of reform whether through formal or informal pathways. The mainstream approaches to international law tend to assign relatively greater autonomy to the legal sphere than realist or critical approaches and are therefore sanguine about reforming the legal order. It is not as if realist or critical approaches are not opposed to determinist and reductionist views of the international legal order. But their views differ from the mainstream, and each other, on the meaning and scope of relative autonomy and the chances of reform. Thus, for instance, Marxist approaches to international law tend to be much more constrained in their understanding of the extent of autonomy possessed by the legal sphere; albeit the charge of economic and political determinism that follows is misplaced, as beginning with Marx and Engels the relative autonomy of the legal sphere has received sufficient weight.[15] But it would not be wrong to suggest that the Marxist approaches are less sanguine about the possibilities of reform through formal or secondary pathways unless supported by dominant ideologies and actors. In fact, some Marxist scholars of international law such as China Miéville simply reject the possibility of progressive reform.[16] Whereas others—like the present writer—concede its possibility in the international legal order. In this view progressive reform can take place. In the instance of reform through informal change it can take place if counter-hegemonic movements seize the opportunities created by internal tensions in the international legal order, construct a degree of consensus around proposed reforms, and approach accessible forums or pathways. Therefore, rather than reach a generalized conclusion on the possibility or the significance of reforms, each instance of formal or informal change has to be assessed from the standpoint of weak groups and states in the global order. But it may be conceded that gradual changes will not substantially transform the character and trajectory of what continues to be an imperial legal order.

In considering the possibility of reform through informal change, the epistemic dimension also deserves consideration, that is, the role that ideas and ideational environment play in facilitating the process, another theme that can be productively pursued. Among other ways, the writings of scholars or opinions of judges can help destabilize existing norms to create space for change. Martínez Esponda aptly points out how ground was prepared for invoking the right of self-defence against non-state actors by 'the deliberate perpetuation of instability in international legal

[15] Chimni, *International Law and World Order* (n 13) ch VI.
[16] ibid.

rules' as it allowed 'actors to purse different courses of action without having to face the hurdles of changing international rules'.[17] The reconfiguring of existing legal categories is another way of bringing about change. In this regard, mention may be made of the role of international commissions and reports. Thus, for example, the Report of the International Commission on Intervention and State Sovereignty (2001) used 'discursive openings' created by the failure of the international community to prevent the genocide in Rwanda in 1994, and Kofi Annan's millennium report (2000) to the UN General Assembly, to advance the doctrine of responsibility to protect (R2P), that is, as against the earlier doctrine of humanitarian intervention.[18] The move has brought about change in the interpretation of the principles of sovereignty, non-intervention, and use of force. These changes also show that informal change is more likely to take place when backed by the ideology of dominant social forces and actors.[19]

A different kind of example of the role of ideas in bringing about informal change can be found in the field of international development law. Thus, for instance, the growth or GDP concept of 'development' and the posited relationship between 'law and development' underscore the importance of institutions that protect contracts and property rights, a view which has crucially influenced developments in the field of international investment law. Corporate actors and their organic intellectuals have used the proposition that foreign direct investment promotes growth in recipient states to produce informal change in the law. For example, in the post *Texaco v Libya*[20] award era, arbitrators and academics supported 'what was theoretically unsupportable', that is, the idea of internationalization of contract relying on 'low-order sources—arbitral awards and writings of publicists—both of which are amenable to the influence of private power'.[21] Obversely, mainstream scholars can create an epistemic environment in which informal change favourable to weak actors is obstructed. Indeed, it would be useful to have some discussion of ways in which informal change is prevented.

If the assumption about the important role of ideas in bringing about informal change has salience, there is a need to promote the critical study of international

[17] Martínez Esponda, this volume.

[18] See ICISS, 'The Responsibility to Protect: The Report of the International Commission on Intervention and State Sovereignty' (2001) <www.idrc.ca/en/book/responsibility-protect-report-international-commission-intervention-and-state-sovereignty> accessed 25 August 2022. See also Kofi A Annan, '"We the Peoples": The Role of the United Nations, 21st century' (UN 2000) <https://digitallibrary.un.org/record/413745?ln=en> accessed 25 August 2022.

[19] BS Chimni, 'For Epistemological and Prudent Internationalism' [2012] Harvard Human Rights Journal (online) <https://harvardhrj.com/2012/11/for-epistemological-and-prudent-internationalism/> accessed 25 August 2022.

[20] *Texaco Overseas Petroleum Co v Libya* (Award) 19 January 1977 (1979) 53 ILR 389.

[21] M. Sornarajah. *Resistance and Change in the International Law on Foreign Investment* (CUP 2015) 134. See however Julien Cantegreil, 'The Audacity of the *Texaco/Calasiatic* Award: René-Jean Dupuy and the Internationalization of Foreign Investment Law' (2011) 22 European Journal of International Law 441.

law in weak nations so that academia and experts can articulate and promote counter-hegemonic ideas and narratives. In other words, the possibilities for informal change can be created by critical scholarship through transforming the intellectual milieu and sensitizing agents of informal change. The Third World Approaches to International Law (TWAIL) along with Feminist Approaches to International Law (FtAIL) are already playing an important role in transmuting the marketplace of ideas in the matrix of which international texts are coming to be interpreted, gaps filled, and indeterminacies in doctrines and practices addressed. But there is a need to be more alert to possibilities of informal change within the international legal order. On a practical level, states should invest in learning and capacity-building as Brazil and China have done in the instance of WTO law or more broadly international trade law.

The global civil society must also appreciate that 'informal change from below' can be brought about when new or competing interpretations of existing rules create the space for norm change or adaptation. Its initiatives are more likely to succeed when there is a crisis in the global order or in a particular domain of law.[22] But civil society movements must have the knowledge and resources to initiate change. For instance, civil society movements have been able to seize the initiative and seek 'change from below' in the field of climate law through invoking science, undertaking education of citizens, and strategizing the pathways that offer greater opportunity for bringing about norm adjustment, such as turning to domestic courts for implementation.[23] In sum, for informal change to happen at the initiative of weak or non-state actors a certain ideational ecology has to be created that influences thinking in different sites of change. In this regard, the relationship between soft law and informal change also needs to be explored as creating the conditions in which change is made possible.

3. The Direction of Informal Change

While this volume is not focused on the direction of informal change but on the processes, conditions, and pathways that produce it, individual contributions have reflected on the question. A precondition for any assessment of the nature of change is the recognition that change has taken place—not always admitted by the actor(s) bringing about change. As Sandholtz points out, 'we need to recognize and understand modes of norm change that do not alter the substantive content of norms.'[24] This kind of change can work either in a positive or a regressive direction.

[22] BS Chimni, 'Crisis and International Law: A Third World Approaches to International Law Perspective' in Makane Moise Mbengue and Jean d'Aspremont (eds), *Crisis Narratives in International Law* (Nijhoff Law Specials 2021) 40.

[23] See generally Samvel Varsatian, 'The Advent of International Human Rights Law in Climate Change Litigation' (2021) 38 Wisconsin International Law Journal 369.

[24] Sandholtz, this volume.

Sandholtz rightly reminds us that 'international legal change is not always progressive but can also move in a non-liberal direction'.[25]

The conclusions of the ILC in the field of customary international law offer an example of controversial informal change. Werner reviews the ILC Draft Conclusions on the Identification of Customary Law and shows that these 'are not just registrations of past practices. They construct certain practices as relevant and exemplary and ignore or delegitimize others.'[26] He rightly points out that 'inchoate and only partially consistent practices are presented anew in the form of a structured report, with numbered conclusions held together by an internal logic'.[27] Werner goes on to submit that the ILC project of restatement is 'openly political'.[28] But what kind of politics do the Draft Conclusions support? A preliminary assessment will suggest that, and there are no surprises here, the conclusions tend to back the perspective of powerful actors.[29] But it is unlikely that the Special Rapporteur who piloted the Conclusions or the ILC as a body will concede this.

However, as was observed earlier, informal change may also work in the interests of marginalized groups or nations. A possible example is the ILC approach to the significance of subsequent agreements and practice of states parties to a treaty. Zarbiyev contends that change is being introduced through modifying the traditional doctrine of interpretation in the matrix of 'a new social ecology' informed by a non-traditional conception of authority. In his view, the 'rise of alternative interpreters' has created an environment in which there is 'room for resistance and contestation' of interpretations advanced by states parties to a treaty.[30] Zarbiyev aptly flags in this regard the role of human rights treaty bodies in progressively interpreting international human rights law and also applying it to new areas. An example is their role in bringing human rights law to bear upon international climate law.[31] Put differently, and to quote the ILC Special Rapporteur on the subject, subsequent agreements, and subsequent practice of states parties in relation to the interpretation of treaties do not possess a 'conclusive, or legally

25 ibid 154 and 172.

26 Wouter, this volume.

27 ibid 131.

28 ibid 116.

29 See Chimni, 'Customary International Law: A TWAIL Perspective' (n 10).

30 Zarbiyev, this volume.

31 For instance, the UN Human Rights Council (UNHRC) has since 2008 passed annual resolutions on the subject of climate change and human rights, focusing each year on a special theme. Human Rights Council resolutions on human rights and climate change are available at <www.ohchr.org/EN/Issues/HRAndClimateChange/Pages/Resolutions.aspx> accessed 25 August 2022. In September 2019, five UN human rights treaty bodies issued a joint statement on human rights and climate change. These were the Committee on the Elimination of Discrimination against Women, the Committee on Economic, Social and Cultural Rights, the Committee on the Protection of the Rights of All Migrant Workers and Members of their Families, the Committee on the Rights of the Child, and the Committee on the Rights of Persons with Disabilities. See Joint Statement on 'Human Rights and Climate Change' (16 September 2019) <www.ohchr.org/EN/NewsEvents/Pages/DisplayNews.aspx?NewsID=24998> accessed 25 August 2022.

binding effect'.[32] This is a significant shift away from the primacy of parties' views, and it might strengthen the role of human rights treaty bodies in progressively interpreting international human rights law and also applying it to new areas. An example is their role in bringing human rights law to bear upon international climate law.[33] However, it needs to be borne in mind that once the doctrine of non-conclusiveness is accepted it can act as a double-edged sword. The principle can be used to give weight to the views of powerful non-state actors notwithstanding subsequent agreement between states parties, such as in the area of international investment law.

Another example of progressive change is offered by Putnam, who shows how without changing 'a single comma' the obligations assumed by member states under the UN Convention on the Prevention and Punishment of the Crime of Genocide have been enhanced.[34] That is particularly the case with the 'prevention element' which now anticipates affirmative measures from states parties. A preeminent negative example is the 1951 UN Convention on the Status of Refugees which has without any formal amendment seen the creation of a non-entrée regime in the Global North.[35]

In analysing and assessing from the perspective of weak groups and states the phenomenon of informal change and the different pathways involved the following general overlapping considerations may be kept in mind.

First, the contribution of each pathway in bringing about informal change depends on the role assigned to it in the international legal order. For instance, given the 'religious faith' of international lawyers in judicial decisions, international tribunals are ideally positioned to initiate informal change that can rapidly gain the acceptance of the international community.[36] But as Zarbiyev points out, the reasons offered for assigning tribunals a special place 'are mostly apologetic'.[37] On the other hand, 'critical perspectives have been largely lacking'.[38] What deserves to be explored from the perspective of weak states and peoples is the 'epistemic and distributional implications' of the 'privileged place occupied by the judicial representation of international law'.[39]

[32] ILC, 'Fifth Report on Subsequent Agreements and Subsequent Practice in Relation to the Interpretation of Treaties by Georg Nolte, Special Rapporteur' (28 February 2018) A/CN.4/715, para 30 <http://legal.un.org/docs/?symbol=A/CN.4/715> accessed 25 August 2022.

[33] See (n 31).

[34] Putnam, this volume.

[35] BS Chimni, 'The Geopolitics of Refugee Studies: A View from the South' (1998) 11 Journal of Refugee Studies 350; T Gammeltoft-Hansen and James C Hathaway, 'Non-Refoulement in a World of Cooperative Deterrence' (2015) 53 Columbia Journal of Transnational Law 235.

[36] Fuad Zarbiyev, 'On the Judge Centredness of the International Legal Self' (2021) 32 European Journal of International Law 1139, 1140.

[37] ibid.

[38] ibid.

[39] ibid 1142.

Secondly, given that the 'community of practitioners' in the international legal arena is dominated by mainstream scholars from the Global North, the bureaucratic pathway is likely to support informal change favoured by dominant actors. Thus, for instance, the reality that official bodies like ILC are unduly influenced by experts from the Global North (partly for the doing of nations of Global South who often nominate individuals without the necessary expertise) has often translated into changes reflecting the ideas and interests of powerful social forces and actors. The process is facilitated by the fact that official bodies like ILC principally rely on state practice for purposes of codification of the law. But given the lack of availability of state practice of Global South nations, it means that the views of Global North nations tend to prevail.[40]

Thirdly, the bureaucratic pathway can yet facilitate progressive change when it involves human rights bodies whether it is UN treaty bodies or UN Human Rights Council special procedures.[41] The treaty bodies have fashioned human rights jurisprudence to contribute to progressive interpretations of human rights conventions. The appointment of a number of international law experts associated with TWAIL as Special Rapporteurs on a variety of human rights subjects (these include Professors Obiora Okafor, Tendayi Achiume, Michael Fakhri, and Balakrishnan Rajagopal) is also likely to contribute to an understanding of human rights that reflect the concerns of subaltern groups.[42] Their individual reports can facilitate informal change through a reasoned analysis of existing norms and practices. But the work of human rights treaty bodies suffers from weaknesses as well, reducing their impact.[43] There are also clear limits to what individual experts can do to produce progressive informal change. Finally, there is the justified lament that the focus on human rights has displaced the discourse of justice.[44]

Fourthly, the role of private actors such as multinational corporations (MNCs) or associations that further their interests (eg the International Chamber of Commerce (ICC)) tend to push 'norm adaptation' in a direction that constrains the policy space of Global South nations. These actors use informal change either to thwart progressive changes or advance new interpretations that facilitate the global

[40] See generally Chimni, *International Law and World Order* (n 13).

[41] According to OHCHR's webpage, '[t]he special procedures of the Human Rights Council are independent human rights experts with mandates to report and advise on human rights from a thematic or country-specific perspective. They are non-paid and elected for 3-year mandates that can be reconducted for another three years. As of October 2021, there are 45 thematic and 13 country mandates.' See <www.ohchr.org/en/special-procedures-human-rights-council> accessed 25 August 2022.

[42] For the list of existing special procedure appointments see *Directory of Special Procedures Mandate Holders* <www.ohchr.org/sites/default/files/Documents/HRBodies/SP/VisualDirectory.pdf> accessed 25 August 2022.

[43] Kerstin Mechlem, 'Treaty Bodies and the Interpretation of Human Rights' (2021) 42 Vanderbilt Law Review 905; Paul Harpur and Michael Ashley Stein, 'The U.N. Convention on the Rights of Persons with Disabilities and the Global South' (2022) 47 Yale Journal of International Law 75.

[44] Samuel Moyn, *Not Enough: Human Rights in an Unequal World* (Harvard University Press 2018); Ratna Kapur, *Gender, Alterity and Human Rights* (Edward Elgar 2018).

accumulation of capital. But the reverse may also happen, though rarely. Thus, for instance, it is said that the *Urbaser v Argentina*[45] and *Aven v Costa Rica*[46] decisions have started the 'trend of acknowledging international obligations for investors—even veering towards a presumption of subjectivity in areas of common concern', albeit it is observed that much theoretical work needs to be done 'to bring continuity and consistency to corporate subjectivity to international law'.[47] The latter observation reinforces the importance of ideas in bringing about real informal change. But a beginning has been made in *Aven* to suggest 'that environmental community interests incur *erga omnes* obligations'.[48] However, it would be a mistake to think that MNCs can be made to respect 'informal change' that enhances their obligations towards nature.

Fifthly, there is a need to be alert to gradual changes substituting for open and transparent changes in the law. In other words, the informal change route may be used to pursue parochial interests when the formal path is blocked by weaker states. An example is how, in the absence of an agreement on the subject of the relationship between trade and environment, the interpretation of bare rules by the WTO Appellate Body has been used to justify green protectionism.[49] Another lesson from the trade-environment interface in WTO is that change impelled by progressive civil society forces in the developed world can have unintended consequences for developing nations. In this regard the use by non-state actors of procedural openings such as access to submit '*amicus curiae*' underscores the importance of both processes and ideas in bringing about gradual change.[50]

Sixthly, the issue of 'accountability and legitimacy' must be addressed.[51] While some may believe that informal change reflects 'thick stakeholder consensus',[52] it is not always the case and therefore must be evaluated from the standpoint of the legitimacy of processes involved and distributive outcomes.[53]

[45] International Centre for Settlement of Investment Disputes (ICSID), *Urbaser SA v Argentine Republic* (Award) (2016) ICSID Case No ARB/07/26.

[46] ICSID, *David R Aven v Republic of Costa Rica* (Award) (2018) ICSID Case No UNCT/15/3.

[47] Kevin Crow and Lina Lorenzoni-Escobar, 'From Traction to Treaty-Bound: Jus Cogens, Erga Omnes and Corporate Subjectivity in International Investment Arbitration' (2022) 13 Journal of International Dispute Settlement 121, 147. See also Christian J Tams, *Enforcing Obligations Erga Omnes in International Law* (CUP 2005) 152..

[48] Crow and Lorenzoni-Escobar (n 47) 148.

[49] See BS Chimni, 'WTO and Environment: The *Shrimp-Turtle* and *EC-Hormone* Cases' (2000) 35 Economic and Political Weekly, 1752; BS Chimni, 'WTO and Environment: The Legitimization of Unilateral Trade Sanctions' (2002) 37 Economic and Political Weekly 133.

[50] Theresa Squatrito, 'Amicus Curiae Briefs in the WTO DSM: Good or Bad News for Non-State Actor Involvement?' (2018) 17 World Trade Review 65.

[51] Pauwelyn, Wessel, and Wouters (n 1) 743.

[52] ibid 762.

[53] Barnett, Pevehouse, and Raustiala note that changes in global governance raise 'issues of legitimacy, fairness, justice, accountability, and other normative scales. And these normative measures refer not only to distributional outcomes but also to process and whether those who are affected by the decisions have a voice in shaping them.' Michael N Barnett, Jon CW Pevehouse, and Kal Raustiala, 'Introduction: The Modes of Global Governance' in *Global Governance in a World of Change* (CUP 2022) 7.

4. Conclusion

In order to respond to changing social and political contexts, every legal system provides for processes and mechanisms that facilitate norm adaptation. These are especially needed in the international legal system, as formal agreements are difficult to arrive at and norms of customary international law take time to emerge. The several detailed studies of gradual change undertaken in the volume make a significant contribution to understanding the conditions and pathways of informal change in the international legal order. However, the direction of these changes, and their cumulative impact, deserve much more attention. From the perspective of weak groups and nations, informal changes tend to be accepted when these subserve the interests of powerful state and non-state actors. Their aim in the final analysis is to promote a hegemonic global order.

Yet to be dismissive of the opportunities that the possibility of informal change offers in enhancing either the policy space of weak nations or the welfare of the poor and marginalized groups is difficult to justify. It opens critical approaches to the charges of determinism, reductionism, and nihilism. But if weak nations or the global civil society have to initiate and bring to fruition desirable gradual change, they have not only to be alert to the possibilities in different sites of international law, but also appreciate the different pathways through which these changes can be brought about and create capacities and facilitative conditions at the level of ideas, institutions, and practices.

Index

For the benefit of digital users, indexed terms that span two pages (e.g., 52–53) may, on occasion, appear on only one of those pages.

Tables are indicated by *t* following the page number